AF291786

Praise for *Power Play*

'Osborn has done what too few researchers and journalists bother to do: take video games seriously as an information environment. The same ecosystems I've watched get exploited for disinformation, the Discord servers, the Twitch streams, the in-game communities, are mapped here with forensic clarity. *Power Play* is essential reading for anyone trying to understand where the next influence operation is being built.'

Eliot Higgins, founder of *Bellingcat*

'Frequently surprising and utterly absorbing whether you're a gamer or not. Osborn shines a vital light on the significant and often troubling impact video games are having on global politics.'

Jonn Elledge, author of *A History of the World in 47 Borders*

'In *Power Play*, George Osborn lays out exactly how we got here: how technology developed for entertainment became a way for political campaigns and regimes to influence millions. He exposes how the Saudi Arabian, Chinese and Russian states and extremists across the world have leveraged the power of games, and how far behind democracies are in understanding or countering this. Anyone who still thinks that video games are trivial will learn from this book exactly why they are not.'

Keza MacDonald, author of Super Nintendo and Video Games Editor at the *Guardian*

'In his revelatory *Power Play*, Osborn masterfully exposes how extremists and state actors have transformed gaming platforms into global gathering places where radical ideas are beta-tested before bleeding into reality. This is an urgent, fascinating read that will fundamentally change how you understand modern power.'

Kelly Clancy, author of *Playing with Reality*

'With the passion of a player and the smarts of a political operator, Osborn shows us how the stratospherically successful video games industry is being co-opted by autocrats the world over. *Power Play* should be required reading for those worried about the future of their hobby – and the democratic leaders who could help change the game.'

Matt Honeycombe-Foster,
Deputy Editor, *Politico*

'George Osborn is perhaps the first to see with real clarity what almost everyone else has missed: that video games are the coffee houses of our age, a vast third-space society connecting billions of people, many of them disenchanted with the world as it is. He shows how this immense network became politically consequential, and how the right has been far quicker than the left to grasp and exploit its potential.'

Thomas Small, co-host of *Conflicted*

'A remarkable account of how and why video games became the most important entertainment space of the 21st century. Osborn writes with authority and passion. Anyone who cares about the intersection of politics and play – and everyone should – needs to read this book.'

Professor Pete Etchells, Bath Spa University,
author of *Lost in a Good Game*

'As a game maker, citizen and industry advocate, I have watched games turn into a key terrain of irregular and cognitive warfare over the last decades. *Power Play* is a great book to introduce you to the most important cultural technique of this century and how it is used by our adversaries to corrode and undermine our democracies.'

Hendrik Lesser, Chairman,
European Game Developers Federation

'At their best, video games a wellspring of joy, ideas, and connection worldwide. But as George E. Osborn makes unnervingly clear in this important book, reactionary movements have increasingly exploited this misunderstood medium. Perfectly accessible for readers who know nothing about video games and frequently surprising even for those who know a lot, *Power Play* uncovers a hidden history of the contemporary world, showing the essential but often overlooked role of video games in shaping everything from the invention of the iPhone to the election of Donald Trump. Osborn warns that bad actors have a big head start in grasping and harnessing the political power of games. This book is the best way for the rest of the world to catch up.'

Rollo Romig, author of *I am on the Hitlist* and
writer for the *New York Times Magazine*

'*Power Play* reveals how the world's most powerful entertainment medium became its most contested geopolitical battleground and is essential reading for anyone trying to understand where culture, technology and power collide.'

Rachel Kowert, PhD, founder of Psychgeist and
Visiting Researcher at the University of Cambridge

'Gaming environments have been a frontier for geopolitical influence and state control for longer than most of us would have thought, yet our collective awareness remains dangerously low. George's book masterfully shines a much needed light on these issues, providing vital wake-up call for anyone concerned with the intersection of technology, power, and global security.'

Dominik Swiecicki, Senior National Expert
at the European Commission

POWER PLAY

Video Games, Politics and the Battle for Global Influence

GEORGE E. OSBORN

First published in Great Britain in Hardback in 2026 by Wildfire
An imprint of Headline Publishing Group Limited

1

Cataloguing in Publication Data is available from the British Library

Hardback ISBN 978 1 0354 2328 6
Trade Paperback ISBN 978 1 0354 2329 3

Typeset in 12.5/15.5pt Baskerville MT Pro by Six Red Marbles UK, Thetford, Norfolk

Printed and bound in Great Britain by Clays Ltd, Elcograf S.p.A.

Headline Publishing Group Limited
An Hachette UK Company
Carmelite House
50 Victoria Embankment
London EC4Y 0DZ

The authorised representative in the EEA is Hachette Ireland,
8 Castlecourt Centre, Dublin 15, D15 XTP3, Ireland (email: info@hbgi.ie)

www.headline.co.uk
www.hachette.co.uk

I have sought to avoid using video game jargon throughout this book. Sometimes, it was unavoidable. Where I have used video game industry terminology relating to hardware, software, business models or subcultures, I have sought to include an accurate accompanying explanation in a glossary located at the back of the book.

Contents

Introduction

When I joined the video games industry back in 2012, I never imagined that it could be a front for political influence. But in April 2022, just a decade later, I received an email from the British government that changed the way I saw games in the wider world.

In February 2022, Russia commenced its full-scale invasion of Ukraine. Vladimir Putin's unjustified aggression against the Ukrainian people shocked the world. This forced Western democracies to take steps to support their allies in Kyiv and do what they could to push back the Russian threat.

The measures were wide-ranging. Russian businesses were banned from accessing the SWIFT international banking system, significantly reducing their ability to trade with the world. Individuals were sanctioned, ranging from Vladimir Putin to former Chelsea Football Club owner Roman Abramovich. Billions of dollars of military equipment and assistance were sent to Ukraine by its allies, supporting its efforts to keep Russian aggressors from the borders.

There were also campaigns to help Ukraine win the 'air war' against Russia within the country itself. According to a couple of sources I spoke to, governments, non-governmental organisations and free media sought to share the truth of Russia's aggression with its population, undermining local support for the war.

There were lots of ways by which these groups were trying to achieve this, including buying adverts in Russian media spaces, hosting 'mirrored' websites which sought to evade the country's censors and promoting local voices who opposed the war. But with fighting raging across the country, every angle was being considered.

It was at this point that someone within the British government had a bright idea. Could the UK games industry create video games, or put messages in its games, which were pro-Ukrainian and then distribute those directly into Russia as another way of sharing the truth about the war with its population?

On the face of it, the suggestion sounds absurd. Video games? As a channel of communication? Aren't they just silly little toys or a waste of time?

But the idea was built on a solid foundation because the government had already worked with the games industry to distribute messages to millions of players during the Covid-19 pandemic to encourage them to keep calm and carry on playing video games.

After a number of businesses had approached the government to offer to post 'Stay Home, Save Lives' messages both in their games and on their social media channels, video games became a channel that other government departments sought to use to their advantage. The sector supported the then Department for Digital, Culture, Media and Sport's Let's Talk Loneliness campaign to tackle mental health challenges by encouraging people to play together. It also joined the global games industry in supporting public health messaging campaigns from the World Health Organisation promoting social distancing and vaccine confidence measures.

But to get support for the pro-Ukrainian messaging campaign, government departments were going to need games companies to back it. And because I was head of campaigns and communications at Ukie, the video games trade association which represented the best part of 600 businesses across the country, I was the person lucky enough to decide how we dealt with the request.

I immediately knew what I was going to say when I read the email: hell no! Partly, I had practical concerns. Games typically take years to make. Asking a member to commit to spending time, money and effort making something for a campaign like this was not something I was going to do lightly.

But my main concern was that asking games companies to share propaganda messages was deeply inappropriate. The vast majority of games businesses we worked with had left Russia immediately, including Nintendo, PlayStation and Xbox. If I'd emailed international games businesses asking them whether they'd like to reinstate their products or services in a sanctioned territory to serve up political messaging on behalf of the British government, I would have been writing a professional suicide note. The outraged reaction of one friendly contact I phoned to run the idea past suggested I was right to be cautious.

After a quick chat with a colleague, we agreed to turn down the request. I responded with a polite but firm email detailing the problems with the idea. Soon after, I received a polite email back implying that my contact was thoroughly relieved that I'd said no. The joys of obeying the chain of command, eh?

That was the end of that. Or was it? From that moment on, I was alert to the possibility that games were being used as a channel of political influence. And in the years following that request, I began to become more aware of a quiet war for influence raging within games.

In October 2023, a friend forwarded me a paper from Lund University that was funded by Sweden's Psychological Defence Agency, an arm of its military dedicated to building resilience to disinformation amongst the country's citizens as part of its overall defence strategy.

The paper warned that video game players were being attacked by malign foreign influences, who were using forty different tactics to turn video game content, the infrastructure underpinning play (e.g. payment structures) and the communication channels that surround them into tools to achieve their goals.[1] And while it was trying its best not to collar any particular group for using games for nefarious ends (probably for pesky diplomatic reasons), it warned that authoritarian states, extremists and populist groups were sharp operators in the space.

Less than a year later, in September 2024, fears that games could be used as a channel for disinformation and undue political influence had grown. During a meeting in New York on the fringes of that year's UN General Assembly, the State Department's Global Engagement Center (GEC), which was designed to counter foreign disinformation, hosted an event with the Kingdom of Sweden to promote the findings of Lund University's paper.

The session's purpose was to bring together government officials, industry experts and representatives from non-governmental organisations (NGOs) to find ways to counter malign political influence, while promoting democratic values. It took place less than a fortnight after the US Department of Justice had unsealed papers revealing a Russian disinformation campaign called Good Old USA Project that targeted eighteen-to thirty-year-old online male gamers, and was opened by James Rubin, then the overall co-ordinator of the Center. He was clear that the video game information space was a channel for influence that democracies underestimated at their peril.

'We share a goal where foreign misinformation finds no fertile soil in which to grow,' he said. 'And it is clear that whether it is through games themselves, or through platforms like Discord, that is where they are.'[2]

But the work was cut dramatically short. Within months of the meeting, following the re-election of Donald Trump, in December 2024 the Center was shuttered. Marco Rubio, secretary of state, would claim in April 2025 that the Center was closed because it wasted taxpayers' money and engaged in 'censorship'.[3]

And while Trump's victory in November 2024 was a 'blow-out' for a number of reasons, his success also showed that Rubin, the GEC and Sweden's Psychological Defence Agency had been right to identify the video game ecosystem as a channel for influence.

In the aftermath of the election result, polling firm J. L. Partners was noted as one of the few 'winners' of the 2024 polling game after they called a Trump win so precisely that they nailed the final electoral vote count of 316 to Trump vs 226 to Kamala Harris.

And when asked about how they did it, James Johnson, one of the co-founders of the firm, told me that the firm was the only one able to reach Black and Hispanic young men – who broke for Trump in unexpectedly high numbers – because they were recruiting them into their polling sample via adverts in the eco-system they trusted: video games.

Video game content, communication channels and communities have become a channel for political influence capable of tilting the world. This book is the story of how on earth this happened.

*

Video games are enormous. In 2024, a year considered by many to be a bad one for the industry, the global sector generated US $182.7bn through software revenues alone and reached over 3.5 billion people around the world. The medium has inspired the intellectual property behind one of the biggest hit TV shows in recent years in the form of *The Last of Us*. It has generated a billion-dollar box office hit through the Minecraft movie. Games have even gone into deep cover in the book clubs of the world through Gabrielle Zevin's thoughtful novel *Tomorrow, and Tomorrow, and Tomorrow*.

Yet despite the rise of games, the medium remains misunderstood or underappreciated within democracies. A number of these misconceptions are surface level and can easily be ignored. Tabloid media fears that video games cause people to be violent have been extensively debunked by researchers at places such as the Oxford Internet Institute. The Oscar-nominated film *Tár* implies that video games are culturally insignificant when its lead character, played by Cate Blanchett, slips from the heights of the Berlin conducting scene to the lows of leading a video game orchestra – a discordant message, given that game soundtracks have revitalised the audience for orchestral music. Niall Ferguson's criticism that games are 'stultifying' simply shows that he hasn't played a good one, rather than saying anything perceptive about the medium.

However, the most misleading trope about games is that the medium is anti-social. Scaremongering pressure groups like Game Quitters, an organisation dedicated to helping people recover from 'gaming disorder', imply that playing games can cause loneliness, social isolation and relationship breakdown.[4] Some academics have attempted to claim that children's social development is negatively affected by play, usually citing wobbly sources like self-reported surveys that have their peers banging their heads on the table in frustration. Teachers in schools report their frustrations that 'boys would rather sit in front of Minecraft or Fortnite than play outside', depriving them of 'real-life' play or social skills in the process.[5]

Yet each of these groups and individuals is mistaken. Video games are not anti-social. Instead, they are, and have always been, a force capable of getting people together, supporting the formation of thriving communities and the creation of an enormous information ecosystem to ensure they make the most of their digital play.

The main reason for this is obvious: play has generally been an influential driver of social communication. A report by the

LEGO Foundation and UNICEF states that play is critical to the development of children because it allows them 'to communicate ideas, to understand others through social interaction', thus 'paving the way to build deeper understanding and more powerful relationships'.[6] The National Institute for Play says that play helps adults to strengthen 'bonds between friends, family, and colleagues and creates a sense of belonging'.[7] A UK charity, the National Literacy Trust, found that play supports the development of communication skills. This includes video games, with one of its surveys finding that youngsters who play video games are consistently reading, writing and talking to one another about their experiences.[8]

Crucially, play is critical to adult life too. In particular, play shapes the spaces where we hang out, talk and form groups: driving the dynamics that consistently transform into political action.

At the heart of this is the concept of the 'third place'. Created by the sociologist Ray Oldenburg, the concept of the third place is simple enough. We have our homes, or the primary place where we exist. We have our places of work, the secondary structure in our life. And then we have the place in between where we meet people outside of those two contexts: the bars, cafés and sports stadiums where groups congregate.

These third places have lots of common characteristics. They're open and inviting. You're welcome to come and go as you please. Conversation is the main activity. But one of the other constant factors is that they are places where you have fun. Specifically, these places generate a 'playful atmosphere' that allows for levelling to take place: creating room for you to meet people, make friends and even, if you're lucky, fall in love.

Video games, despite their reputation, have served exactly the same function since they first emerged a little over fifty years ago. As early as 1972, barely a decade after the first video games were first invented, technofuturist Stewart Brand noted excitedly in an article for *Rolling Stone* magazine that *Spacewar!*, a multi-player space-battling video game that could only be played on mainframe computers, 'served primarily as a communication device between humans'. In contrast to boring computing functions like calculating sums or writing programs, *Spacewar!* was compelling enough to get university students from across the United States together in one room to fight it out in the world's first 'esports' (competitive video-game-playing) tournament.

And in the decades that followed, the video game industry evolved to provide this fun in more places. Arcade machines populated bars across the world. Consoles became a fixture of living rooms, finding a home under the television in millions of households. Home computers offered hobbyists and hackers ways to make, sell and play games into connected communities of enthusiasts who met up at events or swapped tips through magazines. This meant that video games encouraged people to come together, got people talking and led to the exchange of ideas, content and materials that spread news about the medium.

So, like other activities that draw people into third places, such as watching sport, playing darts, or simply having a properly playful gossip, video games proved fun enough to get people into one place. But as a result of their playfulness and their ability to bring communities together, video games ever so gently became a source of political concern for those in power.

Historically, third places have always been something that governments keep an eye on because where people meet, group up and communicate, influence – especially of the political kind – tends to follow. Sweden briefly banned people from drinking coffee in the eighteenth century after its rulers became convinced that coffee houses were 'dens of subversion'. In the 1950s, communist officials in Hungary quickly closed down a scheme which encouraged the peasantry to form reading groups after they immediately started talking politics.[9] Sports have also long provided the perfect mix of playfulness and political chatter, as seen in 2023 when fans of Turkish football club Fenerbahçe were banned from attending an away game after chanting anti-government slogans in defiance of local law.[10] And video games began to attract similar concerns relatively early in their life, particularly in East Germany, where local computing clubs that had got their hands on Western home PCs to play games attracted the interest of the Stasi.

But if the story of video games stopped in the 1980s or 1990s, it would rightly only be considered a minor influence on society. Video game hardware and software were too expensive in the early days for most people to enjoy them, with the market limited to a handful of consumer hubs like the US, Japan and Western Europe. Games' audience was limited to young men who bought technology, or to families who would buy an entertainment device for the home. Games were typically sold as separate discrete products with no way for people who played them to interact with others playing the game. The information ecosystem which evolved around the industry mostly existed to sell games and provide tips on how to beat them (specifically, in my case, the Water Temple in *The Legend of Zelda: Ocarina of Time*).

However, the evolution of the video games market did not stop there. In just three decades between the 1990s and the early 2020s, the push to make the medium a truly global phenomenon fundamentally changed its size, scope and ability to influence the world. The industry's need to ensure people could easily access high-end, low-cost computing devices created the conditions for the mass computing revolution that put a smartphone into billions of hands across the world. The desire to create games led to the emergence of 'democratised' game development tools like Unity and Unreal Engine, which turned the sector from a small cottage industry into a global sector with thousands of developers in all corners of the world. The rise of digital storefronts like Steam and the App Store allowed these businesses to reach customers across the world, transforming digital play from the preserve of young men – who dominated the market because they were more likely to buy technology to play games on – to a truly global, inclusive phenomenon. And the industry's rapid adoption of online play created a digital conversational ecosystem the likes of which the world had never seen before, with players in constant dialogue with each other, their sub-communities and the developers of the game across multiple digital communication channels simultaneously.

As a result, the nature of the industry morphed into something else entirely. Games were no longer the disconnected arcade machines, games consoles, or early PCs that sat in homes or bars waiting for people to congregate around them. Each game was its own third place, with its own thriving community, and with its own tightly connected digital information ecosystem that stretched from the confines of the games, through social media, into the real world. Games stopped being isolated products. Instead, they became individual buildings of an interconnected digital cityscape that allowed people, conversation and ideas to flow up and down the digital highways that connected virtual reality to the physical world.

The hundreds of thousands of games available on the market, and within platforms that allow you to make your own games, evolved into the digital third places where people hang out and talk.[11] *Among Us*, a social deduction game that is best described as *The Thing* for kids, saw its player count grow from the tens of thousands to half a billion active users in one month in November 2020 as people craved entertainment and connection during the pandemic.[12] And in *Fortnite*, Epic Games' action game extravaganza, nearly eleven million people dropped into the game in 2019 to hang out at a concert hosted by dance music producer Marshmello, an event that would spawn similar shows from Daft Punk and Travis Scott.[13] User-generated content platform *Roblox*, which allows players to create, share and hang out in games and worlds of their own, reported in July 2025 that over 111.8 million people entered its world on a daily basis.[14] The *Roblox* PR team confirmed to me separately that well over two billion in-world text messages between its players are generated every day.

But because conversation via in-game chat platforms is often ephemeral and lots of games, like popular single-player video games such as *God of War*, don't include chat functions, games have also become the dominant cultural force across most major social media platforms too. Reddit, the popular forum-based social media platform, reports that r/gaming is its third most popular subreddit in the world with 47 million members. That's more than the number of people who are subscribed to the boards about music (38 million subscribers), film (37 million subscribers) and even world news (which is just behind gaming as of July 2024). Discord, the voice and video chat platform designed initially for video game communities, reportedly serves over 200 million monthly active users.[15] Social video and video-streaming platforms also report vast quantities of games content, with YouTube recording six billion views on games content in June 2024,[16] TikTok reporting three trillion views of video game short videos in 2022,[17] and Twitch, the live-streaming video service founded by esports enthusiasts, drawing 2.5 million people to its service every day.[18]

And while the main reason why people talk in games or around games is to enjoy them, the act of getting people together and letting them talk naturally leads to the emergence of group dynamics we see in the rest of the world. Massively multiplayer online games (MMOs) like *World of Warcraft* and *EVE: Online* have hosted wakes, memorial services and even weddings for its player base.[19] Popular creators who have built massive communities by appealing to players have been able to expand their influence well beyond the industry, with major social media celebrities like MrBeast – the face behind a lavishly funded Amazon TV show – building his audience through videos. Games have also become places where people can exhort others to take action, as evidenced, in hilarious fashion, by the *Games Done Quick* live-streamed event raising hundreds of thousands of dollars for charity by teaching a Shiba Inu called Peanut Butter to 'speed-run' (i.e. complete as quickly as possible) a popular video game to the delight of a baying audience.[20]

Crucially, this transformation is a truly global trend. Over the past decade, China has become the biggest video games market in the world, with spend breaching $50bn per year across its 700 million players. The Middle East, Africa, Latin America and South East Asia have all grown significant games markets as smartphones have unlocked play for all. And with this truly global games market emerging, it means that the enormous social interconnection encouraged by the medium pours across borders. This allows games to connect people to one another across the world, turning it into a window through which people can look at, learn about and think about the way they live.

By slipping the constraints of being locked to one location or a piece of physical hardware, video games both individually and collectively found themselves at the heart of digital society. What happened within a game world, amongst its community, or within the information ecosystem that evolved to support it was no longer trapped in a physical space where games were played. Language, memes and identities formed within game communities could spread, propagate and multiply along digital pathways from the world of the game, through the communication channels players used and straight into the social media world. And with games a defining force behind the language, tropes and tone that dominate social media, what happens in video game communities bleeds out into reality – all the way into our political discourse.

Video game memes like 'Leeroy Jenkins', where a *World of Warcraft* player shouts his name while recklessly charging into a room to doom his companions, has been cited in the US House of Representatives by someone registering their vote for the similarly named representative Hakeem Jeffries. In February 2025, Ezra Klein warned that the Republican right's embrace of the term 'Non-Player Character' (a reference to virtual characters you can interact with in a game world that have little to no meaningful personality or agency) in regards to liberals was a warning to Democrats to avoid dull non-conformity. Games content itself has even been used to deceive in the real world, as seen in May 2022 when retired four-star general Barry McCaffrey was forced to delete a tweet after being tricked by trolls into posting footage of a realistic military video game that purported to be from the conflict in Ukraine.[21] And after investigators discovered that the alleged assassin of Charlie Kirk, the American podcaster who founded the Turning Point nonprofit organisation, had carved references to the video game *Helldivers 2* into his ammunition, it was alarmingly clear that what was happening within the third place of digital games was leaking into reality.

And worryingly, the influence that video games was having on society was noticed. But it wasn't by democracies. Stephen Bush, a keen gamer as well as the associate editor and daily political columnist for the *Financial Times*, told me that the 'middlebrow' perception of games prevented democratic elites from taking the medium seriously. Most major mainstream media outlets lack a video games editor or correspondent, reducing effective coverage of the medium and increasing the likelihood of moral panic reporting that alienates players. There are policy makers and officials who do cover games within government departments, but most of them are typically junior staff or hold a partial brief. And the cultural hangover towards games has led to a mechanical and prejudiced view of the impact of games on society. This has pushed people who play games away from the cultural mainstream. It has also meant that the cultural centre of society has failed to understand that much of the social discourse we see online is shaped upstream in game communities, depriving them of essential insights such as the centrality of humour to online discourse (and when, or if, to take it seriously).

As a result, the potential influence of video game communities and the information ecosystem was left uncontested. This allowed three groups to effectively enter the space: autocratic governments, violent extremists and populists. Less bound by cultural concerns and much more attuned to where social power lies, authoritarians, extremists and populists have spent the past decade trying to harness the force of the medium to their end. The potential power of video games content, communication channels and the communities that sit within them – especially a sub-culture of disaffected young men who feel left behind by the world – has been recognised as a powerful space for ideas to emerge and spread through the interconnected information eco-system around it.

These groups have therefore sought to achieve three goals within video game spaces to strengthen their hold on power: controlling the medium, co-opting it, or collaborating with communities within it to successfully capture the influence of the video game information ecosystem.

Actors may seek to control games to either stop individuals or groups meeting one another to share ideas or to wield the influence of the medium and industry to achieve their own ends. They may co-opt games by funding content and promoting messages in the medium with the intention of 'multiplying' it through the connected social media channels and news outlets that feed public discourse. Or they may collaborate with players or groups of players who share the same world view to promote their messages, encourage digital campaigning for their cause, or take action in the real world.

And by taking one of these approaches, or blending them together, authoritarians, populists and extremists have turned democratic complacency towards games to their advantage. By using an often ignored form of culture to promote messages, erode people's rights, or deploy toxic rhetoric in parts of our world where democracies haven't bothered to support the development of social norms, they've been able to capture parts of the games ecosystem and 'multiply' its influence through the medium's interconnected social channels – tangibly influencing and changing the world in the process.

This book aims to explain how this happened. It will explore how games content, communities and communication channels emerged into a force for mass communication. It will then show how authoritarians, extremists and populists realised its power, turning it into an effective front for political influence in the process. In the first part of the book, we'll discover how video games became a 'flattened' third place where conversation, information and ideas flow freely. By looking at how the medium drove down the cost of high-end computing, democratised the creation of games, made it easy to distribute them to people across the world and plugged it into our social economy, we'll see how an entertainment medium inadvertently transformed into a powerful third place that is both accessible and integral to the lives of billions of people across the world.

Then, in Part 2, I'll explore exactly how authoritarians, extremists and populists are controlling, co-opting, or collaborating with the power of video games to achieve their ends – drawing on the insight of nearly eighty experts from business, academia, civil society and politics to understand exactly what is going on.

I'll outline how Saudi Arabia's Crown Prince Mohammed bin Salman has driven forward a credible and cleverly structured $38bn plan to turn Saudi Arabia into the Middle Eastern hub for video games and esports, sharpening soft power to skewer critics of the regime domestically and internationally with the promise of liberal, modern entertainment at home.

I'll then explore how China has fought to control and censor online video games, examining how it used moral panic around video game addiction to justify mass surveillance of the more than 700 million people who play games in the country, forcing players to access their favourite online games through a login system designed and operated by the country's propaganda ministry.

From there, we will examine how Vladimir Putin's $50bn strategy for video games has turned the medium into another front of disinformation warfare, with state-funded video games, pro-Russian influencers and aggressive state-backed campaigning against Ukrainian developers forming an influential part of its video game arsenal.

The story will then turn to the troubling way that a sub-section of nihilistic video games communities have become a space where violent and extremist communities thrive, exploring in detail how an extremely toxic masculine subculture within games has become a space for radicalisation and self-radicalisation capable of bringing 'gamer-fied terror' to the streets of Charlottesville, Christchurch and Buffalo – and how this links to the assassination of Charlie Kirk.

And we will conclude the second part of the book by discovering how a 'luciferous insight' by Steve Bannon into the power of *World of Warcraft* communities eventually transformed into the creation of the alt-right: wrapping the tropes, tactics and communities within the radical fringe of the games industry into the movement that delivered Trump the White House on two separate occasions.

Amidst the gloom, there is room for optimism. In the final part of the book, I'll show how organisations and institutions that share democratic values or are part of democratic structures have effectively used games as a channel for influence, tapping into the desire of billions of players around the world to demonstrate the value of play to society at large. I'll conclude the book with recommendations on how to protect play from undue political influence, advocating for social solutions to the challenges that games face which encourage democratic institutions to empower developers, players and communities to promote democratic values within games.

The control that authoritarians, extremists and populists hold over games is due in no small part to how seriously they take them. By the end of this book, I hope to demonstrate why democracies and democrats should take them just as seriously to ensure the fun, creativity and power of play as a social force are used to support, rather than disrupt, our world.

Part 1
Building the battlefield

1

Play in every pocket

Video games are able to influence the world because video games drove the mass computing revolution that put powerful devices into everybody's pockets.

The growth of the video games sector has long been seen as a byproduct of technological development, an entertainment format which evolved as the cost of computing hardware allowed games to jump from bulky arcade cabinets in the corner of bars into the smartphones we look at on a daily basis.

That, however, is to misunderstand history. Professional, or as I'd like to say 'boring', uses of computers such as word-processing, filling out spreadsheets, or data analysis provided an impetus for the uptake of computing devices. But video games offered something much more compelling to people who could afford powerful technology, with high-end graphics and the latest features: fun.

And with the games industry dependent on getting those devices into the hands of consumers as cheaply as possible, the desire to play transformed into an almighty consumer catalyst that drove down the cost of computing devices and flattened access to tech. This put connected computing devices in the homes and hands of billions of people across the world, revolutionising the way we communicate in the process.

WAR GAMES

From the moment that the first video game emerged, it became obvious that the only way that games software could ever operate in a viable market was if the cost of computing hardware crashed down.

The first video games emerged from an industry that has a long track record of providing meaningful entertainment for young men through the ages: the US military.

Before the microprocessor was even a glint in the technology industry's eye, enterprising businessmen knew that bored service personnel on military bases wanted to play during downtime and would be willing to pay for it. In 1945, American businessmen Martin Bromley, Irving Bromberg and James Humbert founded a company with the intention of getting entertainment cabinets into military bases. After the United States banned slot machines in 1952, the trio shifted its business to Japan, South Korea and South Vietnam to entertain American personnel. By 1960, Service Games Japan, the branch of the business that was set up after the States banned slot machines, was bought by a new company founded by Bromley and a gentleman called Richard Stewart in Hawaii. That company was called Sega and would go on to become the business that created Sonic the Hedgehog.

But the military was also a natural place for video games to emerge from because it, along with the space industry, was one of the few sectors which had access to powerful computing devices because of their usefulness in the waging of war.

The Colossus code-breaking computer proved how valuable computing devices could be to the conduct of conflict, wheeling its way through thousands of potential combinations of Germany's Enigma code to significantly shorten the Second World War (supported in no small part by the daring seizure of a code book from a German U-Boat in the mid-Atlantic in 1941).[1] The University of Pennsylvania's experimental Electronic Numerical Integrator and Computer (ENIAC) had also shown that computing could greatly improve the accuracy of bombing runs – eventually leading to the use of computing components and software within smart weaponry.[2] The developments in America's military also supported the emergence of its space industry, with the National Aeronautics and Space Administration's (NASA) demand for effective high-end computing components supporting the growth of businesses like Fairchild Semiconductor, which created the necessary components to power the emerging hardware economy.

But the cost of early computing components remained high. It was therefore important for both the military and the space sector to find ways to drive down the cost of computing devices to maximise the benefits of the computing revolution.

In 1957, the US military founded a body called the Digital Equipment Corporation (DEC) to achieve this. It sought to lower the cost of computing devices by simultaneously lowering hardware costs through design efficiencies and swapping outdated and expensive punchcard 'software' for programmable mainframes which used digital coding languages.

This led to the creation of the user-friendly and comparatively cheap Programmed Data Processor (PDP) mainframe computer, which spread to military bases and universities across America. Importantly, the PDP also boasted a visual display – invaluable for the first game creators.

Meanwhile within the space industry, Fairchild was rapidly lowering the cost of its semiconductors because its business relationship with NASA allowed it to produce better semiconductors, at greater scale, while lowering the price. In December 1961, the company's Micrologic chip sold for $120. By October 1962, its price had dropped to $15 – an 87.5 per cent decrease in price in less than twelve months.[3]

The rapid advancement of computing technologies was recognised by Gordon Moore in 1965. Moore, who was a technologist at Fairchild before he co-founded Intel, observed that the number of transistors that could fit on a chip was roughly doubling each year. Although the observation was adjusted in 1975 to suggest chip capacity doubled every two years, his maxim – now known as Moore's Law – has remained accurate to the present day.[4]

But to follow Moore's Law, computing businesses had to find markets beyond the military, the space sector and universities which used their devices. According to the author Chris Miller in *Chip War: The Fight for the World's Most Critical Technology*, 'only consumer markets had the volume to fund the vast research and development (R&D) programs that Moore's Law required'.

So for hardware businesses the challenge was to find markets for consumer devices that had both a mass audience and a need for ever more powerful computing components. And there were a few industries that did emerge which helped to drag down the cost of computing to an affordable level for consumers.

Calculators were one of the first devices to hit consumers across the world. In 1968, Hewlett-Packard released its first calculator, called the HP-9100A, for $5,000. This was cheap compared to buying a mainframe computer like the PDP, which cost at least six figures to purchase, but was still pricey. But just four years later, its HP-35 calculator with snazzy logarithmic and trigonometric functions was on sale for $400. And by 1976, some of HP's rivals had calculators selling for $50 – creating a mass market for consumers to access.[5]

Portable music players, meanwhile, showed that entertainment devices could prove a hit with customers seeking affordable electronics. In July 1979, the Sony Walkman went on sale in Japan for approximately $150 (33,000 yen) and offered customers the thrill of listening to music tapes on the go. By 2010, when the brand was eventually discontinued, Sony had sold over

110m devices.[6] It had also spawned a market for portable music across different 'software' formats, with CD players and eventually MP3 players like Apple's iPod launching in 2001.

The emergence of the personal computing market also significantly increased consumer access to powerful computing devices. The invention of IBM's 4-bit 4004 'computer on a chip' microprocessor in 1971, its more powerful 8-bit successor the 8080 in 1974 and the emergence of timeshare computing (which invented the computer file structure we're all familiar with) led to the creation of the Altair 8800.

Created by Ed Roberts and sold through his Albuquerque-based business Micro Instrumentation and Telemetry Systems (MITS) from 1974, it gave consumers access to a programmable computer featuring an Intel 8080 central processing unit (CPU) that included a series of ports to allow people to plug the device into other components like a screen for $400. This was nearly ten times cheaper than the eighth PDP mainframe computer at the time.

Each sector played a part in building a consumer market for computing products. Calculators offered increasingly easy access to portable calculating devices that could solve mathematical problems on the fly. The cassette player further demonstrated that people would pay for consumer electronic devices that entertained them on the go. The rise of personal computing led to the emergence of an eager hobbyist community that was keen to build connections and businesses to serve a growing market. This included two teenagers called Bill Gates and Paul Allen, who founded Microsoft to sell a tool that allowed people to program software for the Altair via the programming language Beginners' All-purpose Symbolic Instruction Code (BASIC).[7]

But each of these markets initially had a ceiling to their use of technology. Calculators benefited from ever-greater computing power, but lacked visual displays to create meaningful entertainment on. Portable music players created the idea of accessing content on the go, but they were broadly 'mechanical' in the way they read media. Personal computers did have the potential to push the limits of technology (and would), but were initially held back by a lack of imagination amongst advocates. Ed Roberts, for instance, listed 23 uses for a personal computer in MITS's in-house publication *Popular Electronics*. Making games, or entertainment of any form, didn't get a look-in.[8]

However, others thought differently from Roberts. Creative technologists from across the world had already started to dabble with the idea that computing equipment could be used to create fun. And the creators of those early forms of interactive entertainment quickly realised they were a perfect way to stretch the limits of hardware and excite people: opening up a consumer market capable of driving rapid technological innovation at low cost.

BLAST OFF

The first product that we would describe as a video game emerged in 1962 at the Massachusetts Institute of Technology, and somewhat fittingly, it sat at the intersection of space culture, military technology and academic experimentation.

Spacewar!, which Stewart Brand described in an article in *Rolling Stone* magazine as 'the illegitimate child of the marrying of computers and graphic displays',[9] was created by Steve Russell, a computer scientist who would later mentor Bill Gates and Paul Allen on the use of mainframe PCs in the late 1960s, with members of the university's hacking hobbyist group the Tech Model Railroad Club (TMRC).

After MIT got its hands on a PDP-1 in September 1961, Russell and a group of TMRC scientists were inspired to create a 'B-movie' science fiction space game to make the most of the pattern-generating programs which could run via the mainframe's screen.

Following a period of development, *Spacewar!* emerged as a multiplayer game that allowed players to battle one another in a top-down 2D environment. Talented players were able to defeat their opponents by carefully using limited fuel reserves, their stash of weaponry and nearby environmental effects like the gravity well of a nearby star to catapult them to victory. Less able players were, presumably, booed and hissed at.

The game mattered for three big reasons. First, it showed immediately that creating games was a great way to make people better coders and push devices to their limits.

Albert Kuhfield of *Analog Magazine*, who was cited in Stewart Brand's 1972 article about the game, said that students who worked on developing their own versions of the game were 'learning computer theory faster and more painlessly than they'd ever seen before'. L. Peter Deutsch, an employee at Xerox who had not worked on the game but had seen its influence on the industry, suggested that the 1962 game was 'not an outgrowth of any work on computer-graphics, but . . . may have inspired – some of it'.[10] In short, calculators might be useful for doing maths but video games were much better for encouraging the development of computer graphics.

Second, it demonstrated that games were capable of attracting serious interest amongst audiences. As well as proving immensely popular at MIT, the game spread across universities throughout the United States as other students wrote their own versions or deployed code shared with them by TMRC over the Advanced Research Projects Agency Network (ARPANET) – the US military's networked computing forerunner to the internet. The game's distribution was also supported by DEC, which would go on to recommend that institutions installing a new PDP should code the game onto their devices to act as a diagnostic tool to check it was working properly.[11] And as seen in the much quoted article from Stewart Brand, the game had the power to bring together players from across the US to take part in a competitive *Spacewar!* tournament – birthing esports in the process.

Finally, *Spacewar!* banged the drum for the importance of driving down the cost of hardware to access games. The cost of a PDP-1 in the early 1960s was approximately $20,000.[12] DEC may have worked to reduce the cost of mainframe computing. But without a drastic drop in the price of hardware and a way to make money from the games made for it, interactive entertainment risked being stuck in the computer labs of American universities.

From the earliest days of the games industry all the way to the present day, the sector grappled with the hardware question posed by *Spacewar!*: how could it make devices both powerful and accessible enough to hit a mass consumer audience? And between the early 1970s and the mid 1980s, the answer across all parts of the developing games industry was to strike the balance between affordability, technological innovation and delivering entertainment that could reach a large audience.

Atari demonstrated this in the early years of the arcade industry. Its first arcade game, *Computer Space* – which was a single-player knock-off of *Spacewar!* inspired by Nolan Bushnell's time playing the game on Stanford University's PDP-6 – proved something of a commercial flop, failing to sell more than 1,500 units. But its later machines showed how finding the sweet spot of cost, computing and consumer interest could work in its favour.

The manufacture of virtual tennis game *Pong*, which first hit the market in 1972, was initially conceived by Bushnell as a way to test the skills of newly hired ex-General Electric employee Allan Alcorn without pressuring him to release the game commercially.

Alcorn's successful development of a low-cost prototype – featuring a not at all top-of-the-range $75 black-and-white Hitachi monitor – proved a massive hit in both local bar Andy Capp's Tavern and later across the US, selling 8,000 units and becoming the first commercially successful video game.[13] Steve

Jobs and Steve Wozniak, the co-founders of Apple, would demonstrate the value of efficiency versus entertainment by creating the arcade cabinet for single-player *Pong* spin-off *Breakout* (1976) with fewer than thirty chips – well below the 150 chips typically used in an arcade machine at the time.

And while both *Pong* and *Breakout* were landmark achievements for games, the hardware innovation that underpinned them was integral to both the success of the industry and the way the games' creators saw themselves.

'I was lucky enough to speak to Al Alcorn and I called him a game designer quite casually,' said Will Freeman, a freelance games journalist who regularly frequents outlets such as the *Guardian*. 'And he almost got quite offended and said "I'm an engineer", because they weren't using code or software.'

The earliest home consoles faced similar engineering challenges to their arcade counterparts. The Magnavox Odyssey, the first home video games console that could play a simple game of tennis,[14] was released in September 1972 after Ralph Baer, a German computer engineer, had convinced the military consulting company that he worked for to license his 'closed circuit electronic playground' to the American electronics brand.[15]

While the device would sell 350,000 units between 1972 and 1975, it sold a comparatively low 69,000 consoles in the first year after its price point of $100 proved too high for consumers exploring a new market.[16] Price sensitivity would become an ongoing concern for the console industry for years to come.

Home computers, meanwhile, became a space where a combination of hobbyist-led development practices and increasingly powerful home computing devices played a big role in pushing forward the technological credentials of video games.

For example, British game developers in the early 1980s managed to develop games which continually pushed the limit of home computing devices. The 1983 release *Manic Miner* dazzled players with its ability to retain twenty 2D screens in the ZX Spectrum's exceedingly limited memory. But just four years later, in 1987, '3D' game *Head Over Heels* capably stored 300 screens as developers eked performance improvements out of each device.[17]

By the mid 1980s, it was clear that games were becoming the benchmark against which consumer computing hardware was being measured. In 1984, Apple released an advert for its Apple II home personal computer that coached teenagers through the arguments they should make to convince their parents to spend what was a then hefty $1,030 on the device. For unsuspecting parents, the computer was an educational device which doubled up as a tax write-off. But for teens, Apple was explicitly selling them the dream of a powerful motherboard on which to play what it claimed was the biggest collection of games around.[18]

That marketing message hinted at something crucial that had changed in the games market between the early 1970s and the mid 1980s. Until the late 1970s, hardware manufacturers made their money by selling devices into homes. But by 1979, consoles such as the Fairchild Channel F System II – made by the same business that had been producing chips for NASA's space programme – sold itself to consumers on its revolutionary new game cartridge system that allowed players to plug in one of twenty-four cartridges to play dozens of games.[19]

We'll look more closely at what this expansion of games software did to the economics of the industry in Chapter 3. But for now, this mattered for two reasons.

In the immediate short term, the emergence of a glut of consoles and home computers saw the games market soar in size and scale. But as low-quality consoles and games flooded the market and companies across the world sought to capitalise on what was seen to be a home entertainment revolution, the low quality of devices and games led to consumers losing confidence in the sector. And this caused the almighty 1983 video game crash in America, wiping billions of dollars off the nascent industry's valuation in the process.

The crash hammered the games industry. It also prompted a rethink about the market from its biggest players. If consumers were more interested in the quality and breadth of games available on the device, selling a dedicated piece of video game hardware wasn't an opportunity to make money: it was a barrier.

Therefore, hardware manufacturers targeting players had a new guiding principle to build their businesses around. Consumer games hardware needed to be more powerful *and* a heck of a lot cheaper to build a market. And it was this curious mix of a race-to-the-bottom on price and a race-to-the-top on power that turned games hardware into the engine capable of putting low-cost computing devices in every home across the world.

THE EDGE OF THE RAZOR

The year 1983 represented something of a turning point for the industry. While arcades did not end in the early 1980s, the year was considered the end of the golden age of the arcade machine. *Pac-Man*, *Donkey Kong* and *Space Invaders* had all enjoyed their successes. But digital play was shifting away from comparatively costly arcade cabinets that could only play one game, or a handful of games, in a dedicated location towards selling affordable devices to consumers that could offer an exciting – and constantly sellable – variety of games to play.

Partly, this is a representation of the pace of technological change caused by a rapid acceleration in computing power. When *Computer Space* first hit the market in 1971, Bushnell was forced to abandon plans to use a 16-bit computer to build his cabinet because of its prohibitive $4,000 cost. By 1987, the TurboGrafx-16 home console, which used a 16-bit processor, entered the market at $399.

However, the change was also caused by a shift in the economics underpinning the games industry. The rise of devices that could run different games, or software, by inserting new cartridges – whether games consoles, PCs or eventually hand-held devices – meant that software, rather than hardware, became the way that companies made the most money. As a result, hardware manufacturers faced a question: how do we make our devices more powerful while making money?

For console companies, the answer was to suck up the costs as much as possible. By the mid 1980s, games hardware makers such as Nintendo began to apply a 'razor and blades' model to selling their consoles. In return for selling the console at a price that was low margin, broke even or sometimes made a loss, the manufacturer hoped to make up the cost by selling its games software.

The decision to pursue this model had a profound impact on the affordability of powerful computing devices in the home. According to investment firm Konvoy, the average profit margin on the sale of a top games console dropped from 44.28 per cent in the middle of the 1980s to 14.58 per cent by the early 2000s.[20] The result was that the cost of games consoles essentially did not rise in line with inflation between 1990 and the early 2020s, despite the technology within consoles evolving from running games with simple 2D animations to enormous open world games like *Red Dead Redemption 2*, which engrosses players in a cinematically crafted version of the American West.

However, consoles were not the only devices that pursued cost-efficiency as a way of opening up markets. The evolution of handheld devices created a new market for portable computing as typified by the success of the Game Boy. The device rejected the typical games console approach of delivering the most powerful experience possible to players.

Instead, its creator, Gunpei Yokoi, did something else. He

accepted that the Game Boy would not be affordable if he used the best components on the market. Instead, he focused on using cheaper 'outdated' components to allow players to buy the handheld at an affordable price and play on the go. Bundled with the popular puzzle game *Tetris* and sold for $89 at launch in 1990, the Game Boy went on to sell over 100m units. This opened up the portable games market, paving the way for the mobile games industry that dominates the gaming world today.

The early video game PC market, meanwhile, drove efficiency of price at the highest end of computing. Gunpei Yokoi needed to make the Game Boy cheap to sell to families who wanted a device that was akin to a toy. PC hardware makers, on the other hand, were well placed to sell powerful components to its audience because the hobbyist market consisted mostly of teenage boys and men who were willing to fork out for the most powerful devices. This was especially true for those who enjoyed games running in realistic 3D, whether it was a first-person shooter game like *Quake* or simulator games like Microsoft's *Flight Simulator* series.

Nvidia is a perfect example of such a business. Founded in 1993 by Jensen Huang, Curtis Priem and Chris Malachowsky, the company's goal was to make powerful but affordable Graphics Processing Units (GPUs) that it could sell to people who wanted to play high-end PC games. After a wobbly start, which almost saw the business go under in 1997, its RIVA 128 GPU provided an ideal mix of affordability and power to PC players. The chip sold a million units within four months. And the quality of the company's work led to it providing chips for the original Xbox that launched in November 2001. Microsoft's decision to sell the console at a loss of reportedly $250 per console illustrates how willingly companies would drive down the cost of powerful hardware to make sure they had a market to sell software to.

The affordability of games hardware did have an impact on player numbers. While the precise figures are difficult to track across the 1980s and 1990s due to a lack of data, the Entertainment Software Association reported in 2005 that 47 per cent of Americans planned to purchase at least one game over the course of the year.[21] And across the world, Sony would report that it had successfully shipped 79 million PlayStation 2 devices to people between 2001 and 2005 – demonstrating the burgeoning dedicated market for game devices.[22]

However, the impact of video games on the affordability of high-end hardware would stretch beyond games. The highly effective, low-cost hardware innovation that the games industry was driving proved useful for its devices. But those developments also proved invaluable for companies looking to use those technologies in other contexts too – opening up the mass-computing revolution that shapes the world today.

CONNECTING BEYOND GAMES

By the mid 2000s, games hardware had built a player base on PC and console that were ready to be reached. As we'll see in Chapter 4, this created the conditions for communities to use high speed internet access to congregate, communicate and create content. This helped create the conditions for video games to become an influential 'third place', eventually transforming game players and communities into potentially politically influential players.

However, the importance of games as a channel for influence would be significantly lower if the medium had not been responsible for driving the mass adoption of a range of technologies that have changed the way we meet, greet and talk with one another in the digital space. For instance, technological developments within the video games industry are directly responsible for the device that billions of us would deem to be the most important one in our lives: the smartphone. Since the launch of the iPhone in 2007, over four billion people across the world have become an owner of a smart device.[23] Many people credit the smartphone with transforming the games industry. But according to the company responsible for the architecture behind 99 per cent of smartphones across the world, it's actually the mobile industry that owes a debt to hand-held video game consoles.

Established in 1990, Arm is a company that designs chips and then licenses those designs out for companies to produce, allowing it to come up with ideas for components while passing on the cost of fabrication to the hardware giants who want to use them.

'What we do is provide the designs and architecture behind compute [the infrastructure required to process, train and run artificial intelligence models] on all sorts of devices,' said James McNiven, vice-president of product management for the client line of business at Arm. 'That means the design of the CPUs, the GPUs, the bus that binds it all together and other things as well that are effectively needed to build a silicon platform. And then we license that to other companies who will add their own stuff around that, which will eventually come out in the form of a chip or solution.'

Arm now designs chips for everything from laptops to servers. But the company established its reputation as a leader in the field through the design of powerful energy-efficient chip designs. And it did this by becoming the backbone of the hand-held gaming market that powered the likes of *Tetris* and *Pokémon* into the mainstream conversation.

The company's relationship with Nintendo was critical for acquiring this scale. Following the success of the Game Boy, Nintendo needed a chip partner who aligned with its favoured System on a Chip (SoC) model. A SoC is an integrated circuit that includes all the components a computer needs to function, like the CPU and the GPU. But it allows the 'computer' to be much, much smaller: reducing the size, the weight, the amount of energy and the cost of the whole device in the process.

Nintendo's approach aligned with Arm's business model,[24] but initially the companies couldn't find a way to work together. Nintendo approached Arm to ask for a chip design for its Virtual Boy VR console.* While the two companies found common ground, the code density of Arm's chips proved too inflexible for Nintendo to use.

However, the failure to win Nintendo's business sparked an important development within Arm. Dave Jaggar, a CPU designer at the company, set about designing a new core that provided a closer fit to Nintendo's requirements – providing maximum performance under power and storage constraints (a key consideration for battery-powered handheld consoles).

The company unveiled the ARM7TDMI in October 1994. Despite the progress, Nintendo did not initially leap at the prospect of the new core. Instead, it was Nokia that was first to recognise its efficiency by using the chip within its 6110 handset: the first of the company's phones that came bundled with the popular time-sink *Snake*.

Nintendo later recognised the ARM7DTMI's value in significant fashion. The two companies cut a deal to embed the chip into Nintendo's successor to the Game Boy. The Game Boy Advance (GBA) was released in June 2001 and offered players 32-bit graphics in the palm of their hand. Given that players less than ten years before were buying Nintendo's 16-bit home console, the Super Nintendo Entertainment System, it was a huge leap forward graphically for a handheld device.

* The Virtual Boy was a proto-VR headset. The device was riddled with problems, including its red-and-black virtual display. It proved a commercial flop, with its only real legacy proving to be the release of the first Mario Tennis game. A slim achievement.

Crucially, that advancement did not come at the expense of cost or battery efficiency. The GBA launched in the US with a retail price of $100, but offered up to twenty hours of battery life – much more than handheld rivals such as the Atari Lynx. This transformed the GBA into a handheld best seller, selling 81.5m units worldwide against Nintendo's forecast of 24 million units.[25]

The two businesses then repeated the trick with the Nintendo DS. This handheld device, which featured a touch screen, a second visual display and 64-bit graphics comparable to those that drove sales of the Nintendo 64 home console less than a decade before, teamed an ARM7TDMI processor with two new ARM946E-S chips.

After the DS was released in Japan in 2004, the device proved to be an even bigger hit than the GBA. It went on to sell 154 million devices over the course of its lifespan, making it the third best-selling console in history at time of writing.* In doing so, it cemented a partnership between the two businesses which continues to this day, with Arm architecture featuring in the recently released Nintendo Switch 2.

More importantly for the development of smartphones, Arm's work with Nintendo positioned it as the perfect partner for touch screens. Despite Arm being part founded by Apple, Steve Jobs initially approached Intel to provide the architecture for the first iPhone. But after talks broke down, Jobs instead opted to license a chip design from Arm, as it was clear that the Cambridge-based company had the advantage in the market because it had shown its prowess via the Game Boy Advance and DS.

'Portable games were an important early market for Arm, helping it acquire the scale needed to become the standard

---

* The original Nintendo Switch had sold just over 150 million units at the time of writing, meaning it is likely to have overtaken DS lifetime sales in the gap between the completion of this manuscript and the publication of the book.

architecture for mobile devices,' said Chris Miller, the author of *Chip War*, when I spoke to him in September 2024.

The result was historic. The iPhone quickly transformed from a remarkably high-end mobile phone into the starting point for the smartphone economy. Within a handful of years, the number of people who owned smart devices across the world had ballooned past the billion mark. And Arm, as a result of its work with Apple and the flexibility it had learned with Nintendo, was now building its relationship with other tech businesses, leading to companies such as Samsung, Qualcomm and Huawei* licensing its chip designs.

We'll see in Chapter 3 how games powered the mobile economy through software with the growth of free-to-play. But the society-shaking impact of games hardware doesn't end here. The final major way that games hardware has influenced the way we interact with the world is by enabling the success of Nvidia, the multi-trillion-dollar superpower driving the AI economy across the world.

The role of Nvidia's chips in providing the infrastructure underpinning the generative AI services that are disrupting the way we talk, think and are influenced cannot be understated. Oracle announced in May 2025 that it was going to buy $40bn of Nvidia chips[26] to power an OpenAI data centre in Texas to support ChatGPT, a generative AI chatbot, and Sora, its generative AI video service. DeepSeek, the Chinese rival to OpenAI, also reported in a research paper that it trained its rival to ChatGPT using Nvidia chips, according to Gregory C. Allen of the Wadwani AI Center.[27]

And while it is true that the vast majority of Nvidia's business is found in artificial intelligence rather than video games, its role as a video game GPU maker gave it an invaluable cost

---

* Arm would later terminate its relationship with Huawei due to national-security concerns.

and reach advantage over its competitors that it was able to parlay into AI dominance.

In 2005, Nvidia was a relatively successful chip business. It was valued at approximately \$6bn[28] and Tony Smith of *The Register* reported that the company was in the top twenty-five chipmakers in the world. But its market share was under 1 per cent.[29] This compares to the 7 per cent of the semiconductor market it holds as of 2024[30] and the 80+ per cent share of the AI GPU market it is holding on to.[31]

However, Nvidia's focus on building great video-game-ready GPUs gave it an unexpected advantage in the market. By 2009, the company was already writing blog posts about how GPUs were much better than CPUs at performing complicated tasks quickly. Because GPUs were designed to handle complex tasks like throwing together realistic-looking graphics in a video game and displaying them effectively on screen while things constantly changed, GPUs turned out to be excellent at completing thousands of tasks at once. This means GPUs were far better suited to parallel computing, where a computer makes thousands of calculations at once, than CPUs.[32]

Nvidia had the expertise to build GPUs, knew how to assemble them cheaply and at scale, through a relationship with Taiwan's Semiconductor Manufacturing Company (TSMC), and had plenty of GPUs active in the market, having been selling them for years. It just needed something to join those dots together in its favour.

That something turned out to be the company's Compute Unified Device Architecture (CUDA). CUDA's pitch was simple – it allowed developers to repurpose a GPU for whatever purpose they wanted. For example, if you had bought a PC with a GPU to play games you could use CUDA to train a machine-learning model instead – transforming a tool people bought for fun into one they could use for work.

It cleverly inverted Ed Roberts's belief that people would buy computers to be useful, by allowing businesses to use components designed for play for different professional purposes. Crucially, though, Nvidia inserted one catch into the use of CUDA. You could use the software however you liked, but it would only work with the company's chips.

In a stroke, the company had laid the foundation for its dominance of the AI economy. By allowing developers to repurpose GPUs for general computing, Nvidia made parallel computing accessible and effective for a range of markets. But by tying it back to its ecosystem of affordable, yet powerful, games GPUs, Nvidia developed the reach and the price to become the market leader.

And while the advantage did not materialise immediately, Jensen Huang's decision to go all in on AI in 2013, after reading academic research about the state of AI, saw the business ascend to dizzying heights. As companies like DeepMind and OpenAI commenced both the deep learning and generative AI revolution, Nvidia's valuation boomed. In 2017, the company had a market capitalization just shy of $70bn. Eight years later, it had become a multi-trillion-dollar business with CUDA turning its existing GPUs – and more recently developed specialist AI chips – into the backbone of the AI economy.

So while games now form less than 10 per cent of Nvidia's business revenue, the company's history as a video games hardware manufacturer was fundamental to assuming its dominance over the GPU market. The business requirement to make high-powered GPUs at a low enough cost to run on consumer-ready video game PCs spread its components cheaply around the world. CUDA transformed the reach of Nvidia's GPUs globally into a major competitive advantage within the early AI economy. And this allowed it to become its backbone: turning video game hardware into a force capable of driving a global technological revolution.

STRATEGIC SIGNIFICANCE

Video games hardware played an integral role in flattening the cost of high-end computing, lowering the cost of the devices we play on. But it also lowered the cost and increased the effectiveness of computing hardware across the board, acting as the key to unlocking the modern economy and having a significant impact on society in two main ways.

The first is the unexpected overspill effect of games hardware tipping into other parts of society. The low cost and versatility of technology used to power video games has proven useful in ways that are varied, unexpected and occasionally worrying.

Virtual reality (VR) headsets, which emerged in modern form from games company Oculus before its acquisition by Meta, have proven how adaptable low-cost immersive devices created for games can be in the wider economy. Virtual reality has been used to train pilots of cargo ships to steer tankers through the ocean.[33] The headsets have helped train first responders to deal with mass casualty events, offering training that would otherwise only occur in the most extreme circumstances.[34] Hospitals such as Ottawa University use spatial technology to let surgeons see an accurately sized 3D version of tumours they're about to operate on – improving outcomes for patients in the process.[35]

However, the usefulness of games hardware has also led to its adaptation or appropriation in contexts that we'd be less comfortable with. In 2024, Qianer Liu, a journalist at the *Financial Times,* revealed that Chinese businesses had resorted to buying thousands of Nvidia's video game GPUs to help train their AI models after the United States briefly barred the exports of the company's most powerful AI ready chips to the country.[36] A member of the Ukrainian armed forces was spotted using a Steam Deck handheld PC to control a gun turret on the frontlines of the war against Russia.[37] The United Kingdom has imposed restrictions on the sale of game controllers into Russia because gamepads are – as in Western countries – used to pilot drones.[38]

But more importantly for this book, the main side effect of the adoption of video games hardware is that it created the conditions upon which ownership of a cheap, high-powered computer shifted from the dream of consumers in a few wealthy nations to a part of life for billions of people across the world.

Japan, America and Western Europe were early adopters of such devices in the 1980s and 1990s because consumers had the individual wealth which put televisions, CD players and game devices into their homes. They also had access to devices as a result of international trade driven by democratic nations, something that authoritarian countries could not tap into during the Cold War.

Africa, Latin America, the Middle East, parts of Eastern Europe and much of Asia had not been able to participate equally in the consumer technology revolution. But as a result of video games hardware driving down the cost of mass computing enough to make the smartphone economy a viable global business, countries such as China, Russia and Saudi Arabia now had access to both the devices and the games that connected them with peers across the world.

This created opportunities for them to connect, to communicate and to learn about communities across their country or the world in ways that they couldn't before, driving the growth of the digital economy and the emergence of a truly interconnected world.

But it also gradually led to a realisation that the depth of connection between citizens in authoritarian nations and those in democratic countries was greater than ever. And with many of those nations aware of the impact of soft power such as culture during the collapse of Communism in Europe in the 1980s, controlling or influencing the cultural spaces where people could communicate via these new devices – including via games – gradually rose up the political agenda.

But while video games were certainly popular, they were also hard to make, produced in a handful of countries with longer histories of access to consumer technology, and marketed at a limited number of players. The invention of new technologies that have helped democratise game development has transformed the act of making games from the narrow preserve of a small number of developers into a genuinely open form of content creation: allowing games to become a vehicle or a space through which influence can be exercised across the world.

2

Engines of growth

For video games to resonate with billions of people around the world, two things needed to happen. As we saw in Chapter 1, computing devices had to become cheap enough and powerful enough for everyone in the world to become a player. But to reach all these players with games that appealed to them, game development needed to become simpler to allow developers to create more games, more easily.

Between 1970 and the early 2020s, the process of creating video games democratised in an extraordinary way. In the early years of the industry, it would be a struggle to suggest that more than a few hundred commercially developed video games were made each year. By contrast, approximately 150,000 new games (7,500 console, 18,500 PC and 126,000 mobile titles) were released in 2024 on top of the hundreds of thousands of games already available to players.

This glut of games was possible because of the invention of a new, multi-purpose technology: the game development engine. The tool, which was popularised by the companies Unity and Unreal, simplified the process of making popular video games. Whether you were making a giant multiplayer game like *Fortnite*, the real-world monster-collecting phenomenon *Pokémon Go*, or the multi-million-dollar hit *Hollow Knight: Silksong*, game engines made it much easier for development teams of all sizes to overcome the technical and creative challenges of making games.

For the global games industry, the emergence of game engines made it possible to make an enormous variety of creative games to appeal to audiences and demographics around the world. But for the world at large, the game engine served another function too.

The tool acted as the video game equivalent of Johannes Gutenberg's printing press. It turned the manufacture of games into a new way to communicate with audiences through a different form of interaction. In doing so, it created a new arena in which people could be influenced: paving the way for the politicisation of video games and the digital third places they created in the process.

A HIGH DIFFICULTY LEVEL

Since the earliest days of the video game industry, one question has been at the forefront of game developers' minds: how can we make game development simpler, more repeatable and lower cost?

Making video games has always been a uniquely difficult creative challenge. Games have, to some extent, featured many of the ingredients essential to every other cultural form: great writing to tell a story; arresting graphics or visuals to catch a player's attention like a glitzy Hollywood movie; compelling soundtracks that capture the feel of a game in the same way a great musical score does.

Unlike other cultural forms, games must combine all of these elements into an interactive package that responds to a player's command. In contrast to a film, a book or a theatre production, a video game has to give the player meaningful control within a digital world, systems, or game mechanics designed by the developer. And if that world doesn't work because the code is wrong, doesn't feel convincing because the creative aspects of it do not hold together or, most elusively of all, simply isn't fun to play, the game either goes back to square one in development or is killed (whether behind closed doors by the developer or upon commercial release).

The process of making video games can prove remarkably expensive. Sony accidentally revealed in a series of poorly redacted court documents that *The Last of Us Part II* cost $220m to develop,[1] double the budget HBO put aside to fund a remake of the game for TV.[2] Activision Blizzard's *Call of Duty: Black Ops Cold War* cost more than $700m to develop and maintain over its multi-year life-span: nearly 50 per cent higher than the $450m budget for *Jurassic Park: Dominion*, the most expensive film in history. And the reported $2bn budget for *Grand Theft Auto VI* makes Rockstar's newest crime caper more costly than building the Burj Khalifa.[3]

The enormous cost of these projects might suggest that making games is the preserve of multi-billion-dollar businesses alone. Yet the reality is different. *Hollow Knight: Silksong* became a multi-million-dollar hit from the work of three full-time developers and a handful of consulting developers. *Overcooked!*, the BAFTA award-winning multiplayer cooking game, was created by a team of four developers based in a house in Cambridge in the United Kingdom. *Flappy Bird*, the 2014 free-to-play mobile game that briefly went viral and reached hundreds of millions of players worldwide, was made by a solo developer based in Vietnam.

The existence of both a high-end video game production industry and a thriving scene of small independent studios is a by-product of the democratisation of development that has occurred over the past five decades. But back in the earliest days of the industry in the 1970s, the challenge was initially simpler: how do you make great games using a limited number of computing components associated with a single unit of hardware?

To begin with, that meant making games with as little coding as possible. As we've seen already, 1972 arcade game

Pong was literally engineered by Allan Alcorn to run without code at all. But most arcade games like *Defender*, *Donkey Kong*, and *Space Invaders* were made with something called assembly code. The big advantage of using this low-level programming language was its direct relation to the hardware you played the game on – every device (such as an arcade cabinet) intended to run the game would be standardised. You knew exactly what hardware the game would run on, so you only had to make the game work on one device.

However, I'm guessing that you're likely to have already anticipated the problem with this approach: the evolution of the games industry. By the late 1970s and early 1980s, players were beginning to expect that their home consoles, personal computers and arcade machines should be able to play lots of games. Devices that only played a single game were already at risk of becoming out of date. And as more consoles and computers began to hit the market, companies who wanted to serve as many players as possible couldn't risk writing a game that worked on one device alone.

As a result, the industry began to shift towards using 'high-level' programming languages like BASIC to make games that could theoretically be built on lots of devices. BASIC was created by John G. Kemeny and Thomas E. Kurtz in 1964 with the aim of democratising access to computing. 'Our vision was that every student on campus should have access to a computer, and any faculty member should be able to use a computer in the classroom whenever appropriate,' said Kemeny in a 1991 interview cited by a *Time* magazine profile of BASIC in 2014.[4]

High-level languages like BASIC have a less close relationship with the hardware they run on than assembly languages. They also let budding programmers make software using 'natural language' (i.e. the computer understands certain human language) and with standardised processes. This made it easier for people to both make software and to run it on different devices, provided they understood the language. This resulted in a wider shift towards this language over a number of decades.

Throughout the 1980s, the home computing revolution was built almost entirely on the back of BASIC, which ran on pretty much every device released into the market. In the console space, Nintendo and Sony both steadily adopted another high-level programming language called C for their Nintendo 64 and PlayStation devices. Apple used a version of C called Objective-C for its iPhone before eventually switching to its own programming language called Swift in June 2014.

This shift towards higher-level programming languages saw the beginning of a stealthy move towards the standardisation of game development. This has, over the course of decades, led to video games like *Roblox* releasing and running seamlessly on mobile, PC and console devices: opening up play in every context possible.

However, there was a snag with the higher-level programming approach. Games are written using the same coding languages as other software. But they're typically a lot more complicated than software used for the purposes of, say, word processing. Video games need to be visually appealing, which means you need to code in all kinds of great effects like 'particle physics', which is responsible for coding how particle-based phenomena like clouds of smoke waft across a battlefield. Sports games had to calculate the effect of gravity on a ball to ensure it behaved realistically. And so much of the background infrastructure that sits behind a game like the way it works out who to match you with in a multiplayer game, how you use a controller to position your camera, and even the design of in-game menus all need to come together seamlessly.

All of these things are hard to do. And increasingly, it became obvious to game developers that it didn't make sense to rewrite their code every time they made a game. Instead, developers started to take inspiration from something that you wouldn't necessarily associate with fun: factory production lines. By finding a way to create a standardised digital toolset that they could use over and over again, developers could reduce the hassle, complexity and, to some extent, cost of making games.

And in doing so, the games industry created the technology that would break out from behind the closed doors of a handful of well-funded companies into a set of tools that proved to be the industry's equivalent of Gutenberg's printing press: the video game development engine.

ENGINES AT THE READY

'A game engine can mean a lot of different things to different people, but fundamentally it's a set of technologies that allow game developers, artists and creators to realise their vision of creating an interactive 3D application,' says Steve Collins, formerly chief technology officer at game engine firm Unity and former founder of game technology company Havok.*

Mark Brown, developer and the creator of video game documentary series *Game Maker's Toolkit*, says that engines are able to help both individuals and businesses make games because they help them to tackle a lot of common problems using pre-built code in an easy-to-use interface.

'An engine has a bunch of prewritten programming languages which we call libraries, which handle generic tasks that

---

* Havok, if you don't know the company, is responsible for the 'rag doll' physics when a character falls over, gets knocked off a ledge or dies in a game. If you've ever seen a video of someone's video game character being catapulted miles into the air and spinning madly like a limp Barbie thrown across a living room, chances are Havok is behind it.

all games need to have to run,' he explains. 'So from really basic stuff like literally drawing pixels on the screen, to interacting with a controller, to maybe more high-level stuff like physics calculations, the generic tasks that all games need to do are pre-written for you by a person or a provider.'

The purpose of a game engine is to act like buttercream in a cake, glueing together the two halves that make a video game function, namely the software that makes it and the hardware it runs on, into a tasty whole for the player to enjoy.

'Imagine the hardware, the computers, and the consoles at the bottom as a layer,' said Chris Wood, a former employee at Epic Games, the creators of Unreal Engine, and co-founder of development company Tanglewood Games, which worked as a development partner on Warner Bros.' hit game *Hogwarts: Legacy*. 'On top of that imagine a game engine and then, on top of that, imagine the game: the creative fun gameplay, the content, the graphics. The game engine is software in the same way as the game. But it's doing all of the common low-level nitty-gritty technical stuff so that the game sitting on top of it can just be the game.'

And crucially, the point of the engine is to, in the words of Collins, stop them from having to 'do it all from scratch' every time a developer wants to make a game either alone or with a team of people plugged into the same software. 'It allows a developer to write something once and describe something once and have it implemented across all of those platforms in a consistent way,' said Collins.

Initially, game engines emerged in a 'proprietary' form as tools used by one developer to make a specific type of game. A great historical example of this was the video game arm of Lucasfilm, which created one of the earliest and most famous game engines. In 1987, legendary game developer Ron Gilbert created a proto-game engine called the Script Utility for Maniac Mansion (SCUMM). SCUMM made it much easier for the development team to make content for, surprisingly enough, its forthcoming game *Maniac Mansion*, a point-and-click adventure game – i.e. a game where you solve puzzles by picking up items and using them to interact with the world.

SCUMM was later used in point-and-click games like the pirate-themed *Monkey Island* series, incompetent dog and psychopathic rabbit detective game *Sam & Max: Hit the Road* and *Maniac Mansion's* sequel, *Day of the Tentacle*. The engine was useful enough for Gilbert to eventually use it through a licensing deal after he left the company, foreshadowing the business models of Unity and Unreal Engine before they dominated the market.

Proprietary engines remain a big part of game development today amongst some of the industry's biggest companies. Rockstar, the makers of the *Grand Theft Auto* series, have used their own proprietary Rockstar Advanced Game Engine (RAGE) to make the games. Bethesda has used various versions of its 'Creation Engine' to make role-playing games such as its 2008 release *Fallout 3*, 2011 fantasy role-playing game *Skyrim* and its most recent planet/universe-hopping adventure *Starfield*. Electronic Arts (EA) uses its own engine called Frostbite to make games like *Battlefield*, *EA Sports FC* and the *Dragon Age* role-playing series. These home-made tools are particularly useful if you're making one type of game over and over again, or want to make it as easy as possible to troubleshoot problems.

However, home-made game engines had an obvious problem: no one else could use them. The majority of proprietary engines emerged in well-funded games businesses, which could commit resources to building their own toolset, maintaining it and training staff to use it. For most other developers, whose existence relied on making games and hoping they were a hit, committing time, effort and cash to making an engine of their own didn't make sense.

But that, in turn, led to a different question. If most game developers shared similar challenges when it came to making certain types of games (or games in general), was it possible to create an engine that they could use without having to build it themselves? And if such an engine existed, what impact would it have on the industry?

Two businesses, roughly ten years apart from one another, decided to make the engines that they had created available to developers across the world. In doing so, these companies democratised game development: transforming it from a complicated technological process requiring millions of dollars and dozens of staff into something that a single determined person could achieve anywhere in the world.

UNREAL UNITY OF PURPOSE

Unreal Engine, which was created in 1995, and Unity, which launched in 2005, each approached the challenge of creating game engines from a different perspective. But as the market evolved over time, it became increasingly clear that the growth of both businesses relied upon the same outcome – making it easier to create video games for as wide an audience as possible.

Unreal Engine is the 'top-down' game engine. It is the game engine that is used by many of the industry's biggest Triple-A* game developers such as Ubisoft (*Rainbow Six: Siege)*, Take-Two (*Borderlands 4)* and CD Projekt Red (who are using it for their newest game in *The Witcher* series) to make glitzy world-class entertainment experiences that blow the graphical socks off their audiences. Unreal, which is the shorthand used by most of

---

* The reference to Triple-A games is a direct comparison to rating financial bonds. Games are risky to sell. But the biggest games, with the most celebrated IP, that players love are a lot safer to sell than other titles. Hence the reference to the most secure of all the financial ratings . . . at least until 2008, eh, reader?

the industry, emerged from Epic Games, the company now best known for the wildly popular battle royale multiverse *Fortnite*. The company, which was first founded in 1991 by Tim Sweeney as Potomac Computer Systems before becoming Epic,* initially released a mildly successful action-adventure game called *ZZT* before the team decided to work on something a little different.

Epic began to work on a 3D game engine in the early 1990s to create games for the PC market. Like Jensen Huang at Nvidia, Sweeney and his team moved early to try to create a tool that would allow them to develop best-in-class 3D games from the outset.

The first Unreal Engine emerged from this process. Built in C++, an evolution of the C coding language, the engine was designed to help the business make its own multiplayer PC shooter called *Unreal Tournament*. But the features of the engine proved irresistible to other developers, who looked on enviously at its polygonal 3D models, ability to support detailed environmental art and to allow for volumetric fog to waft across its battlefields (a perfect way to animate tricky-to-capture smoke in virtual environments).

Before Epic had even released its game, it had already successfully licensed Unreal Engine to companies like Legend Entertainment and Microprose. This encouraged Sweeney and the team to build upon the engine's success, immediately promising to improve it further following *Unreal Tournament*'s release in May 1999.

By contrast, Unity emerged from a 'bottom up' perspective which saw it court a different audience. Founded by David

---

* Sweeney briefly rebranded the company as Epic MegaGames in an attempt to make his fledgling startup seem bigger than it is. Unsurprisingly, it had precisely the opposite effect and it was dropped pretty soon afterwards.

Helgason, Joachim Ante and Nicholas Francis, the company's aim was to create a toolset that would explicitly seek to democratise game development.

In 2002, Francis posted on a forum that he was having a bit of trouble with a shader – a bit of code that tells a GPU what an object should look like. Ante responded with an offer to help. They eventually developed a shader that solved the problem that each of them was facing on their different engines, inspiring them – alongside Helgason – to find a way to create a 'definitive tool' for easily making 3D games.

The group wanted to create a game development tool that they hoped would work in a similar 'drag and drop' and 'what you see is what you get' visual style of Apple's film-editing software *Final Cut Pro*.[5] After failing to talk Criterion Games, a UK-based business who would later be bought by EA, into using the software, the team released a small game called *GooBall* using their tech before launching the first version of Unity into the market in 2005.

Despite being created nearly a decade apart and more than a continent away from one another (Epic Games was founded in North Carolina, while Unity emerged within Denmark's social democracy), the two engines ended up on complementary but converging paths which resulted in the emergence of an industry where anyone could, theoretically, make a hit game in any corner of the world.

The first thing that both companies did sounds a little counterintuitive in an age when both are now multi-billion-dollar businesses: they made their engines actually useful to their audience.

The problem with third party engines in the late 1990s and early 2000s is that the modern games industry hadn't quite been born yet. Online multiplayer games were popular, but they were new enough for you not to need them to release on every platform possible to get a big player base. Games were beginning to be sold on digital platforms like Steam – much more on that in the next chapter – but those storefronts hadn't yet smashed the games industry's retail gatekeepers in a way that would allow anyone to make money from games. And despite technological advances, there was still plenty of distance between the comparable power of a high-end game PC, a games console like a PlayStation 2 or what we would now call a little unfairly a 'dumbphone' that meant games were still being developed with specific versions of the game in mind for each platform.

The proposition of a general engine for the video game development market to use would eventually prove to be the right one. But in the late 1990s and early 2000s, it was slightly ahead of its time. Fortunately, both companies backed their vision. They each took a series of steps that made their generally useful tools more specifically helpful to a wider audience of game developers.

For Epic, this meant expanding the platforms it could support through Unreal Engine and the genres of games people could make to hit the full breadth of games emerging from the top of the industry. Unreal Engine 2 allowed people to make games for consoles like PS2, the Nintendo Gamecube and the first Xbox, allowing developers of unique first-person shooters like *BioShock* – a shooter set in a dystopian underwater society gone awry – and action games like *Thief: Deadly Shadows* to realise their vision. Unreal Engine 3, meanwhile, was used to create Epic's third-person action game *Gears of War* in 2006 before making an early version of its toolset available for mobile developers working on smartphone games at the end of the 2000s.

Unity, by contrast, focused on making sure its Apple-like game-making tool was the perfect partner for the company's then newly unveiled iPhone. The company moved quickly to create a version of Unity to work on mobile devices after Apple announced that its App Store would carry games. It created a version of the engine to operate on Windows after discovering that most of its early users were being forced to buy Macs to use the first version of the engine. By the end of 2010, the third version of Unity had evolved to become a cross-platform development tool. This allowed developers who had made games to easily 'port' (allow them to run on other devices) to consoles like the Nintendo Wii to increase their audiences on PC or mobile.

Each tool developed functionality to meet the needs of developers working across platforms, with Unity generally preferred by independent and mobile game businesses while Epic served the needs of the biggest console and PC developers. But both companies also shared two crucial similarities that made democratised video game development turn from a theoretical possibility into a practical reality.

Both engines moved to adopt a software-as-a-service model to increase adoption of their tools. As of 2025, both Unreal Engine and Unity can be used completely for free up to a revenue threshold of \$1m and \$200,000 respectively. The cost of each service scales with the growth of the business, with Unity charging more per 'seat' that a developer uses and Epic Games taking a 5 per cent royalty fee from gross revenue over a million bucks. But given that both tools allow developers to build their first game or project essentially for free – with Unity making the move in 2009[6] and Unreal doing so in 2015[7] – the commercial barrier to development was removed.

And equally importantly, both companies sought to remove the skills barrier too, folding their engines into the foundation of developer education. In 2014, Unreal Engine went free for academic use for students enrolled in a range of academic programmes, including the rapidly developing sphere of video game development courses.[8] Unity took longer to make a similar move, announcing a student programme in February 2020.[9]

But in both cases, the decision to allow students to use their engines free of charge was a stroke of genius. By making it easy for students to learn Unreal or Unity the companies helped create the talent pipeline of young creatives willing to have a bash at making a successful games business. This provided trained staff for games businesses across the world who could use the engines proficiently. It also made it much more likely that developers who set up their own business would reach for one of the democratised engines, rather than making their own. This created a virtuous circle, where supporting grassroots talent saw each engine develop their market share (and revenue) as new games businesses took off.

The development of a wider feature set, an affordable price tag, a deep talent base and the emergence of a mass market of similarly powered computing devices allowed both companies to thrive. The result was an explosion in the number of people making games across the world. In March 2024, Unity declared in a report to investors that it drew on the insights of approximately five million developers who used its services for a piece of research it published ahead of the Game Developer Conference (GDC) in San Francisco that year.[10] That was a twenty-five-fold increase on the number of developers that Unity reported as active users in September 2010, when it launched the third version of its service to the market.[11]

By contrast, Epic Games reported a smaller – but still impressive – 850,000 developers actively using Unreal Engine every month at GDC in 2023.[12] However, the company has since launched a special version of Unreal Engine that allows people who play *Fortnite* to make their own games within the world. According to GamesBeat, there are 70,000 people using Unreal Engine for Fortnite (UEFN) to make games: putting Epic's creator count at the best part of a million creators.

But the number of game developers isn't the only way to measure the impact of both engines. It is also important to look at the breadth of games that have been made as a result of both tools existing as a sign of the vitality that they've contributed to the ecosystem, and as a result the numbers of players they'll have brought into it.

Popular Triple-A video games – the ones that feature budgets in the tens or hundreds of millions of dollars – have increasingly been developed with Unreal, with titles like *Star Wars Jedi: Fallen Order*, *Final Fantasy VII: Rebirth* and the next entry in the *Halo* series made in the engine. Independent hits like *Hollow Knight*, *Oxenfree* and *Monument Valley* owe their existence to Unity's simple tools, allowing smaller teams to create critically acclaimed award-winning titles played across the world. Mobile games capable of generating billions in revenue and reaching hundreds of millions of players across the world such as *Monopoly Go!*, *Subway Surfers* and *Call of Duty: Mobile* also emerged from the engine revolution. And perhaps most importantly of all, games which dominate the social lives of players like *Fortnite*, *PlayerUnknown's Battlegrounds*, *Pokémon Go*, *Among Us* and *Fall Guys* were all developed in one of Unreal Engine or Unity.

UNEXPECTED CREATIVITY

Just five decades after game makers were literally engineering their games into computers, game development had democratised to support the creation of tens of thousands of games, made by millions of developers, capable of reaching billions of people.

This revolution transformed the reach of games into the world. One of the ways it did this was to make high-end development affordable for companies operating across the economy. By making it easy to create visually appealing, accessible digital content, game engines made it easier for developers of any interactive content to create compelling experiences. This transformed game engines from a tool used to create games into a suite of tech that could be used in any industry that needed access to the kit assembled by Unreal and Unity, resulting in the emergence of a multi-billion dollar spillover economy in sectors beyond games.

In film and television, Unreal Engine has become the software of choice for companies making the most of 'virtual production' within their project. The methodology, which uses computers hooked up to screens to create realistic virtual backgrounds for people to perform in front of, has become a staple of high-end film and TV production, with shows such as Disney's enormously popular *The Mandalorian* using Unreal Engine as a way to save money on getting Pedro Pascal acting in front of credible-looking planets.

Engines have also been used by companies to support medical communication. Random42, a London-based medical communications business, had been creating engaging visual content using computers for the purposes of sharing a concept – such as how a vaccine works – for decades. But until the early 2010s, the size of the company had been stuck at a handful of people because the cost of making, processing and sharing high-end visual content was too costly, limiting its growth.

However, the arrival of Unity and Unreal changed things. After some initial dabbling with the new engines, the tools proved perfect for making sparkling visual content quickly, easily and effectively.

'We did a whole animation in Unreal in which you could see the future of animations going down the path, where you can dynamically create infinite reams of content within a games engine and just film the experience from a virtual camera within the environment,' said Ben Ramsbottom, Random42's CEO.

By being able to use engines to create dynamic environments, 'film' within the space, and use increasingly powerful graphics processing units – which, again, were strengthened by consumer games tech bringing down the price – the company was able to go from making a handful of animations a year to creating animated videos, immersive experiences and even games with partners like AstraZeneca. As of early 2025, the business's headcount had grown to over 160 employees.

Game engines have also proven to be a boon for the simulation industry too. The military has been quick to realise the potential of video game engines as a way to train soldiers and officials within virtual environments without commissioning bespoke software.

Bohemia Interactive, the creators of hyper-realistic first-person military shooting game *Arma 3*, successfully created a version of its game for use by militaries across the world. The *Virtual Battlespace* service proved to be so adaptable, popular and intuitive for countries from across the world to build on that BAE Systems bought Bohemia's spin-off business dedicated to selling the service for $200m.[13]

Game engines are also very handy for working in tandem with artificial intelligence businesses to create the worlds in which models are trained: providing 'synthetic data' that would otherwise be unavailable in other contexts.

DeepMind's success has long been entwined with games. Co-founded by Sir Demis Hassabis, a former video game AI programmer, the business was acquired by Google after it demonstrated the effectiveness of the model by showcasing it playing Atari video games because, to quote an article released by the business in 2020, 'games are an excellent testing ground for building adaptive algorithms'.

So it isn't a huge surprise that the same principles which DeepMind applied to games have been applied to game engines by other businesses looking to train models to function within certain environments.

'One really nice use for this is self-driving cars and having them operate in what's called safe exploration,' says Dr Kelly

Clancy, author of *Playing With Reality* and a former researcher at DeepMind. 'So you train them in a virtual world where they can go off the rails and go do crazy things. And you need that kind of training data where they're doing things you wouldn't want them to do in the real world so that they understand the consequences of it.' This allows AIs to use virtual worlds created by engines to train, letting them benefit from one of the defining principles of play which, according to Clancy, is 'safely exploring the world and understanding your limits and boundaries'.

But while these applications are interesting, and perhaps worthy of a book of their own someday, game engines matter in this story because the democratisation of development made it easier to make games and create spaces that could reach players across the world.

In five decades, video game development had transformed from a privileged side-project of world-leading academics working on multi-million-dollar computers to something achievable by a student running Unity or Unreal Engine on their laptop. The process has flattened even further since, with *Roblox* and *Fortnite*'s in-game development tools turning millions of children and teens into game makers. And this has ensured that the creation of video games has become a truly global phenomenon, breaking the industry out of its traditional development bases of the United States, Japan and Western Europe – where markets for consumer games electronics dominated in the 1990s – to an industry capable of making games across Asia, Latin America, Africa and the Middle East.

In doing so, the potential for games to influence changed. Game content broke free from the commercial constraints of developing expensive content for a limited market of players to become more expressive. Individual games were able to appeal to niche audiences, become more disposable, and keep pace with the contemporary cultural agenda as the speed of making games increased. This has expanded the market for games. It has also made it simpler to create politicised content. For example, *Roblox*, the user-generated content platform with its own development tools, mostly entices its hundreds of millions of players with popular games like *Grow a Garden*. But the platform also has to contend with its own users creating hundreds of experiences with political messages such as pro-Palestine marches, Ukraine war simulators and even re-creations of the assassination of Charlie Kirk. The democratisation of game development has turned games into active forms of communication, allowing creators – whether acting individually or on behalf of a group or state – to shape the way players think.

In addition to this, game engines have also formed the architecture of many of the most popular online video games that explicitly seek to draw players together. Both Unity and Unreal Engine have evolved to handle the dull, but indispensable, backroom functions that make games like *Fortnite* or *Halo* capable of hosting vast numbers of players: network code that matches players with one another to play games, communication infrastructure to enable conversation, and uploading new game content that keeps players coming back. This has helped games companies create both the entertainment and the spaces for people to connect, making socialising through games ever easier for players across the world.

And the final reason why game engines have proven so important is related to that previous point: games are now being made on a truly global basis. Previously, the games industry was anchored around the countries where consumers had disposable income to buy electronic devices: the United States, Japan and Western Europe. The game engine revolution has flattened game development to create thriving sectors in Turkey, China, Brazil and India, as well as spreading across regions such as South East Asia, Eastern Europe and into North Africa. The development of a truly global games industry has meant that game content made, or in the case of a multiplayer game maintained, in one corner of the world can easily spread to another across borders. This has turned video games into a form of cultural and soft power. But it has also turned game developers into a resource that can be tapped into for the purposes of creating content. And with many of the new hubs for game development emerging within authoritarian nations as their populations began to access play via smartphones, the democratisation of game development clashed with their desire to control. This created new challenges for regimes trying to control what content flows into the country, while raising the possibility to shape what is made within, and, ultimately, what flows out.

But while the democratisation of video game development has built the architecture of a video game information revolution, those games still needed a way to reach an audience. And as we'll see in the next chapter, the democratisation of video game development went hand in glove with a revolution in the distribution of video games around the world: transforming a cottage industry into a commercial leviathan capable of creating, maintaining and growing a digital cityscape with the potential to influence the entire digital world.

3

The video game distribution revolution

In the early 1980s, the video game industry was a nascent entertainment sector with a market valuation of, at best, a few billion dollars. The cost of making, distributing and selling video games was high, the process of release was controlled by a handful of gatekeepers, and the majority of consumers across the world could not participate in the market.

Forty years later, things had changed dramatically. The global games market was valued at $182.7bn, propped up by 3.4 billion players. Digital play had proven to be big business across the world, with 47 per cent of revenue generated in Asia, 28 per cent in North America, 18 per cent in Europe and 4 per cent in each of Latin America and the Middle East and Africa (with both regions growing fast).[1] And play bridges the generational divide. Newzoo's Global Gamer Study found that more than 50 per cent of over fifties across the world play video games. With 67 per cent of Gen X, 85 per cent of Millennials and 86 per cent of Gen Zs playing games, the only thing more surprising than finding a child or an adult who does play them is finding one poor bugger who doesn't.[2]

You might be surprised to see the size, scale and reach of the video game market today. But there's a good reason why it might have caught you by surprise: it only occurred relatively recently. The emergence of digital video game-selling storefronts like Steam and the App Store opened up access to play. Game developers using democratised development tools to make their titles were able to distribute them across the world. Billions of players were able to access games not just with consoles or PCs, but increasingly through the affordable smartphones that were found in every pocket. And the way that video games are sold has evolved to allow multiple business models to thrive: from creating expensive blockbuster hits like *The Last of Us,* low-cost independent games like *Undertale,* the $20bn 'free-to-play' puzzle game juggernaut *Candy Crush Saga* and the 'forever game' of *Fortnite,* constantly adding new content and character outfits to keep players engaged.

By establishing a direct, almost frictionless economic relationship with players around the world, video games grew into an entertainment medium capable of building businesses that were more valuable than Big Tech social media platforms. These include Electronic Arts (acquired for $55bn) and Activision Blizzard King (acquired for $69bn, which is more than the cost of LinkedIn, X and Instagram combined).

But digital distribution had an important social impact on games too. Players across the world could now easily access thousands of games. This allowed people to gather around, or in some cases within, games. And with many popular games becoming 'always-on' services that needed to constantly provide reasons for players to visit, digital distribution created the conditions for games to become ever-on hangouts for dedicated players from Seattle to Shanghai.

This would transform video game software and video game culture from a niche interest on the fringes of the physical world into one of the main reasons why people went online, or entered digital channels together. In doing so, it established video games as a potential 'third place' for politicisation to occur: encouraging the creation of a communication and information ecosystem that would eventually turn this mass congregation of people into an influential force at the heart of the internet.

ANCHORED TO REALITY

As we saw in Chapter 1, video game software was integrated with the hardware it was played on. *Spacewar!* was being shared in universities across America, but you needed a PDP mainframe to run it. Arcade machines like *Pong* were popping up across the country, but you could only play it on the machines that were produced to run it. The earliest games consoles like the Magnavox Odyssey let you play games in the home, but they were hardcoded into the console. So in the earliest days of the industry, making and selling video games was about making a dedicated piece of hardware as cheaply as possible and getting them into places like bars as effectively as possible.

'If you made an arcade cabinet, you had to manufacture those boards, get the cabs [cabinets] out there to the right places, and also then make sure those cabs are generating constant income for the place that hosted them,' said Steven Bailey, senior principal games analyst for Omdia.

The model had an obvious challenge. Early arcade games like *Computer Space*, the first title made by Nolan Bushnell through Atari, could cost hundreds of dollars to make (which would mean a cost of thousands of dollars today when we account for inflation). There was a real risk that a business would spend money making a device, spend thousands on mass producing it and watch it fail to convince punters to part with their pocket change. This could lead to eye-watering losses for manufacturers.

Games were therefore only initially as valuable as the relationship between the cost of assembling a device, whether it was fun enough to pay to play, and whether a distributor could get machines into enough venues to make mass production worthwhile. By the late 1970s and early 1980s, the industry steadily realised that it could reduce its financial risk and increase its return on investment by making it possible to buy or play multiple games on each device: offering players more variety, and more reasons to spend, in the process.

Personal-computing enthusiasts were quick to realise this. Hobbyist developers for the Altair 8800 had realised as early as 1975 that a personal computer could be programmed to play lots of different games, with instructions on how to code dozens of simple traditional games like Solitaire shared across magazines. But the opportunity to sell game software really took off due to a change in the console industry. In an attempt to find a place for its games console in the market, Jerry Lawson at Fairchild Semiconductor invented the video game cartridge. Instead of forcing a consumer to buy a console to play one game, Lawson's invention allowed customers to swap cartridges in and out of the Fairchild games console to play a variety of different games. It was fun. It was impressive. And the market quickly noticed the opportunity.

'Where one company broke new ground, the others could quite quickly get their hands on similar technology and use it in their consoles,' said Mike Diver, former editor of *GamingBible* and writer of *The Console: 50 Years of Home Video Gaming*. By the early 1980s, rivals such as Atari, Sega and Coleco had created consoles that allowed players to plug in new games. Home computers like Apple II, the BBC Micro and the Commodore 64 also allowed owners to plug in software loaded onto media devices like cassettes or floppy disks, or to write their own code to play games. Variety, it turned out, was one of the spices of video game life.

But how could this desire be served? The answer was the emergence of a new business that sought to sell to this market directly: the third-party software developer. Instead of wasting money on building computers or consoles from scratch, these new businesses had a different idea. Come up with ideas for games. Code them. Put them onto readable media compatible with devices. And then sell them to the market through the bricks-and-mortar retail stores that stocked the consoles.

From the late 1970s onwards, the first wave of third-party developers came into existence. This included two famous names that would go on to sell for larger amounts than the biggest Big Tech platforms around. Activision, famed for the *Call of Duty* series, was founded in 1979 and Electronic Arts (EA), the business behind *EA Sports FC* and *The Sims*, came into being in 1982. Both companies took the business of only making game software seriously, with Activision earning $300m from the emerging game market in the year that EA was founded.[3]

A market also emerged for independent creators to make and sell their games informally too. Bailey estimated that 10,000 games were developed for the ZX Spectrum home computer during the 1980s. And although not all of them made it to market, many home-grown developers teamed up with dedicated publishing companies to get their code made into media devices, boxed up and pushed to retailers. In the UK, a wave of teenage 'bedroom coders', typified by twins Andrew and Philip Oliver, who created the *Dizzy* platforming game, were credited with founding the first games businesses that would later turn towns and cities like Leamington Spa and Dundee into the homes of the *F1* video game and a little-known title called *Grand Theft Auto*.[4]

*

By the early 1980s, there was a growing market for games and businesses willing to serve it. There were, however, a couple of big problems. The market for games was growing, but it remained small. Console manufacturers like Atari were able to rack up decent sales across America, getting four million devices into customers' hands in 1982 alone.[5] But most consoles were still too expensive, leading to a plethora of devices that, frankly, didn't sell many units.

There were also too many games entering the market. In an attempt to cash in on what was seen as a gold rush, players were increasingly inundated by low-quality games that were derogatively nicknamed 'shovelware'. And with the cost of physically producing and distributing the game remaining high, consumers were asked to spend as much as $20 (roughly $100 in today's money) to play games of questionable quality.

The combination of a small fragmented market for hardware and an overly expensive saturated market for software led to an almighty market crash in North America's games industry in 1983. Revenue for games crashed from the low billions into the hundreds of millions. Confidence in the industry fell, with analysts and professionals fearing the market had topped out. And the overabundance of crap video games was illustrated in dramatic fashion by the literal burial of thousands of unsold copies of the officially licensed *ET: The Extra Terrestrial* video game in the Nevada desert.[6]

Beyond its short-term effect, the crash proved to be a turning point in video game history. The destruction of the growing video game market briefly left the industry without a viable model to do business. But in the wake of the crash, one Japanese company entered the American market, reshaped the way games were sold, and set the rules for the sector that, even today, cast a surprisingly long shadow on who we think of as players: Nintendo.

The Japanese games business, which started life as a manufacturer of Hanafuda, a form of Japanese playing cards, in the late 1800s, released its first home console in July 1983. The Famicom, better known as the Nintendo Entertainment System (NES) in the West, entered the Japanese market just as the North American market crashed. With the company planning to expand into the American market, its executives were understandably nervous about its prospects in a tough landscape.

However, Nintendo was better positioned than most to sell its hardware to players. The Famicom had been designed more cheaply than its rivals' hardware, largely because of the company's philosophy to use 'mature technology that can be mass-produced cheaply' to lower the cost of its devices.[7] This gave the company some valuable financial headroom to find ways to sell its console to players. One of those decisions was a fun branding choice. To avoid the hassle of being compared to the recently crashed video game market, the company bundled accessories with the console to make it feel more like a toy. The offer for consumers to play a game like *Duck Hunt* using a gun-shaped 'zapper' accessory, or to use its friendly toy Robotic Operating Buddy (ROB) to stack virtual items calmed the nerves of retailers and consumers burned in 1983.

But Nintendo's much more consequential decision was to impose strict restrictions on the 'third party' games that could appear on its platforms. Outside of its own 'first party' games like *Super Mario Bros.* or *The Legend of Zelda*, the company forced developers to prove that their games met its internal stringent quality standards and charged them a licensing fee to appear on the platform. This meant that early partners like Japanese development businesses Konami, Capcom and Taito were initially limited to releasing five games across the year to force them to focus on making the best game possible.

In the years that followed, the NES dominated the market for home video games in North America, selling 30 million units between its launch in 1985 and 1991. Nintendo's success demonstrated that there was a market for consoles and video games in the wake of the crash. This ensured that rivals like Sega, Sony's PlayStation and eventually Microsoft's Xbox were able to enter the market and compete with Nintendo, steadily growing the number of home console players into the hundreds of millions by the early 2000s.

Even more importantly, Nintendo's successful combination of affordable console and great games powered the industry's 'razor and blades' model that was responsible for both the hardware innovation seen in Chapter 1 and the overall growth of the games market. By turning its hardware into a 'platform' for games content, Nintendo created the rules that governed the games sector for the best part of two decades: establishing the importance of the 'first party' hardware manufacturer as the point of access to play, while ensuring that 'third party' partners could add value to its proposition (and make cash) by selling to players.

But underneath this change was a familiar physical model. Software might have been digitally made, but it was still written onto physical media like cartridges, floppy disks and CDs. This meant these items needed to be manufactured, boxed up, shipped to stores and sold. The risk of making too many copies of a game that plagued the arcade industry had now shifted to software makers. And with console manufacturers like Nintendo charging up to 30 per cent of revenue to appear on its platform, developers faced the same problem of making sure that they could find a reliable audience for their games to reduce their risks.

So rather than ask who would buy a game first, the industry did something else. If software could only sell to someone who had bought a console, handheld console or PC, the industry asked itself who had the cash to spend hundreds of dollars on a device upfront. They arrived at two groups: parents and eighteen- to 34-year-old men in countries with thriving consumer electronic markets.

Selling to parents meant leaning into the 'toy-like' nature of games, as Nintendo had so successfully with the Famicom/ NES. Advertising in the 1980s for most consoles zeroed in on families gathering to play around a shared screen. Video game mascots such as Mario, Sonic the Hedgehog and Crash Bandicoot appeared in child-friendly games that, when designed well, also appealed to adults. The industry took selling to parents so seriously that games retailers built their businesses around appealing to them, training staff to act as impartial guides to the various consoles and games and widening shopping aisles to ensure a stroller could easily glide down them.[8] Even today, Nintendo remains firmly in the business of selling to families, with its use of *Mario Kart World* acting as the flagship game release for its Switch 2 console, a sign that it remains committed to supporting wholesome family play (except when I get beaten in the final round of a *Knockout Tour* race, of course).

Appealing to eighteen- to 34-year-old men, however, meant taking a different course. The rest of the console industry and much of the PC sector promoted violent anarchic games that notionally appealed to young men, giving the likes of first-person shooter *Doom*, ultra-violent fighting game *Mortal Kombat* and open-world crime game *Grand Theft Auto* a significant boost. Video games were promoted in an edgy or macho fashion even if they weren't necessarily violent themselves, with the futuristic racing game *Wipeout* promoted with a bloodied image of Sara Cox, now a famous radio host in the UK, that promised 'totally killer graphics'.[9] This was reinforced by the industry's internal culture, which was dominated by men within development roles, commercial positions and in the emerging media covering the sector.

However, there were plenty of other games available within the market that showed the demographic of play was much wider than these two audiences. *Snake*, for example, became arguably the most played game in history after a Danish designer called Taneli Armanto created it to be embedded in Nokia phones. Games like *Solitaire* and *Minesweeper* for Windows PCs helped PC users get used to the then snazzy concept of a visual operating system, while devastating their productivity the world over. In 1998, the unashamedly 'girly' *Barbie Fashion Designer* briefly outsold *Quake*, a popular first-person shooter game, racking up over a million sales in the US.

But these successes were not seen as examples of the potential universality of digital play. They were viewed as unnecessary aberrations from the two 'true' audiences for video games of children or young men. This meant that the audience for games narrowed unnecessarily, making digital play less inclusive and giving audiences like young men overt cultural dominance of the medium. In particular, it excluded forms of play that were typically seen as gendered and implied that games like *The Sims*, where you design your own house and allow people to live in it, were not meaningfully part of the games industry. But as Raph Koster, the lead designer for famous multiplayer online game *Ultima Online* put it, 'The only way something like "playing house" can possibly be "outside the mainstream" is if there's a subculture in charge.'[10] And by putting a subculture of noisy young men in charge of the industry, the sector was inadvertently storing up problems for itself as the internet emerged: allowing male 'gamers' to assume unexpected dominance over digital culture at large.

But for the industry, the major challenge with the model that Nintendo established was that it restricted the number of developers who could release games commercially. As computing devices became more widely and cheaply available across the 1980s and 1990s, and software development began to democratise as we saw in the last chapter, game developers began to pop up all over the world. For example, Poland, Finland and Sweden were all hubs for the 'demoscene' movement where developers would learn how to hack devices like Texas Calculators and make video games on them. The movement, which would later receive UNESCO World Heritage Status, would build up the talent who would staff studios like Supercell (makers of the mobile hit franchise *Clash of Clans*), CD Projekt Red (creators of *The Witcher* games) and Paradox (home of deep-strategy games like *Crusader Kings*).

But these developers, as well as independent creators in territories like the United Kingdom, were essentially locked out of the market, unless they followed the rules of the platform, had the cash to participate in the process of appearing on a major console, and had support to reach a market.

'They were walled gardens,' said Phil Elliot, a video games consultant who previously founded an independent game development publishing business on behalf of *Final Fantasy* makers Square Enix. 'You couldn't pick up a NES or a Super Famicom and think "Oh, I'm going to make a game for this." It was impossible to do. So [the games market] became much more specialized.'

Until the late 1990s, there wasn't any obvious way for developers to kick down the walled garden that guarded the physical releases of games. But as uptake of the internet increased and development tools democratised, the first stores and platforms emerged that allowed developers to begin to sell games directly to players without a physical product or needing the approval of 'first party' gatekeepers. This allowed more businesses to make games and more people to play them, and let companies find more ways to get paid for their work – sparking the emergence of a global entertainment behemoth in the process.

STEAMING AHEAD

The opening of the video games digital frontier truly started with the launch of video game distribution platform Steam.

PC games have always been easier to distribute than other games because the nature of personal computers has always smoothed access to software. Writable, and re-writable, media formats like floppy disks made it easy to copy and share content. Networked computing has facilitated the sharing of content online, whether through fair means or foul (such as piracy). And in the earliest days of personal computing, hobbyists would literally be able to code their own versions of certain games from scratch. The BBC, for example, taught a generation of British youngsters how to make Steve Jobs and Steve Wozniak's arcade game *Breakout* via instructions in a magazine as part of a national drive to develop coding skills.

However, within the commercial games industry, PC games were sold in the same physical retail market as console games. For example, *World of Warcraft*, the multiplayer adventure game which is played solely online, retailed in stores when it launched in 2004. 'The success of your product was made or lost on your ability to be able to sell an effective number of units in a territory, and a lot that came down to production and logistics,' said Chris Davey, a video games consultant based in Australia who used to work for game maker Blizzard. This meant that the business had to literally ship games from abroad, find suppliers in Australia who could create a shiny box for the game so it stood out on shelves, and then work with retailers to get the game into stores.

This was costly, at the best of times. But it was also tricky for PC game developers because their games often needed to be changed after launch in the way console games didn't. Most console games were sold on the basis that what was on the disc or the cartridge was final because you simply couldn't plug it into a computer to update it after it was sold. There was also an assumption that if the game worked on one of the consoles it was developed for, it would work on all other devices.

PC games, however, were different. Games perform differently on different PCs. The mix of hardware that sits within a player's PC, whether made by a games PC company like Razer or built from individual components themselves, meant that a PC game that worked perfectly with one graphics processor unit might completely fall over under another. PC games would therefore often require 'patches' which would fix or optimise the game to run with other components, or to fix issues that appeared after launch.

PC game makers were also much more alert to the risk that their games could be pirated by players too, as it was relatively easy for players to use their PC to crack open the code of a game and copy it onto other readable media. Therefore, these developers were interested in finding a way to update, sell and protect their games without relying on the hassle of selling via physical media.

Steam initially evolved as a private solution to the problems of distributing, selling and updating PC games securely. In August 1996, ex-Microsoft employees Gabe Newell and Mike Harrington co-founded the Valve Corporation on Newell's wedding day (news that Newell's wife presumably received gleefully). Using the cash they had earned at Microsoft, the two men bet that PC games could become as big a business as their console rivals provided that developers were able to get the right support – as Newell had learned by getting popular shooter *Doom* to run on Windows 95.

Newell and Harrington's company did things differently to other games businesses on the market. The duo deliberately named the business in a way that stood apart from the wider market. 'We wanted a name that didn't suggest we were about testosterone-gorged muscles and the "extreme" of anything,' he said, in a 2006 interview.[11] *Half-Life*, the science fiction first-person shooter that made the company's name and is still considered one of the greatest games of all time, was written with the help of novelist Marc Laidlaw to give it narrative heft that went beyond the 'shooting galleries' of other games at the time.

Valve's major concerns back in the 1990s were the challenge of selling its games to consumers without them being pirated, and wanting more control over how it sold its games to ensure it wasn't beholden to the deadlines of external publishers (or paying them revenue they didn't need to).

So Valve did something unusual. It launched a web client called Steam in 2003, which allowed players to download updates to popular Valve games directly from the developer. And in November 2004 it went one step further. Valve allowed players to buy *Half-Life 2*, the sequel to its critically acclaimed shooter, directly via Steam, which they could download straight to their PC over an internet connection.

Initially, Steam received a lukewarm reception. 'I remember the indignation of myself and a lot of other people when we had to sign up for this thing called Steam in order just to be able to run the game,' said Elliott, when reminiscing about booting up *Half-Life 2* for the first time. 'It was shocking.' Valve was also not helped by comparatively low access to broadband at the time, causing grumbles amongst players who had to watch their game download over the course of hours.

Nevertheless, Steam's emergence as a distribution platform was a revolutionary moment for the industry. While Valve still worked with a physical publisher to release *Half-Life 2*, Steam showed that it was possible to build a relationship with a customer directly, offer them a game digitally, and sell it to them without the need for a retailer. Digital media wouldn't just let businesses into the game industry's walled garden; it threatened to blow it away completely. And in the years that followed, Valve realised Steam's potential by turning it into a secure storefront that other companies could use.

In 2005, the company agreed to sell two third-party games through Steam, *Rag Doll Kung Fu* and *Darwinia*. Following their success, it steadily expanded the number of games available for sale into thousands of titles by negotiating deals with other businesses to give them access to the store. By 2012, Steam empowered its community of players to help it decide which games to release on the platform via its 'Greenlight' scheme that allowed players to vote for games they wanted to see on the store. And by 2017, Greenlight evolved into Steam Direct: a scheme that allowed any developer from across the world to release games on the platform in return for a hundred bucks and a cut of revenue it generated.

By opening up, expanding access to, and eventually democratising access to the Steam store for PC game developers, Valve showed hit games could be sold directly to players via digital means in a way that drastically lowered barriers to selling. It allowed independent businesses to sell their games without using a physical distribution partner to get to market. It also enabled developers to more cheaply and easily add, update and sell new content within their PC games after release. Valve itself demonstrated how keenly it values this content at a corporate level. The immensely popular *Counter-Strike* game started life as a 'mod' to its game *Half-Life*, which remixed its single-player game into a multiplayer shooter between cops and terrorists. Rather than booting it off the store, Valve bought *Counter-Strike* outright: adding a game that would become one of the biggest esports titles in the world to its portfolio.

Steam's success within the PC market did not go unnoticed. As the platform grew, Xbox, PlayStation and Nintendo each opened their own online stores to sell games to players directly, make it easier for companies to update their games, or allow them to sell extra content to make more cash after the game had launched. This was popular with businesses but not always appreciated by players, who believed – and in many cases still do – that a game should not ask for more money for additional content after release. This was most famously seen in regard to the role-playing game *The Elder Scrolls IV: Oblivion*, which saw its player community furiously criticise the game's developers for selling optional (and completely mechanically irrelevant) armour for your horse.*,[12]

* The game, which released in March 2006, was eventually remastered and re-released for modern audiences in 2025. Naturally, the developers once again included the armour as an optional in-game extra, this time attracting praise for having a sense of humour about the situation. How times change.

But while PC and console were both growing as a result of digital distribution opening up the market to new players and developers, those changes mostly made it easier for businesses to sell to the existing audience of families and young men. But in 2008, what is now the largest part of the games industry began to take off: mobile games.

THE MOBILE GAME REVOLUTION

Mobile games have long been a part of the games industry. Nintendo's Game Boy handheld consoles proved people would pay to play on the go. The previously mentioned *Snake* remains a formative experience of mobile handsets for anyone old enough to remember when they had keys to tap. Mobile games were also available to purchase across the early 2000s, both through mobile operators and for dedicated gaming phones like Nokia's ill-fated N-Gage gaming phone.

But while there was a market for mobile devices, the market for games on them was not there. Mobile phones were low-powered devices with poor-quality screens, making creating compelling games tricky. The operators allowed companies to sell games through their platforms, but their decision to take cuts of upwards of 80 per cent on purchases pushed prices up. Mobile internet coverage was patchy at best and low quality, which meant that it was difficult to download games from operators without patience.

However, the launch of the iPhone in 2007 gave game developers a glimpse into an exciting future for mobile games that could potentially make the most of its larger than usual display, touchscreen inputs and powerful graphics (all of which were underpinned by Arm architecture, of course).

While Apple initially didn't allow developers to create and release their own games or apps for the platform, in 2008 it changed its mind. It launched the App Store on 10 July, a development which changed the course of the global games industry and the digital economy in the process.

The App Store operated in a similar way to Steam. Developers could apply for an account to upload content. In return for a 30 per cent cut of any revenue generated on the store, initially through sales of apps and later through in-app purchases too, Apple would grant developers frictionless access to the global market of iPhone users. By creating a powerful device to play games and an easy way for players to get their hands on them, Apple had resolved the majority of the problems of mobile game development and distribution by creating both the device that the world could play on and the distribution channel to reach a vastly expanded audience for play. And as mobile internet improved in quality across the world, this opened up a worldwide market for businesses to tap into immediately.

'The iPhone, in true Apple style, made one clean and easy online marketplace that anyone could go into and with a couple of taps download a game,' said Neil Long, editor of mobilegamer.biz and former editor of the European app store ecosystem at Apple. 'The iPhone has literally changed the world, the planet we live on in lots and lots and lots of different ways. But it completely changed gaming.'

Shortly after the App Store was announced, the games industry, naturally, got to work to bring games to the platform. Amongst the first 500 apps to launch on the store, games such as Sega's simian balancing game *Super Monkey Ball*, Namco's retro-hit-reborn *Pac-Man* and a version of popular platformer *Crash Bandicoot* were all available for App Store customers to buy in a snap.

Within three years, the App Store, plus Google's rival Android Marketplace and other stores popping up internationally, had generated breakout 'premium' mobile game stars who had made hundreds of millions of dollars by selling games for a few dollars at a time that were often made using an engine such as Unity. Games like *Angry Birds*, developed by Rovio in Finland, *Cut the Rope*, created by the then Russian based business ZeptoLab, and *Doodle Jump*, which was made by two brothers based in New York, showed the scale of the opportunity for smaller businesses within the rapidly growing mobile games industry.

The emergence of independent development success stories were showing how the mobile-app stores and smartphones in general were reaching every corner of the world. But the moment that the mobile games industry really exploded is when it stopped selling games and started to give them away for free instead.

The rationale behind the move was simple. If a game had a price on it, someone would have to pay to buy it. But if you made the game free, more people would download it. This would mean a bigger audience of players. And provided you could maintain their interest for long enough, you could make money from them by showing them adverts, selling them in-game items to help them, allowing them to buy items that change what their character looks like, buying in-game resources like gold or much more. In essence, you'd no longer sell the game as a product but offer free access to it as a service: turning the process of making money from having a hit to constantly generating revenue.

The move to free-to-play was transformative for the prospects of the mobile games industry and the video game economy at large. The sector was aware that a much wider audience for play existed. This was particularly true after 2006, when Nintendo's Wii console had shown that it was possible to reach audiences like adult women through fitness games, sports titles and the opportunity to waggle a remote control like an idiot.

Free-to-play changed the games industry's prospects because it opened up access. By removing the cost of the initial download, waving players in through their virtual doors, and committing to make money off them later somehow, games suddenly became accessible to anyone with a smartphone. And with the number of devices in the market rapidly reaching billions, free-to-play video games rocketed around the world, massively expanding the audience.

Globally, free mobile games significantly expanded the audience for video games. The app stores were integral to bringing Latin America, Africa, the Middle East, South East Asia and particularly China into the video game economy because access was no longer dictated by who could purchase dedicated games hardware; it was about who had access to a smartphone. This created the conditions for these markets to grow into thriving consumer bases of their own, with developers able to make, market and sell to players in territories that had been excluded from the traditional games market.

Free-to-play games also expanded who played games within existing territories and the rest of the world, building on the lessons of the Wii in a way that traditional market sectors didn't. Where the traditional console and PC games market remained anchored to the stereotypes of eighteen- to 34-year-old men and families with disposable income, mobile free-to-play games chased different audiences. Developers created games like *Words With Friends* that proved popular with pensioners looking for something to do in their downtime. *Candy Crush Saga* became a phenomenon amongst women, with its match-three puzzle gameplay bringing audiences like mums into the industry for the first time. Mobile versions of franchises like *Call of Duty* found their way into markets that had been crying out for a game in the franchise, such as India. And when *Wordle* captivated the world, it was snapped up by the *New York Times* to strengthen its suite of games. The success of its portfolio has been so significant that the company now has a sixty-strong game development team to support the pipeline from players to news readers.

Most significantly, and what will sound counterintuitive, free-to-play games proved to be remarkable money spinners that transformed leading video games from one-off products into always-on services that aim to run successfully for decades.

After bringing billions of players into the games market, the industry realised something important. The majority of players, roughly 95–97 per cent depending on which game economist you speak to, don't spend anything after downloading a game. But the players who do spend do so again, and again, and again provided that you give them reasons to keep coming back. This resulted in a serious shift in the industry's business model. Developers deployed a dizzying array of monetisation tactics – such as showing players in-game adverts, enticing them with in-game purchases, offering regular in-game bonuses through subscriptions or battle passes, and selling in-game content – to encourage their biggest spenders to spend more. And even though only a few per cent of players parted with cash for games, the enormous number of players reached by a top mobile game ensured there were enough to create hits at immense economic scale. *Candy Crush Saga* generated $20bn for its developer King between its launch in 2012 and 2023. Free-to-play mobile viral hit *Flappy Bird* was reportedly generating its Vietnamese developer $50,000 per day through advertising alone when it went viral in 2014.[13] And Tencent's *Honor of Kings*, a heavily Chinese mythology inspired version of the multiplayer battling game *League of Legends*, generated $1.6bn in revenues in the final quarter of 2016 in China alone.[14]

Unsurprisingly, makers of big PC and console games were able to use the lessons from free-to-play mobile game economics to build engaging 'service' games, generating ever higher amounts of revenue in the process.

Grand Theft Auto V, for example, generated over a billion dollars in sales of its boxed game when it launched in October 2013. But it became a near $10bn commercial hit over the course of the following decade because its *Grand Theft Auto Online* multiplayer mode kept its world alive with new game content to play, new items to buy and reasons to hang out.

In 2017, *Fortnite* emerged on console and then across other platforms to transform from a 'last-one-standing' battle to the end and into a virtual connected entertainment universe hosting multiple games, hundreds of brand partnerships and concerts. This has transformed it into a multi-billion-dollar franchise, leading to Disney and LEGO investing in its creator, Epic Games, to ensure they have a stake in its future.

But the extent to which players are monetised, and how aggressively it is done so, has also led to controversy. Electronic Arts, one of the original publishers of third-party games, makes the lion's share of its revenues from the 'service' elements of its sports franchises *EA Sports FC* and the *Madden* NFL games. But the use of buyable in-game currency to purchase 'loot boxes' to unlock players through its Ultimate Team mode sparked allegations that the 'random' rewards you receive from them are akin to gambling. While most gambling authorities across the world have said it doesn't, that hasn't stopped the mechanics – and the games industry more widely – coming under deep regulatory scrutiny in America, Europe, China and Brazil.

CREATING THE SPACE
FOR INFLUENCE

The impact free-to-play games had on the industry can be seen in the rapid acceleration of revenues. In 2010, NPD forecast that they generated \$18.58bn in revenue.[15] By 2015, Newzoo estimated that the market had more than quadrupled in size to over \$91bn with the emergence of the Asian market and a \$20bn smartphone gaming market pushing it up. Nine years later, the market had doubled again to reach the figure of \$182.7bn cited at the start of the chapter. Notably, games hardware sales are only estimated to sit at around \$42bn for 2024 – showing how software, not hardware, drives the modern games industry as much of the sector has stepped away from its historical hardware roots.[16]

The explosion in revenue has been matched by a massive increase in the number of games being released into market. For example, the number of console games increased more than five-fold between 2015 and 2024, while Steam releases have tripled from 6,000 per year in 2017 to 18,500 per year. These figures also ignore the number of experiences created on user-generated content platforms like *Roblox*, which is host to millions of things that could reasonably be described as games.

This has created a tough market for the video games industry to operate in, with businesses suffering tens of thousands of lay-offs and studios closing as the rocket ship growth tailed off after the pandemic. The massive multi-billion-dollar service games like *Roblox*, *Fortnite* or *Grand Theft Auto Online* have become such pervasive hang-out spaces that it is increasingly hard for developers to convince players to move away from them and enjoy alternative games, let alone part with their cash.

But despite these challenges, the games industry has clearly evolved from a small cottage industry into an entertainment leviathan encouraging billions of players to invest their cash into the medium. However, this growth also had a number of side-effects that increased its role as a social space, a place for the exchange of information and, ultimately, political influence.

The industry's ability to commercially support a huge range of games has created more opportunities for different communities to congregate and talk within, or around, different games. In the past two years alone, the industry has been able to support games as varied as *Infinity Nikki* (a free-to-play action game with a strong emphasis on dressing up characters in cute outfits), *Black Myth: Wukong* (a Chinese-developed action game based on *Journey to the West*) and *Balatro* (a game created by one-man development team in Canada that lets players rig poker decks using magical power-ups to rack up high scores). While not all of these games are service titles, they each have their own audience, sub-cultures within their communities, and social infrastructure to talk about the game (often with the developer present to learn about what needs to change). While this is perfectly harmless, fun and entertaining for most players, the potential for games to attract like-minded groups makes the content of games a potentially useful form of political influence. And with companies like Steam operating a content moderation policy that promises to only ban games that it considers to be 'illegal' or 'trolling',[17] it is possible to use games content to rally together supporters to a cause; especially when it exists in a grey area such as a nation state propagandising or a content creator arguing a game with extreme themes is doing so for free-speech purposes.

On the other side of this coin is a different, but interrelated, challenge. The industry's shift towards a global, inclusive audience of players has proven a commercial hit for games businesses.

But this move has antagonised one of the industry's traditional audiences: eighteen- to 34-year-old men, who feel left behind, or ignored, by changes. Whether that is true or not, this group has become increasingly conservative and willing to define what a true game is and what a real player looks like. The sense of grievance, the attempt to form an in-and-out group dynamic, and a willingness to campaign noisily on the point have turned the 'betrayal' of this group by games companies into a rallying cry for the disaffected. This means that this group has unusual power to shape perceptions of games, influence the digital conversation around it, and attack those who don't agree with them – turning them into a powerful campaigning constituency ripe for influencing.

But finally, and potentially most importantly of all, the emergence of games software as the biggest part of the games market, and particularly multiplayer-based service games, transformed the social function of the games industry entirely.

Games were never disconnected, anti-social experiences as some have portrayed them. But they were either anchored to a physical location like an arcade machine or they sat disconnected from one another on consoles, PCs or unconnected mobile devices.

But as games moved online, services grew, and the need to talk increased amongst players of games and the developers who worked with them, it remained nearly impossible for players to socialise together because they were playing physically apart from one another. The industry and its players needed to find ways to connect with one another, both to talk while playing and to keep conversation about the game going beyond the borders of play.

This led to a need to create channels of communication amongst players via in-game chat, existing social media platforms, and new ways of speaking to one another that accounted for the unique strengths of video games. And in the final chapter of Part 1, we'll find out how this happened, how this created a network of interconnected digital third places, and how this led to the creation of a powerful information ecosystem: one that's been capable of pumping influence from games communities right into the bloodstream of reality.

4

A digital third place for influence

Over the past few chapters, we've explored how video games transformed from a niche hobby into an entertainment leviathan because developers made it much easier for people to play any game, on any device, anywhere in the world. The pressures of growing a big enough market for games led to hardware manufacturers crashing the cost of high-end computing to put play in every pocket. The challenge of making great games cost-effectively in a way that works across devices led to the democratisation of development, which opened up game development to the world. Digital distribution allowed those games to reach markets, knocking away gatekeepers to create a larger, more inclusive and truly international games sector.

This, however, is not enough to explain the unique power of games as a channel for influence. Other creative industries such as film, television and music have evolved upon similar lines, with services such as Netflix and Spotify putting affordable entertainment content into our homes. Simply democratising the creation and access of content was not enough to give games a peculiar power. That came from its role in constructing and connecting up digital communications infrastructure.

As video games software detached from video games hardware and moved into the digital world, players and developers had to find ways to create lines of communication with one another to do everything from selling services to enabling ephemeral chatter essential for keeping a space alive.

Companies created channels for communication so inhabitants of online worlds could speak to one another, they built messaging tools that allowed companies to talk (and listen) to players, and plugged into emerging social media channels to spread the reach of their games. Players and communities, meanwhile, found homes in dedicated video game social media sites such as Twitch and Discord to support new ways to talk to one another, creating a third-party ecosystem of media and content creators around games.

The result was that video games stopped being a way to pull people into third places by, say, placing an arcade machine in the corner of the bar. Instead, each video game assumed the potential to become its own space within our digital cityscape: whether it was a massive online multiplayer game which supported deep socialisation inside its game world or simply a beloved indie game capable of activating its own distinct fan culture in social media channels which players flooded to in an attempt to connect with like-minded people.

The popularity of video games, the passion of the communities around the games, and the creation of a direct dialogue between developers and players networked the billions of people across the world who play with one another. And while the purpose of this was to foster play, connecting enormous numbers of passionate people turned players into powerful activists by allowing them to communicate with one another, form their identities together, and give them commercial power to make the fortunes of the games businesses who courted them.

For the majority of people who love games, that activism transformed from efforts to make the games (and game worlds) they love better into attempts to do social good such as charity fundraising, or celebrate and commemorate the people who made their game worlds feel alive.

But where people talk, create and campaign, the potential for politicisation inevitably follows. And as it became apparent that the noisiest video game activists had the power to shape the narrative both within their closed video game communities and the wider social media landscape, the opportunity to use video game content, communications channels and communities as a space for influence grew as an enormous information ecosystem flourished.

And where information spreads, influence follows – encouraging efforts to control games, co-opt them or collaborate with their communities to serve agendas far removed from the fun of play.

PLAYING IN THE THIRD PLACE

Play has always served a social function, including supporting the development of the emotional and social skills necessary to navigate life successfully.[1] But in the context of this book, the most important role it plays is drawing people into third places in which they can congregate, communicate and influence one another.

As mentioned briefly in the introduction, Ray Oldenburg's theory of the third place said that places like bars, cafes and restaurants have a big role in driving our social lives. Their status as the places in between our homes and our places of work allow them to serve a different role, creating a fluid space that can be everything from a hang-out to a den suitable for all kinds of subtle plotting.

When you read Oldenburg's definition of a third place, you'll quickly understand why they're able to serve such a range of purposes. For those of the plotting persuasion, third places are typically open to all, they level off existing hierarchies, they're usually discreet and, crucially, having a chat is the main reason you're there.

However, thriving third places are not austere spaces reserved for cut-throat political action. Instead, as Oldenburg himself points out, the tone of a third place is playful. If the conversation isn't playful or there lacks something to generate playfulness – whether a parlour game, a board game or a sports game running on the TV – then it is unlikely that the third place will create the environment in which that exchange of ideas can happen.

It shouldn't come as much of a surprise that the inherently playful nature of games made them a prime reason for people to come together, talk and distract themselves from the drudgery of their day-to-day lives.

Chess evolved over the course of centuries into a pastime enjoyed by Persian nobles and European courtiers, and a game of choice for visitors to New York's Central Park.[2] The evolution of football from an informal game into a professionalised sport was driven much more by the way that teams such as Sheffield Wednesday provided communal entertainment for factory workers on their day off as it was the rules of the game itself.* And in *The Histories*, Herodotus outlined how the Lydians used dice, ball, and knucklebone games to bring the population together in an effort to distract them from the impact of a famine that ravaged their lands.[3]

Play is a great excuse for getting people together to have a chat. But as we are well aware, when people talk, politics is never far behind. And in many cases, the games and sports that draw people into third places create groups and subcultures capable of transcending them.

In football, the emergence of the ultras in Italy has led to the growth of far-right fan groups (and, in some places, clashing left-wing counter-cultures) from leading football clubs which have

---

* Sheffield Wednesday were named in honour of the day off that the factory workers were given every week. Sheffield Saturday or Sheffield Sunday sound a lot more like newspapers, so we can all be thankful for that.

intersected with the wider political discourse. Biker gangs have assumed a surprising political prominence, becoming keenly associated with political strongmen such as Donald Trump.[4] Figureheads within game-related subcultures can also emerge from their fields to become politically resonant, as shown by Garry Kasparov's transformation from chess grandmaster into one of Vladimir Putin's fiercest critics.[5]

In each of these instances, information ecosystems exist to support them. Social media helps groups to come together, organising around fan pages or private communications channels to guide people into the space. Media and content creators construct the world around the sport or the game, simultaneously growing an audience while feeding it news about developments, figures of note and practical details (i.e. when a big match is on) to maintain engagement. And while there are plenty of official channels informing people where games are being played, which tournaments are on or what the jazzy new board game is you've got to play, the discourse is always supported from the bottom up too – with community groups and figureheads serving the needs of subcultures that may not be supported from the top down.

Video games demonstrated the same qualities as sports and other games from when they first emerged in the market. At the beginning of this book, I referenced an article by Stewart Brand about *Spacewar!* which emphasised how the mainframe computer game gave people an excuse to talk to each other. A big reason why he mentioned this is because he was reporting from what is widely believed to be the first 'esports' event (i.e. a tournament where people play video games competitively against one another for a prize).

Brand had convinced *Rolling Stone* to sponsor what he dubbed the 'Spacewar Olympics', which saw mainframe programmers from across the United States come together to duke it out to discover who had the greatest space combat skills.

Interstellar virtual combat proved to be a remarkably effective way to get some of the most talented programmers in the world together, arguably more so than any run-of-the-mill academic conference.[6]

And within a decade or so of Brand's tournament, the emerging consumer games market was selling itself as a force that was capable of bringing people together to play. Research by Atari that was written up by Paul Trachtman for the Smithsonian in September 1981 suggested that 86 per cent of thirteen- to twenty-year-olds in America had visited an arcade in the previous year. Nintendo, Atari and Fairchild* pitched their earliest consoles as ways to get people playing together, prominently showing families crowding around the television to enjoy their new favourite games.†

Despite the medium's often anti-social stereotype, video games fostered communication. Whether it was players discussing a game, companies attempting to entice people with something new, or people sharing their thoughts about a developing cultural medium, digital play encouraged people to read and write about their hobby. This led to the emergence of an information ecosystem around games that fostered dialogue between players, the communities they started to form, and the businesses driving the games industry.

The top tier of this ecosystem was the information that publishers provided to players to sell games and to encourage them to stick with the games they already had. Companies like Sony

* Television adverts for historic game consoles are widely available on YouTube, but usually through museums or fan channels. The industry's failure to effectively preserve its own history is one of the reasons why its story often fails to cut through in wider society.
† Nintendo also created one advert for the NES which saw a house blast off into the stratosphere as a result of the sheer excitement of the people playing its games. We live in a more cynical age.

funded the creation of media publications for this purpose, with its *Official PlayStation Magazine* achieving a global circulation of nearly 400,000 copies in 1999.[7] Nintendo, meanwhile, was famous for its telephone hotline, which players could call for customer support and, more intriguingly, advice on how to beat games.

Unofficial magazines and publications also sprung up to support the developing sector. Magazines like *PC Gamer*, *Mega* and *Crash* emerged to provide publishers with another route to market through advertising. But in an interview with Keith Stuart at the *Guardian* about the role of fanzines and magazines, John O'Shea, the director of the National Videogame Museum, argued that they 'have a similar lineage to football and music fanzine culture, in that they provide perspectives on the players and the fans and what they were thinking at the time'.[8] The emergence of authentic writing and fandom helped propel a number of writers beyond the sector too, with *Black Mirror* creator Charlie Brooker and *Rogue One* writer Gary Whitta both transitioning from games writer to wider cultural figures.

The emergence of an established culture around creating and playing games led to the rise of in-person events too. Big industry conferences such as the Game Developers Conference and E3 first emerged in 1988 and 1995 respectively. Consumer games events such as the Penny Arcade Expo (now PAX) and gamescom (Europe's biggest consumer game event) emerged in 2004 and 2009. Video games also made their first significant leap into the broadcasting world too, with South Korea televising people playing the popular strategy game *StarCraft* from as early as 1999.[9]

Within a few decades of video games being invented, the medium was big enough to support a large community of players, a specialist information ecosystem and in-person events. Where groups form, politicised chat inevitably follows. And that's why authoritarian governments in the 1980s started to keep a close eye on nascent video game communities, just in case they turned into a hotbed of political dissent.

According to an extensively researched piece for *Die Zeit* by Denis Gießler, the Stasi, East Germany's fearsome secret police, produced a series of reports monitoring how young people interacted with one another at local computing clubs due to fears that they were being exposed to Western technology and ideas.

On 12 January 1988, a Stasi informant produced a memo about an East Berlin club based in a building called the House of Young Talents (HdjT in German) which noted that attendees didn't just own a number of Western-made Commodore 64 computers; it was a prerequisite for joining the club. Considering these devices were notionally barred from the country as a result of rules laid down by the Coordinating Committee for Multilateral Export Controls (COCOM), this naturally attracted the authorities' attention.[10]

And in a taster of what we'll see later in the book, the Stasi's investigation into games quickly turned into an exploration of how it could control them.

A five-page memo was sent by the deputy head of Division XV (essentially the engineering and technology part of the Stasi's framework) categorising 256 games spotted at the club in 1987 by how risky they were to politically control. *Frogger*, the classic game where you try to get your frog across a road without being obliterated, was deemed to be ok. The action game *Raid Over Moscow* wasn't. Ten bucks to anyone who can guess why.

Beyond games content, the Stasi also identified the community as a potential risk to social cohesion. In the 1988 memo, the informant reporting on the House of Young Talents noted 'that there are also members within the interest groups or computer clubs with a verifiably negative attitude toward the socialist state and social order'. Given their exposure to the Western world through imported devices and games, 'there is a potential danger that the interest groups or computer clubs will go in a negative direction.' The informant went on to suggest that this political danger could also be matched by the technological risk that club members could circulate virus-laden Western game disks in the country, which turned out to be an impressive foreshadowing of future technological warfare.

These developments likely influenced conversations amongst the East German leadership about the possibility of creating a dedicated video games strategy, both to counter messages from the West and to strengthen the country's position by providing entertainment akin to what citizens were increasingly seeing smuggled across the border.

'Towards the end of East Germany, there were discussions about how games can convey socialist ideals through playing,' said Dr Jens Schroeder, a key figure in the Australian video games trade association, IGEA, and an academic steeped in the cultural significance of Germany's games sector. These plans 'were not very fleshed out at all' but included efforts to use East Germany's home-grown computing device – the *BildSchirmSpiel* – as the backbone for a consumer games market where products that aligned with the state's values could be sold to consumers.

Nothing meaningful came of this. By the time the East German government had begun to investigate video games and consider creating a plan to use them for political control, the Berlin Wall fell – bringing the Iron Curtain down on the Stasi and the East German state in the process.

But what the Stasi had revealed was a first framework for influencing and controlling games for a political purpose. And even at a time when video games reached millions rather than billions, the instincts of authoritarians to see games content and communities as something they needed to control was established.

Yet at this time, the influence of games was akin to any other subculture. While they were an addition to the cultural and creative mix, video games remained rooted within the physical hardware that they were played on. Players and communities still had to come together in the real world to talk, forge connections and develop an identity, ensuring any influence from a nascent medium would happen in plain sight.

But games, and the world around them, changed. Hardware became increasingly available. Software became increasingly valuable. And as online connectivity steadily rolled out across the world, it was increasingly possible to play online games together wherever you were in the world. This necessitated the creation of new communication infrastructure to connect players, address problems in games and support community conversation: a precondition for the creation of the powerful information ecosystem that would become contested across the world.

MUDDYING THE DIGITAL WATERS

The emergence, evolution and growth of online multiplayer games created the conditions in which the video games industry changed from selling products that people play within a space to becoming an enormous interconnected universe of games, social media channels and influencers capable of changing the way we think.

The transformation started with a game design challenge which emerged when the forerunner of online games was created in the late 1970s. In 1978, Richard Bartle and Roy Trubshaw, two academics working at the University of Essex, invented the *Multi-User Dungeon* (MUD). The game, which was inspired by the first edition of the rulebook for *Dungeons & Dragons* and ran on a PDP-10, allowed academics connected via the United Kingdom's university-to-university online networking structure to enter, participate in and interact within a shared fantasy environment via text inputs (provided they were happy to log on to its thirty-six-player server in the evening to avoid throttling the network).

But even in the early days of MUD's development, Trubshaw and Bartle realised that online games needed to be changed to account for all the people playing at the same time. The game's designers realised that the traditional game design approach of rewarding someone for achieving a goal risked one person having fun at everyone else's expense.[11] 'If you need a lamp to go underground, the first person to grab it prevents anyone else from following,' journalist Aaron Reed wrote in a piece about MUD. 'And once all puzzles have been solved and treasures claimed, what would new arrivals have left to do?'

After toying with ideas like resetting the game every time people played to give everyone individual glory, the designers realised that they needed to change the way they designed the game. Like *Dungeons & Dragons* upon which MUD was loosely based, Trubshaw and Bartle hypothesised that they needed to create a space where people could feel valuable by choosing how they, and their friends, interacted with it. 'The world had to assume dominance, not problem solving,' Bartle said – something echoed by one of the other legendary designers of online multi-player worlds.

'Instead of thinking of myself as a strict game designer. I feel I'm more of a virtual world designer and coming up with the overall structure of the world that is presenting itself to the gamer,' said Matt Firor, who formerly headed up ZeniMax Online Studios and led the team behind the multi-billion-dollar hit online game *The Elder Scrolls: Online*. 'It's setting up a premise,' Firor continued. 'You're setting up a world, you're setting up the rules that define the world, and then [developing] the systems that result from that.'

In short, creating multiplayer online games isn't just about making a fun game; it's about building all the necessary structures that a real world contains to allow people to connect – including ways to talk. MUD's fantasy world, which was somewhat unimaginatively called 'The Land', showed this perfectly. Bartle and Trubshaw focused less on game design and more on making an interesting place for players to spend their time in. Weather effects were added to give players extra challenges to deal with as they navigated the world. Enemies were created that could only be defeated by multiple players coming together (a mechanic now known as a 'raid'). They continually built new content for the game, rolling out new features and new parts of The Land to ensure players who engaged in the world always had something to come back to. The designers created systems to encourage interaction in play, including a 'Captain's Logbook' to leave messages for other players and the ability for skilled players to become powerful 'wizards' whose power made them worth being friends with (or fearing).

The result, according to journalist Nicole Segre, who covered MUD's transition into the home-computing world, turned MUD into a 'means of communication, an electronic forum'.[12] Players left their imprint on the world via an in-game logbook. The game spawned its own language, called 'mudspeke', with shorthand and slang becoming commonplace. MUD inspired a multitude of spin-off games, creating a genre known as MUDs. And the many ways that people chose to play these games led to Bartle creating a taxonomy of player types that identified the four motivations driving their play: achievement, exploration, socialisation and slaying other players.[13]

MUD, in short, was no longer a game first: it was a digital equivalent of Oldenburg's third place that happened to put a game at the centre of it. Yes, play was notionally the reason why people came together. But Bartle and Trubshaw realised that their world gave people an excuse to come together, talk, and hang out. MUD was serving the sociological function of a third place; it just happened to be entirely digital and capable of reaching across the world.

The significance of this shift was noticed but could not be fully realised. British Telecom, the UK's telecommunications provider, attempted to bring MUD to home computers in partnership with Bartle and Trubshaw in the mid 1980s, charging players approximately £2 per hour to play the game.

But the infrastructure to support the concept wasn't there yet. Computer adoption grew in the home-computing era, but there were not enough devices to create a massive online multiplayer game. MUD launched roughly fifteen years before the World Wide Web, twenty-five years before broadband and thirty years before 4G, putting it so far ahead of the networked internet curve that there was no way to support such rich games. The payment infrastructure of the 1980s was also not sophisticated enough to regularly pay developers to add new content to their games through methods we're familiar with today, such as in-game purchases or online subscriptions. This prevented MUD and the many MUD spin-offs from generating enough revenue to support their theoretically never-ending development effort.

However, MUD had already changed the way people thought about making and playing games. Although many of the MUDs that followed Trubshaw and Bartle's work were set in fantasy worlds, 1991's post-apocalyptic *Armageddon* and 1993's education-focused *Diversity University* showed an appetite to create different worlds to play in. A sub-genre of MUD emerged called 'talkers' in which the game was abstracted away to allow people to simply talk to one another in a low-cost, low-intensity online space.

But MUDs also did something else: they gave people and groups power within a game world that they would not necessarily have elsewhere.

Aaron Reed notes that the super-powerful wizards of the first MUD were handed a variety of game-changing spells and powers upon assuming their exalted rank. But rather than act as friendly all-powerful guides to other players, they became 'right bastards', often using their powers to befuddle, torture or kill other players. New entrants to the world were also advised to team up with other people, lest they be set upon by other roving gangs of adventurers who had formed a bond in the name of survival. It wasn't possible for the powerful players and gangs within the early MUDs to project their power beyond the narrow confines of the game's mechanics. It did, however, show the potential for influential people and groups within game communities to accrue power and wield it to their own ends. This foreshadowed the power that game communities could wield beyond online games as they connected to our wider digital world, creating the conditions for these groups to exert their influence for purposes beyond play in the decades to come

MUDs had created the conditions to turn games into societies with social hierarchies, their own language and their own culture. They created new digital third places for people to assemble outside of the physical world. And though the power of these spaces was limited at the time, they would soon put games at the centre of the interconnected digital communication ecosystem that dominates the world today.

MASSIVELY MULTIPLAYER ONLINE CONVERSATION

MUDs demonstrated the potential for networked computing to create a new way for people to play, a new space within which to assemble, and the potential of a new economic model in the industry to support them. But the true transformation of video games from another hobby enjoyed in physical spaces to a cityscape of digital third places started with the transformation of MUDs into commercially successful Massively Multiplayer Online video games (MMOs) across the 1990s.

Early MMOs, which were designed by MUD enthusiasts like Firor and another – Raph Koster – who would soon create *Ultima Online*, took the ideas at the heart of MUD design and updated them for the 1990s: making the most of the emerging mass consumer market for PC games hardware (especially powerful graphics cards) to immerse players in visually appealing virtual worlds that they wanted to hang around in.

Gone was the requirement to turn text-based prompts about fantasy lands into a world in your head. In came role-playing games with 2D (such as 1991's *Neverwinter Nights)* and 3D graphics (including the pseudo-3D assets of 1997's *Ultima Online*), where you could physically see the environment around you and craft your own identity through your character design. This allowed MMOs to take on a truly spatial dimension, driving the efforts of designers to build 'worlds' supporting the fiction of that universe to entice people into play (and, as we've seen across this book, talk to each other).

Advances in networking technologies also created the possibility for online games to support tens, hundreds and even thousands of players at once – moving well beyond the first MUD's thirty-six-player capacity. Communication infrastructure improved, with games creating ways to talk with people or groups for the purposes of making the game world function. Some of those focused on increasing the number of way players could talk through existing text functions, such as *Ultima Online* adding ways to talk privately with some players 'face to face' and also to the wider world. Others focused on fostering group play, with 'party' chat that allowed players to talk to one another in groups popping up in games like *World of Warcraft*. Online games were also an early space for online voice chat, with Sega's

Dreamcast offering voice over internet protocol (VoIP) chat for console players in 1999. Skype, the VoIP platform that was acquired by Microsoft and strongly inspired its Teams service, was launched in 2003 by comparison.

Economically, MMOs benefitted from the emergence of the necessary commercial infrastructure, such as the network of physical video game retailers and nascent online technologies, to sell to a mass audience. And with the roll-out of the World Wide Web across the early 1990s steadily making networked computing accessible for all, it was increasingly possible to reach millions of players across the world with the alluring dream of entering a world alongside your friends (and some new ones you hadn't made yet).

The advancements in game design, technology, economic circumstances and communications infrastructure turned the promise of MUDs into extraordinary commercial successes across the world.

Fantasy Role-Playing Game (RPG) *Ultima Online* was only forecast to grab 15,000 subscribers at its peak when it launched in 1997. By December 1998, the game had over 100,000 paying players supporting the game every month. *RuneScape*, an MMO developed in Cambridge with a medieval feel to it, has seen over 300 million accounts created to play the game online through a browser (or now via a mobile device). *World of Warcraft* became a phenomenon following its 2004 release, peaking at twelve million active subscribers in 2012 and generating over $9bn in revenue by 2017.

This success was also felt in Asia, where MMOs such as *MapleStory* (made in South Korea), *Phantasy Star Online* (created in Japan) and *Fantasy Westward Journey* (developed in China) each accrued enormous audiences and cultural significance. This was crucial in growing both the size and the influence of Asia as the core of the games world, encouraging developers to make online games and adopt some of the service-based business models mentioned in the last chapter ahead of the technological curve – handing them a key advantage when the smartphone market took off.

However, the success of MMOs in the late 1990s and early 2000s also created a problem for both players and developers. The games did enable conversation within them, but in contrast to other digital spaces, that in-game chatter was usually, and broadly still remains, ephemeral to the player. While the business that made the game would record the chat or communication, the expectation for players was that what was said in-game via its communication channels would not last.

This meant players and video game companies had to find, or create, supplementary digital spaces outside of these worlds to effectively grow and maintain them. Where, for example, could players go to learn about how to navigate the world, which quests to pursue, and which areas to potentially avoid without friends? How could groups form to plan their entry into the world outside of the game chat to tackle, say, a challenging in-game 'raid' that required tight co-operation? And how could the developers maintain lines of communication with players to find out what was, or wasn't, working, to allow them to tweak parts of their world, add new features to it and keep players abreast of developments?

At the time when MMOs first emerged, the social media platforms that we consider dominant in the world – like Facebook, X (formerly Twitter) or WeChat – did not exist. Instead, conversation and communication were fragmented across direct messaging apps, early VoIP services like Skype, web forums and, in the case of games, dedicated video game media sites or fan sites where players could talk to fulfil the range of interactions that in-game chat alone could not support.

The result was that the worlds created by MMOs stretched out beyond the borders of the digital space created by the developers. Instead, multiple layers of communication infrastructure were layered one on top of the other to create a two-way funnel where players could flow down from the game into a range of private chats, or up from the private chats back into the game world they inhabited. This changed the relationship between digital play and the communities that engaged with it. The identities, connections and conversations formed within a virtual world began to ripple out into the digital ecosystem, which shapes how we view the physical world around us.

'One of the big things we talked about for many years at Jagex is that the aperture for thinking about the community is not just the game executable, the window into which people look through and see a game world; it is the ecosystem around it,' said Phil Mansell, the former chief executive of Jagex, the creator of the ever-popular *RuneScape* MMO. 'And much of the ecosystem, whether it is *RuneScape* or other MMORPGs, the content is [generated] from the players. There's all of this activity that goes on outside the game that wouldn't happen without the game, but it's also not dependent on the game running.'

In the current world, that means the developers of the games are watching people do everything from post comments on social media, create Discord channels for their guilds, post YouTube videos or stream on a site like Twitch to talk about the game. But while all of that content is created in the name of a game, the motivation behind both why someone plays and what content they consume differs significantly depending on which part of the player base they are in. 'The community will have its own factions and different associations of players who have different beliefs,' Mansell explained. 'They might cluster around activities in the game, player versus player, players or players versus environment types, who like boss monster or raid-like battles. And they will form sub-communities and subgroups and sort of affiliate in these different groups.' Often, these communities would also be shaped by how intensely players associated with the game world they inhabited.

*

'Something that we found with the *RuneScape** games was [that our community operated in] expanding concentric circles, or layers of an onion. You would often have a very core community. These people would play every day, they would play four hours a day. And they would not just be in the game, but they would be on social media and some of the most engaged would be creating content that would span from writing social messages to making a three hour guide on the most deep and niche aspect of the game. But then you go out in the concentric circles of people who just rock up and play for a few hours every few days, or the "weekend warriors".' Mansell even said that there are people who don't play the game any more, but still watch and read content about it because it's been part of their lives for decades and they want to keep across it like they're reading about a sports team in the paper.

So, games like *RuneScape* or *World of Warcraft* became 'a catalyst or unifying force of its community'. And as we will see shortly, the creation of passionate, driven and engaged communities at the heart of the digital world would give these players unusual power within their worlds and beyond. The need for these groups to connect led to the creation of a deeply interconnected information ecosystem, linking the game itself to social channels, forums and other forms of media around the game. This enabled terms, ideas and world views from games to spill into the rest of society because the digital infrastructure that allowed people to talk about virtual worlds was connected directly to the physical one too.

* *RuneScape* is no longer one game. It is instead multiple games: the ever-evolving *RuneScape* game; an 'old-school' version that mimics the game in its earliest versions; and a new title that was announced in 2025. But for ease, I'm focusing on the game name as an umbrella term.

But if the importance of communities to the video game industry had stopped there, its impact might have been limited. Instead, the industry saw the success of MMOs and adopted the tropes, mechanics and tactics they used to forge communities to empower their own: spawning thousands of social spaces where the industry's billions of players could begin to congregate and chat within the process.

COMMUNITY CHANNELLED

Developers, publishers and game platforms realised that connecting communities was critical to business success. Even though the industry was expanding, building a community conferred big advantages on all developers.

For makers of multiplayer or free-to-play games which emerged as the smartphone economy grew from 2008 onwards, a thriving community was as key to keeping the game alive as it was for an RPG. And for creators of 'premium' games – essentially, any title released at an upfront cost – having an engaged community makes it much easier to generate orders for your game before, during and after launch.

So, from the mid 2000s onwards, creating new ways to enable conversation amongst (and with) players, strengthening existing layers of communication, and further raising up the importance of both individuals and groups within game communities became a priority for the industry.

In multiplayer games, developers used tactics and tools that were successfully deployed in MMOs to allow players to express themselves in multiple ways. Adding tools like voice chat, text chat or 'prompt' chat (where you press a button to send a pre-made text message or emoji to other players) to games such as *Call of Duty*, *EA Sports FC* and *Mario Kart* normalised talking to one another in every game. Including other features seen in online role-playing games like profile customisation or character customisation with the help of in-game items or 'skins' (i.e. a different costume for your avatar) simultaneously allowed players more room to express themselves, while generating income for developers.

The platforms that allowed people to access content also integrated social features in different ways to allow players and communities to keep up with one another. Microsoft, Sony and Nintendo all implemented friend and chat systems at a platform level within their console services. This meant that you no longer had to be playing an online game to chat to anyone over a console; you could play any game – such as a single-player action adventure like *The Last of Us* – and still talk to a friend while you played. The implementation of 'screen-sharing' across all major consoles, including the recently released Switch 2, shows how commonplace it is for players to turn what could be considered a 'solitary' experience of playing at home into one they share with others.

PC storefront Steam, meanwhile, went one step further. As well as adding a system to allow people to add friends, talk to them and see when they were online in the store, it also created a Groups feature to allow people to form communities on their platform and made it easy for developers to turn the pages through which they sell their games into an interactive bulletin board for players to talk with them – making Steam function, in many ways, like a barebones social network for PC players.

Meanwhile, the emergence of sustainable major social media platforms across the first decade of the twenty-first century became an obvious space in which players could layer new spaces to talk, create and hang out on top of the existing layers of communication they already relied upon.

'The people who play video games are some of the most online native people,' said Maria Sayans, CEO of the BAFTA award-winning ustwo games and chair of UK industry trade association Ukie. 'They are highly connected. They spend a lot of time online. They are very fluent in how communities get formed and how you influence them.'

And that's why it's not a big surprise that players were quick to enter and assume an important status within nascent social media spaces. Platforms such as Reddit and Twitter became useful ancillary hangouts for video game enthusiasts alongside their games.

Reddit's r/gaming forum blossomed into a community full of over 40 million active users, while subreddits for just about every notable game in existence popped up to allow people to talk about everything from *The Legend of Zelda* to *Cyberpunk: 2077*. Twitter, meanwhile, became the news wire for both players and the industry, with game releases, industry gossip and memes exploding from the space. The industry's immersion in Twitter is a big reason why the Gamergate 2014 hate movement so successfully emerged from the platform, something that we will later discover is a central reason for the rise of the alt-right across the world.

Video sites such as YouTube and live-streaming service Twitch, which was founded as a way to make it easier to broadcast esports tournaments, relied upon video game content creators to drive their expansion, because the ability to record video game footage directly from PC screens made it a great source of rich, engaging media that directly appealed to passionate audiences while smartphones raced to improve cameras to turn everyone into content creators.

By 2020, YouTube creators like PewDiePie, the droll Girlfriend Reviews and documentary series like Game Maker's Toolkit contributed content which powered 100 billion hours of viewership of video game content on the platform.[14] Twitch, meanwhile, evolved into the equivalent of live TV for the video game generation, with popular streamers and major esports tournaments drawing 2.5 million people back to the site on a daily basis.[15] The reach of these creators, also often called 'influencers', encouraged the games industry to court them directly, establishing financial and in-kind relationships that gave these voices additional power within the ecosystem. This provided a foothold to foster their own extensive global communities, giving them unusual power to influence or tilt digital ecosystems.

Even games that had no tie to MMOs could rely upon how much people like to play to power growth. For example, Zynga's *Farmville* path to becoming one of the biggest mobile free-to-play hits was a result of its integration with Facebook and its ability to cascade through the friendship networks of its biggest players. And while *Farmville* is about as far away as can be from a game like *World of Warcraft* in terms of what the game is, who plays it and why they do, it also shows the extent to which games that were part of social communities were already dominating the industry.

And over the course of the 2010s, that relationship deepened. Video games companies of all shapes and sizes developed their games and their businesses by building a deep relationship with their communities across the onion-like layers of communication that sat within games, the platforms they were released on and the social media landscape they fed. This resulted in every game creating its own information ecosystem, which empowered individual members of the community and subgroups within it to assume power. And with games now a truly global medium enjoyed by billions of people across the world, groups who learned to wield that influence could take it beyond the game, influencing the wider world in the process.

At the top of the industry, the biggest video games have evolved into 'games-as-a-platform' style services where people can contribute and create within the enormous multiplayer worlds that developers have created – increasingly as valued, if not yet truly equal, participants.

Minecraft's growth from a small independent video game into a franchise capable of pulling in billions of dollars through video game stores and at the cinema box office is largely due to its open creativity, allowing players of all ages to create their own craftable masterpieces in public and in private.

Fortnite, Epic Games's hugely popular multiplayer shooting game, started life as a zombie-battling game and has evolved into a virtual theme park, where players can dress their character up as everything from Sabrina Carpenter to Darth Vader or create their own games using *Fortnite*'s Unreal Engine powered creator.

Roblox, the user-generated content platform that has over 110 million people within its digital borders every day, has managed to position itself in the market by allowing its creators to make the games that resonate with audiences, before making money through in-game currencies. This includes *Grow a Garden*, a New Zealand-developed farming game that broke the record for the most concurrent players ever in a user game by getting more than 20 million people through its doors in a single sitting.

Even *Grand Theft Auto Online*, a game that is mostly about capering around a crime-filled digital version of what is essentially Los Angeles (insert your own joke here), proved to be enough of a creative canvas for players that two out-of-work actors in the pandemic thought it'd be a good idea to try and stage a performance of *Hamlet* in-game – with predictably chaotic outcomes.*

But below these top 'platform' games, the biggest companies in the games industry have made reaching into its community an essential part of doing business. Electronic Arts has gone to great lengths to build relationships with professional footballers to promote the release of *EA Sports FC* each year, with players arguing

---

* See *Grand Theft Hamlet* to find out exactly what happened: https://www.imdb.com/title/tt28244549/.

over their player ratings in videos shot and shared by their clubs on social media across the world. Mobile games companies have taken advantage of changing competition laws around the world to build 'direct-to-customer' selling tactics, skipping round storefronts like the App Store or Google Play to offer better-value in-game purchases to all players (and custom deals to their most loyal customers). Games like *RuneScape* have grown big enough to become the focus of dedicated fan events, with thousands of players flying in from all across the world to hang out together and celebrate their favourite game.

Even small independently developed games have sought to make the most of the blurring divide between the barriers of video games and social media communities, benefitting from the organic fandom popping up around the game who create content, talk about the game and keep its story going. 'There's a massive community around *Disco Elysium*, which is a single-player game [a BAFTA award-winning role-playing game featuring a cop with amnesia solving a murder within a city on the brink of collapse],' explains Sayans. 'That community is massively invested in the story of the game and what it is.'

And a big reason why it's never been easier for games businesses of all sizes to lean into communities is that the social media economy has evolved further, with the emergence of new channels – or even dedicated services – aimed at adding further important layers to the industry's community network. Discord, the video chat platform that also doubles up as a forum for game enthusiasts, was founded in 2015 to offer an easy hangout for players to voice chat together. At a micro level, Discord can let you talk with people individually, in small groups or within tiny dedicated servers. At a macro level, it's become its own digital cityscape for talking about games with Discord servers for *Minecraft* (409,000 users), Chinese action game *Genshin Impact* (503,000 users) and multiplayer battler *Marvel Rivals* (1.37 million users) boasting city-sized populations.

Short-form video apps such as TikTok quickly became a natural home for the video game content creators who had become central to YouTube and Twitch. By creating new content, repurposing old video, or spawning a new layer of creators who have grown up with short video as their main source of entertainment, TikTok alone saw people watch three trillion minutes' worth of gaming content on the platform in 2023.[16]

Meanwhile, in Asia, the integration of games and social media went even deeper as a result of the top messaging apps from across the region integrating them into their platforms. Japan's Line platform, Korea's KakaoTalk, and Tencent's WeChat have each boosted engagement by making games a key part of their platforms. For example, the invention of 'mini-apps' within WeChat allowed small bite-size games to enter its ecosystem and entertain millions of users across the country. And the importance of game communities to the health of the digital media landscape at large has been demonstrated by how digital play has become integral to traditional news media too. In a 2023 interview with *Vanity Fair*, the *New York Times*'s games team revealed that its portfolio of games – such as *Wordle* and *Spelling Bee* – wasn't simply drawing millions of players every day: it was also successfully upselling full subscription 'bundles' to the entire suite of *NYT* products, with people who played games becoming the most engaged subscribers in the process. And while many of the games look solo, Jonathan Knight, who heads the games team at the *New York Times*, told me that the 'one-a-day' release of puzzles has created a 'social aspect' to its games that is 'often overlooked'. 'Everybody is solving the same puzzle that day,' he said. 'So, no matter whether you started with our app yesterday or three years ago, you're working on the same answer to the same puzzle as everybody else. That really creates this sense of community, especially with something like *Wordle*.' And while those communities might not be sitting on Discord talking over voice chat, they may well be sharing answers together via a

WhatsApp group or tackling *Spelling Bee* together in person, which is apparently a keen activity of Bill and Hillary Clinton's. That speaks to the extent to which digital play is a socially important force within our society: shaping interactions in a digital world that inevitably spill into the physical. And that's why the success of any video game rests on the extent to which it can reach, engage and sell to a community of players.

'It's impossible to succeed today in video games without a strong community of fans, people who feel identified by your game, who feel seen by you as a developer, who feel that the game expresses things about themselves and their values,' said Sayans. 'And they need the ability to like and connect with each other through the game, but [also through] shared interests and shared values.'

A SPACE FOR ACTIVISM, A SPACE FOR INFLUENCE

The emergence of a massive interconnected video games industry, with billions of players who enjoy thousands of wildly different games somehow all identifying the sector as such, is therefore not a story of digital isolation, but of unparalleled connection.

As hardware capable of playing games arrived in everyone's hands, as game engines allowed creators across the world to make the games of their dreams, as digital distribution made it possible to reach all these players with services, and as the lessons of successful online play led to the connection of all these people together, the nature of digital play transformed.

Video games stopped being a one-off activity stuck to a handful of spaces and places like bars, arcades or the living room. Instead, each game became its own space, with its own community, who created its own content, and communicated in its own way amongst itself. This created individual information ecosystems surrounding myriad games that stretched out across social media because video game communities both rely on, and power, usage of these services. As more games emerged across the world that were capable of reaching enormous audiences, the overall size and influence of the games ecosystem grew. And as Sayans alluded to, the communities within games accrued greater power: encouraging players to become activists within games, but also allowing them to increasingly spread their influence beyond game worlds.

This, naturally, ensures that games can have influence on the way huge numbers of people across the globe think because of the reach of the medium and its interconnectedness with the digital communication platforms that shape our world. However, Western democracies missed this development. By clinging to outdated stereotypes of games as anti-social practices, few people saw how the transformation of the industry had increased its potential to project social, cultural and political power. In bringing a world of players to their games, handing them a voice and allowing them to become powerful participants within the game or the community, the industry transformed players from passive consumers of a product into activists and campaigners who believe that the ever-evolving worlds and games they enjoy must reflect their voice. For example, in the context of *RuneScape*, Mansell told me that the company realised quickly that influential players, sub-groups and sub-communities in the game had started to 'lobby' for changes to the game through the content channels they had amongst each other and with the developer. Eventually, the company would agree to implement a voting system into one of its games to allow players to nod through updates – with the rules of what they did or didn't engage players on governed by a 'written' and 'unwritten' constitution.

The 'agency' that people feel when playing games, namely that you control the action in a way that you don't in other mediums, was beginning to translate into a wider feeling of control over the space itself. Once at home in these spaces, and aware of their importance to their ongoing existence, players began to small 'p' 'politicise' amongst themselves. And as the profile of these players, their confidence online and their presence throughout online channels grew, it gave them the knowledge and reach to launch campaigns about games in a digital world that could meaningfully change things within reality: exploiting the enormous information ecosystem surrounding games to achieve their aims.

What those players sought to achieve differed from group to group. Some campaigns were targeted at developers to encourage them to change policies, such as a campaign by the players of *Helldivers 2* that convinced Sony to drop plans to force them to create a PlayStation account to play after thousands of players across the world revolted against it.[17] Other campaigns have sought to cause mayhem for the sake of it, such as the successful attempt to vote Electronic Arts as the worst business in America two years in a row after one of its video games – *Mass Effect 3* – ended controversially.[18] The urge could also prove to be immensely good too, such as the *Games Done Quick* charity event that has raised over $50m through live-streaming people 'speed-running' video games.

Video game players had become unusually savvy at understanding how to use online campaigning to effect real world change. And according to Sayans, who wrote about the activist potential of players over a decade ago, the tactics, language and strategies adopted by groups of players have proven their ability to influence the world today.

'How do you influence people online? So, things like 4chan or Reddit, they're deeply connected to gamer communities and they're deeply online. They are adept at creating memes, with much of the memesphere coming from games. And so the way in which we communicate on social media, and in which ideas spread in modern media, was born, incubated, developed and amplified in gaming communities. And while I'm not a historian, having been involved in gaming communities for, you know, twenty years, a lot of the things that we "first" found in online gaming communities we are starting to see more broadly – those memes, humour and snappy conversation that travels really well.'

Games, therefore, had become a third place where groups could congregate, converse, form identities, and campaign through a range of digital channels that were plugged into each and every game. But in a moment of deep, and somewhat dark, irony, the democratisation of the video games industry encouraged autocrats, extremists and populists to take a much deeper interest in what was happening in its spaces and the information ecosystem around it.

The 'democratised' video game industry that could reach players and countries around the world for the first time ever stretched into territories that were not democratic, many of which sought to control culture following the collapse of the Soviet Union to stop soft power from bringing down their states. Games entered these markets at roughly the same time that social media powered movements like the Arab Spring spread across the Middle East, illustrating that the medium's ability to bring people together to talk with one another posed a risk to power. But equally, the noisy, influential and largely scorned base of video game players also provided these groups with an audience to appeal to: a group that they could court, bring on side and influence to promote their view of the world (or attack their rivals).

The control, co-option and collaboration with video games for the purpose of influencing had begun. And as authoritarians grasped the medium for their own ends, extremists and populists who sympathised with their perspective on the world made a similar grab towards disenchanted game communities. This has led to a medium designed for fun being turned towards reputation washing, a censorship-of-information war, disruption of democracy and the justification of violence on the streets: turning the power of play to insidious ends.

Part 2
The war for influence

5

Saudi Arabia's savvy gaming soft power plan

It was an unprecedented business deal. American video game publisher Electronic Arts (EA), responsible for developing *EA Sports FC*, *Madden NFL* and the *F1* games, announced that it was being acquired for $55bn on 29 September 2025.[1] The deal, which was the second largest in video game history following Microsoft's $69bn purchase of Activision Blizzard, cost $11bn more than Elon Musk's acquisition of Twitter – with EA's new owners benefitting from a direct relationship with 700 million players across the world.

Who, though, were the buyers? The answer may seem surprising. Saudi Arabia's Public Investment Fund (PIF) teamed up with Affinity Partners, the investment firm owned by Donald Trump's son-in-law Jared Kushner, American venture capital firm Silver Lake and bankers J. P. Morgan Chase – who provided $20bn in debt funding – to get the deal over the line. In doing so, the PIF snuck one of the world's most powerful soft power assets out of American hands and seamlessly moved it into Saudi Arabian ownership.

And rather than being the aimless purchase of a trillion-dollar oil fund, the PIF's acquisition of EA was the continuation of a deliberate, carefully constructed strategy to control and co-opt the power of video games for the development of the Saudi Arabian state driven by its de facto head of state: Crown Prince Mohammed bin Salman (MbS).

Underneath public prominent chatter about the country's investment of $10bn[2] into sports such as football, golf and boxing – including whether it was genuine economic investment or 'sportswashing' – Saudi Arabia quietly, and methodically, invested significantly more cash to capture swathes of the games industry. Under the auspices of its National Gaming and Esports Strategy, the foreword of which was penned by the crown prince, the PIF and the PIF-backed home-grown publisher Savvy Games invested tens of billions of dollars into the industry: snapping up shares in businesses like Nintendo, acquiring the makers of hit mobile games like *Monopoly Go!* and *Pokémon Go*, investing in the growth of local Saudi Arabian games businesses, and buying up the biggest esports tournament organisers to turn Riyadh into the home of video-gaming competitions.

According to MbS, the main reason for this glut of investment in games was to bring 'exciting new career, and unique entertainment opportunities, aiming to make Saudi Arabia the ultimate global hub for this sector by 2030'. The seriousness with which the country has taken to the task of developing a domestic games industry has to be taken seriously, especially for the opportunities it is providing to local developers who simply could not participate in the industry as recently as a decade ago.

However, unlike other aspects of Saudi Arabia's economic development plan, video games were never mentioned in the country's Vision 2030 strategy that sought to modernise the economy. MbS's wider vision to deliver modernisation and growth as a way to replace the country's reliance upon oil, provide opportunities for its young population, and move away from its decidedly unfun theocratic roots did not initially include the development of a domestic video games sector.

Their inclusion as a formal part of the country's growth plans came only after MbS, a noted gamer, grasped power in 2017 and had it immediately tested when journalist Jamal Khashoggi was assassinated by Saudi government agents in 2018.[3] As with its sport strategy, the by-product of Saudi Arabia's economic invest-ment into, and ownership of, video game businesses has allowed it to subtly co-opt the cultural value of video games, esports and their communities for soft power purposes: a process described by some writers as 'games washing'.[4]

By owning games companies, buying up stakes within other businesses, and investing heavily in the sector, Saudi Arabia has been able to tilt the industry's axis towards it – encouraging dia-logue, while also suppressing criticism. By buying up esports tournament organisers, hosting major events in the country, broadcasting them to the world and inviting digital influencers to the door, Saudi Arabia has been able to assume commanding control over digital sport, reaching millions with its carefully curated picture of life on the ground.

And by taking advantage of a close relationship between MbS and Kushner, forged during Donald Trump's first term in office, Saudi Arabia has managed to grab control of the one business capable of rippling influence through both the video game and sports ecosystems simultaneously. This acquisition strengthens MbS's control over the cultural and economic narrative sur-rounding Saudi Arabia: enhancing his reputation, increasing his power and curbing domestic dissent in the process.

THE GAMER PRINCE

Understanding how Saudi Arabia, a country that was a full-blown theocracy a little less than a decade ago, has become the owner of the biggest sports video games company in the world requires an understanding of three interrelated factors: how oil went from being the country's primary economic strength to a source of potential weakness; why the emergence of a large population of digitally savvy young people clashed with the state; how MbS's rise to power was based on his grasp of the problems, but was undermined by the ruthlessness with which he pursued power.

Since Ibn Saud founded what we consider to be modern Saudi Arabia in 1932, oil has been at the heart of the House of Saud's control over power. The discovery of it in Dammam in 1938 transformed the country into an oil state, granting wealth to its leadership and allowing it to quash dissent by establishing a generous welfare state. As journalist Tim Marshall put it, 'the people would obey, and the oil money would give them a good life.'[5]

However, the power of the state was buttressed by the support of the House of Saud's Wahhabist allies. And after the seizure of the Grand Mosque in late 1979, a hostage-taking exercise by Islamist Juhayman al-Otaybi and approximately 600 supportive militants which led to the death of over 200 people, the House of Saud leant much more strongly into developing a secretive, austere and theocratic state with its Wahhabist allies to prevent a recurrence. This added a hard, violent repressive streak to the House of Saud's deal with its population: giving it firm control over a population with little connection to the world beyond Saudi Arabia's borders.

But by the early 2010s, oil, the once reliable source of income, was becoming increasingly volatile. Concerns over climate change internationally, the development of fracking technologies in the US and wider geopolitical disruption saw the price of oil fluctuate considerably. The price of a barrel of oil started the new century at $12, rose to $140 in 2008, and then slipped back to $32 a barrel. With oil prices unlikely to return to their previous highs, energy consumption increasing in Saudi Arabia, and the non-oil industry providing only 15 per cent of the country's GDP, Saudi Arabia's historic strength in oil was becoming a modern weakness that, without modernisation, would compromise the bargain struck between the Sauds and its citizens (willing or otherwise).[6]

Fears were exacerbated by the changing nature, and expectation, of the country's population. In comparison with much of the Western democratic world, Saudi Arabia's population is remarkably youthful. According to figures gleaned from its 2010 census, a little under 58 per cent of the population was under the age of 30.[7] In 2022's census, that figure had risen to 63 per cent with a median age of 29.[8] As a result, the population is naturally of an age that, frankly, is more likely to be a source of possible dissent than other age groups. And unlike previous generations of Saudi citizens, they are connected to the outside world as a result of the smartphone economy. By 2018, 92 per cent of Saudis had a smartphone[9] and its citizens acquired a reputation as some of the most voracious viewers of YouTube content in the world.[10] The way they wanted to live their lives at home and interact with the international digital landscape became much more akin to what we see in the rest of the world, rather than what Wahhabist leaders would want for them.

'I lived there for a while and one of the things I noticed is that they have focused on doing a lot more things digitally and through their phones,' said Richard Ball, CEO of Saudi Arabian video games publisher Sandsoft and former executive at Warner Bros. 'Saudis will deal with normal things like online banking through their devices, but if you even get something like a speeding fine it comes to your phone and is linked up straight away.'

By contrast, the House of Saud's increasingly aged leadership looked out of step with its youthful population. Since Ibn Saud's death in 1953, he has been succeeded by one of his thirty-six sons. But by the early 2000s, time was making a mockery of the policy with King Abdullah in 2005 and King Salman in 2015 each assuming power around their eightieth birthdays. The country's leadership therefore faced a potentially existential risk. The oil dividend was weakening and its leadership was ageing. Its youthful population could increasingly see the world beyond the country's Wahhabist borders – they were accessing the same social media channels that protestors in Egypt and Libya used during the Arab Spring, which saw the removal of dictators Hosni Mubarak and Muammar Gaddafi.[11] A revolution could be coming to Saudi society.

But in a development that surprised everyone, including the country's allies, a new leader emerged in the country who had the energy, effectiveness and ruthlessness to turn those challenges into the making of his personal and political fortune. Mohammed bin Salman was never expected to gain power. A son of Salman bin Abdulaziz Al Saud through his third wife Fahda bint Falah Al Hithlain, MbS was considered to be far enough away from the line of succession for major allies such as the United States to know little about him.

His rapid emergence as a major player in the Saudi state changed that. In 2013, MbS was appointed head of the crown prince's court. By January 2015, at the age of 29, he was appointed defence minister by his father, King Salman, shortly after he acceded to the throne. He also retained his position as head of the court and as a minister of state, allowing him to assume wider responsibilities within the state.

As he rose through the ranks, it became increasingly clear that MbS held a considerably different view of the world to a typical junior member of the royal family. Unlike King Salman's direct heirs, MbS chose to steep himself in the intrigues of the Saudi court rather than study or work abroad. He studied and ran a series of businesses, drawing most of his inspiration from the inner workings of Silicon Valley. This gave him a unique perspective both on the challenges that the Saudi state was facing and on how he could position himself to provide the solutions.

'Mohammed bin Salman is a tech guy,' says James Montague, author of *Engulfed: How Saudi Arabia Bought Sport, and the World*. 'He wanted to produce a country that looks more like

California than previous generations [of the Saudi royal family] who would want to maintain a Saudi religious theocratic state.' According to broadcaster Jonathan Rugman, by 2015 MbS was already confiding in people close to him that he wanted to wake the kingdom from a deep slumber by driving a programme of economic diversification and social liberalisation.[12]

But while both liberalisation and modernisation of the economy were on the table, political freedom never would be. According to sports journalist Miguel Delaney, MbS's liberalisation agenda was always intended to work 'hand in hand, iron fist in velvet glove', with efforts to restrain political freedom. MbS was not breaking the House of Saud's deal with the population of a good life in return for political acquiescence: he was reshaping it for a modern age.

The economic and social aspect of the plan was revealed in April 2016. Vision 2030, MbS's ambitious plan for reforming the Saudi state which he drew up in his capacity as chairman of the Council of Economic and Development Affairs (CEDA), was profoundly ambitious. It sought nothing less than to turn Saudi Arabia from a secretive theocratic state up to its waist in oil into a modern technology economy with social freedoms and opportunities for the young people who could challenge the status of the House of Saud.

According to the Vision 2030 strategy document, the plan was to turn Saudi Arabia into 'the heart of the Arab and Islamic Worlds' by making it an 'investment powerhouse' that could connect multiple continents. Channelling billions of dollars from the country's Aramco oil business into its previously sleepy sovereign wealth fund, the PIF – of which MbS had become chairman in March 2015 after it moved under CEDA – Vision 2030 would diversify the Saudi economy by investing in modern technology businesses to bring good jobs to local people, driving social reforms that would wash away much of the cloying hold of the modern theocratic state, and bringing entertainment, tourism and leisure opportunities to Saudi Arabia. Vision 2030 would turn Saudi Arabia into a modern superpower for the benefit of its youthful population.[13] 'Our real wealth lies in the ambition of our people and the potential of our younger generation,' wrote MbS in the foreword to the strategy, demonstrating his handle on the situation.

The launch of Vision 2030 sparked a flurry of investment and activity across the country. Within two years of the launch of Vision 2030, the PIF had formed a $45bn investment fund with SoftBank Group, bought up 5 per cent of electric car manufacturer Tesla and invested $3.5bn in taxi app Uber. By 2020, the PIF's reach had expanded further with investments in Boeing, Live Nation and Meta bringing more technology companies to the country. The PIF also channelled cash into local construction projects to further support its modernisation goal, funding the creation of NEOM, the wildly overambitious technology-powered 'line'-shaped supercity marked for construction on the coast of the Red Sea, and Qiddiya, a new entertainment district located just a short distance south of Riyadh.

The investment in Qiddiya formed part of a wider initial push into entertainment and sport. In 2017, World Wrestling Entertainment (WWE) launched an Arab-language show called Wal3ooha to reach Saudi audiences. Manchester United, meanwhile, signed a five-year memorandum of understanding with Turki Alalshikh, chair of the country's General Sports Authority and close confidant of MbS.[14] The country also announced that it was lifting its ban on cinemas in December of that year, paving the way for Marvel movie *Black Panther* to become the first film shown in Saudi Arabia in thirty-five years.[15]

The reopening of cinemas wasn't just a sign of the country's new focus on entertainment; it also showed that social reforms were on the table. By the end of the 2010s, Saudi Arabia had significantly reduced the power of the country's religious police. It strengthened women's rights, ending gender segregation in restaurants and allowing women to drive. Its tourism board even issued guidance noting that foreign unmarried couples can visit the country and share rooms together, while making it clear that local traditions should be respected.[16]

Vision 2030 was pursued eagerly and energetically, producing genuine rapid change in Saudi society. But its authentic aims have always been rooted in MbS's desire to control the narrative around the state. Prior to Vision 2030's launch, bin Salman had commissioned international polling firms to understand what the world thought of the Saudi state. Economic modernisation, social liberalisation and supporting entertainment are all direct counters to the polling's findings that international audiences saw Saudi Arabia as socially restrictive, closed and authoritarian.[17]

However, entertainment was at this point arguably the least important part of Vision 2030. While investment was taking place and partnerships were being inked, the scale of Saudi investment in sports was nowhere near the level it would reach in the early 2020s. And at this time, Vision 2030 made no reference to video games or esports at all. Partly, this was due to Saudi Arabia's short history with video games. The territory was not a major market for either console or PC games in the early 2000s, owing in no small part to the religious authorities' publicly banning games like *Pokémon*.[18] And while mobile devices steadily opened up Saudi players to video games, there was no driving force within the country to create an industry or external clamouring to enter the market. This left local developers to try to make ends meet in a country that really didn't value games at the time.

'Back in 2013, everyone that is working in the games industry was seen as losers who were wasting their time,' said Meead Aflah, CEO of Riyadh-based game development studio Starvania. 'People thought they were doing something that was only suitable for children, you know, wasting their time.'

Hani Hashem, co-founder of Saudi mobile games company Fahy Studios, concurs. 'I'm a big fan of Nintendo and in my earlier years I had a gaming-related forum that I was managing with around 7,000 people in it. But I never took gaming as a serious career choice. My education was in business and that's why I worked in management consulting for over five years.' PwC's gain was the nascent Saudi Arabian games industry's loss.

So, how exactly did a medium that wasn't even a footnote in the original Vision 2030 document become the subject of a $38bn strategy a little over half a decade later? Quite simply, it turns out that the crown prince loves video games.

'MbS is a gamer,' explains Montague. 'He doesn't like golf and he's not really into tennis. Every time he talks about sport, he talks about gaming. There's nothing else culturally that comes close to it for MbS.'

What games he plays is subject to debate. Some suggested he grew up playing historical-themed military strategy game *Age of Empires*. Others suggested that he played popular first-person shooter *Call of Duty* or battle-royale game *Player Unknown: Battlegrounds*. Montague himself reports that Steve Arhancet, the director of esports organisation Team Liquid, had gone toe-to-toe with the Crown Prince in a game of *League of Legends*.

What is clear is that MbS loves games deeply enough to understand their appeal, their audience and their reach; something that the industry experts working closely with him to deliver the country's games plan have noticed.

'He absolutely is passionate about gaming,' said Mike McCabe, chief operating officer of the Esports World Cup Foundation and former Nike and Epic Games exec. 'I think he's shared this in interviews in the past,[19] but he's incredibly knowledgeable about it as well. I would go as far as saying there is no other world leader that is as knowledgeable or passionate about our industry as he is.'

His love for games is also indicative of a wider intuitive understanding of what Saudi Arabia's generation of youngsters will be looking for from entertainment.

'He's a very young person by international leader standards,' said Brian Ward, CEO of Saudi Arabia's PIF-backed Savvy Games Group and former head of game developer Blizzard, of the currently forty-year-old leader. 'People who are over sixty, seventy or eighty didn't grow up with video games the same way that younger people did. So I think it's a great advantage to Saudi and our sector to have his Royal Highness in the demographic. He's in the sweet spot.'

And importantly, MbS has made sure that other members of the royal family who love games too are also prominently involved in the development of the country's strategy.

*

'[Playing games] has been a lifelong love affair,' said Prince Faisal bin Bandar bin Sultan Al Saud, the chairman of the Saudi Esports Federation and current president of the International Esports Federation. 'I was born in 1980 right after the Atari was launched, at the height of its popularity.' And the prince's enthusiasm for games did not stop there.

'I went through the whole history of gaming,' he said. 'So Atari, you know, Sega Dreamcast, Nintendo 64, Sega Genesis, the whole gamut. And I have very fond memories of each device.' He then told me that he has since thrown himself into understanding the video games that underpin the esports industry, admitting to me that 'I would love to play *League of Legends* [Riot Games's wildly popular online multiplayer battling game],' when I tossed him a question about what he'd like to be able to play at a pro-level.

The Saudi interest in video games is authentic because the comparatively young generation of Saudi royals who now sit at the top of the tree grew up playing the same kind of stuff that I did. However, MbS's pursuit of a video games strategy was only made possible by two side-effects of his rise to power.

First, MbS's successful rise to de facto head of state as the crown prince in 2017 gave him the power and control to direct the Saudi state essentially as he saw fit.

Before his rise to power, MbS was already rumoured to have demonstrated that he was willing to take ruthless steps to assert his power at home and abroad. He allegedly earned the nickname 'Abu Rasasa' (father of the bullet) after it was said that he posted a bullet to a cleric at the land registry office when the official refused to process an illegal transaction on his behalf.[20] It is a rumour that he has never commented on, but one that shows his reputation for looking to control not just narratives, but people too.

His desire to dominate and control continued upon his full ascent to power. After being named deputy crown prince in 2015, the same year that he dragged Saudi Arabia into a bloody and damaging war with Yemen, MbS assumed the mantle of crown prince from June 2017.

Almost immediately, he made moves to consolidate his power. Shortly after the announcement of Saudi Arabia's wildly ambitious NEOM line city on 24 October 2017, hundreds of Saudi princes, business people and government officials were detained in the Ritz Carlton Hotel in Riyadh as part of a 'sheikhdown' instigated by a then newly formed anti-corruption committee headed up by MbS.

A former US government official who spoke to CNN said that the move was meant 'to remind people going forward that their wealth and their well-being would depend on the crown prince and not anything else'. The outlet also reported that 'detainees were coerced, abused and tortured.' Saudi Arabia has dismissed the allegations of abuse as 'absolutely untrue'. NBC News, by contrast, reported that seventeen people were hospitalised and one person died during the crackdown.[21]

The move strengthened the prince's hold on power and the purse strings. This provided him with the latitude to advance his strategy for Saudi Arabia on his own terms, something that likely gave him extra opportunity to fold his beloved hobby – and a medium known for creating high-value technology jobs – into his plans.

However, MbS's approach was not foolproof. In particular, he committed a number of acts of folly as a result of overestimating his ability to take ruthless action without receiving reputational blowback: something that would force the acquisition of soft power onto his agenda.

In November 2017, Saudi security forces detained Lebanese Prime Minister Saad Hariri and forced him to 'resign' from his post by reading a pre-written speech in front of TV cameras. While Hariri, somewhat understandably, withdrew the resignation once he and his family were safe, Saudi Arabia's attempt to forcibly eject him from power prompted widespread international condemnation, putting the state on the back foot.[22]

But it was the murder of Jamal Khashoggi on 2 October 2018 that made the reputational pillar of Vision 2030 crucial to both the future of MbS's project and himself.

Khashoggi was a Saudi Arabian journalist who was born in Medina to the owner of a fabric store. After beginning a career in journalism in 1986, Khashoggi covered both the Soviet War in Afghanistan in the 1980s and the rise of Osama bin Laden. While Khashoggi did rely upon some patronage from the House of Saud to operate as a journalist, his independence occasionally landed him in trouble with the publications that he worked for. This included the Riyadh-based publication *Al Watan*, which sacked him at the turn of the century after he criticised the country's religious establishment. He later rejoined and resigned from the publication in 2010 after publishing another controversial opinion piece.

But by 2017, Khashoggi no longer felt safe to continue to work from Saudi Arabia and moved from Jeddah to the United States instead. The move had been prompted by his mistrust of

MbS, who he believed was not interested in delivering both modernity and freedom. In its obituary for Khashoggi, the *Guardian* described his opinion of MbS as 'more rogue than reformer', citing a March 2018 piece in which the journalist said that bin Salman was shifting Saudi Arabia from 'old-time religious extremism' to 'you-must-accept-my-reform extremism, without any consultation'.[23]

Khashoggi became a target for online abuse that was allegedly co-ordinated by the Saudi state, while he was also accused of being a traitor, an apostate or an ally of the country's fierce regional rival Qatar. But despite this abuse, few would have forecast the brutality with which the Saudi state under MbS would choose to deal with Khashoggi. After entering the Saudi embassy in Istanbul on a trip to Turkey, Khashoggi was set upon, killed and dismembered by a fifteen-man Saudi death squad. They then attempted to cover up his death by having one of its members leave the embassy dressed in his robes, before the participants fled the country to avoid censure.

By 16 November 2018, the Central Intelligence Agency (CIA) had concluded that the crown prince had been involved in the assassination of Khashoggi.[24] Although MbS denied personal responsibility for the assassination, he did accept responsibility for Khashoggi's death as the country's head of state whilst maintaining that it was a rogue operation. This turned the crown prince into an international pariah, damaging his standing internationally and domestically.

As a result, the economic goal of Vision 2030 blended with another one. The country's attempt to economically modernise was no longer solely about moving away from oil dependency; it was now about providing a coat of paint to the country's reputation. And with Saudi Arabia having few soft power assets of its own that were capable of attracting and persuading people back towards the crown prince's state, he did what anyone with enormous amounts of cash would do: he set off to buy some.[25]

'The murder absolutely destroys MbS's attempts to project himself as a reformist figure in Saudi Arabia,' Montague explains. 'And what happens really quite soon afterwards is that investment in sport just goes through the roof. It starts with the purchase of Newcastle United by the Public Investment Fund, which is always seen as a forward operating base for this. But then it goes through boxing, the attempt to take over golf with LIV golf. And all of these purchases and investments basically take place after the death of Jamal Khashoggi.'

Within a matter of years, Saudi Arabia's attempt to wash away its sins turned it into a major financier of international sport. The £305m the PIF spent on Newcastle United turned one of the biggest names in English football into an outpost of Saudi soft power, with the club's third kit briefly splashing the green and white colours of its new patrons.[26] The kingdom's investment in boxing has made Riyadh 'the boxing capital of the world', hosting bombastic fights across weight divisions.[27] LIV Golf, Saudi Arabia's breakaway golfing tournament, has gone from rivalling the long-established PGA tour to discussing a merger, something the BBC News covered with a picture of Yasir Al-Rumayyan – governor of the PIF and the head of the breakaway golf tour – wearing a Newcastle United sports kit on a golf course.[28]

By making an effort to, in the words of Miguel Delaney, 'own competitions and intertwine the state with the infrastructure of the sport', Saudi Arabia's intention was to make itself an irreplaceable, ever-present and, crucially, always visible part of the ecosystem to ensure it served the aims of rehabilitating the state. It has since gone on to demonstrate the strength of this strategy further through its funding of FIFA's Club World Cup tournament in America. The *Guardian* reported that the Public Investment Fund was an official partner of the tournament. Surj Sports Investment, a sports investment company backed by the PIF, brought a stake in broadcaster DAZN and invested $1bn of money into the tournament to acquire exclusive global broadcasting rights: enabling the tournament to reach the world through Saudi-owned infrastructure.[29]

But what if there were a way to do something in a creative industry that had a greater reach into the digital world where young Saudis spent their time? What would happen if the Saudi state were to invest in a sector that had both soft power potential and the economic potential to create jobs in businesses that have shown capability in generating billions of dollars globally? How could investment into the infrastructure, ecosystem and subcultures that underpin it help Saudi Arabia meet young people both in person and online in the spaces they inhabit? And what if that industry happened to be at the heart of the head of state's personal interests, something that would allow him to tie his reputation to a medium he loved?

Video games, and the associated esports industry, were a perfect fit with Saudi Arabia's aims. And in the eight years after the slaying of Khashoggi with a bone saw in a Saudi-owned building, the country's sovereign wealth fund invested more than 100 times the £305m it spent acquiring a Premier League football club to advance Saudi Arabia's digital play plans.

TOWARDS GAMESWASHING

The country's entry into video games began informally at the same time that MbS made his grab for power.

In November 2017, around the time of the 'sheikhdown', MbS's MiSK Foundation, the not-for-profit that the prince founded in 2011 to cultivate learning and leadership amongst young Saudis, entered into a memorandum of understanding with two Japanese games companies. Square Enix, the company behind the *Final Fantasy* series, and Shin Nippon Koki (SNK), the business behind fighting games such as *Fatal Fury*, both agreed to work with MiSK to mentor young Saudi game developers at the foundation's annual forum. The agreement was limited in scope, but its commencement just as MbS assumed near-total control over the Saudi state was notable.

However, the way that Saudi Arabia steadily pursued its objectives to generate economic growth, create jobs for young Saudis and reap reputational benefits in games developed differently within the video games industry, which is focused on selling games to consumers, and esports, which is about using digital games to create competitive sports capable of supporting an ecosystem like football, golf or tennis.

On the consumer games industry side of the fence, Saudi Arabia's early investments were focused on using cash from the Public Investment Fund to acquire game developers or buy a seat at the industry table.

In the years that followed, those first steps turned into strides with both Square Enix and SNK shifting closer to the Saudi state. In June 2021, Square Enix signed a fresh memorandum with the PIF to explore investment opportunities 'in the development efforts of global entertainment content such as games' with one another.[30] SNK, meanwhile, became one of the first assets that a Saudi body invested in, with MiSK taking a 33 per cent stake in the business in 2020 via an affiliated business called the Electronic Gaming Development Company. By April 2022, that stake was upped to roughly 97 per cent in a move that saw MiSK's subsidiary essentially take ownership of the company.

Meanwhile, the PIF began quietly taking stakes in the biggest video games businesses across the world: Electronic Arts, the creators of the *EA Sports* game series, Take-Two Interactive, the publisher of *Grand Theft Auto,* and Activision Blizzard,* the makers of *Call of Duty,* in the fourth quarter of 2020. By May 2022, it had acquired 5 per cent stakes in *Mario* creator

---

* The PIF sold its stake in Activision Blizzard as part of Microsoft's $69bn acquisition of the business in 2023.

Nintendo, in *Street Fighter* maker Capcom and Korea's biggest game publisher, Nexon. It also founded Savvy Games Group as a local Saudi Arabian games business, purchasing a $1bn stake in Embracer Group, a Swedish business which had rolled up dozens of video games companies and intellectual properties, via its new vehicle.

However, its approach to courting the competitive video game-playing industry was a little different. Esports are closely related to the games industry, but have generally emerged as a result of a 'bottom-up' community movement to turn the process of finding out who is best at a popular game into organised sport. How organised, professional and well funded each game is varies from community to community. The biggest esports games in the world, like *League of Legends* and *DOTA 2*, measure the audiences and prize pots for their biggest tournament using numbers in the high millions. Sports-based video games such as *EA Sports FC* or the *F1* games have formed useful relationships with their real world counterparts, with official governing bodies and even genuine sportspeople entering the community to extend its reach. Fighting games like *Street Fighter*, meanwhile, are stuffed full of counter-cultural purists, whose appreciation for the brutal technicality of the genre is much more important than winning cash-stuffed competitions.

But overall, the esports community at large has shared a number of common challenges. There are few central structures governing the esports industry, which means the hundreds of teams competing for cash across dozens of esports games can find themselves stretched thin. There are over half a billion people viewing esports content each year,[31] but the fragmented nature of the ecosystem means it is hard to create a consistent structure around each game in the manner seen in professional sports leagues. Overall commercial viability in esports is pretty poor too, with the industry's forecast $4bn revenue by the end of the decade paling in comparison with the near $200bn market for video games content. This has led to some notable busts such as the David Beckham-backed Guild Esports, which closed down after it failed to sell on the insolvency market.[32]

So while there was a potential economic reason to invest in esports – low cost of entry, large global audience, potentially significant reputational upside – it made more sense for the country to enter through the grassroots, understand its challenges and solve problems once it had a grip on the problems (and the opportunities). In late 2017, the crown prince appointed Faisal bin Bandar bin Sultan Al Saud as chair of Saudi Arabia's national esports association to develop the local industry. This led to the country's first esports event taking place shortly after, something which gave it a sense that it could reach young audiences domestically and internationally if properly supported.

*

'We did our first tournament in March 2018,' said Prince Faisal bin Bandar bin Sultan Al Saud, when I asked him about the country's first steps into esports. 'I had two weeks to put on an event as our first event as a Federation, which was a little bit stressful, not gonna lie. We did FIFA, Super Smash Brothers, Street Fighter, League of Legends, and we had 45,000 people sign up, which caught me completely off guard.'

The tournament would eventually proceed in March 2018 with 1,500 competitors and 1,000 attendees. By 2020, a nationally organised 'Gamers without Borders' esports tournament, hosted during the pandemic in partnership with global organisations such as UNICEF and the International Medical Corps, morphed into Gamers8 – the country's first officially funded esports event.

With a local event off the ground, the state then made a decisive grab for an esports business of scale. In February 2022, Savvy Games acquired ESL and FACEIT – two of the biggest tournament organisers in the esports industry across the world – for a combined $1.5bn and merged them into a single Riyadh-based entity.

In doing so, it snapped up two companies with the skill and infrastructure capable of running esports tournaments for the dozens of games that have esports communities, setting up the broadcast infrastructure to reach audiences on Twitch (including hiring talent like the 'shoutcasters' who commentate games), and using their commercial expertise to make the events at least notionally commercially viable through brand partnerships. In short, the Saudis had done what was close to the esports equivalent of buying up the expertise necessary to run the digital equivalents of the English Premier League, the National Football League, the Formula 1 World Championships and more for $2bn: a comparatively cheap investment in serious industry infrastructure.

By mid 2022, the outline of Saudi Arabia's game plan was emerging. The PIF's investment in games companies reflected the buoyancy of the global games market, which was riding a pandemic wave between 2020 and 2021 to offer the kinds of economic benefits that the Saudis hoped to achieve in the medium term.

It ensured that the Saudis had a direct line into the biggest games companies in the world, ensuring that the creators of top multiplayer video games like *Mario Kart, Call of Duty* and the *EA Sports* series would be incentivised to pick up the phone. There was also emphasis on building Saudi Arabia's reputation as a games ecosystem too, with its MoUs with Square Enix and SNK foreshadowing its efforts to build expertise amongst local developers.

The investments in esports, meanwhile, meant that the state was in pole position to become the centre of the esports economy outside the giants of America and China. By investing only a little more than double the $875m spent on footballers to play in Saudi Arabia's pro football league,[33] Savvy Games had acquired the two tournament organisers capable of putting events on that could reach the half a billion people viewing esports content around the world.

But at this point, the country did not have a formal video games strategy for its economic goals in video games and reputational aims in esports to coalesce. For everyone reading this who doesn't work in the niche field of video game policy, this is perfectly normal. Only a handful of countries in the world have ever commissioned a formal video games strategy, with Germany's strategy of June 2021[34] and the UK's Games Growth Plan from June 2025 rare examples for an industry that's rarely front of mind for policy makers.[35]

'If I take thirteen years in government and seven years as prime minister and deputy prime minister, it was never the most important thing I did in any week or any day during that period,' said Leo Varadkar, former taoiseach of Ireland, when I asked him whether video games ever formed a big part of his thinking during his time heading the Irish state. A little honesty does sometimes go a long way.[36]

Therefore, the creation and announcement by the crown prince of a National Gaming and Esports Strategy in September 2022 marked a significant escalation in the state's plans to make video games a central part of the country's wider national vision. And by doing so, it allowed the state to gradually build its influence and credibility within both games and esports – applying another coat of wash to the country, and the head of state's reputation in the process.

BUILDING, AND EXECUTING, A SAVVY STRATEGY

The National Gaming and Esports Strategy has a simple but ambitious publicly stated aim: to make Saudi Arabia 'the center of the game'.

By 2030, the Saudi state plans to create a video games cluster generating 50 billion Saudi riyals of value for the economy (a shade over $11bn). It also aims to create 39,000 jobs in the country, support 250 game development businesses, become one of the top three countries in the world for developing esports athletes and establish itself as the home of the biggest esports event in the world by 2030 – making the country's industry roughly the size of an established European games cluster like the UK, France or Germany.

The main vehicle for achieving this is Savvy Games Group. After initially being founded as part of the PIF, the group was handed $38bn by the crown prince to advance the country's national video games strategy and was encouraged to crack on with things.*

'Savvy Games Group is the parent company of a number of entities in essentially two business units, plus a third pillar,' Ward explained to me while sitting in front of a frankly enormous portrait of the company's chairman, the crown prince. 'The two business units are video game development [making games] and publishing [distributing them into the market], and esports.' These units house the company's wide range of investments, which we'll come on to in a moment.

The business has pretty staggering commercial ambitions. 'The mandate of Savvy is to build the world's largest games and esports company,' says Ward. 'This is a very audacious objective, considering Tencent [the multi-trillion-dollar Chinese tech company] holds that spot and there are many other great companies above us.' But its intentions go beyond business to becoming the driver of the country's video game strategy.

'The group's mandate is not only to deliver on that objective, but also support the third pillar, which is developing

---

* By contrast, the UK video games industry was practically cartwheeling through the streets when it announced that its national games fund, which supports small video game projects, was offering £30m of funding over the next few years. Chump change in comparison.

Saudi Arabia into the next great global games hub,' Ward continues.

'This is kind of an unusual mandate for a commercial company because it's not revenue oriented or even investment oriented. It's working with other stakeholders in the kingdom to devise the right sort of policies, incentives and programmes to do three things. One, to attract foreign investment in the form of big companies in our industry, bringing leadership to Saudi Arabia to establish a base here, build a studio or some other thing, and hire a bunch of Saudis to work there. Then, secondly, to develop the right sorts of vocational and academic programmes to give young Saudis the skills to fill those jobs. And then thirdly, have the right sorts of operational and financial programmes in place for incubation and acceleration of what is quite a burgeoning entrepreneurial class here in Saudi Arabia.'

Importantly, the video game strategy is close to the crown prince's heart.

'You know, the system of governance here makes it unusual in relation to some of the other countries in our sector,' says Ward, in a curiously sincere manner. 'So when the crown prince says this is an important thing for Vision 2030, here's a strategy for getting there and here are the eighty-six objectives, that gives everyone a high degree of confidence that this is something that will be done and also a high set of incentives towards getting there.'

Savvy Games isn't just a video game publishing company. It is a well-funded arm of the Saudi Arabian state that has the explicit support of the crown prince and has not been shy in its efforts.

On the economic side of the equation, Savvy has been acquiring video games companies with serious commercial, cultural and long-term development clout to create sustainable economic value for the territory in a manner akin to a video game publisher, although much better funded.

It acquired the mobile game developer Scopely for \$4.9bn in April 2023, putting *Monopoly Go!*, the most played and highest revenue-generating mobile game in North America that year, into Saudi hands.[37] In May 2025, the company then concluded the \$3.5bn acquisition of *Pokémon Go* creator Niantic. Less than a decade after religious authorities had banned the game from being played in the country, the game's developer was now owned by the Saudi state and in the process of setting up a base in the country.[38] Quite the turnaround in fortunes for Saudis who had been worried about being caught catching 'em all, you'll agree.

The company has also supported the growth of the wider domestic ecosystem too. Savvy's investment underpins a business called Steer Studios, a local development company managed by a former Ubisoft executive which aims to create top-quality development jobs in the region. After initially talking a big game about releasing Triple-A console titles, its first title was a mobile game called *Grunt Rush*. Even with oil money, the costs and challenges of making blockbuster video games are sometimes best avoided.

More broadly, and outside Savvy's remit alone, the wider Saudi Arabian ecosystem has also snapped into action. NEOM, the ambitious line city, has invested in games companies such as blockchain business Animoca Brands, while also funding accelerator programmes called Level Up which have acted as friendly mini-business bootcamps for developers.

Non-state investors have also plunged into the sector, with firms like Merak Capital putting cash into business support programmes and businesses (including both Starvania and Fahy Studios in 2025). There has also been a concerted effort to educate young people in the skills necessary to get into the games sector, with institutions such as King Saud University offering some of the country's first video game development university courses (something that's been present in academia across the rest of the world for at least a few decades now).[39] In an industry where skills, funding and business advice are key drivers of growth in every video game cluster across the world, Saudi Arabia has rapidly scaled up an ecosystem capable of at least rivalling its neighbours.

The country's strategy towards the traditional video game business aligns pretty closely with the stated aims of Vision 2030 in terms of economic opportunities for the country's young population. But in terms of the all-important attempts at scrubbing the country's reputation amongst international and domestic audiences, Saudi Arabia's substantial investment within the esports industry has wrapped its interests entirely around the fortunes of the sector – ensuring that Riyadh is a major beneficiary if any virtual sports achieve global scale.

Tactically, Savvy has invested in businesses that seek to deepen Saudi Arabia's reach into the established esports economy: the company ploughed $265m into a Chinese esports tournament organiser called VSPO – rebranding it to Hero Esports in the process.[40] This created ties between Saudi's esports project and China's thriving competitive gaming ecosystem, plugging it into a market of nearly 700 million players who love competitive games like *League of Legends*, a similar mobile game called *Honor of Kings*, and shooting games such as *Free Fire*, which is similar to *Counter-Strike*.[41]

But strategically, Saudi Arabia took an enormous step to influence esports audiences around the world by doing something that had not been successfully achieved in the sector before: creating a well-funded, high-profile annual tournament celebrating the medium at large.

In September 2023, the Esports World Cup Foundation was established as a not-for-profit in Riyadh by Mohammed bin Salman to transform the country's Gamers8 event into an annual global competition capable of bringing the world to town.

A month later, the Foundation announced that it was hosting the first Esports World Cup in Riyadh the following year, with the crown prince joined on stage for the announcement at the country's New Global Sport Conference by Cristiano Ronaldo, the award-winning footballer for Saudi Pro League club Al-Nassr, who is followed by over a billion people on social media and is now an ambassador for the competition.[42]

Crucially, teams didn't just win cash for how they performed in each game. They also received money through a 'Club Championship' model, which awarded them pots for their performance across the many different games in the World Cup in the manner of Formula 1's Constructors' Championship. And a year later, 200 teams and thousands of athletes from across the world had participated in tournaments for dozens of games like *Fortnite*, *EA Sports FC* and *Call of Duty* over the course of six weeks – sharing a prize pool valued at $62.5m in the process.

The establishment of the Esports World Cup has become hugely significant to the Saudis for a number of reasons. One of the most obvious is that it provided a genuine solution to the fragmentation problem that the sector clearly had: giving the entire esports sector one big thing to cohere around.

'The Esports World Cup is a really unique opportunity to create a tent pole moment that brings the whole ecosystem together – the clubs, the publishers, the fans and a multitude of IPs,' says Mike McCabe when discussing the purpose of the event. This allows audiences of different games to cross-pollinate together, creating a critical mass for attendance that enables the event to function effectively.

*

'Who would have thought that in one week you could have a *League of Legends* competition, a *DOTA 2* competition, *Mobile Legends, Honor of Kings,* all in the same week,' said Prince Faisal bin Bandar bin Sultan Al Saud. 'You know, you have *Counter*

Strike and *Rainbow Six* all in the same tournament, under the same umbrella of the Esports World Cup, and happy to be a part of it,' he continued.

This brings us to the second reason for the tournament's reception, which is that it provides the communities who follow these games with regular events for them to tune into or attend. Across the course of both 2024 and 2025's Esports World Cups, all of the tournament content was streamed online – including an opening ceremony with Post Malone – while the main arenas for the events hosted up to 3,500 people. This meant that esports enthusiasts from the region could easily come to cheer on a top local team like the Riyadh-based Team Falcon, while the hundreds of other teams were each handed opportunities to fly over their superfans to the event: bringing in high-profile influencers from across the world in the process.

And finally, the Esports World Cup offered up something that the rest of the esports industry simply hasn't been able to support since the pandemic started: cash. According to Prince Faisal, the top team at the 2025 Esports World Cup would walk away with approximately $7m for their efforts. This is not the biggest prize in competitive gaming – winning the *DOTA 2* International tournament will net a team a comparable amount, if not more – but it is a tidy sum.

However, the true genius of the tournament's model is its establishment of the 'trickle down' approach to rewarding participation. Although there is a threshold for the number of games a team has to field esports athletes or teams within to qualify, any reasonable-sized esports organisation, which provides teams to multiple sports and performs reasonably well will be in line to receive a chunk of the tens of millions of dollars that the Esports World Cup hands out as prize money.

With the esports industry at large having suffered a 'winter' as a result of a collapse in brand and advertising money flowing into the sector after the pandemic, the Esports World Cup's ability to provide competitive teams with a source of income on an annual basis that is relatively consistent and predictable is a game changer for them.

But again, this benefit comes at a cost. By propping up the dozens of competitive video games that make up the esports industry, providing desperately needed funding to teams and athletes to keep their organisations afloat, and creating a competitive centrepiece for the esports industry around the world for people to watch, Saudi Arabia's economic investment into competitive gaming gives it a potentially enormous reputational upside amongst the people who will inevitably shape our future.

'We have roughly a hundred million people that leave this world, and a hundred million people that come into this world [each year],' said Prince Faisal bin Bandar bin Sultan Al Saud. 'And those hundred million coming into the world are coming into a world where esport is their sport. So the growth opportunities are endless, and they are for the long term.'

And those opportunities are likely to grow further as a result of the acquisition of Electronic Arts. By buying one of the world's biggest video game publishers, Saudi Arabia has acquired a company generating over a billion dollars of revenue each quarter to support the bottom line of the video game strategy (and bring its business expertise to bear for the benefit of the wider cluster).

It also joins together Saudi Arabia's sports and esports strategy. By grabbing the company behind *Madden NFL* and *EA Sports FC*, the country doesn't just acquire the audience who play the game. It gets plugged directly into the promotional infrastructure that fits behind both of them: the exclusive interviews each game does with sports players to argue over their player ratings; the promotions that leading sports clubs do to celebrate the release of the game with their fans; in the case of professional football, the merging of Saudi Arabia's enthusiasm for virtual competitions featuring *EA Sports FC* with the country's plans to host the 2034 World Cup through global sporting body FIFA (whose name used to be adorned on the boxes of EA games).

These acquisitions may have a business rationale on the face of it. But they also reach audiences in the places they inhabit and the information ecosystems they live in. And with fans of real-world sports almost always enjoying playing their virtual counterparts, Saudi influence permeates through both – nudging fans towards its world view in the process.

REPUTATION GAMES

Throughout this chapter, the Saudi Arabian video game strategy might feel as if it is at the heart of a dichotomy. Is it a serious attempt to modernise the country's economy by creating valuable new jobs and generating new sources of revenue? Or is it merely a reputation-enhancing exercise, subtly spreading Riyadh's influence through games, esports events and the communities that surround them to help the world forget that the country executed hundreds of its own citizens in 2024?

The answer isn't either/or. Instead, it's both. The current success of Saudi Arabia's video games strategy as a means for long-term influence is precisely due to its having taken the business of building a game plan seriously. By investing serious cash, time and effort into building a top-to-bottom plan, the country has gone from having no video game presence to having a local game development sector, multi-billion-dollar revenue-generating businesses in its back pocket, and control of the international esports ecosystem outside China and the US.

By grasping control of soft power assets that achieve the dream of simultaneously reaching audiences and generating revenue, the Saudis are using video games as a perpetual reputation-washing machine. This means it can use income generated through games like *Monopoly Go!*, *Pokémon Go* and, soon enough, *EA Sports FC* to fund eye-catching flights of fancy that can reach audiences like esports events.

It also opens up opportunities for cross-promotion of Saudi Arabian interests developed in sports and games through digital content. MiSK-owned SNK included Cristiano Ronaldo as a playable character in its fighting game *Fatal Fury: City of the Wolves*. The inclusion made little thematic sense within *Fatal Fury*'s story, which is loosely summarised as a battle between martial artists and crime lords in a fictionalised version of Miami. But the footballer's inclusion in a game that starred in the 2025 Esports World Cup shows how Saudi Arabia recognises esports as a potential channel for long term influence - if it takes off as a global force.*

'Esports is still kind of in its infancy, I suppose, when you consider other major sports,' said James Montague. 'The leagues are so almost reminiscent of somewhere like MLS in the United States, right? You have all these franchises. They're not really sure how it works out. There's some popularity to it. They try to work out what works, what doesn't. Some brands fall by the wayside. But eventually they'll get to the point where it's a recognizable major sport in the global system.'

Already, you can literally see how this is working (and could work further in the future). According to figures quoted to me by the Esports World Cup Foundation, over half a billion people watched content from the first World Cup and 2.5 million descended on Riyadh in July and August. And as I watched footage from the Esports 2025 tournament to get a feel for what it's like, I couldn't help but notice the logos of the businesses

---

* The inclusion of Cristiano Ronaldo and DJ Salvatore Ganacci, who also had ties to the Saudis, in the game was heavily criticised by the fighting game community. See more in George E. Osborn, 'Why is Cristiano Ronaldo in a fighting game?', *Video Games Industry Memo*.

featured in the advertising carousel alongside the likes of Pepsi: Aramco, the country's national oil business, Saudia, its national airline, and Qiddiya, the entertainment city south of Riyadh. In return for $2bn of investment in an underserved industry, Saudi Arabian interests dominate the space. In doing so, it makes it impossible for video games and esports to escape its influence.

'No conversation can take place without them [Saudi Arabia] being there,' said Montague. 'If you wanted to extricate Saudi Arabia on moral issues, you'd basically have to kill yourself to do it. It's like the face hugger in *Alien*. They try to take it off John Hurt, but they can't without killing him.'

Internationally, this has led to fears that the Saudis can now actively use the player base and infrastructure of play to influence audiences across the world. Senators Elizabeth Warren and Richard Blumenthal wrote to Scott Bessent, Secretary of the US Treasury, on 14 October 2025 to express concern over the acquisition of Electronic Arts by the PIF on national security and foreign influence grounds. The letter raised concerns that 'the Saudi government's ability to exert its influence through EA would offer the authoritarian regime an effective tool to project power worldwide'. It warned that handing a 'repressive authoritarian government' the data of nearly 700 million players could pose surveillance risks to American citizens and people 'disfavored' by the Saudi leadership. It also noted Jared Kushner's role in the acquisition, raising concerns that the PIF's $2bn investment in Affinity Partners in 2021 – which came shortly after he left the White House – may have encouraged him to step forward as a partner on the deal to navigate future regulatory hurdles; a potential example of foreign influence in action, according to Warren and Blumenthal.[43] Kushner has not commented on the letter at time of writing.

And at home, the emergence of an entertainment economy in Saudi Arabia is not enough to mask the reality that MbS and the House of Saud retain a firm, and brutal, hold on power.

In a piece written for the *Atlantic* about the Riyadh Comedy Festival, Helen Lewis wrote in words that echoed Jamal Khashoggi's words about MbS that 'the old Saudi brand was "austere theocracy," but the new one is "fun, fun, fun, but still with beheading."' This is borne out in 2024, the first year that the Esports World Cup was hosted. Amnesty International reported that executions in Saudi Arabia reached a 34-year high of 198. This included the execution of Abdulmajeed al-Nimr, a former traffic police officer who was arrested for being part of anti-government protests and later sentenced to death for 'confessing' to being a member of Al-Qaeda after having been tortured. As Agnès Callamard, of Amnesty International, puts it, 'Saudi Arabia's authorities are pursuing a relentless killing spree displaying a chilling disregard for human life while promoting an empty-worded campaign to rebrand their image.'

The emptiness of it can be seen in some of the promises made to people who have participated within the Saudi game strategy. In the 2024 Esports World Cup, Steve Arhancet, the gay co-founder of Team Liquid, thought he had made a major stride in advancing LGBTQ+ rights in the Kingdom by negotiating for his team to play in Pride jerseys and wear rainbow-branded merchandise. A year later, Arhancet discovered that the official documentary for the tournament on Amazon Prime cut all mentions of this story in the Saudi release of the series. Turns out you can't contest the video game information ecosystem if someone else mutes it on your behalf.[44]

And for those who don't take part, the steady flow of influence towards Saudi Arabia simply means they're pushed to the side of the industry discourse. In 2025, the creators of the game *GeoGuessr* pulled out of participating in a fringe event at the Esports World Cup after its player community kicked back against the country's human rights record. McCabe told me that the organisers of the tournament 'fully respect their decision and that's fine', which is broadly consistent with the country's line that it wants people to head to Riyadh to form their own opinions. But with other, bigger games such as *Call of Duty*, *Tekken* and *Counter-Strike 2* continuing to form part of the schedule, individual games and communities that do take a stance risk being ostracised. Something that I would suggest is, unfortunately, entirely the point here.

Ultimately, the crown prince and the Saudi state have washed the hard power of its economic resources into video games to emerge with a soft power tool capable of subtly attracting people to its cause, keeping the games industry within its economic orbit, and pushing voices who dissent from it to the fringes. Because it has invested so heavily in the medium, executed its strategy with serious intent, and acquired businesses capable of multiplying influence from games into other channels like sport too, the country has turned a medium designed for entertainment into one that generates influence. And its willingness to work with figures in the Trump administration to get its acquisition of EA approved by regulators shows just how important games are to both the state and its crown prince: suggesting the influence of the Saudi game plan will grow the more it controls and co-opts the industry for its ends.

But how else can authoritarian regimes project their influence through games? In the next chapter, we'll find out how the emergence of the biggest video games market in the world caught a dictatorship by surprise – leading to censorship of both what people play and how they play that's steadily seeping out across the world.

6

Censoring a video game superpower

China has become the world's video game superpower. In the space of two decades, the country has transformed from a minor market in the fringes of the entertainment economy to a market of 701.6 million players spending \$48.7bn each year.[1] And its rise has made its games, the companies who make them and the communities who play central to the video gaming landscape.

Tencent, the multi-trillion-dollar tech giant, is one of the dominant players in the industry, investing in hundreds of businesses such as Epic Games (*Fortnite* and Unreal Engine), Riot Games (*League of Legends*), and the social media app Discord. The country's biggest home-grown games such as multiplayer battling game *Honor of Kings* and open-world game *Genshin Impact* have generated billions of dollars in China alone, while new hits like action game *Black Myth: Wukong* have wrapped Chinese mythology into games bought by millions of players in the West. It is home to the biggest esports sector in the world, boasting the most professional players,[2] and enough fans to sell out the Bird's Nest stadium, the 80,000-seat stadium that was central to the 2008 Beijing Olympics, for the prestigious finale of the *League of Legends* season.

The growth has happened at lightning speed. The country's rapid adoption of smartphones, love for online games and happiness to pay for in-game extras in free-to-download games provided the perfect conditions to grow a massive, diverse market of mobile gamers.

However, China's rise as a gaming superpower presented the Chinese Communist Party (CCP) with a major problem. Where people play, they talk. Where they talk, they form groups. And groups, and the pesky ideas that they develop, have a tendency to challenge authoritarian leaders such as the CCP in ways that they don't particularly like.

So, how could the CCP reap the benefits of a massive entertainment industry, which contributed billions of dollars to the local economy and provided entertainment to hundreds of millions of citizens without ceding control? The answer was not to ban video games; it was to turn this source of immense reach into a new part of the Chinese government's censorship net. By leaning into a global moral panic around 'video games addiction', the CCP cracked down on a creative industry that had previously been outside its control to bring it to heel.

It essentially outsourced the censorship of video game content, access to market, and the process of formally identifying every single online video game player in the country – all 700 million of them – to the games companies who wanted to make the most of its thriving market. In doing so, it established a 'porous censorship' approach to games that allowed most players and companies to feel free in the market while allowing the state to easily crack down on those who transgress.

In doing so, the CCP has made video games a new, powerful layer to the digital infrastructure it uses to police its citizens. But as a result of the sheer size and importance of its market, the impact of Chinese censorship is being felt in games played in the wider world: turning the medium into a quiet transmitter of authoritarian ideals and values in the process.

CONSTRUCTING THE DIGITAL CENSORSHIP NET

To understand how censorship of video games rose up the Communist Party's agenda, we need to understand how the country's approach to controlling its population changed to meet the challenges of a digital age.

In her excellent book *Digital Empires*, Anu Bradford, Professor of Law and International Organizations at Columbia Law School, argues that China's tech policy rests on three pillars: supporting economic growth to keep Chinese citizens content; promoting Chinese nationalism through protectionism, subsidies and barriers to market entry to turn local businesses into powerhouses; and ensuring social control through censorship to preserve 'national unity'. Given that the latter is defined by the Chinese Communist Party, the role of censorship in the system is pretty clear: allow citizens to feel the benefits of economic growth, while steering them away from behaviours, actions or ideas that could encourage them to challenge the status quo.

The roots of this can be traced back a couple of decades to the country's shift towards a more capitalistic system. Jonathan Fenby argues that Deng Xiaoping's introduction of capitalistic elements to the Chinese state in the 1980s was crucial to maintaining the CCP's claim to legitimacy amongst the domestic population. The collapse of the economically moribund Soviet Union following its exposure to Western popular culture reinforced the belief amongst Chinese officials that a wealthy population was important for maintaining healthy support for the CCP. However, economic development of China was never intended to loosen the CCP's control over the state. As concerns grew that rising wealth within China was leading to corruption amongst officials, Xiaoping underlined that economic growth needed to serve national interest by ensuring that it 'really benefits our modernisation and does not take us off the socialist path'.[3] Conservative critics who opposed Xiaoping took the message further. Deng Liqun – a leading party propagandist who favoured a 'traditional' planned economy – warned of the risk of the 'spiritual pollution' of the country's population as result of market reforms. These concerns included the potential for people to engage in obscene, barbarous or vulgar behaviour. It risked people acting treacherously for the purposes of personal gain. And it also led to the risk of the production of articles or speeches that were counter to the country's values and unity – all of which ran in opposition to the CCP's desire for mastery over its population.[4]

Deng Liqun's list of spiritually polluted behaviours would later align closely with the limitations imposed upon video games in China. But until the arrival of the internet, the CCP was able to maintain tight control over what occurred within its borders because the physical challenges of organising against it gave the party significant advantage over its rivals. The flow of information was strictly monitored by the country's propaganda ministry, with dissidents who wanted to oppose it hamstrung by the need to print, promote and distribute literature in person. Groups who sought to challenge the state were forced to meet up physically, providing opportunities to monitor, infiltrate and imprison groups. The massacre of protesters in Tiananmen Square in June 1989 demonstrated that the CCP could brutally enforce its power if necessary.

But the slaughter in Tiananmen Square also showed that the state's approach to censorship had to evolve to meet a modern media environment. Television had allowed people from across China and the world to watch events unfold. This meant that disapproval, dissent or outright rebellion was more likely to form across the mass of the Chinese population.

The arrival of the internet to the country in 1994 took this a step further, bringing the challenge of delivering economic growth for Chinese citizens while maintaining total social control into focus. After initially viewing the internet as a way to allow academics to share research with one another after the first email was sent in the country in 1987,[5] the CCP was quick to realise that it could have a much more profound impact on the way it grew and controlled its society.

Economically, the West was remarkably confident that the internet could crack China's market and make it open to democratic values. American telecoms and technology businesses like Cisco worked with the Chinese government to get the country online because there was an 'alignment of political will and profit motive', according to Michael Robinson, one of the architects of what was soon called ChinaNet.[6] And on the face of it, they were right to say so.[7] The Chinese government promoted the use of ChinaNet in cities across the country, encouraging citizens to get online. By the year 2000, 22.5 million people were online. That figure had more than doubled to 59.1 million just four years later.[8]

The CCP's push to get people online proved to be enormously helpful for local businesses seeking to exploit the new digital frontier. Between 1995 and 2000, many of the biggest names that dominate the Chinese tech industry were born. E-commerce company Alibaba was founded in 1999. Search business Baidu arrived in 2000. Game developers NetEase and Tencent, which was best known in its early years for the messaging service QQ, were founded in 1997 and 1998 respectively. And the Chinese government's broader support for the expansion of the net helped previously established businesses such as Huawei grow, with the company benefitting from hiring international expertise from North America to learn the telecoms business while enjoying hefty government subsidies at home. In the words of Cheng Weigao, a Communist Party secretary speaking in 1994 before the net boom, 'The old wisdom in China was "to get rich, you built highways and then telecommunications. The new wisdom is you build tele-communications networks, then highways." [9] But while Western companies saw a growing digital market to enter, Chinese government officials saw a developing threat. By building telecommunications networks, China was construct-ing digital highways that connected people. By connecting people, you encourage them to talk, share information and connect with one another. This leads to the formation of groups, who can mobilise and campaign. And this solidarity could lead to groups directly challenging the CCP's rule within China, as seen by the Falun Gong spiritual movement – a group that is firmly banned in China – using the early internet to share its narratives with newly connected digital citizens across the country. So even as the Chinese govern-ment embraced the economic potential of the internet, it recognised that it had to take steps to assume control of it across the country.

To begin with, it did so by extending its regulatory powers to ensure the developing internet was firmly under its legal con-trol. In 1996, the State Council issued an order allowing it powers to temporarily control computer information systems. In 1997, it expanded its remit with public security controls that forbid the use of the internet for creating content or messages that threaten security, disclose state secrets, promote the over-throw of the state or encourage morally objectionable behaviours like gambling or violence. In the early 2000s, tech companies operating in the country – including international firms like Yahoo – were forced to make public pledges to self-censor their content.

However, imposing law was not enough for Chinese officials to gain visibility and control over content accessed within the territory. Unlike physically produced literature, the internet allowed content to be created by anyone, anywhere, whether or not they were within the country. Even in the earliest days of the online world, years before social media took off, the internet was going to make it impossible for the CCP to monitor, identify and snuff out dissenting content. It therefore commissioned the 'Golden Shield Project' to create a number of interlocking technologies to address the problem. From the outside the most significant intervention appeared to be what *Wired* magazine nicknamed 'The Great Firewall',[10] which sought to block Chinese access to international sites that contradicted the CCP's view of the world. But the remainder of the Golden Shield project also controlled what people saw internally, both by bluntly blocking content using certain terms and, more interestingly, simply slowing down access to content to dissuade the average citizen from accessing anything that may be transgressive.

What was emerging was a change to China's censorship regime. Instead of seeking absolute control over its entire information environment, the country was beginning to practise a new form of censorship that academic researcher Margaret Roberts has elegantly described as a 'porous' approach.

According to Roberts, censorship regimes generally lean on three 'f's to keep control of a narrative. Fear is used to scare people, either encouraging them to self-censor so they don't get in trouble or making it clear that if they do transgress they risk repercussions. Friction seeks to make it as hard as possible to access censored materials, discouraging all but the most avid rulebreakers to access content. Flooding, meanwhile, makes it hard for censored materials to get a hearing, with official government outlets or media channels churning out materials to drown out rival narratives.

Until the internet arrived, China's censorship approach could mostly lean on 'fear' because it controlled physical infrastructure. But Roberts argues the arrival of the internet led to the Chinese government leaning into the other two 'f's instead. By using the Golden Shield technologies to govern interactions online and ensuring the enforcement of local censorship rules was mostly left to technology businesses which benefitted from online access, most citizens would quietly accept that the 'friction' of accessing censored content wasn't worth the hassle – keeping them in the boundaries. At the same time, the CCP could develop methods to 'flood' the conversation if grassroots online users did express disquiet at the state: directing the likes of state media, digital influencers and a mass movement of people dubbed the 'Fifty Cent Army' (literally a reference to how much they're paid to post messages useful to the state) to manage the messages. This allowed fear to be held in reserve, with the state able to identify people or businesses that were stepping outside the friction-filled information environment and take action against them if they transgressed against the state.

'Porous' censorship sounds less total than the traditional form of censorship. And in a sense, it is. Citizens in China are able to access the entertainment content that they want. They can post on social media, and the government often listens closely to what they're saying. And while technologies like virtual private networks are technically banned in the country, it's commonplace for users to log on to one, virtually hop outside China, and begin accessing the content they want from the rest of the world. For most citizens in China, the online world feels pretty free – a place where they can spend, talk and play in a way that we'd all recognise.

But as Roberts argues incredibly persuasively, the 'porous' method is arguably more effective because it has moved the boundary of censorship beyond the eyeline of the average citizen. As one source told me, the majority of the country's censorship regime is now mostly administered by technology businesses. By encouraging the executives of those companies to feel the 'fear' of breaching the rules, the platforms themselves impose the friction or help enable the flooding that keeps the majority of citizens within the pre-agreed online space. Individuals or groups who then choose to step beyond the technological or cultural boundaries imposed by the censorship net are then much easier to identify. This allows the CCP to take targeted action, cutting off dissent from transgressive audiences while not so gently reminding citizens to self-censor to avoid being caught up.

However, the model that I've described above did not emerge immediately. Between the late 1990s and the early 2010s the censorship net strengthened steadily rather than aggressively. China's need for economic growth meant that the state was willing to give its technology businesses greater freedom to push forward, especially following the 2008 financial crisis, which damaged China's physical export markets. Economic growth did not stop the state from using censorship laws and technology to arrest dissidents, as shown by Yahoo's disclosure of evidence to the authorities that led to the arrest of poet and journalist Shi Tao in April 2004.[11] But it did, at least initially, temper the drive to do so.

The arrival of Xi Jinping as the president of China in March 2013 led to the porous censorship net tightening and gaining an even sharper edge in the name of social control. In a speech in August of that year, Xi claimed that anti-China forces in the West were constantly trying to exploit the internet to topple China. 'Whether we can stand our ground and win this battle over the internet has a direct bearing on our country's ideological and political security.'

After decades of prioritising economic growth, the CCP fought this battle against its own people and businesses in two waves over the course of the following decade. In the first wave, the state strengthened its legal and regulatory structures further. A flood of new rules reminded technology businesses of their place in the country's wider strategy and their responsibility for acting as an arm for the state.

The country's 2015 National Security Law put Bradford's description of the country's policy onto the statute books, claiming that its purpose was to protect 'the political regime; the sovereignty, unity and territorial integrity of the nation; and people's livelihoods, sustainable economic development of society and other major interests'.[12] The 2016 Cybersecurity Law built on this further, defining cyberspace as sovereign and imposing stringent rules on tech companies which included explicitly registering users to services with real names and identities.

New rules rolled out in 2019 for video platforms like Douyin insisted on the importance of these platforms providing 'correct political direction' to users, while also avoiding the promotion of any content which threatens national security.[13] Numerous foreign tech platforms that did not submit to local rules were also driven out of the market, with services such as Discord, Twitch and Snapchat joining Facebook and Google on the country's banned list.

Meanwhile, China's now billion-strong digital-user base was being given clear indications that actions online could have serious real-world consequences. In 2014, China's Uyghur Muslim minority were banned from using social media as part of an attempt to silence their voices.[14] Protestors in Hong Kong in 2019 reported their fear of leaving a digital footprint in case the surveillance state caught up with them.[15]

Chinese citizens at large were also caught up in the net. A 2013 Supreme Court ruling found that posts which share lies or defamatory views (as defined by the state) and were either viewed 5,000 times or shared 500 times could see the protester fined or imprisoned. The announcement of a 2018 social credit system which used the digital footprint that a user left behind them to create a credit score did not necessarily lead to the emergence of a fully dystopian social score, as some media reported, but it did reinforce the idea that the state was always watching you.

But the state's biggest push to impose control over technology businesses came during the pandemic. After Jack Ma, the founder of e-commerce giant Alibaba, made ill-advised comments on stage about China's bureaucracy blocking business innovation, the Chinese state took action against the country's tech giants on the basis of unfair influence on society at large – conveniently asserting the CCP's dominance in the process. The CCP wiped $1.5tn off the valuation of its major domestic tech businesses by embarking on a wave of regulatory actions designed to rein them in. This included blocking Alibaba's enormous $37bn IPO of its Ant Group in November 2020, removing ride-sharing app DiDi from app stores over cybersecurity concerns, and imposing a half a billion dollar fine on food delivery app Meituan for uncompetitive practices.[16] Companies were also encouraged to come to the table with their own social good measures, with Tencent and Alibaba each committing $15bn to 'social responsibility' programmes in 2021. And the CCP also rolled out more rules that aimed to increase its oversight of digital spaces locally. In November 2021, it enacted a data protection law called the Personal Information Protection Law (PIPL). On the face of it, the law looked similar to other data protection rules around the world. In practice, it forced businesses to keep any data gathered in China within the country and open a backdoor to it for national security reasons: deepening the CCP's reach into the wider world.

The purpose of the tech crackdown was to firmly remind technology businesses that the CCP was in charge, that they needed to stay in line, and support the state's goals. Between 2013 and 2023, video game businesses were caught in the same crackdown. And for Western academics such as Bradford, the belief was that the CCP was clamping down on entertainment businesses to try to encourage major companies like Tencent to invest more heavily in other sectors like semi-conductors or AI.

However, that analysis misses a crucial point. Chinese video game businesses had become locally and globally known brands bringing millions of players together in online game worlds. The growth of the industry over the course of two decades had made Chinese businesses an immense amount of money. But it had also led to the emergence of an industry that was under-regulated compared to most, despite the vast amount of time players spent within games playing – and crucially talking – with one another.

And after being caught out by the explosion in size of the Chinese video game economy following the smartphone revolution, the CCP realised it needed to control and co-opt the space for its own purposes: using the immense reach of video games to capture swathes of the population within a new layer of its censorship net; deepening its reach into Chinese society and the world in the process.

FALLING THROUGH THE CENSORSHIP NET

China's censors were caught out by the growth of the games industry for much the same reason that Western democracies have failed to see its true importance: they were too focused on treating them as products, rather than the centre of digital socialising.

In the first few decades of the video games industry, this approach made sense. China was easily able to block or restrict access to games by simply making it hard to buy a device to play on. During the arcade boom of the 1980s, the Chinese government imposed a Trump-esque 130 per cent tariff on the import of any machines into the country to stem the flow of purchases. Between 2000 and 2014, the country banned the sale of games consoles ostensibly on the basis that they caused 'addiction' amongst children. The country would revisit this argument to great effect for censorship purposes in the following decade.[17]

The one console that did famously get traction in the market was Subor's 'Little Tyrant', a bootleg version of Nintendo's

Famicom that was marketed to Chinese consumers with the help of Jackie Chan and the promise of an educational experience that the state's censors could get behind.[18] Importantly, the console was widespread enough to become a popular part of Chinese life over the course of the 1990s. One source told me that the devices were so widely prevalent that they remain a cultural touchpoint for China's video game community, becoming a collector's item in the process.

At the same time, Subor's console showed why established international game developers were not in a hurry to bring their games or devices to the country: rampant piracy. Chinese players who were playing games were either buying pirated versions of console games to run on the devices in the market or were playing pirated versions of video games on PCs. International game developers had little incentive to expand into a market where consumers paid little to nothing for content, while also exposing their intellectual property to risk of theft.

Piracy also mattered because it conditioned China's game developers and its players towards always favouring online games with a strong social element.

*

'The only way they could stop the huge piracy issues in China was to make things that were permanently online like multiplayer games,' explains one source, who worked for nearly half a decade at one of China's biggest games companies. A premium game, that you paid a sum of money up front for and received the full game, could be easily copied and distributed by pirates in the region. But an online game required a permanent connection to the internet to work. This discouraged Western companies from entering the market with their premium games, for fear that they'd be rampantly pirated in China and distributed across the world.

This encouraged companies to make their games 'free-to-play', making their cash by selling subscriptions and in-game purchases to cover costs. And unlike players in the West, Chinese players became used to being sold to from the moment they entered an online game.

*

'When I started at this company, Western companies were very light on monetisation,' said a source who works at a mobile advertising company with knowledge of China's market. 'And when we looked at the Chinese market at games in the same genre, it was monetised a lot more but also with different sorts of engagement systems.' Initially, making money from players was mostly about charging a subscription cost to access a service. But it rapidly expanded to include enormous amounts of in-game rewards for engaging with the game on a regular basis, 'noisy' user interfaces that encouraged people to buy, and a wider range of purchasing options for in-game currencies and items. This encouraged players to spend, something many are happy to do to acquire digital status in China's video game landscape.

*

'China nowadays is a very capitalistic society,' explains the same source. 'Showing off your status, showing off your wealth, is deemed as very important not just in real life but in virtual worlds. So you can buy all kinds of cosmetic items [e.g. a new outfit in a role-playing game] in any Chinese games because those purchases are very, very popular.'

So despite expecting to get access to a virtual world for free, Chinese players were conditioned and willing to spend in 'heavily monetised' online games as they emerged. And this spend had a strong social purpose too. Players who wanted to show off their purchases needed to be able to get online. While China was rapidly coming online, few places had the connection quality to support online games. So Chinese games cultures congregated around 'wangba' or internet cafes, where people would pay to access a PC and play online games with their friends. One of my contacts from an advertising company serving the industry fondly remembered heading to one cafe in the mid 2000s to jump into the multiplayer game *Counter-Strike* with friends, largely because no one had the physical space at home to have a dedicated gaming area.

By the early 2000s, the defining features of China's video game economy had been set. Games were free to access. They were always online. They made their money after release through subscriptions and in-game purchases. And they encouraged people into a space, with players simultaneously socialising with friends in person at the wangba and over the early social networks popping up across China.

The power of this model would not be fully realised in the West until smartphones arrived. But for Chinese video game companies, the free-to-play online video game economy quickly emerged as a thriving consumer market, giving rise to a number of games companies that would become internationally known names.

Shanda Interactive Entertainment was the first to show international markets what they might be missing. Founded in 1999, the company agreed a deal with a South Korean company called We Made Soft to license its multiplayer fantasy role-playing game *Legend of Mir: II* in the Chinese market. After successfully attracting tens of millions of fee-paying players, Shanda successfully listed on the Nasdaq in 2004, briefly catapulting co-founder Chen Tianqiao to the status of the richest man in China in the process.[19]

Home-grown fantasy role-playing hits were possible too. NetEase was founded in 1997 in Guangzhou by Ding Lei. The company's hit role-playing game *Fantasy Westward Journey*, based upon the classic Chinese story *Journey to the West*, quickly established itself as one of the most profitable and popular games in

China, acquiring 25 million paying users to support its growth and briefly holding the title of the most concurrently played game in China in 2010 when over two million people logged on to play at the same time.[20]

Tencent, meanwhile, began its ascent to multi-trillion-dollar status at the intersection of games and social media. The company secured a $32m investment from South African firm Naspers in 2001 after David Wallerstein, the company's man on the ground in China, saw that almost every internet cafe in China had OICQ, the company's forerunner to its wildly popular QQ messaging app, on every PC desktop.

After setting up its QQ Games business in 2004 (and monetising QQ users by selling in-app purchases to customise their avatars like an online game), its games business took off. This in turn led to Tencent securing the rights to license two popular South Korean online multiplayer games – the action role-playing fighting game *Dungeon Fighter* and the multiplayer shooter *Crossfire* – in the late 2000s to establish itself as the coming force in Chinese game development.

China's games market was growing rapidly in a way that suited the country's economic goals. In 2000, the market was estimated to be worth $209m a year. Five years later, it had almost tripled in size to reach an annual valuation of $600m.[21] The growth of a home-made entertainment industry deeply rooted in both online and social communities had not gone unnoticed by the Chinese government. While video games were providing China's nascent technology businesses with a much-needed local revenue boost, its social and creative output naturally attracted the interests of censors on the lookout for 'spiritual pollution'.

Between 2000 and 2010, the country's National Press and Publication Administration (NPPA) and the Ministry of Culture (MOC) worked in tandem with other Chinese regulators to place the first porous censorship net over the top of the industry.

First, they imposed broad-brush content censorship over the industry in line with other sectors. Considering the importance of these laws, it is surprisingly difficult to find out precisely what is or isn't allowed in Chinese video game content. However, Pillar Legal, a law firm with specialist knowledge of the Chinese video game market, listed ten types of prohibited content in its Legal Primer on the NPPA. This included content that 'endangers the unity, sovereignty, or territorial integrity of the nation', 'propagates evil cults or suspicions', 'propagates obscenity, pornography, gambling, violence, or instigates crimes', or 'disseminates rumours, disrupts social order or undermines social stability'. All games that were released into the market were notionally checked for prohibited content prior to release, with games receiving a licence from the state censorship bodies that allowed them to be released.

Next, the state drew up rules to make it legally impossible for foreign game companies to release into the market without local support. The Chinese state treats releasing an online game in China as a 'value add' to telecommunications and that operating an online game is an online publishing service. This makes it essentially legally impossible for any foreign company to set up shop in China and begin publishing a game, meaning that they have to work with a local business like Tencent or NetEase who engage in the relevant legal mumbo jumbo on their behalf.[22]

It also set up a framework to monitor and police internet cafes to ensure that the young people congregating in those spaces were not getting up to any state-subverting mischief. Wangbas were already being monitored prior to 2002, but the spaces became much more heavily policed after two teenagers started a fire at a cafe in Lanjisu which killed twenty-five people. The state had plenty of reasons to be concerned that a number of cafes were unsafe from a health and safety perspective, especially regarding their use of unlicensed and untested technologies. But it also provided an opportunity for officials to brand them as 'opium dens', justifying a crackdown which closed 40,000 cafes.[23]

Lastly, the government also imposed the first 'anti-addiction' measures on players in response to concerns about the apparently addictive nature of some video games. The concerns, which could reasonably be justified due to the aggressive nature of the engagement tactics used by some game developers, led to the issuing of the 2006 Anti-Addiction Notice. It ordered all online game developers to halve the points or score of any player in the country who spent more than three hours on an online game in a single day, reducing their achievements even further to zero if they crossed a five-hour mark that was – probably pretty reasonably, to be fair – not a healthy way to be spending time.

By the mid 2000s, the first version of China's porous censorship for games was in place and functioning in line with the country's comparatively permissive mood towards wider technology.

There were rules in place for the party to ensure content met its nationalist and social control goals, or to ban games that didn't. This included banning the first entry in strategy series *Hearts of Iron*, a game that will come up surprisingly often in the rest of this book, because it was 'distorting history and damaging China's sovereignty', by showing Manchuria, Tibet and Xinjiang in the game world.[24] The CCP had a framework in place to monitor the main spaces where people interacted online, as well as the emergent social platforms around it. It had surrounded its games market with a protective barrier, empowering local businesses to bring foreign cash to the country on its terms. Players were also just about able to pop their heads through the holes of the porous censorship filter, as evidenced by the ongoing existence of a 'grey market' for games consoles in China following their ban at the turn of the century.[25]

The problem is that the Chinese government had built its censorship plans for video games on the assumption that they were played on PCs, in an observable space by a relatively small audience of dedicated players. The censorship net could be enforced more loosely because it was relatively simpler to track and monitor a small subsection of the country.

But between 2007 and 2016, the calculus changed extraordinarily. The half-a-billion-dollar video game market supported by roughly 20 million players[26] in 2005 was washed away. By 2016, revenues had increased thirty-three-fold to over $20bn and China's player count had soared past the half a billion mark – putting it on the cusp of being the dominant global video games market.[27] And to the surprise of just about everyone in the global games industry at the time, the driver of growth in China was not the country's PC games sector that the CCP was monitoring: it was mobile games.

The arrival of the smartphone was transformative to the prospects of the games industry at large, as we've seen in other chapters. But in China, it played an even bigger part in transforming the country's prospects than other parts of the world for four main reasons.

Most obviously, the emergence of the smartphone economy and China's role within the manufacture of devices ensured that all of its citizens could quickly join the mobile gaming revolution. The arrival of China's wave of home-grown high-end handsets from the likes of Huawei, Xiaomi and Oppo, as well as Apple's steady entry into the mobile market, led to 390 million people having 4G devices in the country by early 2010. This built a market for games in China that was larger than the population of all the member states of the European Union.

Additionally, China was also well placed to become a massive mobile gaming market because its player base was conditioned to accept the business model that powered its growth. As it became increasingly obvious in the West that the route to making money was by using a free-to-play model, China's early piracy problem had conditioned its market of players to accept free games with purchases within them. In short, the country's enormous number of players were ready to spend big on the most scalable video games around: giving it immense potential to grow rapidly.

The restrictions around foreign video game developers establishing themselves in the territory also gave Chinese companies control over the market as it grew, with privileged access to an enormous market that was difficult for international businesses to reach, and reason for international developers to license lucrative games through them.

And finally, China's social and digital media landscape supported the propagation of games and fostering a culture that accepted video games as part of daily life. Tencent's QQ messaging service had been a useful 'overlay' text chat for people who wanted to play PC games with one another. But the direct integration of video games into Tencent's super app WeChat via its 'mini-apps', the gamification of shopping services which normalised video game engagement tactics like daily rewards, and the emergence of video sites like BiliBili and streaming services Huya aimed at game players grew the market further.

The result was to catapult China's leading video games companies towards the top of the international entertainment market. NetEase capitalised upon the shift to mobile devices, bringing *Fantasy Westward Journey* to China's players on the go, successfully engaging them despite two of my contacts saying that the early mobile version of the game was 'bad'. MiHoYo, the creators of multi-billion-dollar mobile game hit franchise *Genshin Impact*, started their business in Shanghai in 2012 as the mobile game revolution took off. The success of China's games sector also allowed its games companies to begin to spread their wings internationally, with Chinese internet firm Kunlun ploughing tens of millions of dollars into the Korean games industry after generating nearly $200m in revenue in 2010 as the market took off.[28]

Tencent, however, epitomised how China soared to super-power status in the video games world. *Honor of Kings*, its October 2015 free-to-play arena battling game steeped in Chinese mythological references, became the top-grossing video game in the world despite only being played in China. It would go on to generate nearly $10bn between its launch and 2024, with its international friendly counterpart *Arena of Valor* becoming popular enough to form part of Saudi Arabia's Esports World Cup line-up.

Tencent's international investments also gave it strategic significance across the international video games sector. Its decision to purchase the majority of *League of Legends* creator Riot Games allowed it to bring the action game to the Chinese market, laying the foundation for *Honor of Kings* (which closely resembles the game mechanically) and giving it ownership of one of the world's biggest esports. It acquired a stake in Epic Games to support the expansion of Tim Sweeney's business, giving it a route into the company responsible for the biggest video game engine and, soon after the investment, the immensely popular *Fortnite* virtual universe. It also picked up mobile games company Supercell from Japanese investment group SoftBank, allowing it to publish the company's remarkably popular mobile strategy game *Clash of Clans* within its home market.

Even Tencent's super app WeChat was demonstrating the influence of games. As well as providing a place where people could play literally 'mini-games' like puzzle or pinball games, WeChat, QQ and the non-Tencent-owned Sina Weibo were the route through which 46 per cent of players in China discovered which video games they wanted to play with their friends online.[29]

The result was Tencent's ascent to the top of the international tech world. By 2016, it was the biggest video games publisher in the world – a position it has maintained or competed for ever since. In 2017, it briefly toppled Facebook as the most valuable business in the world. And even after adding a wealth of technology services such as artificial intelligence and cloud computing to its portfolio, Tencent's biggest revenue generator is its games business, accounting for 48 per cent of its wealth.[30]

The growth of China's mobile games market was a resounding economic success story for the country. The problem is that its size, scale and online social reach were running counter to Xi Jinping's wider attempts to impose stricter control on the Chinese technology landscape.

From a practical censorship perspective, the porous net that the government had constructed for the industry proved too open for Chinese game players. Online PC game stores like Steam allowed the country's traditional players to increasingly play Western games. Apple's App Store was functioning in China without full state censorship, allowing unchecked Western games into the market.

And even after the NPPA issued guidance about what mobile game content is or isn't allowed in May 2016, official game approvals through the state's licensing system reached nearly a thousand games per month in 2017, with over 100 of those titles coming from abroad. By contrast, the release of thirty-eight foreign films in China in 2017 across the course of the year was considered a relaxation of its international movie quota by Western media.[31]

The censorship net around games needed to be tightened. The problem was that games had become too popular within China's social media landscape. The ballooning of the player count from tens of millions of people who played to over half a billion reduced the manageability of the potential issues that could emerge from unapproved game content, what communities discussed within video games themselves, and how they interacted with one another in associated spaces.

And as Roberts points out in her book about China's porous censorship model, the massive size of the audience for video games made it more difficult for the Chinese government to impose draconian measures on the population because it was both culturally popular and economically valuable. Limiting access to games through 'fear' of punishment ran the risk of alienating hundreds of millions of people, in a way that risked being at odds with its wider approach to censorship.

The Chinese government therefore needed to find a good excuse to tighten the net around games. It needed a social reason for it to take action, to both prevent the market from 'flooding' with content that the government did not approve of and to impose 'friction' on players accessing social spaces. And it would be useful if it could lean into contemporary cultural trends that would allow it to take action in a way that aligned with concerns amongst Chinese players, including fears around over-playing of games and very aggressive selling of in-game content to players.

Fortunately, it found its solution. Video game addiction has replaced video game violence as the moral panic du jour of the global medical community. Developing concerns about the potential for games to be 'addictive' lined up nicely with China's long-running fears over the effects of 'spiritual pollution' on the minds of its population.

And while the debate about games and mental health would quickly be mired in uncertainty, China leant into the World Health Organization's decision to add a condition called 'gaming disorder' to the International Classification of Diseases (ICD) to strengthen its censorship of games content and communities – dropping its concerns shortly after it had finished tightening its censorship net to the CCP's satisfaction.

ADDICTED TO CENSORSHIP

Between 2018 and 2022, China turned online video games into an extension of its surveillance state. In under half a decade, it moved the censorship of online games under the country's propaganda ministry, drastically reduced the number of games entering the market, and forced all online mobile games in the country to identify their player base within the country's national registration system – adding a new form of surveillance to over half a billion people in the process.

The country justified these moves by saying that it was concerned about the addictive impact of video games on players, a message that resonated with Chinese audiences and, almost certainly, a number of people reading this sentence. What it didn't do was acknowledge the uncertain science around video game addiction, or the country's role in nudging the science towards a conclusion that was useful for its political ends.

There have been concerns that games are addictive for about as long as they have existed. Chess, for example, was viewed with skepticism in some corners of British society in the 1800s, with one physician fearing that the game was a 'rather selfish and unsocial species of warfare' that wasted the time of those who pursued it (and deprived them of contact with other people).[32]

Video games, unsurprisingly, suffered from similar associations. But the technological nature of the medium and its association with children's entertainment has meant that the industry has long suffered at the hands of unfounded moral panics, most of which are based on an innately human misunderstanding of the nature of risk.

In Dan Gardner's 2009 book *Risk: The Science and Politics of Fear*, which is about the nature of risk in wider life, the author wheeled out a nineteen-part taxonomy of risk devised by Paul Slovic, an American professor of psychology at the University of

Oregon and the president of a collective scientific risk research group called Decision Research. It identifies a series of qualities that are more likely to lead to someone overestimating risk, leading them away from a rational judgement of harm in the process.

Video games hit nine of the nineteen criteria. In particular, digital games touch on fears humans tend to have towards new technology, to things that feel unknown to them, to products that simply feel 'new', and to anything that is seen to be targeted towards children. The result is that it is easy for them to become the subject of a moral panic, with people pointing to the innate qualities of video games – they're new forms of entertainment that pop up on tech devices enjoyed by young people – as a reason to overestimate their likelihood of causing harm.

For decades, this fed fears around the idea that video games could be 'addictive'. The phrase, which was carelessly used by bone-headed video game marketers trying to sell to teenage boys, has stuck with the sector. And a clue to the wooliness of the term, as well as its adjacency to which video games happen to be cutting through in the public debate at any given moment, can be found in how concerns over the condition curiously evolved to suit whichever game was dominant in the market at the time. Early panics in the West focused on *Space Invaders* in the arcades in the 1980s, console games in the 1990s and then *World of Warcraft* in the early 2000s.[33]

By 2013, the panic had begun to crystallise into action. The American Psychiatric Association (APA) included Internet Gaming Disorder (IGD) in its handbook as a condition meriting further studies, on the basis that 'gamers play compulsively, to the exclusion of other interests, and their persistent and recurrent online activity results in clinically significant impairment or distress'.

But an attempt by a group of 12 academics to present definitive criteria for what was now being called IGD was criticised at length by a 2014 paper organised by Dr Mark Griffiths, an academic who is sympathetic to the view that games could pose a mental health risk, and supported by dozens of academics.

It warned that there were 'wide-ranging disagreements' over the nature of gaming disorder, that many of the questions used to diagnose its presence – such as asking whether or not a game felt 'exciting or escapist' – were just reasons why people like video games, and that the paper trying to create an 'instrument' to assess the condition had omitted empirical research into the condition from a number of countries.[34]

The paper concluded with the reasonable suggestion that more research was needed, that researchers should work together at international events, and that studies should be conducted on players who spend a lot of time in games without signs of mental health issues to understand potentially problematic play. It also encouraged both sides of the debate to continue their research, avoiding drawing a definitive conclusion when the science couldn't support it.

But in August 2016, efforts to build a consensus over the true nature of the condition were shattered when the World Health Organization jumped ahead of the academic debate and tabled the addition of 'gaming disorder' to the International Classification of Diseases. The final text of the condition would state that gaming disorder was 'characterized by impaired control over gaming, increasing priority given to gaming over other activities to the extent that gaming takes precedence over other interests and daily activities, and continuation or escalation of gaming despite the occurrence of negative consequences' over the course of at least 12 months. It would also put video games into a category of harm known as 'substance use and addictive behaviours'.[35] Playing too much *Mario Kart* over an extended period of time was no longer a sign of enjoying too much of a good thing: it was medically akin to being an alcoholic, smoking or doing drugs.

Professor Chris Ferguson at Stetson University, a co-author of the 2014 paper which highlighted serious disagreement in the field, wrote to the WHO on 20 August 2016 to express his concerns over its inclusion. Ferguson had five objections to the inclusion of the term in the ICD: comparing games use to substance abuse risks 'pathologising' normal behaviour; that there was no symptomology or way to assess problematic gaming; that there was no evidence that games had any additional risk than other behaviours like eating or overwork; that it risked sparking a moral panic and could do 'harm to the reputation of the WHO and medical community more generally'. He also mentioned in a later email, which I've also seen, that the APA was 'getting slammed' on the matter, suggesting that the WHO should consider its position carefully.

Two days later, Ferguson was told an alarming truth. In an exchange of emails with a WHO official, Ferguson was told that the organisation was coming 'under enormous pressure, especially from Asian countries, to include this'.

And while Ferguson was not told in writing which countries were imposing this pressure on the organisation, he told me over a video call, 'I am sure it was China and maybe South Korea'. He does, however, believe that its decision to include it was less to do with the science and more to do with the people whispering in the WHO's ear.

'Obviously, this was a political thing more than a research or clinical thing,' he said. 'They just kind of said "this was a thing", and they never really came up with any criteria for how to define it. I think there were questions about how solid the evidentiary base was to make this a disorder to the extent that people maybe in some cases do overdo games,' he said. 'Is that really a stand-alone disorder? Or is it simply a symptom of depression, anxiety or other mental-health disorders?'

The WHO disputed Ferguson's points vehemently. In a response to an article in video games enthusiast site Polygon,

Dr Vladimir Poznyak, who was the coordinator of the Management of Substance Abuse within the WHO, said that 'there was not any pressure from WHO Member States to include gaming disorder in the [ICD],' that there was no formal request from any member state to do so, and that 'the decision made was based entirely on the available scientific evidence and experiences with such health conditions in different countries.'[36] It then proceeded to include gaming disorder in the draft of ICD-11 in December 2017, ruining the Christmases of a lot of people working in the games industry in the process.

However, the WHO did not publish the evidence that suggested gaming disorder should be included within the ICD.

Professor Andrew Przybylski from Oxford's Internet Institute, whose evidence-based research into video games has consistently demonstrated a 'neutral' effect from the medium on people's mental health,[37] was unconvinced by the lack of transparency. He was also unconvinced about the evidence base guiding the WHO's decision to create the category. So he wrote to it asking whether it would publish the information that guided its opinion, in the interests of open science. Did the WHO release the evidence that led to its decision to include gaming disorder in the ICD?

'No, they've not done any of that. They've just doubled down,' he said. He also stated that it was not normal for the WHO to conceal evidence in this way. 'If it was cancer, it would be exceptionally unusual [not to publish the evidence base]. If it was depression, it would be very unusual. If it was Covid, who the hell knows? But on games I can say I know the science as well as anyone . . . and nothing they've provided is convincing.'

However, the WHO was not entirely immune to criticism of a lack of transparency. In an attempt to side-step the request to see the precise evidence it used to justify gaming disorders' existence, it instead commissioned a separate 'meta-analysis' to analyse publicly available research to justify its decision. Unfortunately, it backfired. The paper, which drew nearly 80 per cent of its data from studies conducted in South Korea and China, concluded that 'the prevalence of IGD ranged from 0.21–57.50 per cent in general populations'.[38] Based on today's gaming population of roughly 3.5 billion people, the meta-analysis suggested that the number of people who could be suffering from the disorder was between 7.1 million people and 1.8 billion. 'It's garbage in, garbage out,' stated Przybylski, in reference to the comically large difference between the figures.

But for the Chinese government, it didn't matter whether or not the science was garbage. The country needed a reason to tighten its censorship net. And the World Health Organization's approach to gaming disorder happened to align usefully with its burgeoning efforts to rein in video game companies in the name of public health, while deftly expanding the reach of its censorship net.

Of course, the country was more than able to expand its censorship net without waiting for an international non-governmental organisation to justify its actions. In July 2017, Tencent implemented a voluntary 'anti-addiction' system in *Honor of Kings* which limited the playtime of under-12s to an hour per day and of 13- to 17-year-olds to a couple of hours, in response to concerns over addiction and overspend. That system was underpinned by a 'real name' identification system, with players linking their real-life ID to the game to manage interactions – explicitly tying the anti-addiction system's goals to one of the main mechanisms through which the state monitors the lives of its citizens.[39]

However, Chinese mobile video games were subjected to much deeper censorship in the years that followed including control of what content they displayed, who could access games and how they could interact with them. And notably, the government turned the legal thumbscrews on developers shortly after the WHO made major announcements about gaming disorder on two occasions before 2020.

The first announcement came on 21 March 2018, just three months after the WHO had included 'gaming disorder' in the draft of ICD-11 and weeks after Xi Jinping had announced the end-of-term limits for the Chinese presidency. The government dramatically froze the issuing of licences for any upcoming video games – stopping any new domestic or international games from releasing. Officially, the move was a result of China's decision to reorganise its censorship bodies in the wider context of the state. The NPPA, the country's propaganda department, was made the main regulator of video games content and was nested within the State Council, sitting directly underneath the Publicity Department of the Communist Party of China.

Unofficially, though, concerns over addiction were being weaponised to extend Tencent's voluntary anti-addiction measures for *Honor of Kings* to encompass all of the most popular games made by the then biggest company in the country. Tencent's big release for the year, the mobile version of *Player Unknown Battlegrounds (PUBG)*, a wildly popular multiplayer action game, was snared up in the licensing freeze.[40] On the face of it, fears over the game's violent content – which sees a hundred players fight one another to be the last player or team standing – led to dramatic changes to its narrative and appearance to keep the censors happy. This meant that the globally known *PUBG* transformed in China only into *Game for Peace*, which saw a brutal battle royale narrative swapped out in favour of allowing players to participate in a blood- and gore-free 'training exercise' by China's military.[41]

The changes to *PUBG Mobile* reflected the government's desire to crack down both on what content was in games and the number of games released into the market overall.

When game approvals restarted in December 2018, the number crashed – dropping to 130 games approved per month compared to over 800 per month in 2017. Everything but the simplest domestically made mobile games (e.g. a simple puzzle game) were subjected to an approval process that examined a game in depth for forbidden content, exploring whether the business seeking a licence was based in China, and understanding whether the online game company distributing it followed relevant local rules (including having NPPA-trained censors on its staff).[42] This led to companies self-censoring their releases for fear of falling foul of the state.

'Companies maybe look at the laws and think, oh do we really want to push that boundary?' a contact said. 'And the Chinese government likes to keep [the content rules] very vague, so they can see what happens and decide if they don't like what they're seeing that they can say "oh you've broken the law". It's a controlling government tactic.'

But dragging games further into the government's digital censorship net was also on the agenda. As part of its attempt to get government back onside and reopen the market to release, Tencent committed in September 2018 to roll out 'anti-addiction' systems it had created for *Honor of Kings* across all of its games. And a year later, the Chinese government moved to bring all online mobile games – i.e. every commercially viable game in China – into its censorship net just as the global public health debate around video games addiction went up a notch.

In May 2019, the World Health Organization finally published ICD-11 and included gaming disorder in it. This resulted in a flurry of research and clinic openings across the world, including the National Health Service's game addiction service in the United Kingdom in October 2019. By 2023, the service had treated 745 people for gaming disorder.[43] With approximately 60 per cent of the UK's 69.3m population playing video games, this amounts to a prevalence rate of 0.000017 per cent. That means you are only seventeen times more likely to be addicted to video games than you are to be hit by lightning. A blessed relief for *Wordle* players everywhere.

But in the same month that the NHS opened up its clinic, China delivered a jolting change in the law which extended the 'addiction' censorship that Tencent had willingly cloaked itself in over the whole industry.

It published a refreshed Anti-Addiction Notice forcing game companies to take steps to prevent supposedly rampant addiction amongst players. Companies were forced to identify who their players were and what their age was. Anyone under the age of eighteen would be set spending limits to reduce the amount of cash they could spend in any game to below approximately $30 a month. Their playtime would also be limited to 1.5 hours per day on weekdays and three hours per day on weekends, with a curfew imposed on playtime in the small hours of the morning.[44]

The measures were, again, framed as a public health concern. Video games were 'harming the physical and mental health of minors', justifying the imposition of limits. But this language cloaked the true intention.

Although the government did not mandate how companies verified the age of players, it said that it was going to 'gradually improve and enrich the functions of an identification system to share gaming time data across platforms' to allow companies to maintain their responsibilities. Inevitably, this meant tying individual player accounts to national identity numbers: ensuring that any player, whether underage or otherwise, was now being tracked in games by state security supposedly on public health grounds.

As these measures were rolling out, the crackdown on games and the community spaces that people congregated within widened. Twitch, the video streaming service, and Discord, the chat forum, were both blocked in China in 2018. Steam, the PC game storefront, signed a partnership with Perfect World to create a state-approved Chinese version of its international PC games store – minus social functionality like groups and chat – to stay in the country. Apple, after years of allowing mobile games to sell in China without a licence, forced developers to display a licence number on its store to release in the territory from the beginning of 2020.

And in the same month that the anti-addiction measures rolled out, a pro-Hong Kong esports player called Blitzchung showed how China's tightening censorship environment could have repercussions internationally. In a live-streamed interview that took place during a tournament for *Hearthstone*, a popular virtual card game that bears some similarity to a card game like *Magic: The Gathering*, Blitzchung said 'liberate Hong Kong, the revolution of our times.' Activision Blizzard, the host of the stream and the tournament, banned Blitzchung and sacked the two hosts who interviewed him. This sparked cross-party concern against Activision's actions in the US, with US Senators Ron Wyden and Marco Rubio speaking out against the decision.[45]

Measures censoring video games continued to deepen during the Covid-19 crisis. As people moved online, China simultaneously expanded its ability to surveil and its willingness to do so. Efforts to prevent the spread of the pandemic provided justification for China to increase its digital censorship at large, both normalising the use of platforms like WeChat for contact tracing and encouraging the state to undertake its wider crackdown on technology businesses.

It also provided reasons for the Chinese state to monitor video game content even more closely. Despite its being technically unavailable for release in the country, China banned Nintendo's peaceful island life simulator *Animal Crossing: New Horizons* after players used some of its features to create signs that promoted messages like 'Free Hong Kong'. The government also removed video games that happened to awkwardly contradict its own narratives. The video game *Plague Inc*, a popular strategy game about spreading a pandemic around the world, shot to the top of the Chinese app stores in early 2020 as Covid-19 raged through Wuhan. Shortly afterwards, it was pulled from sale by the Chinese government on the basis that it featured 'illegal content'. We'll return to that game's story, and the significance of neutering games that fairly inform public knowledge, in Part 3 of the book.

By 2021, the government was ready to tighten the net around games even further. In March 2021, it strengthened its content assessment process to make sure that releases stayed on message. The NPPA introduced a new review process in which it would measure games with a mark out of five on a number of measures, including its quality but also its ideological connotation. Any game with a rolling average of less than 3 or a single 0 in any category was barred from release unless it fixed the issues raised by NPPA. This meant that the content, themes and narratives of China's biggest games became even more firmly controlled by the CCP.

And as the year rolled on, the CCP intensified its efforts to monitor its citizens under the auspices of anti-addiction measures. Unlike in other crackdowns, the move was not presaged by an announcement about gaming disorder by the WHO. Instead, it appears as if the momentum came from within China itself and quite possibly through the government's relationship with the media. In the summer of 2021, Economic Information Daily, a business outlet which is owned by Xinhua News Agency (an official arm of China's state media), claimed that video games were a form of 'spiritual opium' that were damaging China's youth. It also suggested that Tencent, whose game *Honor of Kings* had started the wave of addiction panic in 2015, was largely to blame for the crisis and that China needed to 'watch out for the harm of online games'.[46]

Questions emerged almost immediately after the piece was

published about whether it represented Chinese government opinion. Those who believed it represented the state's position pointed to its criticism of Tencent, which came just at the height of a wider tech backlash that saw its attempt to merge two popular Chinese video game streaming platforms together blocked by regulators. Those who thought it was a rogue operation pointed to the fact that the piece was removed later, after it was blamed for sparking a 10 per cent drop in the share price of both Tencent and NetEase on the Hong Kong Stock Exchange.[47]

What is indisputable is that the publication of the piece was followed yet again by an intense crackdown on game content, game playing and the ability of players to play without being monitored by the government. At the end of August 2021, the government instituted another nine-month licensing freeze that again prevented new titles from releasing into the market. But arguably more consequentially, this new freeze aligned with a deepening of the country's 'anti-addiction' rules that just happened to make it much easier for the Chinese state to find out who exactly was playing games.

The changes did strengthen existing anti-addiction rules to limit playtime. For example, under-18s saw their overall play time reduced even further to just one hour a day every Friday, Saturday and Sunday evening. The offer of an extra hour of playtime on public holidays on top of these limits was not, presumably, much of a concession to young players wanting to enjoy their favourite games.

However, these rule changes coincided with an utterly crucial change in the way that the age verification of players was handled. Previously, companies had been allowed to use their own systems to verify identities against national registration databases. Now, companies had to use special code created by the NPPA within their services to verify IDs to standardise data gathering without exception. Any player who therefore logged into an online game and verified their age with their ID was now being directly tracked by the Ministry of Propaganda. Its reach is pervasive and chilling.

'It is required for all mobile games and apps,' explained another source familiar with the Chinese game-publishing market. 'The first time you open an app after having to download it, you need to verify yourself with your real identity. They know exactly what each user is doing, how long they're spending in apps, and they could send a message to you.'

Through these moves, by April 2022, the Chinese government had cleverly used public health concerns to tighten its porous censorship net around the country's now 700 million gamers. It had brought domestic companies to heel, using their always online games to insert state surveillance into the act of daily play. International games companies were locked out of the market even more effectively, ensuring that their only practical route to entering the market was with a local partner. The anti-addiction measures had simultaneously limited the amount of time young people could play while also bringing all adult players into the censorship net at the same time. This reduced the risk of people congregating together within game communities – denying solidarity amongst groups, as James Griffiths puts it – while adding another layer of extensive personal data on hundreds of millions of people to China's surveillance web.

And with mission accomplished, the public health pretext could be abandoned. In November 2023, the country's China Game Industry Group Committee, a body affiliated to the national games regulator, released a report claiming that it had successfully curbed gaming addiction in the country.[48] But despite this triumphant news, it unsurprisingly did not remove any of its anti-addiction measures, including its invasive identification login rules.

DOMESTIC CENSORSHIP, INTERNATIONAL EXPOSURE

China's crackdown on video games between 2018 and 2022 took a popular, growing and unmonitored online digital space containing close to a billion people and conveniently folded it into the country's censorship network.

The imposition of anti-addiction systems powered by real-name identification systems strengthened social control, restricting the ability of players to communicate freely without fear of backlash and integrating online games companies into the state's arm's length censorship framework. The strengthening of the country's licensing system under the NPPA ensured that national values as defined by the CCP were protected more effectively in games, reducing the number of foreign games officially released into the market while more tightly controlling the content of Chinese-developed games (including the volume). And though the imposition of licensing freezes and the public haranguing of games companies has slowed the economic growth of China's biggest games companies, the country's nearly $50bn consumer market is now mostly tightly controlled and protected: ensuring that businesses such as Tencent and NetEase remain of immense strategic importance to the global games industry.

The result is that the core of the Chinese video games market is the most regulated, most controlled and most politically censored of any video game market in the world. Yet somewhat ironically, the impact of it may be felt outside China more than it is at home.

For players within China, the tight regulation of mainstream games is contrasted by the existence of a 'porous' market for games that allows them to navigate censorship relatively easily. Major video games consoles from nearby regions are so readily available in China that Hideo Kojima, a Japanese video game developer who is known across the world for the stealth game series *Metal Gear Solid*, rocked up to a conference in Shanghai to promote his new release, *Death Stranding 2*, despite it not having a licence to release in the market.[49] The international version of Steam, the PC games store, is so widely accessed by Chinese-language players that Simplified Chinese is the store's biggest language, despite the 'global' version of the platform notionally being banned in the country.[50] Players commonly use digital tools like VPNs or connection 'booster' services to get around, or speed their way past, friction imposed by China's censorship tools. And despite strict rules on who plays games for how long, it's commonplace for young players to either use a parent's device or 'rent' an account from someone online.

For players abroad, escaping the influence of Chinese censorship is steadily becoming more difficult. In April 2025, market data firm Newzoo released a report which showed that the global rate of growth in games industry revenue would struggle to exceed the rate of inflation by 2030.[51] Developers, therefore, need to open access to new markets. And while plenty of new opportunities are developing in Latin America, Africa and the Middle East, China's size, scale and influence in terms of its economic power is simply too much for the industry to ignore – resulting in a number of developments that are turning domestic censorship into a live risk of international influence.

First, China's games businesses have become so central to the global games ecosystem that extracting them from the heart of it is almost impossible. In response to the video game freezes of both 2018 and 2021, Chinese games businesses invested billions of dollars in games businesses across the world to soften the blows landing on them from the CCP. Tencent, for example, has invested in the company that makes the popular *Dark Souls* series (From Software), the business behind the multi-award-winning *Dungeons and Dragons*-inspired game *Baldur's Gate 3* (Larian Studios), the UK's biggest outsource game development business for a billion dollars (Sumo Group), the makers of the *Assassin's Creed* series (Ubisoft) and the video game social messaging app Discord.

Publicly, Tencent and its rival NetEase have sought to present themselves as quiet partners allowing businesses to create what they want on their terms. But the reality is that China's tightened grip on its tech ecosystem has weakened that argument significantly. In October 2023, the Chinese government used its 'golden share' law to take 1 per cent ownership of Tencent: securing the CCP a board seat and additional influence within the business.[52] And in February 2025, the company's founder and chief executive, Pony Ma, attended a business symposium chaired by Xi Jinping aimed at boosting sluggish domestic growth.[53] This means that the only way to get investment from a Chinese business or officially enter its market is by working with companies that are, broadly speaking, tightly controlled by the CCP; an invidious decision for games companies to make.

Second, and on the other side of the coin, the size of the Chinese games industry means that it is creating games big enough to become global hits. This means that games created under the CCP's tightly defined censorship rules can slip out of the porous censorship net into the wider world, allowing the government to co-opt games to spread its own narratives.

To some extent, this process is a reasonable part of cultural exchange. *Black Myth: Wukong* received numerous nominations at the Game Awards, the video game equivalent to the Oscars, in 2024 for providing players with a stunning single-player action game based on *Journey to the West*. The success of mobile game *Arena of Valor*, the Westernised version of *Honor of Kings*, has made it a hit amongst esports communities, leading to its inclusion in the Saudi-hosted Esports World Cup. Fresh hits like *Wuchang: Fallen Feathers*, another single-player action game rooted in Chinese historical references which was released in 2025, showed there is an audience for these games.

But it is also obvious that the CCP reserves the right to determine whether or not the messages these games communicate to the wider world are the right ones. In August 2025, *Wuchang: Fallen Feathers* was subjected to a mysterious update. Players across the world reported that a number of the Chinese historical characters that you fight and kill in the game suddenly stopped dying in the game world, including right at the end of the game. And although it is impossible to say exactly why these changes were made, the game, notably, was initially released without a licence from the Chinese government. It appears as if the content of the game was changed after it became too successful; a perfect example of the porous censorship net suddenly acquiring a razor's edge.[54]

The CCP's desire to control communication can also lead to censorship of conversation around the world. In 2024, NetEase released a multiplayer game called *Marvel Rivals* that allowed players to use popular superheroes like Captain Marvel, Thor and Spiderman to beat the living snot out of one another. The game featured symbols of American democracy such as Captain America in its cast of characters. But that democratic spirit didn't live on its chat. An investigation by *The Times* discovered that the game banned players from using phrases such as 'Winnie-the-Pooh' (a derogatory reference to Xi Jinping that the Chinese president hates) and 'Free Taiwan' in the chat function included in the game. The importance of the Chinese market means developers are increasingly putting its needs first: spreading Chinese censorship and cultural influence indirectly in the process.[55]

And finally, China's warping of the public health debate around video games to tighten its censorship net should act as a warning to the rest of the world about how careless chatter around the medium can meaningfully impact freedom globally.

A seemingly 'moral' attempt to use public health to constrain reasonable freedom to play online games with one another was used to impose a mass censorship net on hundreds of millions of people. And while China has temporarily moved away from heavy-handed regulation of the industry under the pretext that it has 'solved' its addiction problems, the WHO's ongoing maintenance of the term 'gaming disorder' has handed it, and other authoritarians, an extra weapon to enforce control of their citizenry. Assessing whether the condition should exist, be adjusted, or disposed of in the next version of the International Classification of Diseases should be a priority for the WHO to show it is preventing the politicisation of public health.

But while China can influence the world through its video game censorship framework, it is much more concerned with controlling games for the purpose of keeping its own citizens in line under a more explicitly authoritarian framework than Saudi Arabia.

However, there is a nation which is willing to wield political influence via games much more aggressively: Russia. And in the next chapter, we'll see how the state's control over play, co-option of the medium and collaboration with actors across the world has allowed it to wage war on a new digital frontline.

7

Nothing is true and everything is playable

Since 2022, the Ukrainian people have suffered under the weight of Russian attack. Alongside the unprovoked invasion of their country and the incessant bombardment of their homes, the Ukrainian population has also had to suffer under the weight of relentless digital campaigning from an enemy determined to crush its resistance.

But there has been another front upon which Russia has waged its war to spread its anti-Ukrainian narratives: video games. As the war in Ukraine has dragged on, Russia, its proxies and supporters have increasingly tapped video games, video games influencers and the social media services that underpin them as a channel for disinformation.

The campaigns that the Russian state has run within the medium have proven capable of capturing mainstream media attention, with state-developed video games, Wagner Military Group-sponsored game streamers and hackers attacking Ukrainian-made titles popping up across the world.

But while Russia has been able to use games as a tool to unlock a 'media multiplication effect' that spreads its messages around the world, the effectiveness of its campaigning in games is a lot less obvious than its creativity within them.

And while we must take its efforts to turn a form of play and entertainment into a channel for influence seriously, a lack of video game literacy amongst Western media is amplifying the sophistication and quality of Russia's campaigning within video games, allowing Russia to portray itself as much more mighty than it actually is.

DISSOLVING TRUTH

To understand why Russia is using video games for disinformation, you need to understand why it uses disinformation strategically within the digital sphere to aggressively promote its position at home and abroad. And to understand that, you need to know exactly what disinformation is.

'Disinformation is deliberately created content that is designed to cause harm,' says Claire Wardle, an associate professor in the Department of Communication at Cornell University. Where misinformation is defined by someone unintentionally circulating false information, disinformation's purpose is to mislead to help the creator achieve a goal. The lies can be big, such as implying George Soros sits at the centre of a shadowy influence network puppeteering the world order. But they can be insidiously small too.

'Disinformation is intentionally false and created with the intent to deceive, but it doesn't have to fully false,' explains a former State Department official, who worked to counter disinformation through the Global Engagement Center (GEC) and acted as one of the 'bellringers' to inform the world that Russia was commencing the full-scale invasion of Ukraine in 2022. 'It can just be one little detail in a single sentence in a 100,000 word essay that is wrong.'

Disinformation can be perpetuated by a range of actors of differing sizes. The use of disinformation for political influence used to be the preserve of political bureaucracies and intelligence agencies, which engaged in its creation as part of what are called 'active measures' in the intelligence community.[1] Now, individuals, campaign groups and non-state actors can also create disinformation as a result of the democratisation of digital content creation – increasing its scale and distribution, while also making it less stable and coordinated.

The goals of disinformation can vary. According to Wardle's paper about information disorder, a categorisation term that sits above misinformation, disinformation and malinformation, the goal is usually as straightforward as causing trouble for fun, getting hands on cash or using the content to achieve political influence.[2] But when disinformation is used for political influence, it is often wielded as a 'weapon of the weak'[3] by an actor who needs to dissolve the truth to cover its weaknesses, magnify its strength, and give it the space to achieve its objectives – whether on the battlefield or within a wider part of the strategic calculation. This explains Russia's long-term interest in creating disinformation for strategic purposes.

'Russia sees itself as this great power and will do whatever it takes to maintain that status,' says the former State Department official. 'It comes from what it knows is a position of relative weakness relative to China and the US, even though they would never admit this.' The result is that the state has evolved a 'gloves-off approach' to using disinformation to maintain its status in the world, both at home and abroad.

Russia's willingness to use disinformation to achieve its strategic ends has deep historic roots. From the Russian Revolution in 1917 onwards, Russian state actors were willing to go to remarkably creative lengths to spread falsehoods that could prop up the regime. In the 1920s, the Cheka, the Soviet Union's first secret police, blackmailed a sympathiser of the Royalist 'White' movement to create a fake Monarchist organisation within the country to mislead supporters outside the country about the true state of Russia. During the height of the Cold War, Russian agents fabricated US military field manuals to imply the US government was funding far-left groups to stoke dissent domestically and abroad.[4] And Russian disinformation

high-jinks arguably reached their peak in 1964, when an operation dubbed 'NEPTUN' took advantage of media hype
around possible chests full of Nazi gold at the bottom of lakes to
stage the 'discovery' of a box full of documents. Conveniently, it
contained papers from the Nazi era which criticised all of then
West Germany's closest allies: discoveries that were eagerly
reported upon by press who loved the 'docs found in lake shock'
angle.[5]

And despite the Soviet Union falling, those historic roots
have extended into the country's present-day political strategy
because of the background of its head of state, Vladimir Putin.

Putin is a product of the Soviet Union's disinformation
apparatus. After joining the KGB in 1975, Putin steadily
climbed the ranks. He first worked in Leningrad monitoring
foreign nationals, before heading to Moscow to the Yuri
Andropov Institute, named after the former president of the
USSR who served as KGB chairman between 1967 and 1982,
to study. Shortly after that, he headed to Dresden in the mid
1980s until the Soviet Union collapsed at the end of the decade.
Putin implied that he spent his time in Germany drinking beer
and getting fat.

Journalist Catherine Belton disagrees with this account. In
her book *Putin's People*, she reveals that Putin was a liaison for
the KGB with the Stasi and had a first-hand role in a series of
what the Soviets called 'active measures'. An on-the-ground
account of his time there suggested that he was involved in a
number of politically disruptive activities, including allegedly
building a relationship with the far-left terror group the Red
Army Faction, well out of view of Western intelligence agencies.[6] Belton argues that his time in Dresden was crucial for
teaching him about the dark arts of disinformation.[7] And as the
wall fell and Putin transitioned into political life in St Petersburg, the shadow of his time there – and the lessons that he
learned – stayed with him.

'As East Germany was collapsing, he watched what happens when you let slip your grip on the information environment and the reins of control,' according to the former State Department official. 'I think that was a formative moment where [he decided that] the State should never give an inch because as soon as you open up the door or soften up then you're vulnerable.'

As Putin climbed the ladder, control over the narrative, irrespective of whether it was true or not, became key to his rise to the top. By 1999, Putin had left St Petersburg's political scene to head up Russia's security services under Boris Yeltsin.[8] A year later when Putin was elected president, the Carnegie Endowment for International Peace released a report that showed the challenges of understanding the true nature of Russia's new president. On the one hand, the foundation believed that Putin was potentially a reformer who may lead Russia away from a 'feudal order' where the 'people had no say' towards a democracy with a thriving economy. Yet at the same time, the report suggested that Putin had been steered to power by Yeltsin and his oligarchic allies to keep him out of prison. There was also a suspicion that the country had stoked a war with Chechnya to bolster his credentials.[9]

However, international audiences initially had little to go on other than what they were hearing from within Russia itself. And under Putin's rule, the state was using similar tactics to the Soviet Union's active measures campaigns to bombard its population with disinformation. The purpose was to dissolve truth at home to allow Putin's narratives to set in, to keep what was increasingly described as his 'mafia state' in power, and to use that to present the world with a view of Russia that masked his full intentions.

In *Nothing is True and Everything is Possible*, Peter Pomerantsev, the author, television producer and disinformation expert, shows the numerous ways that the Russian information environment was distorted to strengthen Putin's narratives. News outlets like Russia Today with Western staff shared the Russian perspective with the country and the world, with the proviso that staff were directed to claim the Soviet Union saved Estonia, that Georgians were committing genocide in Ossetia and that Putin was personally directing a response to local forest fires.[10] Groups and subcultures such as the Night Wolves motorcycle gang received funding and support from the government because their projected masculinity aligned with Putin's own views.[11] The ever-changing nature of the truth was demonstrated by the arrest and release of Russian businesswoman Yana Yakovleva for supposedly selling a chemical called diethyl illegally, which was much less about the law and much more about two members of Russia's security service fighting (and eventually both being disposed by Putin) over the sale of chemicals across the country's border with China.[12]

And despite numerous examples that the Russian state was willing to eliminate people who did not toe the official line, such as Alexander Litvinenko, the Russian intelligence service defector who was murdered through the ingestion of polonium with a cup of tea, and Anna Politkovskaya, the Russian journalist and Putin critic who was shot dead in an elevator in her apartment block, Western audiences believed the narrative he was selling. Pomerantsev, for example, wrote about an EU official he met in Moscow in the 2000s who signed off projects directed towards developing ties in Russia. He was willing to sign cheques for projects worth hundreds of millions of euros because the country technically was a democracy, with civil society groups and respect for private property rights. The families of Politkovskaya, Litvinenko and later Alexei Navalny, a former political rival to Putin who was allegedly poisoned shortly before his death in February 2024,[13] would disagree.

The sweeping away of truth in Russia has given Putin total power over the narrative at home. This has encouraged the population to do one of two things. Disengage from the debate due to exhaustion over the noisiness of the information ecosystem. Or embrace the official narrative and lean into it for an easier life. And once enough people have decided to do the latter, it becomes remarkably easy for the state to promote whatever narrative it sees fit: even if it is totally removed from reality.

'When they're saying the United States is controlled by a league of shadowy businessmen or that the Bill Gates Foundation is engaging in weaponised research of bioweapons, I genuinely believe that to some extent they believe this,' explained the official. 'That's rooted in the paranoia of the Cold War mentality that "they're out to get us", that they think we do exactly what they think we do and that this is true across the board when it comes to disinformation.'

But as alluded to earlier, Putin's desire to control the information environment is not just about achieving his goals at home. It was also about achieving dominance over its neighbours as part of Russia's attempt to expand into territory that was formally in the Soviet Union. And a handful of interlinked developments made spreading Russia's information environment abroad a priority for the regime.

In the early 2000s, Russia was unsettled by a series of 'colour revolutions' in Georgia and Ukraine, which saw local pro-democracy activists kick back against rigged elections in a series of peaceful movements defined by the colours protestors bore (e.g. Georgia's was the 'Rose' revolution). These movements unsettled the regime because of their proximity to the Russian border. But it was also disturbed by the Arab Spring in the early 2010s, which, again, saw peaceful movements sweep autocratic leaders out of power (at least briefly).

The unifying factor behind these movements was that protestors were not solely organising in the physical world. Instead, they were using the internet, and especially smartphones and social media, during the Arab Spring to organise. The information ecosystems that protestors were using were key to advancing their causes. Therefore, Russia needed to dissolve truth within the global information space to ensure the 'truth' it had assembled at home – a febrile, ever-changing thing – would be strengthened instead of fractured by international discourse.

Russia began to adapt the tactics and strategies of the 'active measures age' – namely, developing creative disinformation, spreading it through infrastructure, using existing groups and subcultures to support it – for a digital age.[14] And in an unfortunate twist, the optimism about the power of social media in the early 2010s as a tool for spreading democracy meant that few measures were put in place to mitigate the impact of hostile campaigning in digital spaces. The result has been that Russia is able to benefit from what Thomas Rid describes as a 'golden age of disinformation', with its creative approach to disinformation proving a perfect match for the digital age.

Russia backed organisations such as Yevgeny Prigozhin's Internet Research Agency, a troll and content farm founded by the former head of the Wagner Military Group, churned out articles, memes and comments on sites across the internet to 'flood' organic conversations with Russian perspectives. The state has used official spokespeople such as Dmitry Loskutov, a former Russian government aide, to promote content useful to its interests (such as a YouTube video of two uncomplimentary phone calls featuring US and EU officials that had been hacked by the Russians, leaked online, but not picked up in the news). It has hit every subculture it possibly can with talking points designed to divide the debate, with the Russian state targeting often seemingly contradictory groups obsessed with gun rights, anti-immigration talking points, Black Lives Matter, and LGBTQ rights with content designed to disrupt ahead of the American elections. It has sought to pay influencers and media to promote its perspectives, including putting cash behind Tenet

Media – a company founded by a number of right-wing media commentators in America – to promote Kremlin talking points (something that the company claimed they were deceived into doing by Russian media executives).[15] And the creativity shown in the KGB's NEPTUN operation is alive and well today, as seen by the Internet Research Agency's invention of a mystic healer called Cantadora who posted content subtly implying that the European Union is a vassal to the United States to disrupt discourse across the continent.[16]

Importantly, it doesn't actually matter whether or not any specific digital disinformation effort is effective in its own right or not. It is, of course, useful if a digital advert, blog post or short-form social video gets views from its audience. But if a measure is covered by the media in any way, whether it's uncritically covering a falsehood or unmasking it, it creates what our former State Department official describes as a 'media multiplier effect' which promotes Russia's message and power. This means that originally ineffective measures like a barely seen advert of Jesus arm-wrestling Satan becomes effective when a news organisation like the *New York Times* covers it and promotes it to millions of readers.[17] And with Russian operatives knowing that officials based in the United States cannot mark campaigns as directed by hostile actors unless it can definitively prove the involvement of a foreign intelligence service, Russia can wash cash and content across the internet through its supporters, supportive organisations it funds and journalists who can't resist a scoop – safe in the knowledge that its rivals will struggle to call it out.

'In the EU and UK, if it looks like a duck, you can check to make sure it's not a duck,' explains the source. 'Here [in the US], you can't even look at the duck unless you know the duck is evil.'

The effectiveness of individual messages may be hard to measure in the digital world, particularly when Russia is constantly quacking at you from all sides. But the cumulative effect of Russian disinformation on democracies is clear. The Mueller Report identified that tens of millions of Americans had been exposed to Russian disinformation campaigns in the knife-edge 2016 election.[18] The UK's Brexit referendum was subjected to significant Russian interference, with the government and intelligence agencies being criticised for the fact that they 'underestimated the response required to the Russian threat'.[19] And in the European Union, digital disinformation campaigns from Russia are deliberately spreading hostile messages about Ukraine, fermenting anti-EU sentiment, and playing up the power of the Kremlin in an effort to tilt the information environment its way.[20] By splattering every digital channel and surface available with its 'firehose of falsehood', Russia has been able to degrade truth, exhaust populations, and replace it with narrow messages that support its strategic aim to grab land in Ukraine and dismantle the Atlantic Alliance. It has also played a significant role in generally weakening democracy, amplifying masculine strongmen and degrading social rights.

But with the information environment constantly changing, and Russia long having a track record of being willing to try just about everything possible to get Putin's perspective into the world, the country has evolved its digital disinformation tactics to ensure that it successfully hits every surface possible with its distorted world view. And with video games, video game influencers and its communities at the heart of a digital third place and contested information ecosystem that can multiply messages across media types, it's no surprise that it has developed sophisticated experimental campaigns within the games industry to open up a new front of its information war – challenging Ukraine, and the world, in the process.

WAR GAMES

Russia's ability to use video games as a channel for spreading its narratives would be possible without it having its own industry. However, Russia has been an important pillar of the global games industry for a number of years, all the way back to the glory days when *Tetris* emerged from the Soviet Union to dominate the world. This means that the state is able to tap into players, developers and games themselves as a resource to spread its message: allowing it to control narratives by co-opting infrastructure (often in collaboration with supportive individuals inside the industry or within its community).

Prior to the invasion of Ukraine, Russia had a sizeable games industry. The Russian Association of Electronic Communications (RAEC) reported in February 2022 that the market generated 158bn rubles (approximately $2.5bn) in 2021 – a figure that'd be much higher if piracy wasn't so rampant within the territory. And despite the invasion limiting Russian players' access to Nintendo, PlayStation and Xbox's console stores due to sanctions and their withdrawal from the country, a June 2025 survey from a Russian government research agency found that 77 per cent of the country play games – with 86 per cent of people playing games via their PC.[21] Importantly, Russian is also the third most popular language on PC platform Steam with nearly 10 per cent of global users favouring it as a first language.[22]

This helps to explain why certain genres of games are popular in Russia. Outside of globally popular games like *Call of Duty*, *EA Sports FC* and *Grand Theft Auto*, three militarised game types dominate the market. 'Slavic shooters' like *Metro: 2033*, which is based on Russian IP; multiplayer military battling games like *War Thunder* where players hop into tanks and pummel each other with shells; militarised strategy games like

Hearts of Iron IV where players can strategically battle out the Second World War again. The thematic link is something that the state has fostered through a combination of censorship and support for 'patriotic game development', as evidenced by a 2024 presidential order supporting games that accurately reflected Russian history.

The prevalence of gaming within Russia means that it has a long track record of producing excellent game developers. Studios such as Saber Interactive (creators of the successful *Space Marine 2*), Wargaming (the developers of the popular multi-player online game *World of Tanks*) and Zeptolab (*Cut the Rope*) were founded in Russia, with many companies in the country becoming outsourced development partners for international games businesses looking for expertise. This means that the country has a base of development talent to support, and that talent is looking for work because many of those businesses have either moved most of their operations elsewhere (Saber has a major base in the US, Zeptolab in Barcelona) or completely left the country (Wargaming has completely exited Russia in circumstances we'll briefly return to later) in the wake of the Ukraine invasion.

Lastly, the PC link means that the Russian state has the ability to project influence through the Steam store that remains functional in the country. Although the company has suspended payouts to Russian game developers in line with international sanctions, Steam's libertarian philosophy means that players in the country can still buy games using its wallet function, still access their existing library of titles, and use communication functions like its chat and groups. The business's frankly naive policy of a blanket removal of 'illegal' content also means it blindly complies with Russia's authoritarian regime to remain online, removing hundreds of pieces of content in late 2024 on behalf of the country's official censorship body.[23] This means that Steam is one of the few social channels that is allowed to operate in the country, alongside Telegram and YouTube (the latter of which has been demonetised).

Russia has all the ingredients to make games, distribute them internationally and use them to project messages. The *Guardian* ran a piece in 2014 about the history of Russian 'patriotic' games, which included references to games promoting scientific education and national narratives around the Battle of Stalingrad.[24] A decidedly average military strategy game called *Confrontation: Peace Enforcement*[25] somewhat blatantly promoted Kremlin narratives around its incursion into Georgia to players in 2008. And in 2010, Russia's Ministry of Communications and Mass Media sought a budget of roughly 500 million roubles (approximately $10m) to fund the creation of six video games promoting Russian historic narratives to counter games that Pavel Zyranov, then a member of the country's youth committee, reportedly said portrayed the country as 'a bunch of villains'.[26] Esports were also included within Russia's thinking relatively early, with Vladimir Putin expressing support for tournaments in schools in 2020 as a way to get Russian athletes competing effectively internationally at a time when they were still banned from the Olympics due to widespread doping.[27]

Its strategy to use games as a channel for influence ramped up considerably from 2022 after most of the global video games industry left the market following the start of the war in Ukraine. In July that year, shortly after the country had invaded Ukraine, Russian business newspaper *Kommersant* reported that the state was exploring the development of a home-grown game engine to support developers who had been locked out of using Unity and Unreal Engine by global sanctions.[28]

By December 2022, plans emerged for the Russian state to invest as much as $50bn in video games via a new publisher called Rosgame – which opened its doors in February 2023. According to *The Insider*, the aim was to fund up to twenty-five games with a budget of approximately $87.5m each (i.e.

blockbuster game releases you'd expect to see advertised on TV) and forty smaller projects by the end of the decade.[29] And judging by comments Vladimir Putin made to a junior game developer in July 2023, Rosgame's success would not be judged by cash generation alone. It would be according to whether they offer 'a mix of art and education' that 'must help a person grow, both within the framework of universal human values, and patriotism'.[30] The country also moved in December 2023 to put in place similar controls to the Chinese government's about where video games data is kept, forcing developers who run multiplayer games to base key technology like servers in the country.[31]

And the following year, the strategy ramped up further. In February 2024, Putin chaired a meeting of Kaliningrad's economic committee that committed to creating a home-grown Russian video game console and a cloud gaming platform like Microsoft's Netflix-style Game Pass subscription.[32] A few months later, Putin issued a presidential order banning games which 'distort' the history of Russia.[33] The new order reinforced a long-held ban on *Call of Duty: Modern Warfare 2*, which included a feature where players were able to participate in a level called 'No Russian' that allowed them to take part in a massacre of civilians at a Russian airport.[34] It also gave the Kremlin power to ban games depending on whether it thought it distorted historical truth, a further strengthening of its ability to determine what is or isn't real in the country.

By the end of 2024, the foundations of the Kremlin's video games strategy were in place. Supporters of Russia had already been promoting messages about the Soviet Union and Ukraine in *Roblox*, *Minecraft* and *World of Tanks* by the summer of 2023, according to the *New York Times*.[35] But in October of that year, the first game that would begin to test the potential of Russia's new disinformation front was announced publicly.

SQUAD DISINFORMATION GOALS

Squad 22: ZOV is a free-to-play strategy game where you control a squad of Russian soldiers participating in the war in Ukraine. Developed by SPN Studio and a publisher called Zarobana Entertainment, both of which have never released a game before, the game allows you to guide your soldiers into a building in a similar manner to a SWAT team letting you check for blind spots, open fire on Ukrainian soldiers, and kill them to clear the mission. Art promoting the game on Steam shows a Russian soldier reloading as a Ukrainian falls to the ground.

The game is not shy about its intent. Each mini-campaign within the game is based on a part of the Ukrainian conflict, with players starting off in Mariupol and being able to buy access to further campaigns such as the 2014 incursion into the Donbass. The game's narrative, which has been localised into American English and Chinese only to ensure it can reach the two biggest languages on Steam, reinforces Russian narratives that soldiers are engaged in a defensive rather than offensive action. The prominent mention of ZOV in the game's title – a reference to the pro-war 'Z' painted on the side of Russian military hardware – is deliberately provocative, leading to the game's ban in Ukraine and Germany.

The development of the game has been led by an individual who founded a business which claims to be able to influence players. Alexander Tolkach, who was formerly a community manager at *War Thunder* developer Gaijin Entertainment and previously worked at Ukraine energy giant DTEK, is named as 'Producer, Game Designer, and author of the idea' for *Squad 22: ZOV* within its credits. In 2014, a full decade prior to the game's release, Tolkach became the CEO and founder at CT Influence Games. Headquartered in Austin, Texas, the company claims that its 'games are not merely for fun' and that they are capable of 'influencing public opinion'.[36]

*

The development of *Squad 22: ZOV* has also been supported by both individuals and institutions who have prosecuted the war in Ukraine. Its advisory board consists of Vlad 'Struna' Golovin, a career army officer who fought in the Mariupol campaign; Vlad 'Chaly', a soldier still serving in the Russian army; Daniil 'Goodwin' Bezsonov, a former militia volunteer in Donetsk who now poses as the head of press for the Russia-backed Donetsk People's Republic. Its development was also supported by the Main Military-Political Directorate of the Armed Forces of the Russian Federation. All of this information is publicly available on the game's website, which has listed all of these details in English.[37]

Squad 22: ZOV is also intended to be educational. The game's Steam description, which is handily anglicised, says that the 'game is officially recommended by the Russian Military for use as a basic infantry tactic manual for cadet and Yunarmiya [the Russian military cadets] training'. This is demonstrated in quite grim fashion in a YouTube video on the game's official channel, where Tolkach discusses the game with a room of dead-eyed Yunarmiya cadets. The video concludes with a montage of boys in oversized military uniforms and girls in red berets and red polo tops with smiles on their faces as they play the game where you kill Ukrainians, all to a perky soundtrack that you'd expect to hear on a generic uplifting corporate video.[38]

This is all eerie stuff. But what is the game like? According to Tolkach, the mechanics of it were inspired by the Romanian-developed game *Door Kickers*, which allowed you to move SWAT teams through buildings strategically using a 'tactical pause' that let each encounter play out like you're pausing a TV show to decide what to do next.

According to Mihai Gosa, the co-creator of *Door Kickers*, KillHouse Games, Tolkach's team had lifted the carefully thought-out and crafted tactical game that his team had made and turned it into a 'shitty propaganda tool'. And after spending some time with *Squad 22: ZOV*, he's bang on the money.

On a wet Saturday afternoon in London, I opened my Steam account, searched for the game and hit download. Five minutes later – maybe six, if you're accounting for the dodginess of my internet connection – the game was ready for me to play. Accessing disinformation has never been so easy.

After being shown a short introductory animated video explaining the stakes, narrated by Golovin because of course it was, I switched language from Russian to American before jumping into the tutorial.

The game had a similar premise to *Door Kickers*. You have a squad of men under your command. You move them around by drawing pathways with your mouse, using button prompts and mouse commands to get people to duck or prepare to open fire. You also have to pay attention to making sure your soldiers are looking in the right direction, otherwise they run the risk of being shot in the back because you decided to fling a door open and look the other way. The tutorial also teaches you how to patch up your squad mates because you don't want to leave any of your soldiers behind (an irony, considering the Russian military's enjoyment of 'meat grinder' combat tactics).[39]

In many ways the game looked similar to *Door Kickers*. In practice, it was a hell of a lot worse. The controls were fiddly, lacking the smoothness that had obviously been a big focus of the original development team. There were bugs in the game that meant it didn't function properly at times and there were obvious localisation blunders. And after finally taking a deep breath to allow myself to click on the Mariupol level, the user interface was so badly designed that I managed to accidentally start the first mission with just a single soldier who, I'll admit, I was quietly delighted to send to his death.

Squad 22: ZOV is an objectively bad video game. It would probably have a higher median play time than 1.1 hours on Steam if it was considerably better than it currently is. Its offer to sell you paid downloadable content by letting you buy in-game extras through Steam's wallet feature, which allows you to circumvent the need for a credit card to buy stuff, would be a lot more worrisome if the content wasn't utterly worthless.

But as with Russia's wider disinformation strategy, the point about *Squad 22: ZOV* isn't whether it is any good or not; it's whether it has been able to generate a media multiplier effect that made the investment worthwhile. And outside of me somewhat oxymoronically dedicating a chunk of a published book to it, its footprint has extended beyond the game through wider information channels.

On the press side, the story of a Russian propaganda game corrupting young minds has hooked the media. Consumer games press sites such as *Eurogamer* and *PC Gamer* covered its release, noting its roots as a Russian information campaign. Ukrainian news media like the *Kyiv Independent* and *UNITED24 Media* each dedicated digital column inches to covering it. British tabloid the *Daily Star* reported, 'Russian army's "official" video game promises more levels if Ukraine doesn't surrender', making it seem as if Putin's cronies are using the threat of a bad time in a video game to force the war to an early end.[40] Ukraine's Ministry of Digital Affairs also released a public statement saying it had written to Steam to ask for the game's removal, which occurred shortly thereafter.[41] The developers of the game reposted coverage of the game on their VKontakte page, recycling the story to their followers.[42]

But *Squad 22: ZOV* also showed via Steam's in-built social functions how a video game and the infrastructure around it create a new surface for attack in digital media.

The game's community pages have transformed into a place for mostly pro-Russian activists to post visual memes denigrating Ukraine. One image shows Volodomyr Zelenskyy standing in front of spectral projections of Osama bin Laden, Manuel Noriega, Saddam Hussein and Colonel Gaddafi, each reaching down to him as American 'allies' who have since been deposed. Another image shows a picture of a pig with a gun to its head, referencing Russian efforts to call Ukrainians 'Nazi pigs'. And in a foreshadowing of the way that video games culture has become a trope in extremist spaces, there's also an image of Russian soldiers in an elevator looking at a camera with the caption 'Remember No Ukrainian' – a darkly tongue-in-cheek reference to that notorious *Call of Duty* level.

Many of the images feature multiple comments from Russian users, whose unimpeded access to Steam's communication channels allows them to share their views on the platform. One comment in response to a pro-Ukrainian user asking whether the developer would donate proceeds of the game to Kyiv asks whether the Ukrainians would like an Iskander missile fired at them instead.[43]

By releasing *Squad 22: ZOV*, Russia hasn't just created a game as a possible channel for influence; it has also encouraged the activation of the platform's surprisingly high Russian-language user base to support its cause. And whether these comments are genuinely from grassroots users or from people creating content on behalf of the regime, Steam's irresponsible content moderation approach has left Russian actors with a channel through which to disinform others and to allow their supporters to congregate.

But it isn't only the Russian military that is using games for influence. The most powerful proxy arm of the country's armed forces was using games for influence before *Squad 22: ZOV* was announced. And in this particular case, it was a video game influencer who helped them lead the way.

THE OTHER PUTIN

Grisha Putin, real name Grigorii Korolev, looks like a typical video game YouTuber. The teenager, who is likely to be an adult by the time you read this, has nearly 25,000 people following his YouTube channel as of July 2025. He boasts about the fact that he's one of the best players of Paradox Interactive's Second World War-themed military strategy game *Hearts of Iron IV*. His social media feed gives glimpses of a typical teenage life. A photo with his classmates celebrating the end of school. A selfie with his mum as he's weighing up his university options.

Then you look at the header image on his X profile and see him posing happily alongside Yevgeny Prigozhin: founder of the Wagner Military Group and the Internet Research Agency. And before you know it, you're tumbling down a rabbit hole that takes you all the way to Burkina Faso.

Grisha, as I'll call him to avoid confusion with the president, is as close as I've seen to a state-backed video game influencer. Between his typical teenage social media posting on YouTube, Grisha washes carefully selected memes which reference Russian talking points – such as its hostility towards LGBTQ+ communities or its thoughts on the Gaza conflict – in a manner that's *just* about careful enough to prevent him from having his account taken down.

By the time you read this, there's a chance that it will be gone. And if it is, we will have lost a resource that can help us understand how he went from a run-of-the-mill Russian YouTuber to the face of Wagner Military Group to video game players in Africa.

Grisha's rise to odd prominence in the eyes of Russia's most notable private military group starts in the way all video game influencer careers did: he made content about his favourite video games.

Before the war in Ukraine, Grisha's videos were so unbelievably run of the mill. His first video on his channel is providing players with recommendations on the best templates to use to create military divisions in *Hearts of Iron,* with Grisha earnestly discussing why one of the templates is the best because it has a good mix of tanks and armoured vehicles. His two most popular videos – which, again, were both released before Russia invaded Ukraine – are memes about how overpowered the in-game railway guns are and that it would have taken the Soviet Union ages to order its troops about if it had to manage its response to Operation Barbarossa in a strategy game. And his main schtick for his Twitch streaming was 'Live Action Role-Playing' (LARPing) as historical generals, dressing up in a variety of hats depending on which national army he was commanding.

By the turn of 2022, Grisha's content started to change. He posted a short video of himself providing opinions on liberals, filming himself throwing an item to the ground before cutting to an explosion. He posts a sombre video of himself standing in front of a statue of Lenin commemorating the thirtieth anniversary of the end of the Soviet Union, eventually wandering up to the statue to lay flowers. His 'New Year Address' to his community of followers – which he says were across platforms like Twitch and Discord as well as YouTube – is a video of Grisha talking over the top of Vladimir Putin giving his annual address.

But the video that seems to have truly set himself on the pathway to becoming Russia's pet influencer arrived on 23 February 2022 – the day before his home country invaded its next-door neighbour. 'How to conquer UKRAINE AS RUSSIA in Hoi4 (GUIDE)' is only seventy seconds long, but shows him running an invasion of Ukraine in a modified version of *Heart of Irons IV* called 'Millenium Dawn' which replaces Second World War soldiers with modern military forces. During the video, he makes references to sending a Russian-language version to Vladimir Putin, talks about taking 'prisoners of war', and rounds off by completing the invasion in seven days.

There's nothing here to suggest that Grisha knew anything more about Russia's invasion plans than what was being reported in the media. However, the video went on to become one of his most viewed pieces of content – accruing 149,000 views.

From that point onwards, Grisha's content became more nationalistic. The uploaded videos on his YouTube channel mostly stopped referencing his favourite game and instead showcased talking points such as his love of the Soviet Union. He increasingly started to appear on the live-streaming channel Twitch in full military camo, cosplaying as a soldier. His You-Tube channel's post history also shows his efforts to try to become a part of the Russian state he loves, failing in his effort to become a police officer before joining United Russia's Youth Wing to drop supplies off to soldiers in Mariupol.

By February 2023, Vaspaan Dastoor of *The Gamer* wrote that Grisha's antics had led to him being shunned by the *Hearts of Iron IV* community who, somewhat unsurprisingly, found his whole schtick a bit odd.[44] But that month also marked the moment that Grisha's relationship with the Wagner Military Group went public.

According to Grisha, the relationship had started at the beginning of the year. After being ostracised from the *Hearts of Iron IV* community, he walked up to Wagner's centre in St Petersburg, went to the reception desk and asked whether he could see the head of public relations to ask if he could live-stream there. They agreed, giving him the chance to run an online multiplayer version of his favourite game to support the war.[45]

Over the course of six weeks, Grisha in full military kit live-streamed games from the group's headquarters in St Petersburg via his channel on Russian streaming site VKontakte.[46] On 4 February 2023, Grisha played a modded version of his favourite strategy game which pitted Russia's proxy Ukrainian republic against Ukraine itself under the auspices of Russia vs NATO. With nuclear weapons turned on in game, Grisha swept through Ukraine, obliterated a number of European capitals, and then eventually agreed a 'peace' deal with another player representing America. Then on 18 February, Grisha set up the game with the same premise minus the nukes. On this occasion, he rolled himself all the way to America's East Coast – crushing opposition before him. His final game of this round of streaming on 18 March put him in charge of Russia's Special Military Operation, triumphantly achieving what Russia's military had not done by steamrolling through Ukraine.

Grisha did not reach a big audience. According to *PC Gamer*, his first stream successfully reached 12,000 people. That's only just enough to fill my beloved Kenilworth Road, home of the almighty Luton Town.

But the stream had an impact. For Grisha, his antics alienated two businesses who made his reach possible. Paradox Interactive, the company who created *Hearts of Iron* and other world class strategy games not about the Second World War, began hitting his Twitch channel with copyright strikes. By the end of 2023, Grisha's Twitch channel had been suspended and was later banned on the basis of promoting terrorist content. Similar concerns would lead to his Discord also being whipped offline, forcing him to set new ones up in an effort to keep his audience in place.

Grisha, however, kept going. As well as meeting Prigozhin in person, who Grisha described as 'chill and respectful' (which is a hell of a thing to say about a mercenary), he returned to Wagner's St Petersburg offices in July 2023 to play the ultra-realistic military video game *ARMA 3*. In the same month, he showed once again that Steam's content moderation policies are non-existent by setting up a Steam group called 'Z Shaker Central' to bring his fans together. At the time of writing, the group remains online, currently has over 400 active members, and has raised tens of thousands of dollars for the Wagner Military Group to support its operations in Ukraine.

The death of Prigozhin in a plane crash, in the aftermath of an aborted rebellion against Putin's regime on 23 August 2023, could have easily forestalled the relationship. A clip posted to Reddit the following day showed Grisha in tears at the news of the death of his PR partner.[47] But instead of waning, the partnership grew further – expanding the disinformation value of Grisha to the group by leaning back into the country's plans to develop games.

Inspired by the work he had done with Wagner, Grisha created – stick with me here – a modified version of the modified version of *Hearts of Iron IV* that he had played on the live stream. *Millennium Dawn* became *African Dawn*. And the objective of the game was now no longer about Russia rolling through Ukraine; it was about African states choosing the right partner to build their future.

According to DFRLab, *African Dawn* lands the player in the middle of Africa in September 2022. After defeating 'terrorists' in the Sahel, a cold war emerges between the Alliance of Sahel States (a real-life pact between Burkina Faso, Niger and Mali) and the Economic Community of West African States. Players must then navigate a war between the various powers involved, eventually deciding whether to side with Russia – who is supporting a free Africa – or France and the US (who plan to return it to its colonial form).[48]

The narrative is explicit enough without mentioning the in-game news stories, which provide Wagner-approved perspectives on news events that happened in the years that followed (including the death of Prigozhin). It was also obvious enough that Paradox unsurprisingly banned the mod: forcing Grisha and his allies to encourage its installation via a separate web launcher.

But once again, the disinformation within the game was turned to a much larger purpose. Wagner, which had been swallowed up by the Russian government and rebranded as the Africa Corps in February 2024,[49] promoted the release of the modified version of the game in Africa itself, using the resources of the African Initiative – a Russian online news service that's based in Moscow but has ex-Wagner staff employed within the business.[50] And in July 2024, Grisha met with the attaché for Burkina Faso – one of the nations featured prominently in *African Dawn* – to once again live-stream a game in which he 'defeated terrorists and demolished Western neocolonialists'.

This, naturally, was too juicy for the media to resist. By February 2025, Grisha's story had spread across the world as the gamer working with the Wagner Military Group. NBC News, the *Wall Street Journal* and Germany's 2DF news broadcaster all carried stories on Grisha between his emergence on the live stream and the time of writing. Even without a huge audience for his streams, Grisha has acted as a multiplier for Wagner narratives through the media to millions of people. The question is what intent lay behind his actions. In an interview with St Petersburg State University, where Grisha is currently studying, he denied that he was promoting Russian narratives uncritically. Instead, he claimed that his activities were focused on 'combating Western disinformation, disseminating accurate information about the special military operation.'[51] Following his efforts to patriotically promote Russian viewpoints, views on Grisha's YouTube channel dropped considerably from hundreds of thousands of views per post to tens of thousands. Audiences were forming their own opinion of his activities.

But his social presence spread into authoritarian spheres in strange ways. In October 2024, Grisha appears to have received an automated message from Donald Trump's X account as the now president continued his efforts to campaign for a second term.[52] He also told History Legends that he has grown a social media following in East Germany and China through his fund-raising efforts for the Russian army, painting anime characters onto shells in return for cash.[53]

Squad 22: ZOV and Grisha Putin have both shown that video games content and creators can be used to create materials that can spread disinformation both within game spaces and as a result of media multiplying the outputs uncritically to their audiences. But what does Russia do when it fears that the other side is trying to use a game to promote its narrative? The answer is they attack it: they try to damage and discredit it in an effort to stop its story from cutting through.

STALKED BY THE ENEMY

S.T.A.L.K.E.R: Shadow of Chernobyl is one of Russia's most popular video games. The 2007 first-person survival horror video game set in the Chernobyl exclusion zone became a hit upon its release, with the title and its expansion packs selling fifteen million copies between its launch and August 2021.[54]

Its popularity is based on a few things. The game fits the 'Slavic shooter' archetype, appealing to local audiences. It was created for PC, meaning it lined up nicely with how audiences want to play. It was also one of the few games set in the region that was also developed there, providing it with authenticity to Russian audiences.

However, the game was not developed in Russia. The game was created in Ukraine by a studio called GSC Game World. And as the studio worked its way through the early years of the war to get its long-awaited sequel into the market, Russian actors turned the studio, its employees and the game itself into targets for its information war.

The development of a sequel to *S.T.A.L.K.E.R.* took a long time to get going. A couple of years after the release of the original game, Sergiy Grygorovych, the founder of the business, began working on a successor to the hit game and announced the company's plans to release it soon. The problem was that he and the team had exhausted themselves developing the first game in the series. This led to the cancellation of the sequel and the entire studio entering hiatus in 2011.

'Sergiy actually started working on the sequel,' said Zakhar Bocharov, GSC Game World's communication lead, a Russian-born citizen who proudly describes himself as 'anti-Putin'. 'But his burnout caused by intense game development, his uncertainty about the quality of the sequel and whether it can be something culturally important at that time caused the company to go nonoperational for quite some time.'

The company ended its development freeze in 2014. Evgeniy Grygorovych, Sergiy's brother and one of GSC's earliest employees, took over as CEO. His wife, Maria Grygorovych, would later take on the key role of creative director.

After releasing a remake of a game called *Cossacks 3*, a strategy title that had established the studio's reputation, the company announced in May 2018 that it once again was working on a sequel to *S.T.A.L.K.E.R.*, using Epic's Unreal Engine to bring it to life in spectacular fashion, with the intention to release it in late 2021. The team scaled up significantly in size, growing from thirty employees to hundreds of workers to meet the scale and scope of the game. In June 2021, GSC Game World announced that the game was nearly ready but its release date had slipped to 28 April 2022.[55]

The delays were frustrating for fans, who had been waiting over a decade for a follow-up to one of their favourite games. But for the team, the long development timeline meant the sequel arrived in a markedly different world from the one into which the original game launched.

Between 2007 and 2021, Russia brought war to Ukraine's door. In 2004, Ukraine had celebrated a 'colour revolution' – much to the displeasure of Russia's leadership. After Ukrainians expressed their keenness to pursue democracy, the Russian state had sought through sympathetic leaders in the country to suppress those urges.

This was a factor behind the 2013 Euromaidan protests following Viktor Yanukovych's sudden decision not to sign an association agreement with the European Union. This led to the country's Revolution of Dignity in February 2014, which saw Yanukovych flee the country after pro-democracy protestors were fired upon by police. In the aftermath of the invasion, Russia annexed Crimea and formally incorporated it into the state. Pro-Russian separatists also seized control of the city of Donetsk, proclaiming it the home of the Russian-backed Donetsk People's Republic.

'For every Ukrainian, the war with Russia started back in 2014,' said Bocharov. This meant that the refounded GSC Game World was no longer developing games in peacetime Ukraine; it was a studio working through a war.

However, the impact of the war would begin to be fully felt a number of years later. As the pandemic began to wane in 2021, Russia stepped up its preparations for a full-scale invasion of Ukraine. GSC Game World adapted accordingly. In a feature for the *Guardian*, journalist Tom Regan remarks that the team hadn't noticed 'the strange buses parked around the corner' of the company's offices in January 2022. The buses had been hired by GSC's leadership team to sit there twenty-four hours a day, ready to ferry employees to Uzhhorod, a small Ukrainian city on the Slovakian border, if war did break out.[56]

A month later, roughly a week before the start of the war, the company's leadership team told employees on a company-wide Zoom call that the buses had been hired to carry them to safety if Russia invaded. They recommended that employees join them. A large chunk of the team boarded the vehicles. For those who chose to remain in Kyiv, 24 February 2022 looms large in the memory.

*

'I genuinely recall this as one of the most dark and chaotic days in my life,' said Bocharov. 'It seemed like the whole territory was bombed on February twenty-fourth. It seemed like everything was irreparably breaking at the moment . . . it feels like a natural cataclysm of some kind, like you're standing and watching how the star explodes in the sky and you're so absorbed in the sheer scale of the event happening that you can't even comprehend how deep the consequences will go.'

The consequences of war were felt almost immediately by the studio. The day after the invasion, Ukraine barred men of military age from leaving the country. A number of GSC employees would therefore remain in Kyiv, in some cases fighting on the frontlines. Volodymyr Yezhov, one of the company's game developers, signed up to fight the day that the war started. He was killed in Russia's offensive against Bakhmut later that same year.[57]

In bleak circumstances, the developers did what they could to resume development. After announcing an indefinite pause to plans to release the game due to the war, the company's leadership set about both supporting the staff left in Kyiv and establishing a new base for the game's development in Prague to house employees who had left for the border – a serious challenge for a large video game development business in the late stage of making a game.

'It's impossible in the business world to plan to open a new legal entity in a new country you've never been to before and you don't know anything about,' said Evgeniy Grygorovych.

GSC's set-up in Prague was aided by the national government and the local game development scene, who helped speed up the company's establishment. This allowed it to restart work on development of the game in May 2022, working with the remaining staff in Kyiv. The practical consequences of creating in the midst of a war were felt daily.

*

'Workwise, it means practically you can be on a Zoom call, the air raid starts and the Ukrainian part of the team goes off, they stay in the shelter, then they come back, and continue working,' said Bocharov. The Prague team also adapted to Ukrainian staff working between blackouts, establishing schedules that lined up with when the country announced it was turning out the lights each day to protect citizens from bombardment.

The psychological effect of the war also had a major effect on the team, with staff balancing the day-to-day stresses of creating games with the reality of being at war.

*

'We had a huge challenge on how to solve our psychological reactions to the war,' explains Evgeniy. 'It's both hard to operate normally and be efficient when you are reading the news about your friends, families, [and] what's going on. And you have to fight for yourself, your health and also the team, which is huge. It's the experience other companies are not facing. There is always a crisis when someone is doing the work for three years on a project. But it's nothing compared to the existential crisis of the national scale when, like, someone is trying to erase your nation from the Earth.'

Like so many organisations and businesses based in Ukraine, GSC Game World used their profile to support the defence of the country. On the day that the full-scale invasion started, the company posted on social media encouraging people to donate directly to the country's coffers. By the end of April 2022, GSC had raised $800,000 through sales of its existing games to support the country's Come Back Alive Foundation, which funnelled cash to the Ukrainian military to combat the invasion.[58]

The company was also recognising its ability to act as a form of soft power for Ukraine's cause. In March 2022, the company announced that it was changing the subtitle of its sequel to include the Ukrainian spelling of 'Chornoybyl'. It added Ukrainian folk and jazz music to the game's soundtrack to give it an authentically Ukrainian feel. By June 2022, the company had announced that the game would not be localised into Russian, sold in Russia or contain Russian-language voice acting in response to the war.[59] The Ukrainian government also recognised its contribution to the cause, with the country's Ministry of Defence posting an English-language tribute when the death of Volodymyr Yezhov was publicly announced.[60]

GSC Game World's public stance on the war was brave. It also made them a target for a range of actions from Russian actors, who sought to damage, discredit and intimidate the development team in response to its support for Ukraine.

Almost immediately after the war began, the studio started to suffer attacks from Russian hackers who sought to leak confidential information from the business. After fending off waves of attacks in cyberspace, the company announced in March 2023 that hackers had breached its defences and were threatening to release private documents about the game and the people working on it if GSC Game World did not comply with their demands.

'It was not only a way to steal our internal materials like concept art, story or some early builds of the game,' said Evgeniy. 'It was also the personal data of our employees, like their passport identity data [which was kept by the company's human resources team within their personnel files]. And a lot of this was just on the internet.'

What was intriguing were the demands of the hackers. Rather than asking for cash, the community who had hacked the game posted a handful of demands that were entirely oriented towards the developer's decision not to localise the game into Russian.

As *PC Gamer* reported, the hackers wrote in Russian that GSC needed to 'change your mind, rethink your attitude towards players from Belarus and Russia, apologise for the unworthy attitude towards ordinary players from these countries'. The hacker also said that the game required 'the return of ru-localisation' because 'it is not necessary to spoil the game for people because of politics'.[61]

GSC Game World did not give in to the hackers, leading to the release of materials across the web. Fortunately, the company had the backing of the game's wider community. Despite having the opportunity to have an early look at the game before release, supporters of the game resisted the urge to look at leaked materials and suppressed their spread through community social media channels – tempering the effectiveness of the campaign.

Rather than weakening *S.T.A.L.K.E.R. 2*, the hackers inadvertently strengthened it by encouraging the rest of the game development community to row in behind it.

As development of the game continued into 2023, the company was able to strike a deal with Microsoft to bring the game to its Game Pass subscription service from launch after Bocharov directly emailed Xbox boss Phil Spencer using an email address he stumbled upon on Reddit. This provided much needed funding for the studio, helping it to expand its staff to nearly 500 people. It also gave the game a major boost in profile, with it featured across multiple Microsoft showcases. By the time the game launched, Bocharov told me that the main trailer for the game had been viewed over 2.5 million times. That was more views than for *Halo: Infinite*, the most recent release in one of Xbox's most popular franchises.

The impact of the war on the game's development meant that its release date stretched further into 2024. But when it did finally release on 20 November 2024, Russia's media and political machinery whirred into action. *S.T.A.L.K.E.R. 2* suffered a wave of attacks designed to disinform audiences at home and abroad about the game.

According to Evgeniy, Russian broadcast media including Russia Today began denouncing the game as 'fascist' propaganda and warned that it could turn Russian young people against the rest of the country.

'I think for the local market, their audience and especially for non-gamers, it worked,' he explained. 'Some grandfathers and grandmothers that have nothing to do with games were listening to reports about Ukrainian propaganda teams that are doing some propaganda project to [get players] to fight against their mother and something like that. So it had some effect.'

Players in the country who were considering playing the game were also warned off with the threat of potential criminal sanction. Anton Gorelkin, the deputy chairman of the state Duma's Committee on Information Policy of Russia, said that the game could be banned due to GSC's support for the Ukrainian armed forces and unspecified 'extremist' content. Mikhail Mushailov, a Russian legal expert, told United 24 that buying the game via an international storefront could be defined as supporting a 'hostile force' – potentially leading to Russian players being prosecuted under local terrorism laws.[62]

Finally, the threat that *S.T.A.L.K.E.R. 2* posed to the authorities led to the creation of an international disinformation campaign aimed at discouraging Ukrainian people from playing it. 404 Media reported in late November 2024 that Russian actors were circulating a false video bearing the watermark of media outlet *Wired* which claimed that the game was being used to find young men who'd dodged the draft.[63] The video was localised into English to ensure it spread further.

But Russia's campaigning did not stop the game's release from becoming a moment of celebration in Ukraine. Within days of launch, *S.T.A.L.K.E.R. 2* had sold over a million copies around the world. The Ukrainian parliament offered celebratory remarks on the day of the game's launch, while the *Kyiv Independent* reported that soldiers on the frontlines were joining a national 'frenzy' to play the game throughout their downtime.[64] By January 2025, GSC Game World had been invited to Davos, where they spoke about the game on behalf of the Victor Pinchuk Foundation.[65]

Russia's attacks on the game had not dampened enthusiasm for it. Instead, it turned it into a national phenomenon that the team could barely believe.

*

'It was a huge success all over the world, but particularly in Ukraine. It was a national scale moment, something like the football World Cup and everyone was talking about *S.T.A.L.K.E.R*,' said Evgeniy, with genuinely earned pride. 'Everyone understands that it's a project made in Ukraine by Ukrainians in a situation of war. It's a symbol of surviving and still having an impact.'

And for Maria Grygorovych, successfully releasing the game was a sign to the world that Ukrainians would not give up in the face of Russian aggression. 'It's a kind of resistance. You can do whatever you want to us. But we will do projects. We will make games. And we will do great things. You can try to kill us all, but it's just impossible. We will survive.'

Russia's attempt to crush the spirit of a Ukrainian game developer contesting its narratives had failed. But its aggression shows the seriousness with which the country's supporters are willing to contest the video game information space: attempting to suppress their rivals to try and forcibly control the way we view the world.

PLAYING WITH TRUTH

In his book about active measures, Thomas Rid warns readers to apply a critical eye to Russian disinformation campaigns.

While he writes that Western democracies often underestimated the effectiveness of Russian campaigning, he also warned against the dangers of overcorrecting and providing undue credit to their operations.

And when we cast a critical eye over the actual effectiveness of Russian disinformation campaigning within video games, there is little sign that measures – whether active or otherwise – have had much impact in the games space alone.

Squad 22: ZOV had accrued a measly 16,000 downloads at time of writing; a disaster for a free-to-play video game. Grisha Putin's organic social media profile has collapsed almost entirely since he traded in being a video game streamer for that of a Wagner mouthpiece, while also being mocked online by influencers from the *Hearts of Iron IV* community that he was ejected from.[66] Russian campaigns against *S.T.A.L.K.E.R. 2* turned a popular video game into a symbol of Russia's aggression against Ukraine, transforming it into a source of genuine national pride and international prestige for Ukrainians under fire.

The country has also embarrassed itself via its use of games for disinformation before the Ukraine conflict, after the Russian Ministry of Defence posted a screenshot from a video game as apparently irrefutable proof of American activity in Syria. 'Even Russia Today published a bit saying, you know, look how silly the Russian MoD is,' said Eliot Higgins, founder of Open Source Investigative journalism outfit Bellingcat. 'You know they've really fucked up when Russia Today is talking about it.'

And while Russia has talked a good game about creating its own industry ecosystem, its big measures have added up to very little in practice. *Squad 22: ZOV* is one of the only games to emerge from its strategy so far and its low quality suggests that Russia's big-budget games will struggle to succeed.

Plans for Russia's video games console were revealed in late 2024 and were immediately mocked by Redditors, who suggested that the 'Putindo' console was laughably underpowered for modern tastes.[67] The weakening of Russia's games industry as a result of its actions in Ukraine can be seen by the state's decision to seize a studio called Lesta Studios from its previous owners Wargaming, one of Russia's biggest games developers who exited the country after the outbreak of the war and immediately began fundraising on behalf of Ukraine.[68]

Yet Russia's use of video games within its influence campaigning and military machine continues to evolve, despite these failures. Exiled Russian news outlet *The Insider* reported that children who played a game about protecting bears from bees stealing their honey were participating in the first stage of a multi-step recruitment programme for the next generation of drone pilots, with effective players funnelled towards the military by Russia's Agency for Strategic Initiatives.[69]

Meanwhile, online campaigners – whose links to Russia are hard to prove or disprove – have used footage from games more successfully than the Russian Ministry of Defence to disrupt democratic discourse. The creators of realistic military shooter *ARMA 3* were forced to release a blog post in October 2023 warning people that footage from the game was being edited and shared on social media with the aim of claiming to be from live warzones such as Ukraine and Gaza.[70] And as recently as June 2025, Estelle Nilsson-Julien of Euroverify reported that footage from an *ARMA* YouTube site called UMC had been clipped and reshared falsely as footage of Ukraine's Operation Spiderweb offensive against military targets across Russia – demonstrating how thin the line can get between user-generated game content and social media deception.[71]

And then there's the curious case of *Atomic Heart*, which was created by development studio Mundfish that was founded in Russia and is funded by investors including Tencent, Gaijin (the creators of *War Thunder*) and GEM Capital, a firm founded by Anatoly Paliy – a man described as an 'executive in Gazprom entities for over ten years.'[72]

The role-playing game, which is set in a stylised future of the Soviet Union where a **KGB** operative investigates robots who have gone rogue and launched almost exactly a year after the full-scale invasion started, is notionally 'apolitical', with the studio distancing itself from claims that it is part of Russia's propaganda machinery after the army used iconography from the game within its adverts.[73]

However, Ukrainian players have discovered numerous disparaging references to their country in the game, including blue and yellow painted tins of 'pork', postcards of Donetsk which implies ongoing Russian ownership, and flying robots holding flowers that look like 'geraniums' – a term used by Russian soldiers for Iranian-made drones used on the frontlines.[74] And while Mundfish's website no longer lists Russia as a development base for the business, the game was celebrated in a November 2022 Soviet Union-themed party hosted by VKontakte in St Petersburg.[75]

It is nearly impossible to tell whether the game's references are sarcastic, tasteless or an influence campaign. Mundfish continues to assert that it is operating entirely independently from state actors. But with Mundfish securing a twenty-minute showcase for the sequel to the game, and other titles in its portfolio, during the 2025 Summer Game Fest video game showcase – which was watched by tens of millions of people across the world – it is important for the video games industry to resolve the ongoing ambiguity about Mundfish's ownership (and, by extension, its intentions).

Ultimately though, the measure of the effectiveness of Russia's video game campaigning is not about what happens in a video game itself; it's about how effectively the messages, narratives and disinformation it has generated gets 'multiplied' through media outlets with the aim of flooding the discourse. And by co-opting, controlling and collaborating with developers and influencers across the space, either through direct influence or simply by shaping Russia's internal narrative to encourage people to believe the state is telling the truth, it is able to reach audiences both directly and indirectly through often credulous reporting of the effectiveness of its campaigning through legacy media and on social media – dominating the conversation in the process.

While much of this chapter has focused on the use of games to promote narratives around the war in Ukraine, the effectiveness of the medium as a multiplier for messaging has encouraged Russia to use games to attack audiences across the Atlantic too.

In September 2024, *Wired* reported that the US Department of Justice (DOJ) had unsealed documents alleging that Ilya Gambashidze, a Russian working for state-backed disinformation channel the Social Design Agency, had identified eighteen- to thirty-year-old men in America as ideal targets for a disinformation campaign called 'The Good Old USA Project'.

The documents, which the DOJ claims are written by Gambashidze, state that the 'community of American gamers, users of Reddit and image boards, such as 4chan' were a key audience for the campaign. They went on to describe this category of players as the 'backbone of the right-wing trends in the US segment of the internet', marking out their value to Russia's campaigning goals.[76]

Separating this group of people from the rest of society was therefore considered key to helping Russia exercise wider influence in the US and beyond. And as we'll see in the final two chapters of this part of the book, the successful isolation and radicalisation of people within this demographic has had alarming consequences at the ballot box and on the streets of the world.

8

The gamer-fication of terror

On the afternoon of 14 May 2022, Buffalo in New York State was rocked by a mass shooting at the Tops Friendly Market in the city's east side.

An eighteen-year-old white supremacist armed with an assault rifle, a shotgun and a loaded bolt-action rifle, and cloaked in camouflage fatigues, stepped out of his car at approximately 2.30 p.m. His aim was to walk into the store and 'never stop firing' at its Black customers.[1]

He kept to his word. The shooter murdered three people in the parking lot, injuring another. He walked into the supermarket and killed Aaron Salter Jr., the store's security guard, who laid down his life in an attempt to stop the shooter. Shortly after, he would murder another six Black customers in the store. The murderer only stopped the killings to apologise to a white store worker who he accidentally injured during his rampage.

This act of terror devastated Buffalo's Black community and left the families of the victims bereft. Kimberley Salter told investigators for New York State's Attorney General that 'my best friend was taken from me. The love of my husband was taken from me.' Garnell Whitfield Jr, meanwhile, described the murder of his 86-year-old mother Ruth Whitfield as feeling 'like somebody reached inside me and pulled the best part out of me.'

But while the attack was committed by one teenager, the shooter did not act alone. Before entering the parking lot, he had strapped a camera to his chest to live-stream the shooting to mimic both the feel of a first-person shooter video game and footage from a 2019 mass shooting committed in Christchurch in New Zealand.

Despite the footage being pulled from streaming services like Twitch in a matter of minutes, it wasn't enough. A community of toxic gamers, which had grown and festered in little-seen or unmoderated corners of the internet, had grabbed enough footage from the stream to clip it for social media services, distribute it via public channels, and circulate it through closed groups like Telegram.[2] The same community also re-created the attacks in games like *Roblox*, recording themselves playing these transgressive creations so they could distribute the footage of their recreations on social media.

The perpetrator's attack showed a disturbing overlap between the evolution of violent extremism and toxic gamer subcultures. Nihilistic young men across the world have increasingly become 'self-radicalised', mixing together hateful ideologies and content to create their own reasons to enact violence on the world. But in many instances, these men still need a group dynamic to justify their action.

Immersing themselves in toxic video game fandoms congregating around sites such as 4chan or 8kun (previously known as the 4chan spinoff group 8chan), 'gamer-fying' terror by draping it in the aesthetics, references and in-jokes of video games, has emboldened these individuals to act, encouraged the glorification of their actions and aided the spread of their dark world view through a horrified media.

The results have been the deaths of hundreds of people across the world, including Charlie Kirk, the right-wing political commentator who was assassinated by a shooter who had allegedly carved video games references into the ammunition found at the scene of the crime. And without action to decisively sever the link between video game culture and nihilistic groups who seek to co-opt it for their own ends, a medium designed to entertain billions will continue to be used, and tarnished, by people who seek to repurpose it for disgustingly violent means.

THE CHANGING FACE OF VIOLENT EXTREMISM

Extremism, which is defined by the Institute for Strategic Dialogue (ISD) as 'the advocacy of political and social changes in line with a system of belief that claims the superiority and dominance of one identity-based "in-group" over an "out-group"', has always been a challenge to society.

But over the past few decades, the emergence and spread of the internet has changed its character. What was once a comparatively ordered, organised and definable problem has become individualised, chaotic and unpredictable. People who commit acts of extremism, particularly violent ones, increasingly do so on the basis of a world-view they've constructed entirely for themselves: changing the rationale behind their actions in a way that is immensely challenging for society to respond to.

At the turn of the twenty-first century, acts of violent extremism tended to be committed within a traditional, 'offline' structure. Usually, a group would form an ideology of hate. The leadership of that group would direct its members to engage in violent acts. And those acts would rely upon physical networks of connection to enable them to take place.

The 9/11 attack showed how this worked in practice. The attack itself was shocking, with the use of passenger jets within a suicide attack an utterly unexpected inversion on the traditional terror group practice of abducting planes for the purposes of hostage taking. But the 9/11 Commission Report showed how the attacks were organised within a typical violent extremist approach. The attack was directed from the top down by Osama bin Laden and Khalid Sheikh Mohammed. The rationale for the attack came from a coherent, although pungent, ideological view, rooted within a fundamentalist interpretation of Islam which encouraged holy war on behalf of their religion. Physical networks played a key role in determining who took part in the attack, with the large numbers of Saudi men involved in the attack a direct result of the demographic make-up of Al-Qaeda's training camps.[3]

However, extremists and terror groups were already exploring the possibilities presented to them by newly emerging online channels of communication. In 1995, Don Black, the Grand Wizard of the Ku Klux Klan and member of the American Nazi Party, created the Stormfront online forum because the internet provided the far right an opportunity to 'reach an audience . . . so easily and so inexpensively'. By the mid 2000s, extremist groups operating across the spectrum of hate had reached the same conclusion. Islamic State (also known as Daesh and ISIS), for example, became effective at churning out captivating digital propaganda, localising it and spreading it across social media to recruit individuals for its war in the Middle East.[4] It also, in an early foreshadowing of the gamerfication of terror a decade or so later, started to appropriate gameplay footage from military video games to use the aesthetics of games to lure young men into its cause.[5]

Towards the end of the 2010s, the impact of digital channels in encouraging people to commit violent extremist acts began to rise up the political agenda. A wave of terror attacks in the UK in 2017 led to the country's prime minister, Theresa May, warning that Islamist ideology had found a 'safe space' in the corners of the online world and was using that position to spread carnage into the real world.

But while Daesh claimed responsibility for attacks in London and Manchester, such as the murder of seven people in Borough Market in June 2017,[6] a report by David Anderson QC that profiled the attackers showed something different. It found that

Daesh had 'employed its formidable propaganda effort to inspire rather than to direct acts of terrorism'. The individuals who carried out the attack were solo actors or small groups, who did so without direction from the centre. And although nearly half of the individuals were part of proscribed terror groups or were known to the security services, half weren't. It wasn't just the police who didn't know where the perpetrators had come from; Daesh didn't either.

At this point, it was becoming increasingly clear that the nature of violent extremism was changing in the online world. Traditional extremist or terror attacks were still being directed, or encouraged, by hateful organisations. But increasingly, individuals were starting to 'self-radicalise'. Instead of becoming a member of a group directly, meeting up with other like-minded people, and following orders from the top down, people were taking a different path.

Young men, typically aged between their teens and thirties and often with a mental health problem, were riffing on multiple sources of hate to construct their own chaotic ideology. After starting with a common form of hate such as misogyny or racism, individuals built their violent world view from the sources they cherry-picked on the internet. At times, their view could be informed by propaganda shared by a terror or extremist group. But equally, they might be inspired by hateful online communities who share footage or reproductions of school shootings for transgressive thrills.[7] They could have been driven to act by insidious 'com' networks, which have been responsible for spreading real-world violence by extorting vulnerable teens to commit crimes.[8] Or they could have drawn part of their inspiration from 'gore' communities, where people can relatively easily access and share content such as beheading videos or the aftermath of terror attacks with one another.[9]

Whatever the individual pathway, the risks of this form of radicalisation were becoming abundantly clear. In July 2024 in

Southport in the United Kingdom, an eighteen-year-old killed three girls attending a Taylor Swift dance class. Despite being referred to Prevent, the country's multi-agency counter-terror programme, on three occasions between 2019 and 2021, the attacker's case was closed because he lacked a fixed ideology or motivation which aligned with existing proscribed terror organisations.[10] But in the wake of the attack, it was revealed that the attacker had accessed a dizzying array of violent, hateful content. This ranged from possessing Al-Qaeda training manuals on the production of ricin (a chemical poison) to researching school shootings during computer lessons at his own school in 2019.[11]

In response to a Home Affairs Select Committee investigation which is currently seeking to investigate Prevent's remit following the attack, the ISD submitted a paper summarising this new form of violent extremism.[12] It said that extremism 'has undergone a fundamental shift characterised by decentralised online networks and hybridised ideologies rather than informal groups'. It warned that the demographic of extremism was changing, with four times as many minors being arrested for terror offences. And it identified a 'high frequency of neurodiversity and poor mental health' amongst those who committed acts, reframing this new form of terror as a social problem as much as a law enforcement issue.

However, the ISD and other researchers in places such as the European Union's Radicalisation Awareness Network have all drawn a crucial conclusion about 'self-radicalisation': it never truly occurs by itself. Someone may embark on their own distinct pathway to violent extremism, drawing upon multiple sources of hate to spark action; but in the background, seemingly lonely, nihilist, violent individuals are drawing upon, or appealing back to, an online subculture that they are part of.

In the rest of the ISD's submission, it noted that male-dominated spaces, known to most of us as the 'manosphere', was blurring the line between self-help and ideological grooming. In doing so, it helps connect nihilistic, violent young men with one another. This enables hateful practices like misogyny to grow within the group. And as the group communicates amongst itself and with the wider world in language that is increasingly superior and violent, the conditions for violence to spill over from the digital world into the physical one grow, causing carnage on the streets.

But the ISD noted something else too. People drawn towards hateful or violent forms of content still need a push from a community to keep accessing material. And in this case, the push often comes from groups who engage in a shared language of darkly transgressive jokes that encourage people to continue accessing content: encouraging individuals down the path through a warped sense of camaraderie.

And at the heart of this shared language is a strong hint at how the gamer-fication of terror emerged. 'Memes, aesthetics and gaming motifs' have become common linguistic currency amongst people who are on the pathway towards self-radicalisation – leading to the culture and communities that underpin video games being co-opted for mass, despairing violence.

THE PROBLEM WITH TOXIC GAMERS

For a long time, the main concern around video games and violence was that playing violent video games could lead to horrifying actions in the real world. The industry was subjected to waves of moral panic over the possible link in the late 1970s, particularly in connection with the supposedly shocking violence of a game called *Death Race* (which was so crudely animated it's hard to even see the violence while you're committing it). Separate panics emerged in the 1990s following the release of ultra-violent fighting game *Mortal Kombat*, which led to the US games industry being subjected to a series of hostile US Senate committee hearings, and the release of a sadistically violent game called *Manhunt 2* in the mid 2000s, which ended up being the subject of a high-profile court case in the UK after local content-rating agencies refused to certify it for sale. The popularity of video games amongst school shooters has also, unfortunately, been a common theme, with the perpetrators of shootings decades apart in Columbine (1999) and Uvalde (2022) both playing games.

However, one counter-terror researcher who spoke to me on background pithily summarised that the mechanical link between violent video games and someone becoming violent is 'bullshit'. Extensive academic research from organisations such as the Oxford Internet Institute has long debunked the idea that teens who play violent video games become more aggressive.[13] In 2019, Patrick Markey, director of the Interpersonal Research Laboratory and professor of psychology at Villanova University, told CNBC News that 'The research is not there to suggest that there is a link between violent video games and these horrific acts of violence' and that when people do play games consistently 'we actually see a dip in violent crimes . . . and we don't see an uptick later on'.[14] There is also no evidence that violent games are encouraging people to carry out violent extremist acts, with a paper from the European Radicalisation Awareness Network in 2022 suggesting that 'there was no evidence to suggest extremists were utilising games to directly recruit'.[15]

However, the same paper also noted that 'multiple recent terror attacks with strong links to games' have occurred over the past decade, including the murder of Charlie Kirk. This therefore leads to one big question: if video games content isn't a cause of extremist behaviour, why is there a connection between video games communities and the emergence of this new form of 'self-radicalised' nihilist extremism?

Galen Lamphere-Englund is the co-founder of the Extremism and Gaming Research Network (EGRN). After working for over a decade as a conflict researcher, and having been a keen *World of Warcraft* player during his childhood, he noticed a disturbing rise in extreme, hateful far-right content on popular video game streaming sites during the pandemic. And after raising the alarm with counterparts from across the world and investigating what was causing it, he concluded that the power of video games as a digital third place was leading to significant detrimental side-effects.

'Games are social spaces,' he told me over a video call. 'They're social environments and the social ecosystems around them involve intense interpersonal relationship building that has a quantitatively and qualitatively stronger aspect of relationship building than what you're seeing in traditional social media platforms.'

*

Playing with friends, hanging out in shared social spaces, creating groups to play together and overcoming challenges with one another lead to what Lamphere-Englund describes as 'different layers of identity building' for individuals and 'strong connections of both in-group and out-group dynamics'.

If you're struggling for a second to picture what that looks like, Lamphere-Englund and collaborator Menso Hartgers likened the way that games create group dynamics online with what it is like to watch your favourite sports team.[16]

You decide to watch your team or a particular sport because you enjoy it. You head to a stadium or a space like a bar to watch a match. While there, you congregate and chat with other fans about the game. In doing so, you build connections with each other. So maybe you say you'll see them in the same place next week, swap phone numbers or recommend you follow each other on social media. You can then stay connected with one another, in person but also by sharing content about your team, the sport they play or just about anything else in the process.

Games work in much the same way. Players can pick up their favourite game and start talking to each other within it, if it has communication services, through a connected voice chat platform like Discord, or watch and participate in a live-stream broadcasting of another party playing. Within these spaces, players can deepen existing relationships with friends, meet new people in open voice chat, or interact with a wider community on social media or a stream's live chat. As with the world of sport, those relationships quickly move out of the game into forums, news sites or physical spaces like meet-ups, esports competitions or fan events. And within this ecosystem, identities form as players share stories with one another of what they experienced in-game, create in-game personalities based on the way they play, or use things like in-game purchases to express their identity visually in the world.

But in the world of sports, there has long been a problem with how places like stadiums have been used by people with malicious intent. When lots of people congregate together, there's a chance for people – whether as part of a group or on their own – to identify someone who looks lonely or vulnerable, take them out of the safety of the shared space, and encourage them to participate in a group whose intentions are significantly less community-minded than peacefully being a sports fan.

In the UK and across Europe, this dynamic is a major driver behind the emergence of football hooligan communities who drape the cultural identity of sport over themselves to justify the nihilistic violence they commit against one another. Lamphere-Englund suggests that, like with sports, video games are inappropriately co-opted by narrow nihilistic violent subcultures to provide a warped rationale for their actions.

'Similar to football, the [video] game is not the reason why hooliganism existed in the 1980s and became a massive issue. Rather the community around it developed various forms of social extremism that were created by nefarious actors inside of the community, who are seeking to radicalise individuals and bring them into their own, often violent, cause,' Lamphere-Englund explains. The challenge, therefore, is not to taint video games and video game communities as a whole, but instead to interrogate who is bastardising the space. 'If you see a swastika on the side of a stadium, the conclusion should not be "football is inherently terrible and is making people Nazis",' he explained. 'The conclusion should be "that's a horrible symbol" – who painted it, why did they paint it, and what can be done about it?'

So, who are the people sitting within this subculture that are providing the people, the community and the language to justify extreme acts of violence? In an attempt to provide an answer, I'm adopting a term used by Take This, a nonprofit that aims to foster positive mental and emotional health in games, to give this diverse, diffuse and sometimes quite confusing subculture a name: toxic gamers.

Toxic gamers are to video game communities what football hooligans are to football communities. They are people who use a love of video games to conceal, and in some cases justify, a wide range of transgressive behaviour on the internet. Emerging from communities like 4chan, 8kun and Kiwi Farms, toxic gamers use a range of tactics like 'doxxing' (revealing someone's personal details online) or 'swatting' (sending the police to people's homes warning that the person in the property is armed or unstable) to harass victims, and, in extreme cases, perpetrate violence in the streets to demonstrate their credibility to the group around them.

Toxic gamers often appear to be the 'traditional audience' for video games which are men aged between their teens and their 30s. But members of the group are also more likely to be lonely, isolated, and suffering from poor mental health. Games provide them with a sense of community that they don't get in the rest of their lives. But if they end up in the wrong corners of the online world, things can turn: becoming increasingly nasty.

The nastiness that festers within this community occurs for a number of reasons. Transgressive toxic gamers are likely to make remarks that are racist, xenophobic or homophobic because, well, those are transgressive things to do. But almost always, toxic gamers are misogynists. They believe that video games are for men alone, especially those who have grown up as the 'traditional' audience for the medium. Therefore they want to create an environment within games that kicks women out – stinking the space out, while spreading ideas that increase hate towards women in the real world.

'I call it the cyclical nature of exclusion,' said Dr Rachel Kowert, a researcher on the uses and effects of digital games who has worked with the Department of Homeland Security on the risks that toxic gamer subcultures pose to online spaces in general. 'In games, you have the games and the culture in the games studios are male dominated. They create content that is kind of male skewed. And then you have the parents who buy more consoles for boys than girls, and then you have more boys go into STEM (science, technology, engineering, maths) subjects, and then more boys go into the industry. What happens is that the culture becomes dominated by men, and then when women want to enter the space there's some hesitancy because they're like, well, this is our space and why are you encroaching on it.' Toxic gamers, in short, have turned the industry's shift away from young men as the dominant audience for play as a form of betrayal: encouraging them to further spread transgressive behaviours.

Unsurprisingly, video games are particularly important to toxic gamers. But in comparison to football hooligans, whose relationships with clubs are less important than their loyalty to the group, their love of gaming is central to their identity. Their cultural interests are likely to be narrow, usually restricted to online subcultures and games exclusively. Their taste in games is narrow, favouring 'traditional' genres like first-person shooters, strategy games and a handful of creative multiplayer games.

There are reasonable concerns that such players play and circulate modified versions of these games with hateful or far-right messages, including the first-person shooter *Doom* and strategy game *Hearts of Iron IV*. But given that the group dynamic is important to these players, they're just as likely to be in a major online game playing it 'silently' via the platform and keeping hateful conversation to a separate, less moderated channel.

Beyond what they choose to play, toxic gamers have ensured that their language is infused with gaming memes and cultural references to ensure they can easily identify like-minded members of their clans. And crucially, their social circles are predominantly online groups that are themselves obsessed with games. This means that their 'in-group' dynamic consists almost entirely of other toxic gamers, with many of their deeper interactions formed in places like private game servers, chat channels like Telegram, and 'alt-tech' video-streaming platforms like DLive or Rumble which offer similar functionalities to Twitch but with much less moderation.

Where toxic gamers do overlap into wider culture is largely through an affiliation with another group that has found masculine, misogynistic, racist toxic gamers to be useful allies or supporters of the cause: the far right. Spaces like 4chan have proven to be excellent places for the far right to spread its ideas and mobilise recruits. This has created an invaluable symbiosis, where toxic gamers – concerned about their culture being commandeered by people not like them – could help the far and alt-right grow while receiving support.

'I would say that in the last decade, there has been a very strong mobilisation in online spaces by far-right actors and also by the alt-right,' said Dr Julia Ebner, a researcher at the University of Oxford's Centre for the Study of Social Cohesion, who is the author of *Going Dark: The Secret Social Lives of Extremists*. 'The alt-right really hijacked a lot of existing online platforms and spaces, or other hobby platforms, and saw an opportunity there to politicise or derail discussions, spread disinformation, and radicalise people towards far-right, extremist or anti-minority views.' And though Ebner says only a 'very small percentage of people' have been specifically radicalised within these spaces, the alt-right has allowed them to 'twist the entire conversation' in forums such as 4chan and 8kun. This has enabled extreme, performative and loudly transgressive voices to dominate: creating conditions for emboldened individuals to take action in the real world in devastating ways.

Toxic gamers share one other similarity with the far right as a result of the merging of their information space: a strong belief in conspiracy theories and conspiratorial thinking. More in Common, a charity founded in the aftermath of the murder of the British MP Jo Cox in 2016, shared polling at the Cambridge Disinformation Summit in April 2025 about how to reach video game players across the country with media literacy interventions designed to stop people from falling victim to misinformation online.

The main findings of the report were alarming. It discovered that highly online, frequent video game players were more likely to say that they were confident in their ability to 'know what's true', that they doubted the intentions of traditional media organisations and instead focused on getting their news from niche information sources like content creators, YouTube personalities and independent podcasts. This was especially true of a mistrustful section of the population that the firm describe as 'disengaged battlers', who feel like they're struggling to keep their heads above water but are being overlooked, or ignored, by the system.

Unfortunately, what they believed to be true – well, just isn't. More in Common's polling suggests that 44 per cent of people who play games every day believe that it is certainly or probably true that 'secret groups control global events' and 33 per cent believe that extraterrestrial life is being hidden by the authorities.

By comparison, only 21 per cent of people who don't play games believe in shadowy cabals affecting the world and just 15 per cent believe that the presence of alien life has been concealed on earth.[17] Many of the people who are within the toxic gamer subculture therefore believe they know the truth, but that the truth they know isn't shared with the world – increasing their ostracisation in the process.

Finally, toxic gamers may begin as isolated individuals, sharing transgressive viewpoints in the dark corners of the internet. But they also have a remarkably strong sense of agency too, encouraging them to take action both online and offline in troubling ways.

Toxic gamers are effective at deploying the 'in-group' identity that they've formed online to campaign noisily against players, developers or critics who disagree with their narrow definition of who should be able to play.

The Anti-Defamation League found in 2024 that 80 million players in America were exposed to hate and harassment, with women and Black men particularly affected by a communications landscape driven by the toxic gamer subculture.[18] The subculture was also responsible for driving the 2014 Gamergate hate movement against women working in the games industry, swelling its influence and membership by harassing, doxxing and threatening people on the basis of false allegations that a game developer had slept with a journalist.

We will return to the full impact of Gamergate on the world in the next chapter. But according to Ebner its success in securing media coverage and bullying businesses gave extremists confidence that their activities in the digital space would naturally pour over the porous border between it and reality itself. 'It showed "no, actually, we can have a real impact here." The online world is the real world and we can make politics or even intimidate our opponents and have a massive impact on the ongoing debates.'

It also encouraged one other seemingly contradictory quality within the community too: the empowerment of individuals to 'go it alone' with their own hateful ideas and acts on behalf of the amorphous groups they sit within.

By combining a tech savviness that allows them to navigate the shadowy parts of the internet, a deeply conspiratorial mindset that has emerged from communities responsible for driving theories such as QAnon into the mainstream, and immersion within a creative subculture that played a big part in turning live-streamers and video content creators into superstars, toxic gamers have developed a warped boastful individualism and the agency to act upon it. Sharing vile memes, harassing people online or even committing acts of violence in the real world marry the ego of the actor with the desires of the group. This encourages the worst actors in the group to 'self-radicalise' and engage in violent acts that are dripping with video game references, turning their gamerfied terror into social capital that they can forever cash in within the subculture that reveres them for it.

In short, the most toxic gamers align uncomfortably closely with the characteristics of the nihilistic modern extremists who perpetrate acts of harm and violence. And as we've seen over the past decade, the way that individuals within these closed-off groups have used video game communication channels, motifs and sometimes content to do harm has transformed – bringing violence to our streets in the process.

SOWING DISCORD

The use of video games, communications channels, culture and content for violent extremism has evolved in the past decade from the opportunistic use of infrastructure to an alarmingly self-referential form of violence that seeks to co-opt play for the purposes of dealing out nihilistic terror.

The gamerfication of terror began in Charlottesville in August 2017. On 11 August, the Unite the Right rally gathered together America's far right – including the Ku Klux Klan, neo-Nazi groups and white supremacist organisations – for a night-time tiki-torch rally. White men in matching khaki trousers and Make America Great Again (MAGA) caps chanted anti-Semitic slogans such as 'Jews will not replace us'.

The next day, the groups gathered to rally around the statue of General Lee in the town. In the late morning of the 12th, the rally was called off and a state of emergency was declared as counter-protestors confronted the far-right activists.

As the protestors dispersed, violence began to spread through the streets. It reached a devastating culmination when a neo-Nazi who attended the rally ploughed his car into a crowd of protestors. This action led to dozens of serious injuries and the death of 32-year-old paralegal Heather Heyer, whose final post on social media before she attended the counter-protest in Charlottesville read 'if you're not outraged, you're not paying attention'.

Reflecting on events in the town five years after the attack, Ian Solomon, then dean of the University of Virginia's Frank Batten School of Leadership and Public Policy, said that the events in the town in 2017 showed that 'hate is quite brazen to show its face proudly.'[19] But to show its face proudly, hate needed somewhere to organise. And it chose a video game chat platform as its channel of choice.

Discord was set up in 2015 by Jason Citron and Stanislav Vishnevskiy. The pair had been working on an online mobile video game called *Fates Forever* that was similar to the popular multiplayer game *League of Legends*. While making the game, they created voice and text chat functions to make it easy for people to talk to one another. The game itself was not a success. But Citron and Vishnevskiy realised the problem that they were solving in the development of *Fates Forever* – namely, that it was surprisingly tricky to find easy ways for people to talk to each other while playing online games in one space – was shared by most games and most players. As a result, they turned the tools they had built into the backbone of Discord and offered everyone access to the service they had built.

It quickly proved a hit amongst players. After launching a mobile and PC app in 2015 to let people text and voice chat to one another, the pair evolved the service quickly over the course of the next two years to allow it to 'overlay' games (i.e. keep working while you played a PC title), set up group chats, enabled direct messaging, and even customised emojis that could be used to show off your personality or reward other people in your forum with perks. The service quickly swelled in size, getting 45 million users as the promise of both open and private servers dedicated to all kinds of games and game communities enticed people through its virtual doors.

However, Discord had a moderation problem. The service was in its infancy, which meant it had little staffing power to attempt to moderate what people were talking about online. This led to a softer approach to content moderation. And with plenty of people in the toxic gamer community looking for a place to hang out, Discord became the chat channel of choice for the far right by the time of its second birthday in 2017.

In her book *Going Dark*, Dr Julia Ebner outlines in great detail how a flexible chat app built to encourage people to play video games together became the space in which the far right successfully organised the Unite the Right rally.

Jason Kessler, under the username MadDimension, turned his closed Discord forum into a digital communications command centre to bring the far right together in a single rally under one banner. And from her time sitting inside Discord in the build-up to the event, Ebner shows how he achieved it.

Kessler himself used Discord's user-led moderation tools to appoint senior figures within the right into positions of authority within the server. Richard Spencer, who was previously the president of 'alt-right' think tank the National Policy Institute, and Mike Enoch, the host of far-right podcast *The Daily Shoah*, were given VIP status in the forum to anoint their importance – creating a hierarchy and therefore a command structure within a deeply argumentative Discord server.

Kessler, along with other leaders in Discord, then used the server as the focal point for the entire operation of the march. Adverts for the Unite the Right march in spaces ranging from Facebook to Twitter and through to 4chan encouraged people to join the march, while also pointing them back to Discord. The organisers of the protest took great care to use the server to order attendees to follow instructions aimed at legitimising the cause as much as possible, including informing attendees of the khaki trousers requirement and dissuading anyone seen as aesthetically unpleasing from staying away from the event.[20] The server also became a space where supremacists would hang out and talk, discussing ideological differences amongst their chaotic communities or lamenting the loneliness of a forum member called Convo who had been without a romantic relationship, or meaningful friendship, for nearly half a decade.

The Unite the Right march was the 'first time they bring this [online] activism into the real world', according to Ebner. She was tempted to fly to Charlottesville to attend the rally, until discussions amongst the Discord group turned to whether or not to bring firearms to their event. As users increasingly leant towards arming themselves, Ebner chose to stay away and watch from afar instead.

In doing so, she was able to watch the drama of the two days unfold from Kessler's command centre in Discord. The first day proved celebratory, with posters in the server waxing lyrical about the effectiveness of the rally in generating publicity for the far-right's disparate groups of neo-Nazis, right-wing militia groups and KKKers.

But on the day of Heyer's murder, the mood changed. Live streams from neo-Nazis caught up in the suddenly cancelled rally were flooded with racist and violent comments aimed at Black people and the counter-protestors. Shortly after the murderer had driven his car into the pack of protesters, some were already sharing distasteful jokes such as posting 'do you like my car' underneath pictures of the battered motor vehicle.

In the aftermath of the attack, the use of Discord by the far right attracted enough attention to neuter its effectiveness as a highly public command post for organising future hateful attacks. The company moved quickly to remove far-right servers from the platform, growing its trust-and-safety team in response to the rally, developing new policies that allowed it to work proactively when extremists sought to use the platform again to support the insurrection at the Capitol Building on 6 January. It said that it planned 'to continue standing firm against ideologies of hate that violent extremist communities espouse', explaining that its goal was to 'ensure that another event like Charlottesville isn't planned on our platform.'[21]

However, the Unite the Right rally had already set a precedent. Whether organisers were trying to hide from view on sites like Discord or moving to alt-tech platforms where moderation was looser, the use of video game communication channels to organise rallies and harassment campaigns helped extremists to evolve their tactics. Ebner told me that 'the way the platform works makes it easy to create a trolling army through a very strong game-like structure,' where participants are assigned ranks, receive points and can climb the ladder within a well-organised server: gamifying far-right campaigning.

On its own, this gamification of hate would be worrying enough. But the misuse of Discord's hierarchical system designed for appointing moderators has proven to be the tip of the iceberg when it came to bringing video game tropes into the sphere of violent terror.

The presence of young men who were deeply invested in video games and part of the toxic gamer culture within these alt-right, far-right and chaotic online spaces gave the medium's culture some incredibly rare social capital. This enabled some people, in Ebner's description, to make a 'departure' from solely being interested in games culture to acquiring a radical, dangerous and, on occasion, politicised edge to their violence.

And less than two years after the Unite the Right rally had taken place, one person who had been submerged by the culture launched an attack that would dress a massacre in the cultural tropes of video games: 'gamer-fying' mass murder in the process.

THE STREAMER SHOOTING

The deadliest act of terror in New Zealand's history took place on 15 March 2019. At 1.40 p.m., a 28-year-old white supremacist and self-described 'ecofacist' entered the Al-Noor Mosque in Christchurch while holding weapons painted with far-right slogans. There, and shortly afterwards at the nearby Linwood Islamic Centre, he murdered fifty-one people and injured forty. Jacinda Ardern, the country's prime minister, described it as 'one of New Zealand's darkest days.'

It was also a grim first for the world. Shortly before the attack commenced, he posted a message on the /pol board of 8kun: 'Well lads, it's time to stop shitposting and time to make a real life effort post. I will carry out and [sic] attack against the invaders, and will even stream the attack via facebook.' He then posted a link to a stream that he was hosting as he carried out the atrocity, turning Christchurch into the first mass-shooting event to be broadcast live online to thousands of viewers.

The Christchurch incident bore similarities to an attack on a Norwegian youth camp in July 2011. The shooter was deeply racist and active in extreme-right forums online, and like the man

who committed the Norway atrocity, he created a lengthy manifesto which sought to justify his actions on the grounds of the racist
'Great Replacement' conspiracy theory, which wrongly suggests
that white populations are being culturally and demographically
replaced by non-white groups (especially Muslims). He had
donated money to groups like the National Policy Institute, which
had participated in the aforementioned Unite the Right rally. He
also intentionally distributed the manifesto minutes before the
shooting, sending it to approximately seventy media outlets and
the generic contact email addresses for New Zealand's prime minister, leader of the opposition and speaker of the Parliament.[22] He
also stated explicitly in his manifesto that he was inspired by the
'Knight Justiciar' responsible for the Utoya attack in Norway,
whom he described as the 'true inspiration' behind his act.

But the shooter's world view and tactics were also inspired by
the toxic gaming communities that he spent time in online.
Although his manifesto contained his own warped racist theories, Robert Evans, a conflict journalist working for Bellingcat,
wrote on the day of the attack that the manifesto was an exercise
in 'shitposting', which is the act of posting content online that is
deliberately designed to be provocative. While it was notionally
designed for external audiences, its litany of memes and deeply
'online' references were directed towards the racist online 'in-
group' which had formed around forums like 8kun.[23] And
unsurprisingly, he drew video games into his document.

In a section about supposed motivations for his attack, he posed
to himself the question of whether he was 'taught violence and
extremism by games, music, literature, cinema'. He sarcastically
wrote that child-friendly platformer *Spyro the Dragon 3* had taught
him ethno-nationalism, while *Fortnite* 'trained me to be a killer' and
taught him to 'floss [dance] on the corpses of my enemies', before
decisively answering his earlier question with 'no'.

The murderer's message was deliberately mocking people
who believe that video games cause violence. And though it may

have been a joke for his toxic community of players, it was consistently picked up by news outlets in the aftermath of the shooting. UK press outlet Sky News, for example, put the comments next to remarks the shooter made about ethnic cleansing in Bosnia, creating an equivalence of the two in the minds of its readers.[24]

While the killer mocked the idea that video games cause violence, his desire to burnish his racist reputation within a toxic community of video game players did shape his actions.

The perpetrator trusted members of his community enough to allow them to inadvertently support his attack, with New Zealand's Royal Commission discovering that a 'gaming friend' had been used as a referee to acquire a firearms licence.[25] He deliberately used a GoPro camera to film the attacks to create the aesthetic of a first-person shooter. And just before he commenced his attack, he sarcastically said on stream, 'Subscribe to PewDiePie': a throwaway reference to a popular video game YouTuber that appealed to the in-group of gamers and became the subject of fervent discussion within the media.[26]

The significance of the shooter's decision to live-stream the attack cannot be understated. 'His video was not so much a medium for his message insomuch as it was the message, even more so than his actual manifesto,' wrote Graham Macklin from West Point's Combating Terrorism Center following the attack.[27] He had set out 'to make a video of someone killing Muslims,' with the aim 'to incite violence, retaliation and further divide between the European people and the invaders currently occupying European soil.'* His references to other mass shooters also suggested that he sought to increase his personal reputation within his community.

---

* The reference to European here is figurative rather than literal. The shooter is referring to racist terms for a wider racial struggle in the context of the Great Replacement Theory, not referencing distinct geographic areas.

Depressingly, the shooter achieved his goals. The Facebook live stream was viewed thousands of times before it was removed, but clips and screenshots of the attack would later reach millions as a result of the shooter's supporters sharing his content. While some members of boards like 8kun rightly feared that his actions would see their community taken offline, others were delighted. 'OP fucking delivered, I just saw him kill so many hajis,' wrote one poster. Another wrote that 'memes have done more for the ethnonationalist movement than any manifesto.' And the filming of the attack in the manner of a live stream, with cultural tropes and references included, represented a form of 'dark fandom', providing a small percentage of hateful people with transgressive content that they could celebrate, post, and consider repeating themselves to bathe in the perverted glory that the shooter had generated.[28]

The result was a new form of far-right terror that wouldn't have existed without video games culture: gamer-fied mass violence. Between March 2019 and February 2020, three further attempts were made to live-stream far-right attacks that either riffed upon, or were inspired directly by, Christchurch.

One man attempted to stream his attack on a synagogue in Poway in the USA on 27 April 2019, where he killed one woman and injured three other people, but it failed to work. Another shooter who attempted to live-stream his attack on a Walmart in El Paso on 3 August 2019 was also unsuccessful, but his actions nevertheless took the lives of 23 people. Later that year, an attack on a synagogue in Halle in Germany on 9 October 2019 was successfully live-streamed on video game site Twitch with the neo-Nazi killer broadcasting both his murder of two people and extremely anti-Semitic views to watchers.[29] The perpetrator of an attack on an LGBT bar in Bratislava in October 2022 further captured the influence of the Christchurch attack, admiring how the Christchurch live stream 'felt different' and crediting it for introducing him to the racist communities that he would be radicalised within.[30]

But these attacks also showed something else: the gamer-fication of terror was evolving as other video game tropes and tactics were laid on top of the New Zealand shooter's work.

Prior to the Halle attack, the killer also released a manifesto alongside his live stream to explain his actions. Suraj Lakhani, a researcher who examines the links between violent extremism and video game communities, noted that he had created a 'gamified' scoring system.

The shooter had set himself 'objectives' for the event, but he also had a range of 'achievements' that he wanted to 'unlock'. The two latter terms are closely tied to the way that almost every popular video game on a major platform provides players with extra challenges to complete in return for badges or trophies, suggesting a clear link between the perpetrator's thinking and the games he was playing.

More disturbingly, he also suggested that he would award himself points 'for killing Jews, Muslims, Christians, blacks, children and communists' and for using different weapons. Considering that 4chan and 8kun spaces contained references to individuals 'beating the high score' of New Zealand, his system should be considered as an attempt to merge gamification – the process of using game mechanics to encourage behaviours – with the cultural gamer-fication of terror.[31]

For now, that frame of reference hasn't been adopted – potentially because much of the Halle killer's live-streamed attack was chaotic, disorganised and ineffective compared to its inspiration.

But his willingness to further gamify terror in the months after Christchurch showed that there was more room for extremists to use the medium for ill – something that would become obvious in the aftermath of the Buffalo shooting in May 2022.

TERROR REPLAYED

Within twelve months of the Christchurch shooting, the gamification of terror by the toxic gamer subculture had transformed from a one-off event into a template for action that lone participants were inspired by, encouraged in and able to follow with the support of the narrow community of nihilists who supported it. The Buffalo shooter followed the template to spread his atrocity far and wide.

The killer fit the archetype of both the modern extremist and someone who could be radicalised within the toxic gamer subculture. He played video games, spending some of his time playing the survival game *Rust* according to logs of his Discord diary. Benjamin Goggin, currently the deputy editor for technology at NBC News, noted on X that the Buffalo shooter 'directly ties an interest in nationalism and guns to playing *Roblox*', citing two experiences – *Apocalypse Rising* and *Blood & Iron* – as influential to his thinking.[32] As with the Christchurch killer's comments about *Spyro the Dragon* and *Fortnite*, treating his words literally risked playing into his hands. But it did definitively show that the murderer was interested in games and that they formed a key part of his identity.

Demographically speaking, he also matched the archetype of both groups. He was just eighteen years old at the time of the attack. His diary would reveal that he felt in poor mental health after the pandemic, framing his decision to attack the Tops Supermarket as a choice between killing others or committing suicide.[33] And like the other shooters mentioned above, he was an active member of racist online communities such as the 4chan and 8kun image boards where a love of games could offer lonely young men a way to gain warped social standing.

The execution of the attack on Buffalo followed the playbook established by the Christchurch killer beat by beat. The

Buffalo shooter kept a private log on Discord of his thoughts, transforming a personal diary full of personal, often racist, ramblings into a manifesto that stole large chunks of content from the New Zealand killer's work. He bought cameras to allow him to live-stream the attack, setting it up to run not only on Twitch but also within a private Discord server to share with approximately 15 handpicked community members. He also painted his gun with slogans and far-right references, ranging from 'White Lives Matter' to references to subheadings of the manifesto distributed by the Christchurch shooter.[34]

As the Buffalo killer's attack commenced, his actions led to a chain reaction amongst community members that was similar to other attacks. Twitch, to its credit, managed to identify the video as an active shooter incident within two minutes of going live – preventing it from reaching an organic audience through the platform. But his backup stream in Discord allowed the dozen or so people watching his stream to create video clips and share them online through their communities. These would go on to accrue millions of views and lead to further glorification of mass shooters amongst the toxic subculture.

The Buffalo shooting was another step towards gamerfied terror that could be replayed in different contexts across the world. By the end of 2022, the gamification of terror had shifted back to Europe for the Bratislava attack. And in August 2024, a Turkish teenager killed five people with a knife in Eskişehir after posting 'hateful and extremist content' on Steam.[35]

But the shooting was the moment when organisations realised that there was a new way for people within deep video game communities to celebrate his work: they were using democratised game development tools to turn the footage of the shooting into playable experiences.

Roblox was most affected by this, with its content moderation team moving quickly to take down a number of experiences created by players who wanted to glorify the shooter's actions. It has publicly responded to concerns over users making extremist content by claiming it has 'a strict policy prohibiting content or behaviour that incites, condones, supports, glorifies, or promotes any terrorist or extremist organisation or individual.'[36] The company also released a public blog post in August 2025 highlighting how it uses AI moderation tools, human moderators, and partnerships with law enforcement to develop 'extensive safety systems' capable of capturing extremist content.[37] PC games storefront Steam also hosted re-creations of the Buffalo shooting made by players of a game called *Garry's Mod*, which were eventually removed in 2025 during the writing of this book.

As seen in the chapter on Russia, the extent to which these games are played or able to influence people by themselves is questionable. For instance, the game *Hatred*, which puts players in the shoes of a nihilistic shooter, made little impact despite remaining available on Steam in the UK at the time of writing.[38]

However, the ease with which games and experiences can be developed by communities associated with toxic subcultures like the active shooter communities is leading to a game of what Lamphere-Englund describes as 'whack-a-mole' as user-generated content platforms like *Roblox* struggle to deal with them.[39] Social media sites like TikTok are full of videos of these experiences live in action: multiplying the effect of the original media within social channels and encouraging the press to pick the story up.[40]

And while few people will play these games, and even fewer people will enjoy them, the multiplication effect means that it organically reaches isolated, unhappy and often mentally unwell young men whose disaffection with the world can translate into nihilistic hate.

This turns video games and the content created about them from a source of entertainment into a tap-on-the-shoulder moment for someone who may be prone to self-radicalisation. And this leads them towards a subculture that perverts play to encourage on-the-edge individuals to commit atrocities, perpetuating them further by recording, promoting, and celebrating their actions to create a horribly circular form of individualised hate.

Playing games does not cause people to be violent. But in a similar vein to nihilistic violent subcultures in the world of sport, the groups, spaces, communication infrastructure and even tropes of games can be appropriated by hateful people and communities to provide a cultural foundation to individualised theories of hate. This means that any attempt to deal with the underlying causes of extremism in society – including addressing mental health harm, tackling toxic behaviours and working out how to guide vulnerable people away from poisonous 'in-group' dynamics – must look at how we can collaborate with games businesses, associated social media companies, and the communities who make up the vast majority of players to normalise behaviours that move us away from harm.

But we must act quickly to do so if we want to protect our fundamental democratic rights too. The assassination of Charlie Kirk, the podcaster and founder of the strongly right-wing Turning Point political movement, as he took part in an open-air political debate on 10 September 2025 shocked the world. And in the hunt for the shooter, the police discovered that Kirk had fallen victim to a gamer-fied killer: someone who had carved his bullets with references from satirical anti-fascist multiplayer game *Helldivers 2* amidst a wider mix of chaotic cultural references that amounted to an atypical self-radicalised world view.[41] And like the Buffalo shooting, players re-created the murder within platforms like *Roblox*, with the company removing dozens of experiences in response to justifiable outrage at the glamorisation of murder.[42]

The developers of both *Helldivers 2* and *Roblox* do not want their games or platforms used in this way. The fans who make up the majority of the game's multiplayer community were aghast. But one individual was willing to remix those references for extreme, anti-democratic violence before others voluntarily promoted his actions with disturbing re-creations for the purpose of appealing to other members of a toxic subculture. And while it might seem like a big step from someone using video game references in an assassination to the collapse of our political order, think again. The British government's recently updated definition of extremism argues that it can represent a threat to our democratic system and democratic values. If that's the case, and the Kirk assassination underlines that (irrespective of my personal queasiness over some of his views), tackling the problems emanating from toxic gamer communities is not a minor problem in a distant online community: it's crucial for keeping our values and our citizens alive.

Democratic nations must take the political challenges posed to their systems by groups such as these seriously if they wish to survive. But beyond shocking acts of extreme violence, there is another reason why democracies must not underestimate the effect that influence can have on the political leanings of those who play.

The use of Discord by the organisers of the Unite the Right rally showed that the perpetrators of extreme violent acts are at the thin end of a much thicker wedge of disaffected young men whose political identities have been formed within gaming groups. And as we'll see in the next chapter, the influence of those groups has been significant enough to play a major role in bringing populism to power in America: threatening liberal democracy with it.

9

The Gamergate to populism

To conclude this part of the book, we briefly need to return to the beginning of the story. In early September 2024, I was rudely reading my emails at a friend's drinks event when an unexpected invitation landed in my inbox.

I opened the message and discovered that I'd been invited to a conference hosted by the State Department's Global Engagement Center, which, at the time, was responsible for helping the US government and its allies to 'recognize, understand, expose, and counter foreign state and non-state propaganda and disinformation efforts'. I'd been invited in my capacity as someone who writes about video games and politics intersecting to cover the event, sharing the lessons with the readers of my newsletter.

The meeting was taking place in New York at the fringes of a UN General Assembly Meeting, and was exploring how the State Department, the Kingdom of Sweden's Psychological Defence Agency (an organisation dedicated to building resilience amongst the country's population to psychological 'offence' campaigns) and companies in the games industry such as Microsoft and Roblox Corporation were seeking to counter disinformation campaigns from foreign states channelled through video games.

A few weeks later, and with my wallet at least a few thousand dollars lighter, I made my way to Microsoft's office to hear James P. Rubin, a former Clinton-era official and at the time the special envoy and coordinator of the GEC, state that the information ecosystem which surrounded video games had become a space where influence – whether ill or otherwise – could be exercised.

'We share a goal where foreign misinformation finds no fertile soil in which to grow,' said Rubin, as he opened the meeting. 'We are focused on meeting people where they are . . . and it is clear that whether it is through games themselves, or through platforms like Discord, that is where they are.'

And Dr Magnus Hjort, who heads the Psychological Defence Agency, agreed that the ecosystem was being abused for the purposes of influence, referencing the work of Russian actors that was covered in Chapter 7.

'Video games are being used as propaganda to influence the way we think,' he explained. 'Russia is expanding its work in the field with games like *African Dawn*. Game images and video clips are being published with claims that they're from war zones. Historical war games are being released, where people can rewrite histories in favour of threat actors.'

When I spoke to officials from the GEC and the Psychological Defence Agency after the event, it was clear that both organisations were worried that foreign actors like Russia could be trying to tilt the outcome of the forthcoming US election by means of influence campaigns directed through games.

*

'Some numbers say that we have over three billion gamers in the world,' says Dominik Swiecicki, a Counsellor for Psychological Defence. 'For an antagonistic actor, this digital space can be seen as an infrastructure to deliver influence campaigns, to deliver messages in a digital space. We recognised the situation from [the 2016 US election].'

As I was leaving the event, Swiecicki told me that he feared 2024 could be the moment when the information ecosystem around games was infiltrated and corrupted for political purposes by those who did not support democracy. The fear of a foreign threat appeared to be justified after the Department of Justice unsealed documents showing Russian agents actively targeted eighteen- to thirty-year-old American gamers through a major disinformation campaign called 'Good Old USA Project'.

However, there was a problem with both the GEC and Swiecicki's analysis. The State Department, naturally due to its international remit, saw the threat to players as a new, external challenge. But the challenge facing America was neither of those things. American 'gamer' culture had become a political force a full decade before the GEC's event took place after a hate movement called 'Gamergate' was harnessed by Steve Bannon to energise the hard right.

As a result of what the journalist Joshua Green described as a 'luciferous insight' into the power of game communities from a Hong Kong business deal gone wrong, Bannon, and the columnist Milo Yiannopoulos, collaborated to turn fringe hateful concerns of a minority of players into the first front of the culture war.

By tapping into the emergence of an organic video game hate movement in 2014 called Gamergate, giving it credence via his media company Breitbart, and driving the story into the mainstream, Bannon's intuitive understanding of the power of toxic gamer communities created the digital-activist base, the tactical playbook and the strategic approach necessary for 'mainstreaming' populist far-right ideas within the online media ecosystem.

In doing so, Bannon started a process that resulted in the capture, mobilisation and mainstreaming of this community's values into the political right. It created the online 'shock troopers' who powered Trump's campaign forward. It spawned the alt-right, QAnon and other movements that fed into the mainstream. It even gave Elon Musk and Trump an audience to court directly to help them achieve their campaigning ends.

And by 2024, the capture of that information ecosystem meant that the Republican Party had attuned itself not just to the white young men who formed the movement, but also the

Hispanic and Black men who trusted little else than the games they enjoyed on their phone every day. And by playing video game communities so effectively, Team Trump found its way into the White House on two separate occasions: turning the power of game communities towards achieving sharp, political power.

UNINTENDED CONSEQUENCES

A central theme of this book has been the unexpected way that community spaces and information ecosystems that sit around games can have political influence. And there probably isn't a better example of this than *World of Warcraft*, the immensely popular, massively multiplayer online role-playing game, and its role in the birth of the alt-right.

World of Warcraft (also known as *WoW*) is a cultural phenomenon. Set in the fantasy world of Azeroth, the game lets players create their own fantasy character, pick a faction such as the Alliance or Horde and then head out into the world to explore, meet other players and complete quests. On launch in 2004, its enormously engaging 3D fantasy universe blew the minds of MMO players who had grown up playing text-based MUDs.

'I went to *World of Warcraft* when it was in the beta and I was completely won over,' said Holly Longdale, executive producer & vice president for *World of Warcraft*, when I interviewed her at a publicity event in London celebrating the game's 20th anniversary. 'I played it all the time, even though I was working on another game at the time. It really made MMOs accessible.'

That accessibility turned it into one of the most successful games of all time. The game generated nearly $10bn of revenue between its launch in 2004 and 2017. It did so by attracting a country's worth of players, reaching over 100 million account registrations a decade after release.[1] By April 2022, the game's official X account confirmed that players had spent nine million years within its world.[2] If we were to go back in time from today by that length of time, we would emerge in the Miocene epoch for a front-seat view of the formation of the Sierra Nevada mountain range. Not a bad way to spend your time, I'd say.

It also became a cultural phenomenon. *South Park*'s most successful episode 'Make Love, Not *Warcraft*', saw the show's lead characters go to, erm, extreme lengths to hunt down a player who had hacked the game to allow them to permanently kill off other people's avatars. The game found its way into other creative mediums, including featuring in Jesse Eisenberg's opening monologue near the start of the 2009 film *Zombieland*.

It has even spawned memes capable of entering the political discourse. The phrase 'Leeroy Jenkins' emerged in 2005 from an in-game skit arranged by players of the game, where one enthusiastic character decides to forego the careful planning of an entire guild to attack a room full of monsters while shouting 'Leeeeerooooooy . . . Jenkinssssss' down the microphone. In January 2023, Jared Huffman, a representative for the House of Congress, announced his vote for Hakeem Jeffries as the next speaker of the house with the same delivery as the meme: bringing *WoW* to the heart of the US political institution in the process.[3]

World of Warcraft became an immensely valuable community space to the millions of people who inhabited it. And though the primary use of that space was for role-playing fun, its combination of character design tools that let you express your identity, flourishing in-game economy and communication channels transformed digital play into real world impact.

Official charity events fundraisers within *World of Warcraft*, where players can complete actions like buying an in-game item and having the fee donated to a good cause, have raised over $15m for organisations like the Make A Wish Foundation, the American Red Cross and Doctors Without Borders since 2009.[4] The family of Mats Steen, a disabled teenager from Norway who died in 2014, were joined at the funeral by a group of people who had travelled from across the world to pay their respects to a friend they made in Azeroth.[5] *Cosmopolitan* ran a story in June 2016 about three couples who got married after meeting in *World of Warcraft*. They included Jeremy and Amanda from Elgin, Illinois, sharing that they met one another while raiding a Horde-controlled village in Ashenvale.[6] Try beating that for a first date.

WoW emerged as a big part of internet culture as the internet really took off. And although it was a place where anyone could play, and plenty of people did, it was demographically similar to the rest of the internet. While it is difficult to say exactly who played *World of Warcraft*, a 2010 paper from the University of Michigan exploring the experience of women within the game estimated that roughly 79 per cent of its players were men. Meanwhile, a self-reported survey about the habits of *WoW* players in 2012 saw every respondent answer that they were aged between their mid teens and mid thirties.

So while *WoW* became home to communities across the world who were dedicated to play, it also, naturally, interested communities such as those explored in the previous chapter, who wanted to be more active, more transgressive and trolling online too. This included members of the now notorious image board 4chan.

4chan is essentially an online forum for people to share images and chat about what interests them. The board hosted spaces for people to talk about everything from anime to technology to maths. It also had spaces dedicated to politics (/pol) and was home to the 'lolchat' board, which birthed many of the early internet memes and language that would shape online culture.[7]

In its early days before it acquired a darker reputation, 4chan was a chaotic mixture of welcoming and transgressive. It did offer people a great place to hangout online, especially if they were a teenage boy looking for laughs. But it did have a darker side too, with use of transgressive language a normal part of the experience – in this case, usually sexist, racist, anti-semitic or homophobic terms.

For the teenage boys who gravitated towards 4chan, it was a genuinely fun place to be for at least part of your life.

James Ball, the author of *The Other Pandemic: How QAnon Contaminated the World* and an avid *World of Warcraft* player in his youth, spent plenty of time on the board between 2004 and 2008 because he was 'a teenager, didn't have many friends, and [he] was better at making them on the internet.' For Ball, 4chan was at this point silly, nerdy and fun. And where there were silly young male nerds having fun online, video games were not far behind: becoming a noisy part of the board's culture from the outset.

'I think the most vocal core of video games culture is teenage boys and young men. It's perhaps the only cultural medium they dominate, and it's perhaps the most vilified medium,' he told me. 'I think there's an odd thing about gaming where there is resentment that it's not taken seriously. It's a huge creative industry. It's a huge job creator. It's got all these huge spaces. And it's only covered in "does it cause school shootings, does it make people violent, is it radicalising your son". Some of that crap is absolutely infuriating.'

The instinct on the Chan boards, which includes 4chan but also references its edgier cousin 8kun, from the earliest days was to defend the cultural form where so many of them found happiness. This included appropriating parts of video game culture for the purposes of defining who was in the group (and who didn't get it).

In some cases, this meant the fairly benign adoption of terms from games as part of the language of the 4chan boards. The adoption of the phrase 'kek' from *World of Warcraft* was one such example. *WoW*'s in-game chat function scrambled the text chat between Alliance and Horde factions so you couldn't see what your enemy was up to. 'Kek' in *WoW* speak simply meant 'lol'. But for many far-right researchers, 'kek' has become synonymous with memes such as Pepe the Frog that increasingly have racist connotations. Ball told me that the misunderstanding has driven him mad, with the incorrect assumption that the term is solely 'hard coded as right wing' missing the importance of its innocuous roots. It also, by extension, leads to 'incredulous' misunderstanding of games in general, which deepens the divide between those who play peacefully and the world in the process.

Disillusionment with mainstream culture and the desire to have fun in online spaces also led to the 4chan boards doing something else. They started to spill over into other online spaces, including games, to cause trouble that was arguably beyond transgressive.

For example, members of the board raided the game *Habbo Hotel* en masse solely for the purpose of being annoying, forming swastikas out of in-game characters controlled by 4channers and blocking access to the in-game swimming pool on the basis that it was closed due to 'aids'. A senior executive in the games industry told me that a major reason for *Habbo Hotel*'s decline in popularity was its failure to prevent attacks like this from happening, driving players away from the space.

However, at this point, the power of disaffected gamers as potential campaigners in a political environment had not been spotted. But *WoW* had inadvertently created conditions through which campaigning could happen: it had built passionate communities who cared immensely about its game world; those communities were keen to defend the world they loved, including by defending it from outsiders who undervalued or underappreciated communities; they were capable 'activists', whose digital activities had the potential to nudge real-world actions.

While Blizzard used these conditions to drive social good like charitable fundraising, one company sought to exploit global passion for the game to build a business that offended the game's many players. And its downfall proved to be surprisingly influential to a man who has reshaped the world we live in: Steve Bannon.

BANNON FODDER

Online games acquired value amongst players because they allowed them to express their identities, hang out with friends and be part of a wider world they loved to play in. But by the late 1990s and early 2000s, that value could be expressed in another way too: cold, hard cash.

MMOs, and other 'service'-based video games, needed to find a new way to get players to pay for their games because they required ongoing maintenance. Unlike traditional boxed video games like a *Mario* platforming game, MMOs had upkeep. Staff needed to be paid to maintain the game or add new content to it. Servers had to be paid for, office space had to be rented and so forth.

So in keeping with Bartle's observation that online games had to be worlds, MMOs evolved into economies. Even though players generally paid a monthly subscription for upkeep, items in the world became valuable. And whether players got their hands on those items by buying them directly from the developer, unlocking them through play or trading them with other players, virtual value quickly became expressed in cash terms. Players of *EVE: Online*, an MMO set in space, estimated that the 'Battle of B-R5RB', a conflict fought between 7,500 players over the course of twenty-one hours, saw over $300,000 of in-game content wiped out.[8] Game economies were also subject to the challenges that our real-world economies face too, with Yongcheng Liu and Qinfang

Ying, game designers at Chinese MMO-friendly firm NetEase, talking at length at famous games conference GDC about how to stop inflation tanking your game economy.[9]

However, there was a problem with all of this. Technically, game developers restrict the sale or trading of in-game items outside of the game worlds in their terms and conditions. This stops video games from being treated as 'real money' games like gambling. It discourages the use of game items or currencies as proxies for other forms of cash, something that inventive money launderers have attempted to do.[10] It also handily ensures that the developer keeps the economic benefits of games to themselves. The rotters.

In 2001, a new business was founded that attempted to turn the shadow economy around games into a functional one. Internet Gaming Entertainment (IGE) was formed by Brock Pierce, a former child actor who popped up in two of the *Mighty Ducks* movies and later as an independent candidate for president in the 2020 election, to create a unified marketplace to sell game accounts, items and currency accrued in online multi-player games.

During a stint in the Spanish seaside town of Marbella, the nineteen-year-old Pierce discovered and fell in love with the popular MMO *EverQuest*. After demonstrating his prowess in the game, he realised that there was real-world value in acquiring powerful 'Fungi Tunics' from an in-game enemy that other players found hard to beat. By running six computers at the same time, he could get an item that would normally cost 50,000 of the in-game currency to buy (equating to roughly 150 hours of play) and simply sell it directly to players on eBay. This saw him rake in $500 per transaction in a career known in the games world as a 'farmer', reaping what he was virtually sowing.

But Pierce had bigger ambitions than one-off purchases. In May 2001, he founded IGE in an office in downtown Marbella with the aim to build a $100m business professionalising the sale of in-game items. The idea was to roll up the various market-places offering different in-game items through one dedicated platform, generating cash from all the sites in the process. This in turn would supposedly give IGE leverage with games businesses, encouraging them to do a deal with Brock's platform to 'legalise' item sales in return for a cut of the profits.

The company grew quickly, advertising its own site, buying up competitors, and creating its own 'gold-farm' in Shanghai. The company then relocated to Hong Kong to make sure it was nice and close to the growing Chinese games market where buying accounts, in-game items and currencies on grey markets was considered a-ok by local players.

But the launch of *WoW* was IGE's big opportunity. On the one hand, the popularity of its game made it a prime target for IGE's business model, allowing its gold farmers to get to work farming content for Azeroth's eleven million players. On the other hand, players hated gold farmers. In January 2006, *Eurogamer* reported that *WoW*'s players had started to test players on the quality of their English to prevent gold farmers from joining their groups. Chinese players were unhappy. So too was developer Blizzard, who saw a key market being discriminated against.[11]

So IGE changed tack. Instead of changing what they were doing, they realised they needed to change the way people thought about in-game item sales. They needed professionals to help them tidy up the image of gold farming, sell it to skeptical executives and back IGE with enough cash to continue its investment. And after getting Goldman Sachs in to help them secure their investment, the company found the man who was destined to represent them.

Bannon, who was at the bank at the time, had previously made a pretty penny by negotiating the sale of TV show *Seinfeld* to Castle Rock Entertainment.[12] He was recognised as someone with the necessary entertainment experience to help the company out. And by 7 February 2006, he had pulled together cash from Goldman Sachs and a number of private funds to give IGE the firepower to dominate the market, making the most of the *WoW* boom.

However, Bannon's deal proved to be the highpoint for IGE. In the middle of 2006, Blizzard began a crackdown on gold reselling, having previously made their disdain for IGE's model clear by blowing off its executive team at a business meeting shortly beforehand. This caused the company to lose hundreds of thousands of dollars of inventory every month, pushing it into the red. But Bannon's moment of revelation was not caused by a change in corporate policy at a major business. It happened after a dedicated *World of Warcraft* player called Antonio Hernandez dealt IGE its final killing blow through the courts.

The 28-year-old, who claimed to play *WoW* for thirty-five to forty hours a week, filed a class action lawsuit in May 2007 against IGE on the basis that its actions were 'substantially impairing' the experience of playing the game. As well as seeking financial damages for every dollar it made on selling *WoW* content, he also sought to ban IGE from selling anything *WoW* related in the future too. He also claimed to be doing so on behalf of the community of players who enjoy the game, with his lawyer saying that IGE was 'polluting that entertainment' by allowing people to buy their way into the game in that manner.

Hernandez's effort pushed IGE over the edge. A couple of months prior to the suit, Pierce jettisoned IGE's failing item-selling business to a rival. The rest of the company split into two units, with Affinity Media holding on to IGE's video game news sites and IGE US remaining as a husk of a holding company. The latter would eventually be barred from selling any currency from *World of Warcraft* for five years as Hernandez sealed a symbolic victory in court.[13]

For Bannon though, IGE proved to be both an intriguing lesson and the beginning of an opportunity. As Joshua Green outlines in his book *Devil's Bargain*, Bannon had viewed the *WoW* community's outpouring of vitriol online and in the courts as a form of remarkably effective campaigning.

These communities, who were passionate for the cause but supported by people who were steeped in the tactics of the Chan boards, had strength, with their 'leaderless' white male communities demonstrating their ability to knock over organisations in the real world. This revelation occurred in the same year that Bannon co-founded Breitbart.com with Andrew Breitbart, a hardline right-wing news site. This created a subtle tie between IGE's fall and the emergence of the Breitbart doctrine, which states that politics must always be seen as downstream of culture.[14]

And while stories like Hernandez's class action lawsuit would pop up in the papers, no one else made the connection that the campaigning nature of video game communities could be turned to another purpose – let alone that they should be engaged.

So Bannon kept his eye on the community to see whether it could have that value in the future. In June 2007, Bannon was made head of Affinity Media. He went on to retain an interest in three *WoW* MMO sites – *WoWHead*, *Alakhazham* and *Thottbot* – to remain on the pulse of an online-game community that had shown it was able to take radical, effective digital action to deliver real-world change.[15]

THE PATHWAY TO GAMERGATE

For the best part of seven years, Bannon's connection to the online games industry didn't translate into political opportunity because he had nothing to campaign for.

However, between 2007 and early 2014, three changes occurred within the media landscape, the traditional 'gamer' community and Bannon's position that enabled the emergence of a video game hate movement which would birth the modern American far right.

The first factor was the adoption of smartphones and the accompanying growth of social media with it. In 2014, Comscore estimated that 167.9 million people in the United States owned a smartphone. This meant that the smartphone had gone from not meaningfully existing in 2007 to being in the hands of roughly 70 per cent of the American population, connecting them to the digital world more meaningfully than ever.[16]

Putting connected computing devices into peoples' hands inevitably led to significant growth for social media sites. Facebook had amassed 1.35 billion monthly active users by 2014,[17] with YouTube also crossing the billion-user mark. Digiday, meanwhile, revealed that Instagram and Twitter both had user bases of approximately 300 million people per month at the time.[18] Even comparatively niche or new social media platforms were generating impressive user counts, with Reddit recording eighty-five million monthly users[19] and Snapchat, then a new entrant into the market, boasting approximately seventy million across the same time scale.[20]

And despite having wider usage, video games were at the heart of the growing social media economy. The most watched YouTube channel in 2014 was PewDiePie, the Swedish video game YouTuber who generated 4.1 billion views over the course of the year to outgun pop stars Shakira and Katy Perry.[21] The games industry was an early and eager adopter of Twitter, with an article in IGN reporting that year it had become a 'powerful' tool for building communities, connecting to consumers and even funding projects.[22]

Games were one of the major pillars that the social media economy rested upon. And though most people went online to watch their favourite YouTubers play a game, talk about crowdfunding campaigns for interesting new releases or take part in the mass 'Twitch Plays Pokémon' experiment – where millions of players simultaneously played an early game in the battling series by posting prompts in the chat – other parts of the video game community were also well placed to influence.

This leads into the second reason why a strange video game hate campaign could bleed into the mainstream: the steady radicalisation of the fringe video game player base in spaces such as 4chan. In particular, the players who had grown up in these digital places, but did not find meaning in the wider physical world, remained anchored to them: transforming a transgressive culture into an increasingly racist and misogynistic one which retained an 'activist edge'.

'I think you get people who are left behind, who don't find that life starts for them,' Ball explains, when reflecting on his experience of leaving the Chan boards around 2008.

'Most follow a path like mine. You get very obsessively into gaming, very obsessively into online communities. Some of them are a bit dark, a bit dodgy. And then life starts, your real world kicks in and you migrate out of them. But the more people you have left behind and staying in, the more they toxify those communities. And the more dangerous it gets.'

By 2014, the signs were already there that the toxicity within these communities was both present and was proving that it could be just as effective at campaigning noisily online as the efforts waged by the *WoW* community against IGE's gold-farming efforts.

In 2012, the ending of *Mass Effect 3*, the final game in an epic science fiction role-playing action series that put your choices as the hero at the centre of the story, became the subject of a controversy amongst players online. The final act of the game, which saw players choosing to destroy, control or merge with a race of sentient alien spaceships destroying the universe, was anticlimactic, reducing the choices players had made across hundreds of hours of game playing down to one of a handful of underwhelming animated videos. And under pressure from fans, BioWare, the developer of the game, created a new ending to the game with extra content that both wrapped up the story more effectively and showed the impact of earlier decisions.

However, both the creators of the game and a number of the game's performers were subjected to intense, and inappropriate, online abuse as part of what was dubbed the 'Reclaim Mass Effect' campaign – which trended on social media. The emotional and mental health toll of this campaign was increased by the translation of the activity into the real world, with some fans sending differently coloured cupcakes to the studio to sarcastically lampoon the original ending. Though it was likely an ill-judged joke more than an intentional threat, it was an unsettling reminder that digital campaigning could have meaningful real-world consequences for those who were being campaigned against.[23]

Additionally, it's also important to remember that this campaign happened against a changing backdrop for the industry itself. The 2008 financial crash, the arrival of the mobile game economy and a need to engage new audiences were all leading to the industry shedding its 'gamer' reputation.

In a world where games like *Candy Crush Saga* were becoming the money makers of the games industry, generating billions of dollars a year by 2014 while targeting an entirely different audience of players, disaffected young men in parts of the gamer community began to frame the expansion of the audience as a betrayal of them, the true gaming audience. Within these dark corners, reaching women and people of different sexualities or races was increasingly seen as straying from the true course of the industry, something that would be mobilised to deeper ends in the years to come.

But even though some video game communities were developing toxic tendencies and were showing their ability to tilt the conversation on social media to achieve real world ends, their ability to influence political discourse was limited. Without a platform, a champion, and a wider base of support to promote their work, gamer campaigns were likely to sit on the fringes of the social media landscape.

It was the transformation of Steve Bannon from a Goldman Sachs executive to the man masterminding the American right's political media ecosystem that led to the opportunity for narrow video game campaigns pushed by a small subsection of players to infuse the country's political discourse.

Bannon's influence over the political right had been increasing since the IGE debacle. His efforts to dismantle and reassemble the political right to fight back on behalf of Judeo-Christian forces opposing Islamic ideology first found a home within the Tea Party movement. He would write and direct two films – *Generation Zero* and the ironically named Sarah Palin documentary *The Undefeated* – to continue to mainstream the movement following its injection into the Republican Party establishment in the 2008 election.

By 2012, he had also assumed complete control of the Breitbart media empire following the death of its co-founder Andrew Breitbart. Bannon tilted it away from a moderated form of conservatism approved by his co-founder towards his more aggressive, punchy and, at times, pungent form of political discourse.

And Bannon's control of the outlet allowed him to handpick the staff who would turn Breitbart into a noisy force capable of projecting his ideas into the mainstream. This led to the appointment of a technology journalist who would connect toxic gamer campaigning with the political mainstream: Milo Yiannopoulos.

I know that Yiannopoulos was a controversial figure when he popped up at Breitbart because I knew him. I had met him briefly in person during my time at the University of Cambridge, when we were both writing articles for the new online tabloid called *The Tab*. I was also paid to write a piece for his long defunct tech media news site *The Kernel* when I first was a freelancer in my early twenties about what it's like to share a name with a famous person on social media. The fact that I pitched the idea in and wrote it for the site has, frankly, made me feel deeply queasy ever since.

What usually happens here is that someone says they had no idea what that person would go on to become. I will say here that I at no point expected him to get embroiled in scandals as diverse as being banned from Twitter for harassing the actor Leslie Jones in 2016, causing enough controversy in Australia to have his visa cancelled by the national government in 2019, or briefly acting as the campaign manager for Kanye West's aborted run at the presidency in 2024.

I will also say that I had no sense that he was a 'nihilist', as Bannon would later claim. What was true is that he was undoubtedly smart. He had a sharp tongue. He was a provocateur. He was an opportunist. He was chaotic. He was certainly conservative.

After bouncing out of a job at the *Telegraph* and skipping away from his own debt-saddled publication,* Yiannopoulos took on a news role at Breitbart with an angle towards tech, where he also had the opportunity to cover games as part of his beat.

He was, it's fair to say, not a public fan of the medium prior to joining Breitbart. He had previously described adults who were excited over the idea of new video game consoles as 'pungent beta male bollocks scratchers', which is not the best way to win over the audience.[24]

---

* They would later be settled up and a new body called The Kernel Media would briefly exist separately from Yiannopoulos, before it too was snuffed out of existence.

But Yiannopoulos's ability to identify an opportunity and make the most of it meant that his disdain for games could turn on a dime if it proved useful.

So when a video game hate movement emerged online in summer 2014, Yiannopoulos proved to be the perfect cheerleader for its point of view. And with Bannon, Breitbart and the emergent alt-right following in behind him, the momentum of a niche hate movement transformed into a wave that eventually swept Donald Trump into power.

GAMERGATE, THE RISE OF THE ALT-RIGHT, AND THE ELECTION OF DONALD TRUMP

Gamergate was a storm in a teacup that somehow broke through the porcelain and ripped the foundations of democracy away with it.

The invented scandal slowly came into being following the release of a text-based video game called *Depression Quest* in 2013. Developed by Zoë Quinn, with writing support from Quinn and Patrick Lindsey, the game is essentially an interactive novel where you navigate a day in the life of a person suffering from depression, and was originally released for free online.

Depression Quest does not fit the typical archetype of video games that are thrown around in the popular conversation about the medium, but that didn't mean it was unusual for the industry. The sector has long had a counter-cultural independent development scene, where people are happy to hack together games on the cheap to tell a story. *Depression Quest* may have benefitted from using democratised development tools and distribution platforms to reach a wider audience, but it was part of both an established industry culture and a developing 'golden age' for thoughtful independent game development at the time.

However, it became a target for the toxic gamer subculture from the moment it was released. In a January 2014 article about how Twitter changed the games industry, Cassidee Moser wrote that Quinn had taken to the platform to slam anonymous trolls for the 'egregious amount of sexism' that she had suffered in the wake of the game's release.[25] The gamers attacking Quinn focused both on the game's themes as straying too far from the traditions of the industry, as well as the perception that the game was injecting politics into games; an irony that would be completely lost on them.

The trigger for the abuse to turn into a fully formed hate movement eventually came in August 2014. After the game had succeeded as a free release, Quinn and the team convinced Steam to 'greenlight' it through a programme it had introduced to filter great indie games onto the platform. *Depression Quest* released on Steam, allowing it to reach a new audience whilst introducing a 'pay what you want model' that donated part of every sale to a suicide prevention hotline.

But that month, Quinn was accused of improper behaviour by an ex-boyfriend. He alleged that Quinn's success had been achieved through a sexual relationship with a journalist called Nathan Grayson, who worked at a games publication called Kotaku and, he claimed, had promoted her work to ensure it achieved commercial success. Members of aggressively toxic video games communities immediately seized upon this as evidence of 'collusion' between game developers and games journalists to eradicate the 'gamer' identity in the name of 'political correctness'.

The campaign was demonstrably and blatantly false. It was true that Grayson and Quinn had been in a relationship with one another. However, Grayson had only mentioned Quinn once across his entire body of work at Kotaku (which happened prior to the start of their relationship). He had never written about her or reviewed any of her games after starting the relationship, including *Depression Quest*. The game itself was also free to download at the time, squashing the suggestion that there was any commercial benefit to the two being together. The reasonable conclusion, therefore, is that the post was a poison pen letter designed to discredit Quinn unfairly.

However, that did not matter to the online communities who had already abused Quinn following the release of *Depression Quest*. 'The Zoë Post' was seized upon and shared through 4chan, 8kun and Reddit by malicious gamers. Quinn became the subject of an immediate harassment campaign, leading to the revelation of her personal details via a 'doxxing' attack and a wave of misogynistic harassment under the Twitter hashtag dubbed the Quinnspiracy.

But a fenced-in hate movement began to morph into something bigger. After initially being framed as a scandal involving one developer, the actor Adam Baldwin, mostly known for a passable turn in the sci-fi Western TV series *Firefly*, posted about the controversy on social media using the hashtag Gamergate.

This amplification encouraged the harassers to draw more women into the abusive campaign, with the critic Anita Sarkeesian and the developer Brianna Wu both being harassed to the point where they fled their homes for safety. The creation of the term Gamergate gave a 'leaderless' movement a shared identity. And the conversation also created a deeply conspiratorial mindset, with motivated online campaigners creating absurd interconnected networks of industry professionals as part of a disciplined campaign of harassment.

'The thing that gets me about this being the start of Gamergate is that you look at it and it is so clearly unhinged,' said Keza MacDonald, who is currently the games editor at the *Guardian* but was Kotaku's UK editor during the worst of the campaign. 'It is an unhinged rant against somebody who you know has been dumped. But it expanded to include all women, game developers and journalists, all being targeted as a part of what became a very coordinated harassment campaign.'

'And when I say coordinated harassment campaign, there was paperwork,' MacDonald continued. 'They had documents. They had strategic planning that they thought they were being very clever and secret about but was very easy to get hold of.' This included one person creating a plan on how to 'make her [MacDonald's] life a misery' because she worked for the same publication that Grayson was a member of. The documents were discovered in a Sub-Reddit called 'KotakuInAction', which plotted much of the harassment that occurred within the Gamergate movement and remains active today.

In late 2014, it should have been obvious what Gamergate was to any reasonable outsider who was observing it. But the problem was that the campaign sat in the blind spot of most democratic media. It was a deeply online movement. It was focused on an entertainment industry that few major outlets understood. And there seemed to be little willingness to engage with the subject to work out that it was a hate campaign sparked by a poison pen letter.

As a result, the opportunity to cover Gamergate was left open. Yiannopoulos at Breitbart seized it. After picking up on the issue early, he quickly framed it as a 'culture war'. Towards the end of the year, he would claim that the 'basement-dwelling nerds' who pushed Gamergate forwards were 'heroes and inspirations' for resisting a 'poisonous incursion into their culture' by 'feminists' who smeared an 'inclusive' community.[26]

In doing so, Yiannopoulos successfully grasped that grabbing Gamergate could win him support amongst the audience and bring noisy activists to the political right – cloaking their toxicity in return for their help. Arguably even more importantly, Breitbart's promotion of the Gamergate campaign also gave it undue influence in the media debate around the topic.

Outlets such as the *New York Times*, who had mostly missed the story, covered Gamergate in October 2014 as the hate campaign raged on for years. And while they did focus on the harassment and hate directed towards the likes of Sarkeesian and Wu, they also suggested that the threats they faced were the extreme actions of people aligned to Gamergate's supposed concerns around ethics in games journalism.[27] Breitbart, in essence, was helping to wash a toxic message shared by extreme groups through the media into a more palatable right-wing talking point: guiding audiences in positions of power towards its political perspective and away from accurately reflecting the nature of the Gamergate movement.

'An enormous factor in Gamergate's success was the fact that traditional mainstream journalists, broadcasters, researchers, politicians and the police did not understand how the online world worked at all,' explained MacDonald. In her case, she was told that the way to stop being threatened online by Gamergate supporters was to stop being online – an impossibility for a journalist working for an online news site.

But more fundamentally than that, the washing of Gamergate into the public debate without proper critical engagement emboldened the movement, allowing them to advance their hateful aims further.

*

'A lot of people well meaningly assumed there must be something to it, right? Because they're like, there's all this fuss. What's going on here? What are these people's legitimate grievances? And they assumed that there was a legitimate grievance, which resulted in a lot of coverage of Gamergate that well intentionally washed the intent to harass women out of it,' said MacDonald.

In the immediate short term, this handed Gamergate the power to tip the industry. While the US games trade association the Entertainment Software Association condemned the violence and harassment in the piece in the *New York Times* about the campaign, developers such as Electronic Arts, Blizzard and Activision Blizzard stayed silent. The lack of a meaningful response allowed Gamergate to 'coagulate', allowing it to incorrectly claim that it represented the voice of the wider video games community.

Intel pulled advertising from a games media website following a pressure campaign by Gamergaters, which was also simultaneously targeting Leigh Alexander, the site's editor, for harassment.[28] Intel eventually apologetically returned its advertising to the site, but not before Gamergate supporters on Reddit had gleefully suggested the move would bury the site and its workers.

At the time, it appeared as if Gamergate had been a nasty, virulent and hate-filled campaign that had caused disruption and distress to large parts of the games industry. But its political impact was much bigger than that. Gamergate's effectiveness in causing noise online, disrupting the social media discourse, shifting the perspectives of the media, and delivering real-world campaigning outcomes was the moment that the political right in America and beyond started to dominate the political debate.

'I think Gamergate still has a major influence today on the tactics that we see being part of the far-right playbook,' says Dr Julia Ebner, author of *Going Dark*. 'It was a turning point in mobilising support for anti-liberal and anti-progressive moments because what went really well for Gamergate and the people driving the scandal was that there was a lot of reporting on it in the media.'

And between the end of 2014 and the end of 2016, its influence began to show itself in a number of ways that meaningfully shaped the emergence of the alt-right and their rapid ascent to power in America.

The first was its tactical success. Gamergate provided the toolkit for campaigners to bring toxic ideas into the mainstream. It showed its ability to shape popular language en masse, mainstreaming the phrase 'social justice warriors' so effectively that the campaign was credited with its inclusion in the dictionary.[29]

Its ability to drastically tonally shift depending on its audience allowed it to evade scrutiny, presenting a serious face about 'ethical concerns' in public that spoke to liberal democratic values, while engaging in racist, sexist, homophobic and anti-Semitic language in closed corners of the internet that few people went into.

It also showed how concentrated digital campaigning could be used to tilt the discourse, tipping algorithms on Twitter or Reddit to display Gamergate's concerns to a wider audience with relatively little effort amongst a concentrated audience.

This translated into the second major significance of Gamergate, which was the way it changed the strategic playbook for the right at large.

It established the playbook for washing extreme ideas into the political discourse by taking an idea that emerges on the fringes of the internet and giving it credibility through aligned individuals by promoting through their feed or washing through a media outlet such as Breitbart or Fox News.

This, in turn, naturally encouraged other press outlets to try to discover what the fuss was about, covering stories that have been strategically pushed into the debate uncritically – allowing the right to choose the political mood music.

And lastly, Gamergate was not a part of the alt-right: it helped birth it. The movement's main activists were banned from 4chan in late 2014 for breaching its rules about 'no doxxing, no raids [diving into someone's social media channel and flooding it with hate]' on the basis that it was likely to cause legal headaches for the board's founder, Christopher Poole.

But rather than dissipate, they instead found their way into spaces where the new political right flourished. 8kun, 4chan's despairingly edgier cousin, became the home for many Gamergaters where, as seen in the last chapter, their efforts to secure approval led to them draping a video game aesthetic over mass terror.

Although the alternative right existed prior to Gamergate, use of the term 'alt-right' within gamer subcultures attached to the hate movement increased while the alt-right co-opted its campaigning tactics. In his book *Alt-America*, David Niewert described Gamergate as the force that 'heralded the rise of the alt-right and provided an early sketch of its primary features: an internet presence beset by digital trolls, unbridled conspiracism, angry-white-male-identity victimization culture, and, ultimately, open racism, anti-Semitism, ethnic hatred, misogyny, and sexual and gender paranoia.'

The 'unbridled conspiracism' also explains why Gamergaters proved to be easy recruits for the mad conspiracies of QAnon, where the 'skills' divining massive networks of supposedly inter-related games industry professionals proved to be the perfect way to propagate its ideas. Pizzagate – the absurd conspiracy theory that the Democrats were running a paedophilia ring out of a pizza restaurant in Washington DC – likely shares its linguistic heritage with the video game hate movement, rather than Nixon's impeachment over Watergate.

Crucially, the tactics, strategies and people that made Gamergate such a success were naturally courted by Bannon to support a candidate for president who had the characteristics to maximise the effectiveness of its digital shock campaigning: Donald Trump.

Trump is not a gamer, nor is he ever likely to be. But he shared three qualities with the Gamergate-ified alt-right that meant he was perfectly placed to form a symbiotic relationship with the people pushing it.

His language, style and approach proved to be a perfect fit for this new activist base. The vulgarity of his language, his propensity towards sexism and racism, but also, frankly, his ability to be simultaneously more entertaining and chaotic than an average presidential candidate was a great fit with the anarchic leanings of the Gamergate community.

His consumption of news media, and the way he distributed it via Twitter, also increased his strategic value within the 'ideas-washing' framework that Gamergate had demonstrated the value of. By running stories on Breitbart aligned to his interest, encouraging him to place pieces on the site, or by simply steering the hosts of his favourite Fox News shows towards a certain position, Bannon and the alt-right could reasonably rely on Trump to 'mainstream' extreme ideas that were once or twice removed from their original source. In doing so, he would project talking points that emerged from fringe video game communities and digital spaces to a new wider audience: providing them with credibility in exactly the same way that Gamergate did.

Finally, and related to the last point, Trump's digital presence – especially via Twitter – ensured that his support for alt-right talking points on social media delivered credibility back to the audiences who served it up to him.

While Trump would not explicitly praise Gamergate in the way Yiannopoulos did, his success provided reflected glory on the campaign groups who supported him. This was why members of the Chan board vociferously celebrated his 2016 election win, gleefully posting that the country had elected a 'meme president'.

But interestingly, and importantly, the influence that Gamergate had on empowering the alt-right, creating the strategic framework for the 'mainstreaming' of extreme ideas, and the digital campaigning power that it unleashed went surprisingly unnoticed in much of the coverage leading up to the 2016 presidential election.

A BBC journalist who profiled Trump's 'shock troops' interviewed Yiannopoulos in August 2016[30] and noted that he had written a guide to the alt-right on Breitbart detailing its rise and factions, but missed the explicit link Yiannopoulos made between the success of the Gamergate campaign and successfully mainstreaming radical conservatism.[31] Similarly, a profile of Bannon in *Mother Jones* by Sarah Posner in the same month titled 'How Steve Bannon created an Online Haven for White Nationalists' failed to mention the impact of video game communities, the Chan boards or Gamergate in establishing this landscape.[32]

This meant it wasn't until December 2016 after Donald Trump had defeated Hilary Clinton in the election that the journalist Matt Lees, a video game critic by trade, was able to say what everyone had been missing. Gamergate's 2014 hate campaign was not just a harassment campaign of women on an unparalleled scale; the 'hashtag was the canary in the coalmine and we ignored it'.[33] And despite the importance of these game communities to tilting the 2016 election in Trump's favour, the 2024 election showed that the canary is still being ignored in liberal democratic circles.

MUSK, GAMERGATE 2, AND THE CAPTURE OF THE GAMER VOTE

By 2016, Bannon's 'luciferous insight' that online communities protesting at the sale of virtual gold could be used to tip the political scales had been realised. Through media channels, its network of influencers and the simple act of approving patronage, America's conservative right gave a cadre of controversial, but highly effective, groups of online campaigners whose identity was rooted in video games culture a level of approval that they had never received before.

This encouraged them to fuse their identity with the far right, organically feed into the activist base that supported it, and turn their campaigning firepower from games towards Trump – turbocharging the movement that fed his own impressively influential social media machine.

This proved effective in 2016, when Trump shocked the political establishment and seized the presidency. The question is how much the influence from some game communities has remained within the political right, and the extent to which it explains the continuing dominance of Trump over American politics.

Between 2016 and 2020, there was a reasonable question over whether the chaotic coalition that had transformed a video game conspiracy into a founding myth for a political movement could hold together.

The alt-right's fortunes stalled temporarily in the wake of the Charlottesville Unite the Right rally, after the links between toxic game communities and the American far right were exposed in terrifying fashion following the murder of Heather Heyer. Steve Bannon, who had by this point risen to the post of Trump's chief strategist was turfed out of the White House just days after the rally following multiple clashes with the president.[34] Yiannopoulos, meanwhile, suffered his fall from grace in February 2017, when an old recording emerged of him defending relationships between older men and younger boys – leading to his resignation from Breitbart.[35]

But as mentioned above, gamers who had formed the backbone of Gamergate had found themselves at the centre of the political right – using their reach on social media to establish themselves in positions of influence over our digital political discourse.

This included Calvin Robinson, the right-wing vicar who had founded a video game news site called God is a Geek; Ian Miles Cheong, a Malaysian political influencer and former games journalist with 1.2 million followers on X who was integral to pushing Gamergate amongst his audiences;[36] and Mike Kern, aka Grummz, who managed to say the quiet part out loud in February 2025 by saying 'Gamergate did change the world', suggesting that the movement transformed the conservative right and has 'won the long game' against 'social media censorship'.[37]

The extent of that victory, and the influence it has had on an influential part of the American electorate, could be seen in early 2024 when the community who had fermented Gamergate orchestrated a re-run targeted at a company called Sweet Baby Inc.

The business, a consultancy that helps video game developers tighten up their storytelling, was founded by Kim Belair and David Bédard in 2018. While the company offered lots of services, one of its unique selling points was to advise on how to tell stories with diversity, equity and inclusion in mind. If video game businesses were willing to hire historians to make sure their historical video games felt accurate, it made perfect sense to make sure that characters from a range of different backgrounds were written effectively and sensitively to resonate with the audience.

Sweet Baby Inc. quickly found a business audience in the games industry because companies genuinely wanted, and continue to want, their services. The company worked with leading businesses like Sony, Warner Bros. and Remedy Entertainment to provide narrative services to titles such as *Spider-Man 2*, *God of War: Ragnarök*, and *Alan Wake 2*.

Their work on the final game, however, proved to be too much for long-dormant Gamergaters. In October 2023, posters on Kiwi Farms suggested that the company's involvement in the development of *Alan Wake 2* was 'one of the biggest scandals in gaming history'. It was suggested that the company had been responsible for ensuring that Saga Anderson, the lead character in the game, was a Black woman. This was decisively debunked as 'absolutely not true' by Kyle Rowley, the director in charge of the game's development,[38] but once again, the truth didn't matter. The Kiwi Farms post cascaded through 4chan and the KotakuInAction subreddit. A Steam group called 'Sweet Baby Inc Detected' was set up to direct gamers away from titles that the company had consulted on, supported by a Discord server that deliberately skirted the firm's terms of service.

And as with Gamergate, the company soon found itself at the centre of an insanely imagined conspiratorial web. It was allegedly using funding from investment firm Blackrock to insert unpopular ideological content to cause leading video games to fail. The 'social justice warriors' weren't just invading games spaces; they were apparently actively crashing the gaming economy.

This was, of course, untrue. A contact at the business described the theories as 'wild conspiracies' that were used to justify a targeted campaign of harassment against the studio, its leadership and its workers. This included the flooding of the company's generic contact email address with toxic materials and constant messages to members of staff imploring them to 'kill yourself', all of which were coded with alt-right terminology.

The second round of Gamergate 2, although horrifying to the staff of Sweet Baby Inc., did not take off in the same way because the original 'took people by surprise', according to James Ball. The 2014's hate movement's function as the 'coalescing of a new young male political angle and force around an incredibly trivial set of incidents' meant it was always going to be more impactful than the effort to stoke a scandal that reheated many of its talking points.

However, the second wave of hate targeted at Sweet Baby Inc. did reveal how deeply video game coded thinking was within the alt-right. This was demonstrated by the decision of one of the political right's leading figures to weigh in behind the second wave of the hate movement: Elon Musk.

Musk has long been a video game fan and desperate to court the affection of players. In an interview with shock jock Joe Rogan, Musk claimed that he was one of the top players in the world of an action role-playing game called *Diablo*. His skills were later called into question after he was forced to admit that he had cheated while playing a similar game called *Path of Exile 2*. Somewhat ironically, his cheating crime was to pay someone to 'boost' his account to make his character better; a version of the services offered by the Bannon-advised IGE during its heyday.[39]

Nevertheless, Musk's desperation for an in with gamers on the political right saw him prominently posting about Gamergate 2 on X when the storm truly broke in March 2024. As well as reposting accusations from Grummz about the nature of the scandal under the caption 'wow', Musk also reshared a video from right-wing influencer Matt Walsh which claimed Sweet Baby Inc.'s work was attempting to indoctrinate children. Musk claimed that video games needed to 'get rid of this woke BS' and stop lecturing people with 'tedious propaganda'.[40]

Yet Musk's post was itself propaganda aimed at strengthening ties between gamers and the political right ahead of the election. And unlike in 2016 or 2020, Trump himself leant into the group too.

In August 2024, he joined the live stream of a game streamer called Adin Ross on a service called Kick. Ross, who had built a follower base of seven million people on Twitch before initially being ejected from the platform in 2023, had assumed an unusually prominent role within the 'manosphere'. Specifically, Ross appeared to have been inadvertently responsible for the arrest of Andrew Tate in March 2024 after announcing on one of his live streams on Kick that Tate was considering leaving Romania. Tate, who was under investigation for rape and human trafficking offences in the country at the time, was picked up by local police shortly after the stream.[41]

But despite Ross's links to Tate, there was no stopping Trump from turning up on his live stream. And over the course of his time with the streamer – and a mini-studio audience – Trump was given the chance to reach half a million concurrent viewers shortly after he had survived an assassination attempt. Sporting a Make America Great Again cap, Ross thanks Trump for his time by handing him a Rolex and a customized Tesla. Not bad work for an afternoon, if you can get it.[42]

Trump's appearance, Musk's support for Gamergate 2, and the soon-to-be-made revelation that Russian agents were targeting young male online gamers with their messaging demonstrated gamers' importance to the fortunes of Trump's political project.

And the importance of targeting, reaching and engaging this audience within the video game information ecosystem was demonstrated by the success of one polling firm when it came to calling the outcome of the 2024 presidential election.

As in 2016, the pollsters narrowly called the election incorrectly. In an article for BBC News on 7 November 2024, Natalie Sherman explained that national polls 'under-estimated' Trump for a third election in a row. And while the state-by-state polls were 'within striking distance' of Trump's actual performance, pollsters were faced with the tricky truth that their call of a tight contest had been disproved by the president's 'commanding victory' over rival Kamala Harris.

According to Sherman's piece, most firms had missed the mark for two reasons. Traditional polling methods had failed to 'anticipate the depth of the swing amongst Latino voters and young voters towards Trump', and had also failed to capture the extent of the Trump vote, with many of his supporters distrusting traditional media and institutions enough to be out of reach of typical polling techniques.

For most pollsters, another Trump victory meant that it was time for another post-mortem on polling failures. But for polling firm J. L. Partners, it was a time for celebration.

The firm was crowned one of the few winners of the 2024 election, having successfully called a Trump victory from 24 September 2024. It even correctly forecast Trump's electoral college count, precisely calling his victory at 312 electoral votes versus Harris's 226.[43]

One of the main reasons behind J. L. Partners' success was its mixed methodology in reaching Trump's supporter base. Rather than relying on a single method of outreach to recruit its samples like getting on the phone to people, the firm instead used a variety of channels to arrive at its results.

And J. L. Partners was reaching Trump supporters in an information ecosystem that no one else was looking at: mobile video games. By running adverts in popular mobile games that can reach an audience by showing them a message and incentivise them to interact by offering in-game currency, J. L. Partners hit demographics that other pollsters missed because they targeted the spaces they trust and spend their time in.

*

'The demographic [of the players targeted] is broadly what you would expect,' explains James Johnson, co-founder of J. L. Partners. 'They're younger, by which I mean under the age of thirty-five. They're more likely to live in cities and more likely to have busy lives, which is quite interesting. You might think the average gamer is somebody who is dedicating hours and hours of their life to it, but actually the average video gamer in our definition is anyone who plays for sixty seconds a day and is usually doing it on their way to work or in the middle of doing other things.'

Importantly, the in-game advertising method also captured groups such as Hispanic and Black men who do not respond to traditional polling outreach.

'There's also a big skew to non-white people and men,' Johnson continued, when explaining who responds to in-game advertising. 'Young non-white men are a really difficult audience to reach using traditional polling because they tend to have lower social trust of traditional methods.'

By accepting that these groups have pretty well-founded reasons to distrust traditional media sources and institutions – including their behaviour towards themselves, members of their families or communities – J. L. Partners instead leant into games as a space they did trust.

*

'My archetype definition for this person who we're picking up is your twenty-year-old man who lives in Pittsburgh, Pennsylvania, who is on the bus to work, and who absentmindedly loads up his phone to play whatever game he's got on. That's the voter that I think we picked up on.'

For Johnson, the use of in-game advertising to reach players was central to J. L. Partners' success in calling the 2024 election.

'It's also the reason why I think we were the most accurate because we were picking up a lot of these disengaged non-white men who, as we know, swung to Trump in numbers that we haven't seen before 2024 for the first time ever. We think part of the reason why we got it right is because we picked up people using exactly this technique.'

And while it might seem surprising that Black and Hispanic men swung towards Trump when much of the 'gamer' movement behind him held white supremacist values, the right's embrace of the stereotype of video games and video gamers as part of its political movement meant they won the information ecosystem that sat around the games that people were playing on the bus – helping to shape their world view in the process.

*

'Every voter has a bubble around their head,' Johnson said. 'It builds a view of the world based on a range of sources. Friends and family. The people they work with. Social platforms like Reddit. They're all part of it. Games are part of the information ecosystem. It's one of the platforms, viewpoints and lenses through which people develop their view of the world.'

And with democrats and liberals rarely seen within gamer subcultures that they struggle to understand or take seriously, the conservative and populist right has been able to secure a dominant hold over an information ecosystem reaching people in disconnected corners of both our digital and physical communities: turning Steve Bannon's *World of Warcraft*-inspired video game plan into a surprisingly powerful – but lesser spotted – supporting pillar of the populist right shaping the free world.

But is that advantage unassailable? Are there ways for liberals and democrats to engage within games to influence them? And can we contest, or unpick, the hold that authoritarians, populists and extremists have within the space?

The answer, I believe, is that we can. And in the final part of this book, we'll explore how it can be done and what we need to do as a society to win back the space from the control of malign actors.

Part 3
Fighting back

10

A serious game for democracies to play

Over the past five chapters, I've explored in detail how authoritarian regimes, violent extremists and populists have sought to control games, co-opt their infrastructure and tropes, and collaborate with companies and communities to achieve their goals.

In doing so, they've each established strong positions within a cultural medium that forms a series of digital third places capable of multiplying messages from within its borders, along the highways of social media and into society: reshaping the world around us.

In response, democracies have done little to nothing about it. No democratic nation has a video game strategy akin to Saudi Arabia's, which recognises its cultural value beyond being an economic asset.

There is currently no democratic counter to Russia's influence campaigning vehicle in games or to China's censorship of games, allowing both to directly or indirectly project their views, values and influence across uncontested, unmoderated spaces like Steam.

Strategies for countering violent extremism or online toxicity that shape extreme and populist opinions rarely look at games as anything more than a vector for transmission for ideas. This has left players, communities and developers within democracies under-resourced and under-supported to fight an influence war that's raging in a community meant for the purposes of play.

But if you briefly look past the challenges for a moment, you'll see something else. While much of this book has looked towards the more challenging, more problematic and fringe elements of the games community, there are still billions of players enjoying games peacefully, connecting with one another and campaigning to raise money for good causes, make digital spaces more inclusive for all and support public information campaigns on everything from public health to the environment.

That's because there are the foundations for the emergence of a truly 'democratic' movement to counter the challenges I've identified across this book. The invention and evolution of a 'serious games' movement has recognised the influential power of games. The effectiveness of campaigning activities by the UN, World Health Organisation and the Department of State prior to Trump's re-election has shown that games communities are drawn to, will organically promote and can support messages with democratic intent. And where players are engaged through games and spaces in the spirit of co-operation, collaboration and community, democratic values can follow.

However, democratic campaigning through games has been hamstrung by inconsistent institutional support towards games projects, limited funding and the sometimes well-founded accusation that organisations are offering up 'chocolate-covered broccoli' to players. And with autocratic regimes, populists and extremists happily leaning into the fun of games for their own end, democracies need to embrace play wholeheartedly if they want to compete in the space.

SERIOUS GAMES, PERSUASIVE AIMS

The idea that play can influence the way we think, including within democracies, is not a new one. In a 2016 paper titled *A Brief History of Serious Games*, academic Phil Wilkinson ponders, amongst many other things, Plato's fondness for the value of play as an intellectual exercise, the use of an early form of chess for 'militaristic' purposes in seventh-century India, and the morphing of 1902 satire *The Landlord's Game*, a cautionary lesson for renters about the potential rapacious demands of their landlords, into *Monopoly*, a game which rewards you for crushing the dreams of friends and family members who've always wanted to own a waterworks.[1]

Even some of the earliest video games showed this too. Between 1964 and 1966, *The Sumerian Game*, a project designed by a teacher called Mabel Addis, developed by William McKay, and co-founded by IBM and a New York county education board, put children in charge of the ancient civilisation and saw how their choices across three distinct in-game ages affected Sumerian society. It is credited as the first simulation game and first narrative game. It also arrived half a decade before *Pong* did, showing that organisations did recognise the value of play.[2]

However, *The Sumerian Game* butted into a problem that would become familiar to the industry at large: play was viewed, and arguably is still envisioned today, as childish. For games to be accepted as a way to impart ideas in a formal manner, someone needed to make an argument that there was a fundamental value of the medium beyond entertainment alone.

Clark C. Abt, a German-born academic researcher based in the United States, was the person who made the argument to take games seriously as a way to deal with something we're all guilty of: brainless thinking. In 1970, Abt released a monograph in which he argued that society needed to create 'serious games' to solve an incoming crisis in Western society. Previously, reading, writing and numeracy were valuable enough skills to allow anyone to navigate through life. But the rise of technology, including computers, meant that those skills were becoming less useful if someone was unable to abstract them for other purposes. The twin problems of 'physically inactive thought' and 'mentally inactive action' would become the 'diseases of civilised men', leading to conflict and strife as an increasingly underskilled and dispirited population kicked back at the world.

So Abt had an idea. Leaning on Plato's classical Greek ideal that the creative world of children 'embodied both thought and action' in a way that adult life didn't, Abt argued that developing games with a 'serious' mission could bring the dynamism of childhood into the adult world. Games developed an optimistic view of the world, where failure wasn't permanent, ideas could be tried out and the best outcomes were achieved by those brave enough to take action. In short, playing a game whose intent was purely serious first – and fun second – could be the way to teach people the abstract skills they need to succeed.

Let's be frank here: Abt's thinking was, and remains, wonkish. But it matters because the 'serious' academic framing allowed 'adult' organisations to begin to experiment with games within their work stream. In the two decades after Abt's monograph was released, computer-made 'serious games' began to pop up in a number of contexts. According to the introduction to Abt's updated monograph in the mid 1980s, nearly '400 major war computer games' had been developed by the US military for training purposes.[3] Healthcare professionals began to explore the use of games to build rapport and support socialisation in psychotherapeutic situations. Microsoft's *Flight Simulator* games, which first emerged in the early 1980s, entertained players around the world, while also encouraging the development of increasingly realistic commercial flight simulators that closely resembled their video game counterparts. Edutainment games such as *The Oregon Trail* showed that 'serious games' continued to grow within traditional education too, traumatising millions of American children through tales of grim misfortune befalling families exploring the American West.

However, Abt's argument that games could be a force for serious good were undermined by the limitations of his own thinking. By arguing that games didn't need to be fun to achieve their goal, Abt encouraged early serious games creators to make stuff that bored players stiff. The result was the memorable description of serious games as 'chocolate-covered broccoli' by Amy Bruckman, then assistant professor at the Georgia Institute of Technology, at the Game Developers Conference in 1999.[4]

But Abt's narrow view of 'serious games' began to be challenged from an unlikely angle: other game developers. A number of hit video games proved that players would engage with serious, chunky, realistic issues provided that the game was fun first. Sid Meier's *Civilization*, a game where you found your own empire in the earliest ages of history and lead it (hopefully) to glory over the course of thousands of in-game years, became a wildly popular strategy game, especially amongst the kinds of people who form our political elites today.[5] Microsoft's *Flight Simulator* games, became so inspirational to its legion of aviation-loving players that its community circulated guidebooks on their favourite routes to fly around virtual America.[6] *Sim City*, a game where you design and run your own virtual city, was used as a way to 'test' candidates in Providence's 1990 mayoral race. According to Kelly Clancy, Victoria Lederberg, one of the candidates in the race, suggested that negative media coverage of her performance in the game cost her the election.[7]

So if players were willing to play games with 'serious' messages just because they were fun, what could that mean for the strategic deployment of games? In 2002, Ben Sawyer, a game developer, and David Rejeski, an industrial designer, released a paper titled *Serious Games: Improving Public Policy through Game-based Learning and Simulation* that proved to be the foundational text for the use of games within a public policy context.

According to the Serious Games Society, Sawyer and Rejeski's paper was a 'call to use the technology and knowledge from the entertainment video game industry to improve game-based simulations in public organisations'.[8] It argued, like Abt, that games could be deployed for deeper purposes beyond entertainment alone, that building games with wider societal purposes could positively impact society, and that the communication of public policy could benefit significantly from unlocking the power of the medium.

However, in a subtle shift from the previous definition of serious games, Sawyer defined them as 'any meaningful use of computerized game/game industry resources whose chief mission is not entertainment'. This linguistic tweak meant that the serious aim of the game was still key, but that fun was no longer secondary. Additionally, the use of the phrase 'industry resources' also gently pushed the door open to co-operation between governments, individual game designers and game development businesses. This was the democratic equivalent of collaborating and co-opting games for purposes beyond play; a framework built upon consent, negotiation and shared good.

Shortly after publishing the paper, Sawyer was given the opportunity to turn his newly defined movement into something bigger, forming a new body in January 2004 that turned his ambitions into a part of day-to-day life for parts of the federal government.

'The Serious Games Initiative was originally started with the radical idea that games can be used for good, but also specifically for policy engagement,' said Elizabeth Newbury, former director of the Serious Games Initiative at the Wilson Center, a DC-based think-tank founded as a memorial to former president Woodrow Wilson.

The Center supported the creation of a number of video games which taught potentially tricky or, let's be completely honest here, drily dull public policy matters in a way that would leave players feeling meaningfully engaged. And as mentioned above, that meant ensuring that the games they made were fun.

For example, a game called *Fiscal Ship*, which sees players stopping a metaphorical tanker from crashing by weighing up policies – each of which is explained and contextualised in easy-to-read language – aimed at reducing America's debt, received 4.5 million plays from people across the world. Another game, *The Plastic Pipeline*, which gave players a good look at environmental policy and the impact of single-use plastics, was found to have meaningfully changed players' understanding of environmental issues. Newbury, who is a game designer by trade, believes that these experiences successfully got messages across to players by engaging the superpower of video games compared to other creative industries: the ability to control what happens.

'One of the things that we learned is that by making it [*Fiscal Ship*] fun and engaging and really putting the ownership and the agency in the players' hands – passing their own politics, not prescribing any particular political platform, letting them choose what's important to them, and mapping the budget to it – it really did afford them the opportunity to have lots of ownership over the learning process and policy itself.' This helped Americans get more engaged with public policy, while also inviting international visitors to the games website to join in too: quietly communicating political values further.

The Serious Games Initiative became the main convener for serious games work across the US government. In comparison to democracies across the rest of the world, the existence of the Initiative – and the foundation of the complementary, industry-backed Games for Change movement – allowed US government departments, not-for-profits, academics and industry to convene around the movement. Representatives from the State Department, the Department for Education and the Smithsonian contributed to the Initiative, through expertise and through funding for relevant projects. And the initiative's foundation within the Wilson Center as part of what Newbury described as a 'non-partisan' approach helped its reach grow further, leading to the establishment of an annual conference to convene the movement and the foundation of a Federal Games Guild to provide a forum for serious games experts from across government to convene. Newbury told me that the Obama administration particularly 'got' the value of games as a method of communication, which is unsurprising given that the successful 2008 campaign included an advertising buy in Microsoft's online Xbox Live service.[9]

The idea that games could be used for influence within democracies, therefore, had serious currency in the US. But even as the serious games movement grew, there was something missing. The definition of it still excluded developers who created games that had a serious message which had emerged from the 'bottom up' from their mission to entertain or provoke new ways of thinking. And it fell to academic Ian Bogost to slot in the final piece of the puzzle in 2007 to provide the serious games movement with a broader definition that allowed it to work more effectively with the rapidly democratising games industry.

In his book *Persuasive Games: The Expressive Power of Videogames*, Bogost argued that the term 'serious games' risked denying the rhetorical power of all games. He coined the term 'persuasive games' instead, in which he argued that games offer a new form of rhetoric in which you convince people of a point of view by getting them to play with a system.

For example, *Papers, Please*, a 2013 game developed by an independent designer called Lukas Pope, puts players in the role of a border guard of a fictional Soviet republic called Arsotzka. After dutifully manning the border post in line with the rules of your glorious government, you quickly realise there's no way to earn enough money to keep your family fed and healthy if you stick within the system. So when another security guard at the border tells you that they get a cash bonus if they arrest a certain number of people in a day and that they're willing to split it with you, what do you do: do your job and suffer or arrest innocent people to get the cash you need?

Pope's game left players with a serious message about the grey, grim realities of life in an autocratic regime. But his intention was never to make a 'serious' game. Instead, he thoughtfully engaged with a political topic, translated it into game mechanics, and reached over five million people across the world in the process.[10] In short, Pope didn't need to be ordered by someone from the 'top down'; he was better placed to reach an audience by tailoring the content of the game to achieve 'bottom up' success within the games world.

And that is why Bogost's shift from 'serious' to 'persuasive' games was so important. Rather than saying that video games needed to have an explicitly serious end goal to make headway in our world, Bogost's argument was that *all* games could influence through their mechanics. Sure, Pope's *Papers, Please* showed how this could be done by getting people to play one game with a very specific set of mechanics. But beyond that, every video game had a range of systems, mechanics and design choices that could influence players. This included the design of in-game characters, the functioning of in-game advertising networks keeping the game afloat, the option to use in-game purchases for charity fundraising campaigns, and even tapping into the rapidly growing communications infrastructure sitting around the game (including ties to social networks).

So in comparison to autocracies which have sought to promote their narratives by buying up games businesses, censoring content, or developing their own materials to influence, democratic organisations steadily realised that the best way to counter that was not to follow their tactics. Instead, it became about collaborating with video game developers to enhance, promote and celebrate their creativity in solving the big messaging challenges of our ages: unlocking an even bigger 'multiplier' effect in the process.

A VIRAL MESSAGE

Over the past ten years, it has become increasingly difficult for leaders and institutions to promote messages to the public directly. The democratisation of social media discourse, rising mistrust of traditional democratic institutions, and the emergence of new influential voices across our media and political landscape have weakened trust in 'top down' messages within democracies – making the sharing of expert information increasingly challenging.

However, that institutional trust has not entirely evaporated. Experts and institutions still hold value to audiences across the world. Many of them have excellent traditional communication structures to broadcast their messages. And for those willing to adopt a collaborative approach with new forms of media capable of engaging audiences from the 'bottom up', there's plenty of room for trusted messages to engage millions of people organically.

The video game *Plague Inc* demonstrates how this works in a public health context. The game, which launched way back in May 2012, has a cheery offer for players. They take on the role of their own home-made pathogen. They must then evolve it to ensure it spreads widely and lethally across the world, causing as much pandemonium as possible before scientists snuff it out with a vaccine.

It's a grim premise. But the game proved to be immensely popular. Since 2012, *Plague Inc* has been downloaded more than 185 million times across the world. And despite it never carrying the moniker of 'serious game', it turned out to be a remarkably effective way to communicate a serious message about pandemics: the dangers of exponential growth.

James Vaughan, the creator of *Plague Inc,* thought up the idea for the simulation game when he was bored while working as a management consultant.

After playing a flash game called *Pandemic,* which released in 2008 and had a similar premise to *Plague Inc* of inflicting mass viral death on the world, and watching the film *Contagion* on a transatlantic flight, Vaughan thought he could make a strategy game based on pandemics that was 'so much better' than anything he had played on the market.

After doing some research to understand how pandemics work, which started on Wikipedia and ended with Vaughan 'reading a lot of disease books', he quickly discovered the existence of publicly available data sets that he could use as the basis for his in-game pandemic model.

'The real world was definitely useful for us because there's a lot of data sources that are available,' Vaughan said. 'You've got World Bank data sources where you can plug in data rather than having to invent it. If you have to invent data, you have to balance it as well. Whereas if it's in the real world, you balance the game around the real world data a little bit instead.'

After playing around with the data and working on the game, 'as a hobby over weekends and evenings' – Vaughan achieved what game developers describe as 'finding the fun' by swapping slavish adherence to the demands of the data set in favour of offering players the 'core truth' about how pandemics functioned.

Due to the limits of mobile devices at the time, and the fact that the devices have always favoured easier to play games due to touch screen controls, Vaughan accepted that he could not create a game that was 'hyper-complicated or impossible for the player to understand'. So he smoothed off the edges of the model. The game did not compromise on the central pillars of how a pandemic spreads, including its capacity to mutate, the importance of transport hubs in spreading a virus, and how damaging exponential growth is compared to linear increases.

But it did streamline some aspects to keep things simple, such as by making every transport hub spread the virus broadly equally (rather than accounting for the volume of passengers travelling through, say, London rather than Madagascar).

Upon *Plague Inc*'s release, it was clear that Vaughan had got the balance right to release a hit game. It became in his words – and seemingly with no pun intended – 'a real viral success story', becoming the fifteenth most downloaded iPhone game in the US in 2012 and receiving the Best Strategy Game Award from IGN after captivating players across the world.

It also, however, positioned itself as something else: a potential public health tool. Dr Ali S. Khan is the dean of the College of Public Health at the University of Nebraska and author of the book *The Next Pandemic: On the Front Lines against Humankind's Gravest Dangers*.

In March 2013, when Dr Khan was the director of the Office of Public Health Preparedness and Response, the Centers for Disease Control and Prevention decided to host a conference on finding ways to talk about health topics in a way that would be engaging to the public. And with his mind firmly focused on the risks of pandemics, Dr Khan stumbled upon a fun, culturally relevant topic to spark a lively public health conversation: combatting the (fictional) rise of the living dead.

'During the horrific tsunami and the Fukushima event, there was a lot of chatter of "oh, is this going to create a bunch of zombies" because of the original Romero film where zombies were created by radiation,' Dr Khan explained. 'And I realised that zombies were a big deal.'

To tap into the zeitgeist, Dr Khan created a post for the conference called *Preparing for the Zombie Apocalypse* to put a fun frame around the meeting. The post became one of the most widely seen CDC posts, becoming a globally seen viral hit for the organisation off the back of a marketing campaign that Dr Khan estimated cost a princely 'couple of hundred bucks' to run.

And though the premise might have sounded odd on paper, Dr Khan had identified that it was significantly easier to talk about public health topics when they were related in a fun, accessible way back to the audiences the CDC was trying to reach.

'The point of that was that everything you need to do for a zombie apocalypse is everything that you need to do for a natural disaster,' said Dr Khan. 'That was a better way to educate people about what they needed to do than give them the usual message.'

So Khan assembled a range of speakers to make the point. He spoke to National Public Radio and the producer of the film *Night of the Living Dead*. And shortly after that, Khan spoke to Vaughan about *Plague Inc* – discovering, after a little bit of hesitation, its ability to contribute to the debate.

'When I first spoke to James, it was all about killing people and how to kill the most people. I told him it's kinda hard for the CDC to get behind killing lots of people,' Dr Khan said. 'But it is exactly the inverse too: how do you think about incubation periods, how do you think about disease transmission modes and how does that help you think through prevention strategies – such as vaccines or social-distancing strategies – to keep people safe.'

And according to Vaughan, the reason why *Plague Inc* was particularly effective at shaping the way people thought about pandemics is that it turned the abstract risk of the rapid viral growth of a pandemic into a systemic reality: bedding the dangers into the minds of players who engaged with it.

'Exponential growth is a very hard concept to understand intellectually. You can understand it, but emotionally, you don't really understand it until you see those numbers changing. They don't work the way your mind thinks they should,' he said. 'A really powerful message that you can get from playing *Plague Inc* is seeing those numbers go up not by a bit but that they're getting bigger and bigger and bigger. It is both fascinating and terrifying.'

As a result, Vaughan spoke at the CDC conference and was later praised by Dr Khan for the game's success in engaging 'the public on serious public health topics' through 'non-conventional methods to communicate with the public.' *Plague Inc*'s success would later inspire Dr Khan to support the creation of other public health games such as the child-friendly *Zoodemic* to communicate similar concepts to younger players.

In the aftermath of the conference, *Plague Inc*'s value in the public health conversation was principally informal and driven by player interest. Between 2012 and 2019, downloads of the video game spiked in response to the Ebola outbreak in Western Africa in 2013 and the emergence of a strain of avian flu in Japan in 2015. But it was the arrival of the Covid-19 pandemic in January 2020 which cemented *Plague Inc*'s role as a public educator in partnership with public health bodies.

Vaughan was one of the first people to see the public's reaction to the emergence of the virus. By 23 January 2020, he was receiving media requests as a result of the game leaping to the top of the mobile game stores in China – a direct result of players flocking to content to explain what was happening to them. And as the pandemic spread across the world, the game's sales soared with people swarming to it as a way to understand the world around them.

In the wake of *Plague Inc*'s Covid success, Vaughan donated $250,000 to the World Health Organization's (WHO) and the Coalition for Epidemic Preparedness and Innovation's (CEPI) Covid-19 solidarity response fund.[11] Following the donation, the CEPI, the WHO and the Global Outbreak and Response Network (GOARN) began conversations with Vaughan about how to use *Plague Inc*'s platform to reach players with relevant public health messages – stretching out from the game and the developer's communication channels to engage players directly.

The major method for achieving this was the development of a new mode for the game called *Plague Inc: The Cure.* Released in March 2021, and advised by CEPI, the WHO and GOARN, the new mode offered players the inverse experience that Khan had suggested: making players responsible for creating a vaccine to eradicate a pandemic running rampant across the virtual world.

According to Andrew Pattison, team lead for digital channels at the WHO during the crisis, the move was not opportunistic; it was a strategic effort by the organisation to head out into the digital cityscapes people inhabited.

'One thing that really attracted me to the industry was that it had so many creative people within it. That means they can take our messages and make them relevant, interesting and exciting,' he told me. 'So rather than bring people into our Facebook page, Twitter account or Instagram account, what we try to do is meet people where they are in their digital journeys. We'll turn up on apps that they use every day, whether it's Google maps, Google search, YouTube or Tiktok to get our content into people's lives.'

The WHO had already partnered with game communities prior to the *Plague Inc* campaign, supporting the industry-led #PlayApartTogether campaign in 2020 which encouraged people to stay connected through play to support social distancing. The irony that it was supporting this less than a year after creating the gaming disorder mental health condition was not lost on everybody.[12]

But the *Plague Inc: The Cure* campaign offered more direct benefits to the health organisations that supported it. Due to the original game's enormous reach, the *Plague Inc: The Cure* update was widely played: becoming the main driver of traffic to CEPI's publicly available resources about the pandemic in the process, according to Vaughan.

By collaborating with a developer who understood their community and role within the world, public health bodies had been able to negotiate access for their messaging to reach a community of millions of players. This allowed it to multiply its message across those channels, providing the WHO, CEPI and GOARN with the benefits of adjusting its messaging and tactics to meet millions of players in the digital third place they spent their time in.

PLAYING FOR THE PLANET

Plague Inc's success as a tool for messaging was the result of one developer creating a game that was useful in a public health context, allowing for global organisations to partner with Ndemic Creations to promote their messages.

But how effective could video games be as a medium for sharing messages if there were deeper collaboration between a wider variety of games businesses and organisations seeking to promote positive societal messages? The success of the United Nations Environment Programme's (UNEP) Playing for the Planet initiative in reaching billions of players with messages and changing behaviours suggests that it could be significant.

In 2019, UNEP launched Playing for the Planet in the fringes of the 74th session of the United Nations General Assembly. Created with an explicitly educational goal, its aim was to work with the games industry to find collaborative, constructive and effective ways to reach its audience of billions of players with messages about the importance of taking action on the climate in the games they love.

And according to Sam Barratt, who runs UNEP's Youth, Education and Advocacy Work and helped found Playing for the Planet, one of the big ideas behind the movement was a hunch that game spaces and communities had the power to project messages to players.

'I've always been curious to think about how people come together, in what fora and how change can happen through that convergence,' he explained. 'You've seen that throughout history either individuals or communities can generate agency by speaking out, whether it's Rosa Parks or Gandhi. I've always been curious about the power of change and how different spaces and places can deliver that.'

Having grown up with games himself – and watched his son grow up playing games – Barratt was keen to tap into the uniquely passionate dialogue between players and games companies to bring climate topics up the agenda.

'Having worked to get millions of people marching on climate or against different movements in my past, I wanted to think about how you can build a sense of agency and power through new kinds of creative mediums in the games industry. It kind of out-competes most other entertainment media because it has a call and response that no other media has.'

But this, according to Barratt, led to a question internally: how exactly could UNEP mobilise this? After commissioning Trista Patterson, who served as director of sustainability at Xbox, to write a paper exploring options, UNEP – with the support of games industry experts – created a plan of action based on sustained collective action.

Instead of commissioning a game to promote its message, UNEP formed the Playing for the Planet Alliance to convince games companies to commit to supporting decarbonisation of their businesses and the world more generally – using their influence, communication channels and games to bring those messages to players in the process.

First, the Alliance sought to win big endorsements from industry from the moment it founded: folding the biggest games companies in the world into its movement. 'Securing the support of Jim Ryan [at that time president of PlayStation] in California and then talking with Phil Spencer's team [Xbox's overall lead within Microsoft] to get them to collaborate together unlocked a wider movement to come beneath them.' This provided the Alliance with a credible base of committed partners, encouraging dozens of other businesses, including industry giants like Tencent, to commit to the Alliance and its goals.

Next, it created an accountability framework that ensured companies in the movement set goals to decarbonise their businesses and encouraged them to contribute to the wider work of the movement to raise standards behind closed doors. Since its foundation, the Alliance has been able to use its collection of industry experts to advise businesses across the sector about how to calculate their carbon emissions (a specialist task that had not been done before), share best practice on reducing waste in the production of games (e.g. reducing plastic packaging), and advising industry events on how to cut back on carbon. The Alliance has also sparked a meaningful race to the top amongst the biggest games platforms to reduce their emissions output at scale, with Microsoft and Sony both implementing significant power-saving updates on their consoles to reduce energy consumption amongst millions of players.

But the true secret to the Alliance's success has been how effectively it has empowered developers to promote green messages to its player base by inspiring them to develop content for their games that really resonates with their audience.

In comparison to commissioning a video game for social good – which is potentially a costly process with an uncertain outcome – the Alliance created an annual event called the Green Game Jam that allowed it to promote its messages to hundreds of millions of players through games that already existed. Initially founded in 2020 by John Earner, formerly of a mobile games company called Space Ape Games, and Mathias Gredal Nørvig, the founder of Sybo, who are the creators of the enormously popular game *Subway Surfers*, the 'Jam' encouraged game developers to think about an environmental theme, create inspiring content for their games based on it, and share it with their players. The most creative campaigns were then celebrated through a series of awards judged by other members of the Alliance and independent third parties, like journalists.

Over the past five years, I've been lucky enough to both head the panel for the Media award for the Jam and twice act as the independent auditor for the Alliance at large. In both capacities, it is clear that the design of the Green Game Jam has led to enormous adoption amongst Alliance members: driving environmental messaging to millions of players in a way that has had meaningful impact.

By making the competition a reliable part of the industry calendar, encouraging the creation of both game content and complementary messaging, and pushing developers to support tangible real-world actions – such as raising funds for a charitable cause through in-game spending or ensuring that in-game actions lead to, say, a tree being planted – the Jam gives games companies the latitude to create. And when they do, the best campaigns resonate with players in a way few others do.

For the 2022 Jam about preserving forests, Ubisoft created an activation for its open-world biking game *Riders Republic* that saw players explore a version of Sequoia National Park, which had been devastated by wildfires (and gave them an in-game opportunity to march against climate change), that was picked up by the press.[13]

In the 2023 edition of the Game Jam, Supercell created an entire storyline called Turtle Division for its mobile game *Boom Beach* – pitting players against an in-game villain who had stolen a horde of baby turtles. The campaign, which was designed to raise awareness of sea turtle populations as part of an animal conservation-themed Jam, raised hundreds of thousands of dollars for the Sea Turtle Conservancy and reached nearly 200,000 players with a documentary about the issue.[14]

And in the 2024 edition that sought to inspire people to take small actions against climate change, Tencent launched a 'Play for Green' campaign inside the mobile version of *Player Unknown: Battlegrounds*, which saw players battling in a version of a popular in-game map devastated by a century of climate change. The popularity of the game was decisive in ensuring the 2024 Jam reached well over 200 million people,[15] taking the total number of players exposed to environmental messages to 1.4 billion people.

Crucially, the Alliance's in-game campaigns via the Green Game Jam have had a meaningful impact on the world too. The 2023 Jam aimed at protecting habitats generated $700,000 for charities supporting the conservation of creatures in the Amazon, Himalayas and the West Indian Ocean.[16] The forestry campaign in 2022 saw game developers and players team up to support the planting of 2.5 million trees across the world.[17]

And the reach the Alliance has with players has allowed it to sustain its action by demonstrating to industry the value of supporting green activations. It worked with Playmob, a platform for understanding what players think through in-game polling, to find that 81 per cent of 400,000 players surveyed in 2022 wanted to see environmental content in games if it fitted the world.[18] This both justified the Alliance's work and gave a sense of the true voice of players who sit outside the narrow (and noisy) gamer demographic – giving the movement the confidence to act assertively in the digital third place.

'I think the power that games have both in terms of reach and engagement is unprecedented,' said Barratt when I asked him about the impact of the programme. 'I think we're seeing a lot, particularly in Gen Z, of people who are looking for games to represent not just what they like to play but also who they represent as individuals as well. The opportunity for games is to give the potential for players to play not just for pleasure, but to play for purpose. And that's what the Green Game Jam is testing.'

WINNING THE DISINFORMATION GAME?

Public health and environmental communication are two messages that are democratically adjacent, given the importance they place on values such as the truth. But both issues affect people across the world whether or not they live in a democracy. Therefore it's reasonable to ask a question: can games be used as a messaging channel for public service campaigns that do serve obviously democratic purposes? And if so, how?

The answer, as you'll probably have guessed, is that I think they can. But before I get to some examples of how it could work, it's worth leaping back to the request from the British government that I opened the book with and why it couldn't work.

As mentioned in the opening chapter, there was no hope that I was going to ask games companies whether they fancied inserting themselves into an information war with Russia on behalf of the UK's Cabinet Office.

But beyond the obvious risk of asking whether international businesses fancied propagandising on behalf of a national government, the request represented a deeper systemic problem in the way that parts of the government talked to me: its belief that it could order communications from the top down.

Political communication operations within governments, political parties and campaigns rely on a certain level of authority. There is a reasonable belief that when the centre talks, the information ecosystem around it jumps to attention: willingly snapping up its talking points for discussion, arguing furiously over them and promoting them through their channels.

However, communications within the video game information ecosystem work differently. The dual dynamic of highly empowered player communities and the extent to which game developers control what messages do or don't appear to them means that the industry has a strong grip on what 'official' messages cascade through the environment.

In these digital worlds and communities – which stretch across national borders and platforms – communicators and campaign organisers at the centre of a national government have little to offer developers if they're perceived to be ordering them about. And having fielded multiple irrelevant requests from government for the industry to participate in campaigns that ranged from the tangential (a blood donation drive) to the thematically silly (a suggestion of running anti-speeding campaigns in racing video games), it is easy for communicators who are used to commanding a media grid or advertising spend fall flat on their faces in these negotiated spaces.

However, we were able to run messaging campaigns in partnership with the government when we had the opportunity to take a message and adapt it to different contexts.

The original UK partnership between games businesses and the 'Stay Home, Save Lives' messaging campaign at the start of the Covid-19 pandemic came into being because games companies like Activision, Electronic Arts and Rebellion (a UK business which is also known as the rights holder for hostile future cop Judge Dredd) asked to do it and suggested ways to implement it.

Later in 2020, I worked with the Department for Digital, Culture, Media and Sport's communications team to adapt its Let's Talk Loneliness campaign into a 'Play & Talk' campaign that saw UK games businesses encourage all players to spend an hour playing games with a friend, family member or colleague online to get a much needed conversation in. Later that year, polling firm Ipsos Mori found that UK players were nearly 10 percentage points more likely to say that playing made them feel less lonely, less anxious and happier than European counterparts who weren't hit by a similar campaign[19] – implying enough campaign impact to justify me getting my annual bonus that year.

But putting my personal finances to one side for a moment, the serious point is that government campaigns for a wider range of issues can be multiplied through video games effectively *provided* that they allow the participants the agency to tell their own story. Similarly to *Plague Inc* in public health contexts and Playing for the Planet in the environmental sphere, the biggest way for democracies to participate in the space is to stand back and allow their participants to actively tell the story for them: multiplying reach much more effectively than even authoritarians can hope to achieve.

The evidence for this can be seen within a project that demonstrates clearly how government support, or lack thereof, can significantly affect the impact of an information campaign within games: the Ctrl+Alt+Disinfo project.

Ctrl+Alt+Disinfo is another 'Game Jam' project, but with a different twist on the Playing for the Planet model. Instead of offering a group of game developers a theme to design around each year, the Jam – which is run by an organisation called Global Game Jam (GGJ) – encourages grassroots developers from across the world to create games which teach 'media literacy and critical thinking to increase skepticism around propaganda and disinformation'.

Maria Burns Ortiz is the director of the Global Game Jam. Having previously worked as a journalist for ESPN, she cofounded an educational games company which worked with the US federal government, groups like the National Science Foundation, and even the Chilean government to create serious games for educational purposes – giving her insight into both the power of the movement and its potential as a form of communication.

Shortly after being appointed as the organisation's executive director in 2024, she received word of an intriguing opportunity. In July 2022, the State Department's Cultural Heritage Center, the US Embassy in Warsaw and Poland's GovTech ministry teamed up to host a 'United with Ukraine' game jam to create games that celebrated the country's heritage following Russia's full-scale invasion.[20] A little under two years later, the State Department's Global Engagement Center was ready to expand on that work.

'I came to Global Game Jam in May 2024 and probably within my first week I came across a Request for Proposal for a game jam around Ukraine,' Burns Ortiz said. 'I had the background in writing federal grants, I knew a number of the folks kinda within that space, and it just made a lot of sense to me to create games that would raise awareness and increase skepticism around disinformation.'

Creating games that tackled disinformation was not a new idea within the space. Games such as *Harmony Square* and *Cat Park* both put players in the middle of relatively entertaining games about tackling the issue at a thematic level. But Global Game Jam's pitch offered a few big differences to those two titles.

First, the competition was not framed as an educational activity. Despite the potential to educate through the Jam, she avoided using the word 'education' within the pitch 'because most educational games are boring'.

Next, and somewhat evident in the name, GGJ made it clear that the jam would be led by what the developers created. While they would need advice and guidance about tackling disinformation to inspire their work, it was crucial that they made games to tell the story.

'The entire point of Ctrl+Alt+Disinfo was to create games that wouldn't just say "disinformation is bad" but would teach you how to identify disinformation, how to be skeptical of it, and then train developers how to be able to do that,' she said. Top-down interference in messaging would get in the way of creativity, not support it.

And finally, Burns Ortiz believed that the organisation's deep reach into Ukraine meant that it could connect with developers on the ground who really understood what was at stake given Russia's efforts to bombard them (and the world) with disinformation about the war.

'We have a very strong core in Ukraine,' she explained. 'We have a regional organiser, we have hundreds of game developers, and hundreds of jammers that are part of our community there.'

Unsurprisingly, the Global Game Jam won the bid. But after securing the grant, there was one mostly positive surprise in store for the team.

*

'We got the grant and we got the notification [saying we had won it], but they said that we want one change,' she said. 'And you know at this point you're like, "ok whatever the changes are, let me know." And they said we really loved it, but we wanted to include twenty-five other countries because disinformation is a global issue.'

This presented an opportunity, but also a challenge for the team. By expanding to what would eventually become twenty-seven countries, the Jam had to ensure that participants truly understood that disinformation is not the result of 'a single threat actor, but it is really this global issue and it's important to help people understand what it is'. Making sure developers understood what it meant outside of the context of one conflict became even more important to allow the Jam's message to multiply.

*

'Once you start training people to understand what disinformation is and recognise it through the medium of games, that carries over into real life,' said Burns Ortiz. 'I know that from having done education [games], where you teach kids how to multiply in the context of a game. When they turn off and go away, it means they still know how to multiply, right? And so that's the same thing that we took through the approach to disinformation.'

By reaching into the community, teaching developers about disinformation, but leaving them to choose what they develop, Ctrl+Alt+Disinfo was in many ways perfectly placed to succeed. By January 2025, it was ready to roll out across three stages in the following months with a pitch event to be held in Poland later in the year.

And the top twenty games that did eventually emerge from the Jam included some fantastically inventive explorations of how disinformation works, including *Medieval Courier* (where a cunning messenger fox tweaks messages sent between two courts to sow mayhem), *Polar* (a game where you manipulate information by playing tarot cards with different propagandising effects) and *My Little Conspiracy* (which puts you in the shoes of an early online moderator capable of guiding the conversation online).[21]

Ctrl+Alt+Disinfo was a perfect example of how democracies could work with the games community to promote messages. It funded a scheme by a popular grassroots movement that was trusted by developers (and fought for its interests). It worked with developers from across the world to convince them of the challenges of disinformation, but allowed them to interpret the problem in their own way. The games that resulted from the Jam were clearly good enough to be commended too, increasing the chances that the messages contained within their mechanics would reach players across the world.

But the work was significantly damaged by the election of Donald Trump in the United States. The closure of the Global Engagement Center in late 2024 as part of the Trump administration's deprioritisation of disinformation as an issue was followed shortly afterwards by Elon Musk's Department of Government

Efficiency (DOGE) reviewing spending across the federal government. The new administration decided that the funding it had assigned for the Global Game Jam was no longer a useful way to spend money. This led to the government reclaiming cash it had already assigned to the organisation directly from the not-for-profit's bank account. 'That's one of the things that I've never seen before,' said Ortiz Burns, somewhat despairingly.

'Getting DOGE'd,' wiped out the hard work of the Global Game Jam team. But it also hit the rest of the serious games sector too. Following an executive order from Donald Trump, the Wilson Center was ordered to return to its statutory minimum funding amounts. The Serious Games Initiative was therefore put into cold storage, with many of the officials who worked across departments such as the Department for Education cut down by DOGE. This has forced the movement to consider new sources of funding and new ways to convene to circumvent the challenges put in its way.

PLAYING WITH DEMOCRACY'S FUTURE

Having spoken to a few contacts about the cuts, it is hard to suggest that DOGE deliberately cut budgets relating to the serious games movement and the use of games to support democratic messaging. Few people thought that DOGE had anywhere near the knowledge of how the federal government works to successfully do that, let alone the skill with the fiscal knife to cut accordingly.

But the fate of Ctrl+Alt+Disinfo and the Serious Games Initiative tells us where we currently stand when it comes to the promotion of democratic messages within the multiplying environment of the video game digital third place.

There are democratic organisations interested in games as a channel for influence. It is possible to create effective structures such as the Serious Games Initiative to support collaborative work across departments. The Playing for the Planet Alliance and the World Health Organisation have shown how games and the systems that underpin them can be co-opted for good, with the right relationship with industry and players. Other international organisations are taking the influence of games as a strategic channel for communication seriously, with NATO hosting a conversation about the use of games as a channel to promote narratives – both positive and negative – at a conference in Riga in October 2025.[22]

But despite having a head start in the development of serious games for positive societal good, democratic organisations and governments are on the back foot when it comes to contesting the information ecosystem that pulses around the industry.

While more and more organisations are taking games seriously as a medium for influence, there is still widespread skepticism about the medium that makes it hard for people who do believe in the power of play to access funding, in-kind support like access to infrastructure or simply cultural approval within a company. The extent to which explicitly pro-democratic messages are being shared within and via games is questionable, with most of the examples in this chapter serving wider global public good purposes than specifically supporting democratic norms. Video game industry support for initiatives remains patchy, with companies often fearing backlash from fan communities who are either wary of being served 'chocolate-covered broccoli' or from 'toxic' subcultures who seek to aggressively control the space by harassing businesses, developers and individuals who disagree with them. And with what was previously a global centre of serious games knowledge being cut back considerably by a government in the United States propped up by supporters whose instincts are authoritarian, there is a vacuum within democracies for an organisation that can protect democratic values in games from the attacks of authoritarians, extremists and populists.

But this chapter shows there is hope. Games can be persuasive for socially good and democratic causes. Game communities, including developers, platforms and players, are willing to participate in campaigns and project messages effectively across the digital cityscape. And there is more than enough evidence from public health professionals, global NGOs and even governments that games can work as a channel for influence for good.

However, we do have to take the challenge facing us seriously, put effort into resolving the problem, and commit to doing so in the long term to reclaim the persuasive power of games. And in the final chapter of this book, we'll discuss how exactly we should do that.

Conclusion: Free to play

Video games have assumed an important role at the heart of our social worlds. A medium that was once bound to mainframe computers in laboratories inside American universities has transformed into an interconnected digital cityscape where games, the infrastructure that underpins them and the people who play them congregate for the purposes of playing, relaxing and chatting with one another.

In doing so, they have brought entertainment to billions of people around the world, created a market with a valuation nearing \$200bn and, much more importantly, provided fun, relaxation and reasons for people to socialise in a world that has felt increasingly fragmented and isolated.

But where people meet, talk and hang out, identities and ideas can form. When that occurs, influence isn't far behind. And in the absence of a sustained strategic effort by liberal democracies to understand, appreciate and participate in this new world, the digital third spaces created by video games have been left uncontested – encouraging others to take control.

Over the past decade, authoritarian regimes, extremist groups and populist political movements have successfully controlled, co-opted and in some cases collaborated with video game subcultures to achieve outcomes that strengthen their causes at the expense of democratic norms.

Saudi Arabia has used its economic might to capture and co-opt video games and esports companies to scrub the international reputation of the state and use 'bread and circuses' to satisfy its population, covering political repression in the process.

China's emergence as the superpower of the global games industry has allowed it to trap hundreds of millions of players into the mesh of its new censorship net, dragging all domestic games companies, their international partners and even non-governmental organisations into supporting its enforcement.

Russia's investment in video games as a channel for promoting its narratives has handed it a new weapon within its disinformation arsenal, allowing it to 'multiply' its messages through supportive streamers, existing media channels, and Western news outlets which often lack the necessary video game literacy to adequately critique its effectiveness (or otherwise).

Violent extremists who have developed their own chaotic ideologies have gamer-fied terror, co-opting the aesthetics of games and collaborating with like-minded nihilists across the world to power a toxic online debate, commit atrocities in the real world, and promote – or even re-create them – through the games that provided these deeply isolated individuals with a shared culture.

And in America, Steve Bannon's 'luciferous insight' about the power of online game communities washed the extreme political beliefs, language and participants behind the Gamergate hate movement into the political mainstream: birthing the alt-right, supporting Trump to two victories in the presidential election, and creating the conditions for the White House social media accounts to post AI-generated memes that you'd usually see on a chan board to a despairing world in 2025.

As a result of this, democracies have been caught on the back foot by the transformation of video games from products into influential social spaces. Tired stereotyped thinking about who plays games and why has seen democratic institutions shove games out of the mainstream, ceding the fun of the digital third place to actors with varying levels of hostility to democratic norms. And with democracy suffering from a wider malaise that leads people to question its very existence, failing to contest an influential ecosystem and then appearing to be boringly humourless in comparison to authoritarian regimes, extremist groups and populist movements that have seriously embraced the importance of play are actively damaging democracy's chances of survival.

But democratic complacency over games has, at least, one benefit: it leaves an enormous amount of room to do better in games. The absence of strategies to engage players in games, the lack of institutional support or funding to do it, and the failure to take games seriously are all problems. Yet this also means that small changes could potentially have a big impact on the effectiveness of promoting democratic values in games. Importantly, we have the right ingredients within democracies to change this. The vast majority of players want to play and talk with their friends and family in peace, without being threatened or influenced. Most video game developers want to provide fun and safe spaces for people to play, but need help dealing with challenges that prove problematic for nation states (let alone entertainment businesses). The popularity of video games within society means there is definitely a cadre of grown-up players who will be in positions of authority – whether in political office, working at regulators, in law enforcement or in the press – who would support a push to ensure games remain democratically safe spaces.

And as we saw in the last chapter, players, developers, NGOs and governments can team up to project democratic values through games in a way that respects the right to play (and could counter authoritarian efforts to control the space effectively).

So, how exactly can we address the complicated challenges raised over the course of this book within the video games space? What do we need to do differently to ensure that democracies have reasonable and fair influence within the medium? And what can you do to address the problems?

I've come up with a list of seven recommendations that I hope can provide a framework for how democracies can create a new proactive and collaborative relationship with players and game developers to counter efforts by hostile actors to use the power of play for ill intent.

1. UNDERSTAND THAT THE PROBLEM IN GAMES IS PREDOMINANTLY A SOCIAL ONE, RATHER THAN ONE OF CONTENT OR TECHNOLOGY

The range of problems raised across this book are varied, deep and often trickily complex. And within a number of chapters, the content of games has been used for purposes of influence – directly and indirectly.

Propaganda games like *Squad 22: ZOV*, China's censorship of video games content, and the use of platforms such as *Roblox* to re-create mass shootings are all worrying developments that show how the democratisation of game development can be twisted to a darker end.

But in all of these instances, the content is less important than the network that promotes it. Russian propaganda games rely on unwitting journalists to project its content well beyond the meagre number of players who engage with it. Indirect influence of Chinese games censorship ripples out of the country by dint of it being the biggest games market in the world, which therefore encourages developers to design for it first (or as one of its highest priorities). Extremists know that experiences on *Roblox* will get shuttered quickly, on the understanding that their main purpose for doing so is to raise their credibility in narrow toxic game communities who find re-creations of mass shootings funny.

Therefore, the shared challenge across all the issues raised in the book is not the content of games but their context as social spaces within our digital landscape. In the same way that football authorities did not tackle the challenge of violent hooliganism in the UK by trying to change the rules of football, fighting malign influence in games is about guarding the social space that people play in.

This means that the challenges have to be handled by developing a strategy to shape norms in game communities towards positive democratic behaviours, to warn players and communities of risks of harm, and to provide the industry with institutional support – and the occasional judiciously targeted regulatory crack of the whip – to affect social change.

Otherwise, the transit of people, ideas and influence up and down the social highways connected to leading video games will continue to go ungoverned: handing opportunities to hostile actors in the process.

2. PROTECT PLAY, DON'T PREVENT IT

Having dealt with the press while managing comms on behalf of the UK games industry, I know that there will be plenty of knees ready to jerk into action in response to this book.

I don't dispute the fact that I've raised major issues that require solutions. However, the severity of what has been raised demands a thoughtful, long-term and considered response. What it doesn't need is a new wave of moral panic, calls to limit or prevent access to games, or coming down like a ton of bricks on the industry.

We've tried the panic-like-idiots approach in the past and it has failed miserably.

Even though games are more a part of our culture than ever, the 'high' democratic discourse around games treats them as trivial, threatening and niche, as if we were still stuck in the 1980s or 1990s. As a result, it reinforces a number of pre-existing challenges that will simply deepen the problems we're facing.

This includes annoying communities of players who already feel like they're ignored, encouraging an industry that's used to being tarred to hide behind cover, and ceding the space to the authoritarians, extremists and populists who are gleefully running rampant there anyway. A knee-jerk, 'ban this sick filth' approach consolidates their control by driving video game fans away from the mainstream towards them. And given what I've argued across this book, I don't think that's a good idea.

Instead, democracies should do something bolder: claim the right to play as a fundamental democratic right in opposition to authoritarianism. According to UNICEF, every child should have the right to play. But once those children hit adulthood, that right is whipped away.

Despite the fact that most people who play video games are adults, despite the fact that play is a central reason why people come together in third places, and despite the fact that organised sport – both professional and amateur – is a massive part of the world, my understanding is that nowhere in the democratic world actually recognises the joy, expressiveness and freedom of play as an adult right.

So the way to begin solving the influence problem is to start to embrace the idea that playing online is a democratic right, that people should have freedom to play, that it supports freedom of expression and assembly, and that efforts to restrict it, pervert it or attack it are anti-democratic.

This simultaneously counters the intention of hostile actors and allows us to label a lot of what I've written about as harmful. And even more importantly, it rehabilitates play: bringing players, communities and developers towards democratic values in the process.

'The thing that we need people to understand is that human play is an important fundamental technology,' said Professor

Andrew Przybylski from Oxford's Internet Institute. 'It's how people learn about the world, how they experiment with the world. And because our world is so mediated by the internet, freedom to play within it, and freedom to play safely, is one of the most precious things that governments can offer people.'

3. BUILD COALITIONS WITH PLAYERS, DEVELOPERS AND OTHER PARTICIPANTS IN THE SPACE

Democracies are generally bad at digital communication campaigns because institutions are locked in remarkably autocratic ways of thinking about information spaces.

Eliot Higgins at Bellingcat told me that our information landscape has transformed from a fairly narrow pillar, where stuff is mostly shoved down from institutions at the top, to a flattened landscape where individual influencers, communities or organisations can get their voice heard much more easily from the 'bottom up'.

Most governments and democratic institutions remain stuck in the old model, aiming to command the public debate by using its authority to lead the news agenda.

Yet as we've seen across this book, most of the influence to emerge from game communities is coming from the bottom up. Grisha Putin streamed at the Wagner Military Group's headquarters because he knocked on their door to ask them. Breitbart's strategic mainstreaming of hard-right and far-right ideas started by promoting Gamergate into its communities. Saudi Arabia is inviting influencers to its esports events to allow them to promote Riyadh on their own terms to their communities, balancing the risk of negative coverage against the likelihood of self-censorship. No wonder China wants to censor games spaces so badly.

So democracies need to change tack. Rather than ordering messages from on high, it needs to learn from groups like the Serious Games Initiative and the Playing for the Planet Alliance that it is much easier to build bridges with players, communities and developers when it brings its value – such as expertise in tackling societal challenges, its power to convene and its credibility in traditional institutions – to the table as a broadly equal partner.

Doing so isn't simple. Given the range of issues raised in the book and the number of stakeholders you'd need to get around the table, there would likely need to be the creation of either an arm's length body or not-for-profit that has the funding, the institutional support and the credibility to take informed positions on problems emerging from the space, convene people to discuss how to address them, and execute campaigns able to tackle concerns (or foster positive behaviours).

While it would be hard to do, it would be the right thing. Not only is this a more effective way to operate, but it is also much more democratic. And by projecting the positivity of these values to players and developers, it makes it much easier to highlight how much financial brute force, manipulation and autocratic control form the foundation of authoritarian strategies for influence – strengthening arguments against those parties in the process.

4. TARGET SPECIFIC SOCIAL ISSUES THAT ADDRESS THE LARGEST CAUSES OF HARM

The temptation when reading this book is to immediately think about the different ways democracies could create game-specific strategies to address disinformation, national influence campaigns or far-right campaigning. It is a good idea to think about these issues in this way and come up with plans to deal with them.

However, there are a number of social harms that have been identified within this book that stretch across both the issues and groups we've studied extensively. And while walking up to games businesses and saying 'we need a strategy for tackling right-wing extremism in your communities' will likely spook the international companies who make large amounts of their cash in America, abstracting back to tackling social harms through a 'no fault' framework (i.e. social spaces always have challenges, let's solve them together) makes it easier for developers to support campaigning through their games.

In particular, there are three social harms that should be tackled through campaigns to support the promotion of democratic norms in games, their communities and beyond.

The first is addressing the risk of grooming in game communities generally. It is easy for nefarious individuals and hostile groups to enter online games, forums or live streams and subtly draw people away to darker spaces. This is true of child sexual predators, terrorists, nihilistic extremists and hostile political actors. Developing education campaigns to run in schools, in games, in social media and in the wider world to create a rubric in the minds of players about what a groomer does is useful for both safety purposes and addressing questions of influence – creating a double benefit.

Next, addressing misogyny in games is a clear requirement. As Galen Lamphere-Englund told me, misogynistic comments about women are common amongst the nihilistic groups spawning solo mass shooters, terror or extremist organisations tapping up the space, and the far right. Zero tolerance towards misogynistic content or communication in games, both through content moderation and by setting a wider social standard that it isn't ok, is therefore crucially important for preventing toxic communities and radicalised individuals projecting undue influence on games.

Finally, and related to the point above, combatting racism is as important in video games communities as it was for addressing the challenge of nihilistic hooligan communities within football. And like the world of football, it will take a combined campaign that encompasses players, the developers who set the standards for in-game spaces, social media platforms (or, if they're intransigent, community moderators) and the authorities to make sure that its normalisation by toxic communities ends.

The video game industry has done much more work on this than is often publicly spoken about. Ubisoft worked with UK police to train its customer support and community management teams to fight toxicity in their games, including how to report it. Tools such as Modulate, an AI-powered chat moderation service, reported in 2024 that it had filtered 45 million interactions within Activision's popular shooting series *Call of Duty*. Riot Games, meanwhile, has changed the terms of service of its leading games to allow it to temporarily or permanently ban players who engage in unacceptable behaviour within their games *and* on other platforms – ensuring it can snuff out toxic voices at source.

However, a lot of these actions are either one-offs by developers or applied unequally across games that utilise a technology. Combining forces to tackle hatred of women (and, it must be noted, other sexualities) and hate for other races, and to alert players to the risk of grooming or influence via joint industry-supported campaigns like Kick It Out – the anti-racism body that has been enormously influential in football's battle against hooliganism – is crucial for maximising the effectiveness of campaigns.

And by picking these three issues to campaign on, it won't just make game communities safer and more positive in a way that'll boost business; it'll also promote democratic values that are the precise counter to groups like the far right who boost nihilistic violence or Vladimir Putin's machismo disinformation.

5. TARGET GAME PLATFORMS THAT CAN'T, OR WON'T, DEFEND DEMOCRACY WITH REGULATION

If creating campaigns aimed at tackling harm is about multiplying democratic values across the world, there also needs to be a corresponding effort to dampen the multiplicative effect of hostile messaging across video games at every layer.

And while the only way to achieve this is with a multilateral approach, there are specific areas of risk that merit special attention as a way to clamp down on transmission.

The first is on the coverage of games, games companies or esports events that are aligned to influential actors. It is incredibly difficult to find the right balance between exposing an issue and trotting out talking points, as you can probably see when I tried to get to the bottom of what's happening with games in Saudi Arabia.

However, a consistent theme across the book is that credulous coverage of video games by media outlets that often lack any dedicated video games experts on staff – or sideline them – has allowed propaganda, soft power plays and outsized grievances from toxic communities to lead the discussion that shapes public and political perception of the medium.

Balancing that risk by being both more critical of potential power plays in games and by simply covering the day-to-day of the games industry more effectively will dilute the strength of such campaigning: hosing it down with content that is rooted in a serious – and still, when necessary, critical – approach to the industry.

Next, storefronts like Steam must be subjected to regulatory scrutiny until they stop enabling authoritarians at the expense of democratic values. Its 'nothing illegal, no trolling' content moderation policy actively multiplies authoritarian influence at home and abroad, allowing them to control access to content under the auspices of local laws, while dampening democratic norms. If states lack the legal powers to force Steam to pull blatantly propagandist games from its store, lawmakers should hand them the means to act to withdraw them from sale. And if the industry wants to maintain its seat at the table, make it clear to all games businesses – from the smallest independent developer to the largest publisher – that if you work with storefronts like Steam, which lack meaningful content policy, that the cut you give to them for displaying your game funds the time they spend emailing Russia's censorship authorities to remove content on their behalf. Unhappy with that? Then demand better and stop treating stores like Steam as eccentric wealthy relatives, whose crank political views are best ignored.

Finally, there is a big question – and problem – around how social media platforms directly tackle groups and communities who cause harm. Once again, Steam has covered itself in shame with a slack moderation policy for its social channels that has allowed fascists, extremists and actors working on behalf of organisations like the Wagner Military Group to organise freely.

But other social media platforms like YouTube, Discord and arguably *Roblox* – which is also still available in Russia, at the time of writing – have also acted as home to communities who use games to advance influential aims. And while each of those platforms has at least to some extent implemented moderation tools or closed off routes into foreign markets, others like X – which remains hugely popular amongst players and toxic communities – have given up entirely.

Regulators have increasingly been handed the powers to deal with these platforms via rules like the European Union's Digital Services Act and the UK's Online Safety Act, but they have failed to pick a fight or extensively scrutinise services that are seen to be closely aligned to the current American political landscape. If democracies want to survive, they'll need to be a lot braver and take action there – to stem influence both from games and from the wider social media landscape in the process.

6. ATTRACT GAMES COMPANIES BACK TOWARDS DEMOCRACIES

Sticks can be used to great effect to punish bad behaviour. However, the games industry and its communities have been subjected almost entirely to stick-based beatings from democracies since they first emerged. This has allowed other groups to use carrots such as Saudi Arabia's $38bn investment fund or Steve Bannon's loose, but realised, promise of a meaningful voice within the wider world to entice them to their side.

And while it isn't right, or possible, for democracies to go toe to toe with a PIF-backed publisher or Vladimir Putin's reported $50bn investment in a Russian games publisher, the truth is that democracies can entice developers, players and communities towards them with targeted support that boosts the health of democracy in general.

For example, most of the groups mentioned across this book could do an awful lot of good with not very much money at all. The Extremism and Gaming Research Network operates almost entirely unfunded, despite the fact that it regularly convenes a global network of experts that has produced much of the world-class research which has made this book possible. The Wilson Center's Federal Games Guild acted as a top-class convening body for the Serious Games Initiative across the country while operating on a shoestring, and initiatives like the Global Game Jam's Ctrl+Alt+Disinfo achieve huge reach in return for relatively small investment of a few hundred thousand dollars. One Ukrainian games researcher I spoke to for the book said that they wanted to create a database of Russian propaganda games but lacked just €50,000 to make it a possibility.

Furthermore, there are plenty of ways to incentivise the development of democratically significant games through policy tweaks, existing forms of public funding and simple social proof.

On the policy front, a number of countries like the United Kingdom, Australia and Ireland award tax credits for games made in the country, usually on the basis that they represent 'cultural' values within their development. Amending these credits to either award extra points in the application process or more cash to developers who promote democratic values is a positive way to reward organic interest in societal good.

Next, there are an enormous number of funding pots – both public and private – that could promote democratic value in games. Organisations like the UK's National Lottery could, for example, help put money towards supporting the domestic esports sector at a grassroots level to promote national interest within it. Meanwhile, there's plenty of room for other funding sources such as charitable foundations, philanthropic trusts and individuals' private wealth to fund groups or campaigns addressing issues in games – something that could have a lot of upside for comparatively little cash input.

There's also some good old-fashioned value in simply taking pride in video games and the video game industry as a part of the cultural conversation within democracies.

In 2025, French President Emmanuel Macron managed to get himself a round of favourable press coverage after praising the success of the remarkably successful Gallic-tinged and French-developed role-playing game *Clair Obscur: Expedition 33* on social media. Meanwhile, the former Chancellor of Germany Angela Merkel had a memorable appearance on the front pages of the German press after being caught high-fiving a man dressed as Mario during gamescom. Member of Congress Alexandria Ocasio-Cortez's use of Twitch streams during Covid-19 to reach hundreds of thousands of people worked because she authentically engaged with game communities on their terms. She picked a platform popular with players, brought on board influential game streamers who supported her message, and played the then wildly popular social deduction game *Among Us*. She did not compromise on her message. But she did meet the community where it gathered, generating influence in the process.

It might seem like a small thing to do. But when done authentically, celebrating video games or the work of a leading games business is a great way to signal to the community that it is included: reducing exclusion and providing a valuable signal to other societal participants to back it.

7. TAKE GAMES SERIOUSLY, WHATEVER ROLE YOU PLAY IN THE WORLD

Finally, I am leaving the simplest, but most important, recommendation until last: we all need to take video games much more seriously if we are to protect play and prevent it from being controlled, co-opted or collaborated with to clamp down upon our freedoms.

From cult-hit indie games to major Triple-A single-player games, to competitive multiplayer esports, through to creative platforms like *Roblox*, *Fortnite* or *Minecraft*, the popularity of video games has put them at the heart of our digital landscape, made them a prime place for people to hang out and created a thriving information ecosystem. This has turned the space into a multiplier for ideas, concepts and influence: giving games serious cultural and social power that is meaningfully shaping political power downstream, as Andrew Breitbart notoriously argued.

So I want to round this book off by addressing some key audiences independently across the big pillars of our democracies with advice on how to take the medium seriously.

For elected officials at the top of the democratic tree, view video games as a major cultural medium, their spaces as influential to our social discourse and their players as an adult audience you need to court to succeed. Strengthen the right to play, encourage industry to raise its standards within its spaces, and support the creation of institutions that address concerns in a measured, serious way. And remember, doing this well and learning to embrace the fun can win you elections by helping you look more in touch, more authentic and less stuffy than your rivals.

For political officials, civil servants and other participants in civil society who are thinking hard about how the digital and real worlds interact, develop video game specialism within your organisations. Stop handing individuals or incredibly small teams the remit to examine everything that happens in the biggest social landscape ever invented. Instead, invest in expertise, find people who can tackle harms, and build relationships with industry to translate practical problems within counter-terror, law enforcement or the upholding of wider civil standards into game-appropriate messaging.

For academics and academic institutions, support researchers who are looking at video game topics that exist beyond the usual landscape of topics like violence or addiction. Yes, you can continue to support them and you should do so as part of the fact that academic freedom is integral to democracy. But look at the range of issues raised in the book and the challenges I've had truly measuring what is going on as an opportunity. I've done my best to be fair, but I know that the depth of your expertise can build upon, or challenge, the wider foundations I've laid here.

For the media and press, elevate games into the public debate with the seriousness they deserve. You are already aware that audiences love to read about play – hello, the sports pages – that they're engaged with culture, and that games are literally retaining readers for publications as big as the *New York Times*. Investing in covering video games effectively is a great way to grow your audience, but also to reach into interests of your existing audience that are currently under-served elsewhere. And just in case you're worried it somehow isn't serious enough, I hope that this book has shown you that what happens within the video games industry, within its communities and sometimes within games itself spills out into the real world – making effective coverage of the medium necessary to give your readers the full picture of the world they live in

For the developers and games industry at large, it is time to stop thinking that our medium is a niche or undervalued part of society. Your games, your communities and your entire medium are able to wash the reputation of authoritarian states, spook the Chinese government and even inadvertently shove at the sides of democracy. I know from working in the industry for over fifteen years that the vast majority of people making games do so to entertain, not to repress. So embrace the role you have as a big part of our society that is capable of shaping the way a truly free, fair and open society functions. It is a privilege to hold such responsibility and it should be openly embraced, through leadership at the top of the industry, through the wider development community and through meaningful work with – and, in some cases, investment into – organisations across civil society that can help to tackle the challenges you're facing.

For players and communities, keep speaking up about what you truly want from your games and the spaces you inhabit. The importance of a narrow audience of exceptionally noisy players has been prioritised for too long. But if you keep demonstrating how serious games are to your life, how important they are to your social bonds and why they deserve protection, you have a part in making play a democratic right worth protecting – both in games and beyond.

Finally, if you do not play video games – or, more likely, think you don't even when you're dipping into *Wordle* on a daily basis – the easiest way to take them seriously is to simply accept video games as a normal part of social society for people of any age.

By tolerating video games – or even trying to understand why the people in our life play – you play an important part in rehabilitating a medium that sits at the centre of our digital social lives. And if everyone does that quietly in great numbers, we can slowly, steadily and effectively bring the power of digital play back towards democracies: strengthening our societies in the process.

Acknowledgements

I thought that writing a book would be a solitary activity, but I quickly realised that this was a team effort. So it is time to thank all the behind-the-scenes players (do ya geddit?) for doing their bit.

First, I want to thank you for reading this book. I've tried my best to fairly represent an underreported, little known-about and developing space of political influence, while trying to make it as clear as possible that games are great, should be celebrated and, in this context, protected. Any failure to achieve that, any errors within the book and any bad jokes made throughout the course of the book are my fault alone. Failing to laugh at the jokes? That's on you, I'm afraid.

Next, I want to thank the people who made the book possible. Jared Shurin got the ball rolling by listening to my vague idea for a book and telling me he wanted to introduce me to someone to discuss it. Max Edwards, my agent, kindly transformed a rubbish written proposal into something much better, sold it successfully on my behalf, and proceeded to celebrate every milestone with *just* the right number of beers. Alex Osmond, his former assistant, was charmingly supportive through our time working together. Emily Randle, who managed the book's international rights sales, passionately pushed my work at every opportunity.

Joe Thomas at Wildfire was the perfect editor for *Power Play* and for me. His enthusiasm for the book, his love of games, and his understanding that I wanted this to be a book about the world first (and the games industry second) convinced me that he was the person I wanted in my corner. His thoughtful, supportive and precisely critical edits proved me right. Jake Bonar at Prometheus, meanwhile, showed remarkable faith to bring the book to North America and champion its importance. I am also enormously thankful to all the staff at Wildfire, Prometheus and my other international publishing partners for the hard work you've put into promoting my work.

I must also say an enormous thank you to everyone who I interviewed for the book. Over the course of a year, I spoke to over eighty people on the record, for background purposes and occasionally off the record to bring the book to life. As time went by, and my focus narrowed, a lot of great interviews had to be cut for the sake of narrative coherence in a way that I feel, even now, deeply uncomfortable about.

I'd therefore like to thank all of the following people for contributing their expertise on the record, irrespective of their inclusion in the book: James Johnson, Prof. Andrew Przybylski, Dr Julia Ebner, Anne Craanen, David Sweeney, Keza Macdonald, Holly Longdale, Prof. Chris Ferguson, Will Freeman, Simon Carless, Galen Lamphere-Englund, Rachel Kowert, Fred Langford, Eliot Higgins, Prof. Claire Wardle, Elena Lobova, James Montague, Mike McCabe, Prince Faisal bin Bandar bin Sultan Al Saud, Brian Ward, Tami Bhaumik, Jens Schroeder, Chris Wood, Chris Davey, Steve Collins, Neil Long, Steven Bailey, Phil Elliott, Mike Diver, Prof. Pete Etchells, Meg Jayanth, Ben Porter, Maria Burns Ortiz, Yaraslau Kot, Mark Brown, Lee Mather, Kelly Clancy, Jonathan Knight, John O'Shea, Matt Firor, Andrew Pattinson, Leo Varadkar, Paul Fogolin, John O'Shea, Meaad Aflah, Hani Hashem, Nawaf Alnaghmoosh, Dirk Bosmans, Jed Dawson, Ron Curry, Paul Callaghan, Clara Reeves, Maxwell Scott-Slade, Chris Miller, Dr Ali S. Khan, Alex Stewart, Elizabeth Newbury, Ciaran Brennan, James Vaughan, Dan Chequer, Nicholas Lovell, Sarah Ticho, Ross O'Brien, Phil Mansell, Sam Barratt, Maria Sayans, Adrian Webb, Ben Ramsbottom, Zakhar Bocharov, Evgeniy Grygorovych and Maria Grygorovych. I am also enormously grateful to those who spoke to me on background or off the record.

I want to thank the physical spaces that have made this possible. The British Library was an invaluable research base. My office at the co-working space Clockwise provided a little sanctuary for me to write. I'm also grateful to every library and bookshop stocking this book. Cherish their value as much as you can.

On top of the faces and spaces that made the book possible, there are a number of people I need to thank in my personal and professional life for helping me reach this point.

Professionally, I'd like to thank Dr Jo Twist OBE, former CEO of Ukie, and Ben Greenstone, now of Milltown Partners, for the professional, financial and personal support for getting the book over the line. I want to thank Tom Regan and George Young for keeping my newsletter, Video Games Industry Memo, afloat during my time on book leave. James Whatley and Emily Britt proved to be both excellent mentors and friends.

Speaking of which, there are a few other friends I need to give particular thanks to. Carl Anka is the man you want in your corner in life. His constant check-ins, his calm reminders to keep on writing and his thoughtful listening kept me afloat during my hardest moments (book or otherwise). Rachael Kells and Dane Satterthwaite provided emotional support and a base for research in the US, while their daughter Libby offered some friendly burbles on WhatsApp calls during my final few months of writing. Fiona and George Kimberley-Brown were there to celebrate my successes and commiserate with me when I was 'deep in a writing hole', usually at Hot Milk Cafe – the finest café in London – with their handsome hound Watson in tow.

I also want to thank Steve Burns, Alysia Judge, Gillian Allen, Alex Humphreys, Dominik Swiecicki, Anna Poulter-Jones, Grace Shin, Eleanor Rose, Bibek Mukherjee, Sally Kevan, Leo Danczak, Rachel Wang, Jess Bonner, Alex Russell-Moyet, Kathryn Eastwood, Sophie Densham, Mark Knight-Sands, Paul Fischer, Nicole Alexander, Matt Honeycombe-Foster, Dr Celia Pontin, David Mills and Paul Almond for making *Power Play* possible. Whether you read chapters, checked in with me to make sure I wasn't going out of my mind, or made me a sticker chart to celebrate every thousand words written, I wouldn't have been able to achieve this without you.

Finally, I must round off by thanking my family for their support too. Mum, Dad, my siblings James, Lizzy and Will, and my in-laws Ailsa and James were consistently supportive throughout the whole process. This included the brief period of time between late 2024 and the middle of 2025 when things were looking a bit hairy for a while (something that definitely wasn't causing my editor to sweat profusely).

I'd like to end this book by dedicating it to my wonderful nieces and fantastic nephew who have enriched my life immensely. To Maddy, Clemmy, Hettie and Leander: thank you for your love, for your support, and for only occasionally ganging up on me when we play video games together. I love you all.

And if your silly old uncle can do this, you can achieve anything you set your hearts and minds to.

Glossary

4chan – an anonymous English-language social media forum focused on the posting of images, known as both a centrepiece of internet culture and a home for transgressive content. Founded in 2003.

8kun – an image board founded in 2013 as 8chan by a disenchanted 4chan user. The forum became a home for racist and anti-semitic content, as well as child abuse material. Rebranded as 8kun in October 2019 after being connected to three mass shootings earlier in the same year.

8-bit – third era of video game development commenced in July 1983, which gave developers basic audio and visual functionality to build games from. Games include *Super Mario Bros.*, *Contra* and *Ninja Gaiden.*

16-bit – commencing in 1987, 16-bit games benefitted from an ability to use larger sprites, stereo audio, and parallax scrolling that created early 3D effects. Games from the era include *Sonic the Hedgehog, The Legend of Zelda: A Link to the Past* and *Donkey Kong: Country.*

32-bit – expanded on the capability of 16-bit consoles to translate 2D experiences into 3D experiences during the early to mid 1990s. The original 32-bit PlayStation sold over 100m units, with hits including *Gran Turismo, Final Fantasy VII* and *Spyro the Dragon.*

64-bit – further boosted 3D rendering power, leading to consoles such as the Nintendo 64 and the PlayStation 2 from the mid 1990s to early 2000s. Famous games from the era include *Super Mario 64*, *The Legend of Zelda: Ocarina of Time* and *Grand Theft Auto: San Andreas*.

Action game – a genre of game which emphasises the player's physical skills, such as their reaction time and mastery of a game's control scheme. Examples include fighting games like *Street Fighter*, arcade games like *Streets of Rage* and 'hack and slash' games like *Dynasty Warriors*.

Adventure game – a game genre where a player assumes the role of a protagonist in an interactive story, usually with emphasis on puzzle solving or exploration. Examples include *Zork*, *Escape to Monkey Island* and *The Stanley Parable*.

Battle pass – a tiered reward system which offers players extra content for completing challenges. Usually has a free track, which offers a small amount of basic rewards, and a paid track, which provides subscribers with rewards more frequently.

Bit – the smallest unit of digital information, representing a 0 or 1. Bits can be grouped into bytes (typically in groups of 8) to create more complex data.

Boss – a tough-to-defeat enemy, usually located at the end of a section of a game world, level or game.

Central Processing Unit (CPU) – the 'brain' of a computer which processes data and instructions and controls the rest of the computer system.

Console – a specialised device dedicated to playing video games, which typically requires connection to a screen and the use of other accessories like a controller to function. Examples include the PlayStation 5, the Xbox 360, the Nintendo 64 and the Sega Dreamcast.

Developer – can refer to both the individual coders who make video games and be used as shorthand for a game development studio.

Discord – an instant messaging and social platform that allows communication through voice calls, video calls, text messaging and media through user-generated servers. Discord 'overlays' video games, allowing people to play while retaining access to the service.

Downloadable Content (DLC) – additional content sold by game developers after release to expand their games and increase revenue. Typically takes the form of new levels or expansions to stories, but extends to in-game purchases too (see below).

Esport – an organised, competitive video game tournament in which players compete for ranking, prizes and often cash.

First party – a game development studio owned or directly affiliated with a device manufacturer such as Nintendo, Sony or Microsoft.

First-person – a camera angle that allows the player to experience the game from the perspective of the character they are playing as.

First-Person Shooter (FPS) – a game where players shoot enemies from the perspective of the character they are controlling. Examples include *Call of Duty*, *Doom* and *Goldeneye 64*.

Free-to-play – a video game that is free to download and play, which makes money after installation by selling extra content, through subscriptions, or via other means like advertising. Examples include *Roblox*, *Fortnite* and *Candy Crush Saga*.

Game engine – a software development tool which combines multiple functions needed to make a game in one place to make production easier and faster. Examples include Unreal Engine and Unity.

Gamification – the application of game elements or mechanics such as scoring points, ranked competition or winning trophies to other areas of activity. Commonly seen in use in contexts such as dating apps, language learning platforms and corporate training.

Gamer-fication – a term invented for this book to describe the application of video game references, terminology, or aesthetics to foster an 'in group' dynamic within a gamer subculture.

Graphics Processing Unit (GPU) – the PC component that allows the computer to rapidly process images and videos. Essential for video game play.

Handheld – a battery-powered games console designed to be played portably, usually with the control buttons placed either side of or just below a screen. Examples include the Game Boy, the PlayStation Portable and the Nintendo Switch.

Hardware – the physical components that form a machine upon which video games can be played. Examples include game consoles, smartphones, and personal computers.

Indie developer – a loose term used to describe an independent development studio which makes its games without being owned by a publisher.

In-game purchase – a purchase made by a player within a game to access extra currencies, lives, or cosmetics in order to enhance their experience.

Localisation – the process of adapting a video game for a different market, ranging from translating in-game text to adjusting content for different markets.

Loot box – an in-game item that provides players with randomised content such as new outfits for their character. Players do not know what content they will receive, but they will always receive something. These are sometimes purchased with real world money, sometimes earned by completing tasks within the game.

Massively Multiplayer Online game (MMO) – allows people to interact with large numbers of other players in a persistent online world. Examples include *World of Warcraft*, *EVE: Online* and *Fantasy Westward Journey*.

Mobile game – a game played on a smartphone or tablet. Examples include *Candy Crush Saga*, *Wordle* and *Monument Valley*.

Mod – a modification of a game created by the player community to change the core experience. Mods can change how a game looks, its rules, or add new content. Modding is typically reserved for PC games, where players can easily create and upload new content to games.

Open world – a video game that allows players to explore freely within a world, choosing when to interact with missions and other in-game content. Examples include *Grand Theft Auto V*, *The Legend of Zelda: Breath of the Wild* and *Ghost of Yōtei*.

Patch – a piece of software designed to update a video game after release. Patches are used to fix bugs, to add new features or to rebalance a game (e.g. making an enemy easier to defeat if it is too hard).

Publisher – a business which supports the publication of video games through physical distribution, managing digital distribution, and often through ancillary services such as marketing and promotion.

Role-Playing Game (RPG) – a game where players assume a fictional role in a virtual landscape, where their decisions affect the world around them and shape their narrative. Examples include *Skyrim*, *Baldur's Gate 3* and *Final Fantasy*.

Simulation game – a genre of game where the objective is to closely simulate the real world to offer players the chance to experience it. Examples include *Microsoft Flight Simulator, Football Manager* and *Plague Inc.*

Software – the program that tells a computer what to do. In a video game context, it is the collection of instructions, rules and data that allow the game to function on a device.

Steam – the world's most popular PC digital video game storefront, akin to the App Store or Google Play on mobile. Managed by Valve Corporation.

Third party – a studio that develops games for a platform independently of the platform maker (e.g. Electronic Arts, who make games for major consoles and PCs without producing their own device).

Third-person – a video game where the player's perspective is behind the character, allowing them to see the avatar they are playing as. *World of Warcraft, Tomb Raider* and *Fortnite* all offer third-person views.

Triple A (AAA) – the most expensive, highest production value video games made across the world. Budgets typically stretch into the hundreds of millions of dollars. Examples include *The Last of Us, Call of Duty* and *God of War.* Triple A is a direct reference to financial bonds.

Twitch – a social media service which allows people to share video and audio of themselves playing video games and engaging in other activities to a live audience.

Virtual reality (VR) – a computer-generated 3D environment that a person can explore spatially while wearing a dedicated headset. Famous VR games include *Tetris Effect, Half Life: Alyx* and *Superhot.*

Bibliography

Abt, Clark C., *Serious Games*, University Press of America (1987)

Applebaum, Anne, *Autocracy, Inc.: The Dictators Who Want to Run the World*, Penguin Books (2025)

Ball, James, *The Other Pandemic: How QAnon Contaminated the World*, Bloomsbury (2023)

Belton, Catherine, *Putin's People: How the KGB Took Back Russia and Then Took on the West*, William Collins (2021)

Bogost, Ian, *Persuasive Games: The Expressive Power of Videogames*, MIT Press (2010)

Bradford, Anu, *Digital Empires: The Global Battle to Regulate Technology*, OUP (2023)

Ceruzzi, Paul E., *A History of Modern Computing*, MIT Press, 2nd edn (2003)

Chen, Lulu Yilun, *Influence Empire: The Story of Tencent and China's Tech Ambition*, Hodder Paperbacks (2023)

Clancy, Kelly, *Playing With Reality: How Games Shape Our World*, Allen Lane (2024)

Csíkszentmihályi, Mihály, *Flow: The Psychology of Optimal Experience*, HarperPerennial (2008)

Curran, James and Joanna Redden, *Understanding Media: Communication, Power and Social Change*, Pelican Books (2025)

Delaney, Miguel, *States of Play: How Sportswashing Took Over Football*, Seven Dials (2024)

Diver, Mike, *Retro Gaming: A Byte-Sized History of Video Games – from Atari to Zelda*, LOM Art (2019)

Dreunen, Joost van, *One Up: Creativity, Competition, and the Global Business of Video Games*, Columbia University Press (2020)

Ebner, Julia, *Going Dark: The Secret Social Lives of Extremists*, Bloomsbury (2020)

Faroohar, Rana, *Don't be Evil: The Case against Big Tech*, Penguin Books (2020)

Fenby, Jonathan, *The Penguin History of Modern China: The Fall and Rise of a Great Power, 1850 to the Present*, Penguin Books (2013)

Gardner, Dan, *Risk: The Science and Politics of Fear*, Virgin Books (2009)

Grayson, Nathan, *Stream Big: The Triumphs and Turmoils of Twitch and the Stars behind the Screen*, Atria Books (2025)

Green, Joshua, *Devil's Bargain: Steve Bannon, Donald Trump, and the Storming of the Presidency*, Penguin Books (2018)

Griffiths, James, *The Great Firewall of China: How to Build and Control an Alternative Version of the Internet*, Zed Books (2019)

Hillman, Jonathan E., *The Digital Silk Road: China's Quest to Wire the World and Win the Future*, Profile (2022)

Hope, Bradley and Justin Scheck, *Blood and Oil: Mohammed bin Salman's Ruthless Quest for Global Power*, John Murray (2020)

Humphreys, Alex, *Playing With Reality: Gaming in a Pandemic*, Renard Press (2022)

Kent, Steven L., *The Ultimate History of Video Games, Vol. 1: From Pong to Pokemon – the Story behind the Craze That Touched Our Lives and Changed the World*, Crown (2001)

———, *The Ultimate History of Video Games*, Vol. 2: *Nintendo, Sony, Microsoft, and the Billion-Dollar Battle to Shape Modern Gaming*, Crown (2021)

Kim, Tae, *The Nvidia Way: Jensen Huang and the Making of a Tech Giant*, W. W. Norton and Co. (2024)

Lean, Tom, *Electronic Dreams: How 1980s Britain Learned to Love the Computer*, Bloomsbury Sigma (2016)

McGonigal, Jane, *Reality is Broken: Why Games Make Us Better and How They Can Change the World*, Vintage (2012)

Markey, Patrick M. and Chris Ferguson, *Moral Combat: Why the War on Violent Video Games is Wrong*, BenBella Books (2017)

Miller, Chris, *Chip War: The Fight for the World's Most Critical Technology*, Simon & Schuster (2023)

Marshall, Tim, *The Power of Geography*, Elliott & Thompson (2021)

Montague, James, *Engulfed: How Saudi Arabia Bought Sport, and the World*, Blink (2025)

Murray, Janet H., *Hamlet on the Holodeck: The Future of Narrative in Cyberspace*, Simon & Schuster (1997)

Narula, Herman, *Virtual Society: The Metaverse and the New Frontiers of Human Experience*, Currency (2022)

Nordström, Kim, *Up Down Up: Why Some Game Companies Succeed, While Others Fail*, Kim Nordström (2024)

Nye, Jr., Joseph S., *Soft Power: The Means to Success in World Politics*, Hachette (2005)

Ower, Jude and Mathias Gredal Nørvig, *Gaming for Good: Unlocking the Power of Gaming to Create a Better World for Us All*, Rethink Press (2024)

Pomerantsev, Peter, *Nothing is True and Everything is Possible: Adventures in Modern Russia*, Faber & Faber (2017)

————, *This Is Not Propaganda: Adventures in the War against Reality*, Faber & Faber (2019)

Rid, Thomas, *Active Measures: The Secret History of Disinformation and Political Warfare*, Profile (2021)

Roberts, Margaret, *Censored: Distraction and Diversion inside China's Great Firewall*, Princeton University Press (2018)

Rundell, David, *Vision or Mirage: Saudi Arabia at the Crossroads*, I. B. Taurus (2021)

Schlegel, Linda and Rachel Kowert (eds.), *Gaming and Extremism: The Radicalisation of Digital Playgrounds*, Routledge (2024)

Schreier, Jason, *Blood, Sweat and Pixels: The Triumphant, Turbulent Stories behind How Video Games are Made*, Harper Paperbacks (2017)

————, *Press Reset: Ruin and Recovery in the Video Game Industry*, Grand Central (2021)

Sheff, David, *Game Over, Press Start to Continue: How Nintendo Conquered the World*, Vintage Press (1994)

References

Introduction

1 Jesper Falkheimer, Elsa Isaksson, and James Pamment, 'Malign foreign interference and information influence on video game platforms: Understanding the adversarial playbook', Lund University, 23 October 2023, https://www.lunduni versity.lu.se/article/how-video-games-are-being-used-foreign-actors-and-extremists

2 George E. Osborn, 'How video games became a front of the global information war', *Video Games Industry Memo*, 26 September 2024, https://www.videogames industrymemo.com/p/how-video-games-became-a-front-of-the-global-information-war-26-09-24

3 Daphne Psaledakis, 'US State Department closing office aimed at countering foreign disinformation', *Reuters*, 16 April 2025, https://www.reuters.com/business/media-telecom/us-state-department-closing-office-aimed-at-countering-foreign-disinformation-2025-04-16/

4 Cam Adair, 'The Social Effects of Video Games', *Game Quitters*, https://gamequitters.com/social-effects-of-video-games/

5 Claire Cain Miller and Amy Fan, 'How Video Games Are Shaping a Generation of Boys, for Better and Worse', *New York Times*, 3 October 2025, https://www.nytimes.com/2025/10/03/upshot/video-games-boys-young-men.html

6 'Learning Through Play', UNICEF and LEGO Foundation, October 2018, https://www.unicef.org/sites/default/files/2018-12/UNICEF-Lego-Foundation-Learning-through-Play.pdf, p. 7

7 'The Importance of Play for Adults', National Institute for Play, https://nifplay.org/play-note/adult-play/

8 Irene Picton, Christina Clark, and Tim Judge, 'Video game playing and literacy: a survey of young people aged 11 to 16', National Literacy Trust, 12 August 2020, https://nlt.cdn.ngo/media/documents/Video_game_playing_and_literacy_report_-_National_Literacy_Trust.pdf

9 Ray Oldenburg, 'The political value of third places', *The Way We Live Now with Karen Christensen*, 7 November 2024, https://karenchristensen.substack.com/p/the-political-value-of-third-places

10 Isil Sariyuce, 'Turkish soccer fans who chanted anti-government slogans banned from stadium', *CNN*, 28 February 2023, https://edition.cnn.com/2023/02/28/football/turkey-football-fans-banned-government-spt-intl

11 'Roblox Reports Second Quarter 2025 Financial Results', 31 July 2025, https://ir.roblox.com/news/news-details/2025/Roblox-Reports-Second-Quarter-2025-Financial-Results/default.aspx

12 Adam Bankhurst, 'Among Us Reportedly Had "Roughly Half a Billion Monthly Active Users in November"', *IGN*, 23 December 2020, https://www.ign.com/articles/among-us-reportedly-had-roughly-half-a-billion-monthly-active-users-in-november

13 Frances Perraudin, 'Marshmello makes history with first ever Fortnite in-game concert', *Guardian*, 3 February 2019, https://www.theguardian.com/games/2019/feb/03/marshmello-fortnite-in-game-concert-edm-producer

14 'Roblox Reports Second Quarter 2025 Financial Results', 31 July 2025, https://ir.roblox.com/news/news-details/2025/Roblox-Reports-Second-Quarter-2025-Financial-Results/default.aspx

15 David Curry, 'Discord Revenue and Usage Statistics (2025)', *Business of Apps*, 24 March 2025, https://www.businessofapps.com/data/discord-statistics/

16 Henry Worthen, 'The State of Social H2 2024: The Dynamic Rise of Gaming Content', Tubular Labs, 4 October 2024, https://tubularlabs.com/blog/the-state-of-social-h2-2024-gaming/

17 'Introducing the What's Next: Gaming Trend Report', TikTok Corporate Site, 12 July 2023, https://newsroom.tiktok.com/en-us/whats-next-gaming-2023

18 Nathan Grayson, *Stream Big: The Triumphs and Turmoils of Twitch and the Stars Behind the Screen*, Ayria Books (2025), p. 1

19 Michael Waters, 'Game Never Over', *Slate*, 26 September 2018, https://slate.com/technology/2018/09/video-game-memorials-players-death-community-mourning.html

20 Megan Meyers, Four-legged gamer nearly breaks world record at charity event, *Fox News*, 19 January 2024, https://www.foxnews.com/tech/four-legged-gamer-nearly-breaks-world-record-charity-event

21 Andrea Blanco, 'MSNBC contributor and retired four-star general Barry McCaffrey deletes tweet showing Russian plane "getting nailed" by Ukraine that's from a VIDEO GAME', *Daily Mail*, 18 May 2022, https://www.dailymail.co.uk/news/article-10827315/Retired-four-star-general-shares-video-game-footage-claims-Russian-war.html

Part 1: Building the battlefield

1. Play in every pocket

1 Hugh Sebag-Montefiore, 'The boarding of U-559 changed the war – now both sides tell their story', *Guardian*, 21 October 2017, https://www.theguardian.com/world/2017/oct/20/enigma-code-u-boat-u559-hms-petard-sebag-montefiori

2 Chris Miller, *Chip War: The Fight for the World's Most Critical Technology*, Simon & Schuster (2023), p. 7.

3 Ibid., p. 21.

4 Gordon E. Moore, Science History Institute: Museum & Library, https://www.sciencehistory.org/education/scientific-biographies/gordon-e-moore/

5 Paul E. Ceruzzi, *A History of Modern Computing*, MIT Press, 2nd edn (2003), p. 212.

6 Kentaro Yamazaki, 'Sony discontinues production and sales of cassette Walkmans', AV Watch, 22 October 2010, https://av.watch.impress.co.jp/docs/news/401936.html

7 Bill Gates, 'Celebrate 50 years of Microsoft with the company's original source code', *Gates Notes*, 2 April 2025, https://www.gatesnotes.com/microsoft-original-source-code

8 Ceruzzi, *A History of Modern Computing*, p. 230.

9 Stewart Brand, 'S P A C E W A R: Fanatic Life and Symbolic Death Among the Computer Bums', *Rolling Stone*, 7 December 1972, https://www.wheels.org/spacewar/stone/rolling_stone.html

10 Ibid.

11 Stephen L. Kent, *The Ultimate History of Video Games: From Pong to Pokémon – The Story Behind the Craze That Touched Our Lives and Changed the World*, Crown (2001), p. 19.

12 Bill Logudice, *The History of Spacewar!: The Best Waste of Time in the History of the Universe*, Game Developer, 10 June 2009, https://www.gamedeveloper.com/design/the-history-of-spacewar-the-best-waste-of-time-in-the-history-of-the-universe

13 Kent, *The Ultimate History of Video Games*, pp. 53–4.

14 The similarities between Ralph Baer's table tennis game and *Pong* were not lost on Magnavox or Baer. The company sued Atari for copyright infringement; Atari eventually paid $1.5m to Magnavox as a licensing fee for the console.

15 Kate Willaert, 'Pixels in Print (Part 2): Advertising Odyssey – the First Home Video Game', The Video Game History Foundation, 20 March 2020, https://web.archive.org/web/20200511162130/https://gamehistory.org/magnavox-odyssey-advertisement-history/

16 Magnavox Odyssey, Victora and Albert Museum Collection, https://collections.vam.ac.uk/item/O1580096/magnavox-odyssey-videogames-console-baer-ralph-h/

17 Tom Lean, *Electronic Dreams: How 1980s Britain Learned to Love the Computer*, Bloomsbury Sigma (2016), p. 200.

18 '22 Fascinating Vintage Computer Ads for Families From the 1980s', *Vintages Everyday*, 13 July 2021, https://www.vintag.es/2021/07/computer-ads-families-1980s.html

19 'Fairchild – Channel F System II with Milton Berle (Commercial, 1978)', https://www.youtube.com/watch?v=bkbzerx2qfc

20 'Evolution of Console Business Models', Konvoy VC corporate blog, 4 April 2025, https://www.konvoy.vc/newsletters/evolution-of-console-business-models

21 'Essential Facts about the Computer and Video Game Industry', *Entertainment Software Association*, 18 May 2005, https://www.theesa.com/wp-content/uploads/2024/02/2005-EF-FINAL.pdf

22 Steven L. Kent, *The Ultimate History of Video Games, Volume 2: Nintendo, Sony, Microsoft, and the Billion-Dollar Battle to Shape Modern Gaming*, Crown (2021), p. 158

23 'Smartphone owners are now the global majority, New GSMA report reveals', *GSMA*, 11 October 2023, https://www.gsma.com/newsroom/press-release/smartphone-owners-are-now-the-global-majority-new-gsma-report-reveals/

24 Ben Walshe, *A Brief History of Arm: Part 1*, ARM corporate website, 21 April 2015, https://community.arm.com/arm-community-blogs/b/architectures-and-processors-blog/posts/a-brief-history-of-arm-part-1

25 'Nintendo 2010 annual financial report', https://www.nintendo.co.jp/ir/pdf/2010/annual1003e.pdf

26 'Oracle to buy $40 billion of Nvidia chips for OpenAI's US data center, FT reports', *Reuters*, 23 May 2025, https://www.reuters.com/business/oracle-buy-40-billion-nvidia-chips-openais-us-data-center-ft-reports-2025-05-23/

27 Gregory C. Allen, 'DeepSeek: A Deep Dive', Center for Strategic and International Studies, 8 April 2025, https://www.csis.org/analysis/deepseek-deep-dive

28 For the current value of Nvidia, see 'Market capitalization of NVIDIA (NVDA)', Companies Market Cap, https://companiesmarketcap.com/gbp/nvidia/marketcap/

29 Tony Smith, 'Nvidia to out-sell ATI in 2005 – analyst', *The Register*, 2 December 2005, https://www.theregister.com/2005/12/02/nvidia_ati_2005_sales/

30 Simon Jones, 'Nvidia now holds 7.3% of the semiconductor market', *London Loves Tech*, 18 March 2025, https://londonlovestech.com/nvidia-now-holds-7-3-of-the-semiconductor-market/

31 David Jagielski, 'Nvidia Is Dominating the Artificial Intelligence Chip Market, but Apple Has Been Securing Supply From Another Tech Giant', *Nasdaq*, 11 August 2024, https://www.nasdaq.com/articles/nvidia-dominating-artificial-intelligence-chip-market-apple-has-been-securing-supply

32 Brian Caulfield, 'What's the Difference Between a CPU and a GPU?', Nvidia corporate blog, 16 December 2009, https://blogs.nvidia.com/blog/whats-the-difference-between-a-cpu-and-a-gpu/

33 'Power of AR, VR, and XR', Maersk Training, https://maersktraining.com/services/training/digital-learning/ar-vr-and-xr

34 Nicholas E. Kman, Alan Price, Vita Berezina-Blackburn et al., 'First Responder Virtual Reality Simulator to train and assess emergency personnel for mass casualty response', JACEP Open, Vol. 4 (1), February 2023, https://www.sciencedirect.com/science/article/pii/S2688115224001541

35 'A Canadian surgical first at the Ottawa Hospital using VR technology', Ottawa Hospital Foundation, April 2024, https://ohfoundation.ca/be-inspired/a-canadian-surgical-first-at-the-ottawa-hospital-using-vr-technology/

36 Qianer Liu, 'Chinese companies resort to repurposing Nvidia gaming chips for AI', *Financial Times*, 10 January 2024, https://www.ft.com/content/eeea7c4d-71f0-454f-bd16-b2445cb3bbb0

37 Edwin Evans-Thirlwell, 'The Ukrainian armed forces are reportedly using Steam Decks to remote-control gun turrets', *Rock Paper Shotgun*, 10 September 2024, https://www.rockpapershotgun.com/the-ukrainian-armed-forces-are-reportedly-using-steam-decks-to-remote-control-gun-turrets

38 Linus Höller, 'The UK banned sending game controllers to Russia. What's the point?', *Defense News*, 2 May 2025, https://www.defensenews.com/global/europe/2025/05/02/the-uk-banned-sending-game-controllers-to-russia-whats-the-point/

2. Engines of growth

1 Stephen Totilo, 'PlayStation games cost as much as movie blockbusters to make, exposed budgets show', *Axios*, 29 June 2023, https://www.axios.com/2023/06/29/playstation-game-budgets-leak

2 Will Lennox, 'Here's how big the budget of "The Last of Us" first season is going to be', *GQ Australia*, 19 January 2023, https://www.gq.com.au/culture/entertainment/the-last-of-us-budget/image-gallery/7f6baa18ed3ccd82778206aff793466d

3 'Did GTA VI really cost more than the building of the Burj Khalifa?', *The Rest is Entertainment*, 26 July 2025, https://www.youtube.com/shorts/wqda7lvuQ4w

4 Harry McCracken, 'Fifty Years of BASIC, the Programming Language That Made Computers Personal', *Time*, 29 April 2014, https://time.com/69316/basic/

5 John Haas, *A History of the Unity Game Engine*, 2014, https://digital.wpi.edu/downloads/2f75r821k

6 'Unity 2.6 Released And Now Free!', Unity corporate blog, 28 October 2009, https://unity.com/news/unity-2-6-released-and-now-free

7 Tim Sweeney, 'If You Love Something, Set It Free', Epic corporate blog, 2 March 2015, https://www.unrealengine.com/en-US/blog/ue4-is-free

8 Ray Davis, 'Unreal Engine 4 Goes Free for Academic Use', Unreal Engine corporate blog, 4 September 2014, https://www.unrealengine.com/en-US/blog/unreal-engine-4-goes-free-for-academic-use

9 Ellie Harisova, 'Unity Student Plan Announced', *80LV*, 26 February 2020, https://80.lv/articles/unity-student-plan-announced

10 '2024 Unity Gaming Report Highlights Game Studios' Continued Resilience As They Boldly Stretch Resources Amidst Shifting Market Forces', Unity Investor Relations, 18 March 2024, https://investors.unity.com/news/news-details/2024/2024-Unity-Gaming-Report-Highlights-Game-Studios-Continued-Resilience-As-They-Boldly-Stretch-Resources-Amidst-Shifting-Market-Forces/default.aspx

11 'Unity Technologies Delivers Unity', *Global Newswire*, 27 September 2010, https://www.globenewswire.com/news-release/2010/09/27/1251895/0/en/Unity-Technologies-Delivers-Unity-3.html

12 Marie Dealessandri and Alex Forbes-Calvin, 'What is the best game engine: is Unreal Engine right for you?', *Games Industry Biz*, 21 November 2023, https://www.gamesindustry.biz/what-is-the-best-game-engine-is-unreal-engine-4-the-right-game-engine-for-you

13 'BAE Systems completes acquisition of Bohemia Interactive Simulations', *BAE Systems*, 7 March 2022, https://www.baesystems.com/en/article/bae-systems-completes-acquisition-of-bohemia-interactive-simulations

3. The video game distribution revolution

1 Michiel Buijsman, 'How did the global games market reach $182.7B in 2024 – and what's next?', Newzoo, 24 June 2025, https://newzoo.com/resources/blog/global-games-market-update-q2-2025

2 'How consumers engage with games today: 2024 edition', Newzoo, 2 July 2024, https://newzoo.com/resources/trend-reports/global-gamer-study-free-report-2024

3 Joost van Dreunen, *One Up: Creativity, Competition, and the Global Business of Video Games*, Columbia University Press (2020), p. 32.

4 Alex Wade, *Playback: A Genealogy of 1980s British Videogames*, Bloomsbury Academic Publishing (2016).

5 Joost van Dreunen, *One Up – Creativity, Competition, and the Global Business of Video Games*, Columbia University Press (2020), p. 81.

6 Alex Godfrey, 'A golden shining moment: the true story behind Atari's *ET*, the worst video game ever', *Guardian*, 30 January 2015, https://www.theguardian.com/film/2015/jan/30/a-golden-shining-moment-the-true-story-behind-et-the-worst-video-game-ever

7 David Sheff, *Game Over, Press Start to Continue: How Nintendo Conquered the World*, Vintage Press (1994), p. 28.

8 Van Dreunen, *One Up*, p. 32.

9 Sara Cox in *Wipeout* (1995), IMDB, https://m.imdb.com/title/tt0262903/media-viewer/rm2346534144/

10 Raph Koster, 'What core gamers should know about social games', *Raph Koster's Website*, 18 March 2010, https://www.raphkoster.com/2010/03/18/what-core-gamers-should-know-about-social-games/

11 Geoff Keighley, 'The Final Hours of Half-Life', *GameSpot*, 1999, https://web.archive.org/web/20110223141855/http://uk.gamespot.com/features/halflife_final/part22.html/https://www.docdroid.net/nuj22KX/the-final-hours-of-half-life-pdf

12 Emma Neeson, 'Oblivion Remastered Including One DLC Could Be Controversial', *GameRant*, 17 April 2025, https://gamerant.com/oblivion-remastered-horse-armor-dlc-potential-controversy-why/

13 Daniel Terdiman, 'No, Flappy Bird developer didn't give up on $50,000 a day', *CNET*, 11 February 2014, https://www.cnet.com/tech/services-and-software/no-flappy-bird-developer-didnt-give-up-on-50000-a-day/

14 Masha Borak, 'World's top-grossing game Honour of Kings is coming to Europe and the US', *Technode*, 7 July 2017, https://technode.com/2017/07/07/worlds-top-grossing-game-honour-of-kings-is-coming-to-europe-and-the-us/

15 Dean Takahashi, 'Video game sales were down 6 per cent in 2010', *Gamesbeat*, 13 January 2011, https://gamesbeat.com/video-game-sales-were-flat-or-down-1-percent-in-2010/

16 Shubham Munde, 'Gaming Hardware Market', October 2025, https://www.marketresearchfuture.com/reports/gaming-hardware-market-11513

17 'Who Gets To Be On The Steam Store?', *Steam News*, 6 June 2018, https://steamcommunity.com/games/593110/announcements/detail/1666776116200553082

4. A digital third place for influence

1 British Academy, 'Play and socialising are vital to early childhood development', 25 March 2020, https://www.thebritishacademy.ac.uk/news/play-and-socialising-vital-to-early-childhood-development/

2 Ismail Tasdelen, 'The Cultural Impact of Chess: A Historical Perspective', 10 July 2023, https://ismailtasdelen.medium.com/the-cultural-impact-of-chess-a-historical-perspective-16826d053da4

3 Herodotus, *The Histories*, translated by George Rawlinson, Roman Roads Media, 2013, p. 44, https://files.romanroadsstatic.com/materials/herodotus.pdf

4 Josh Wood, "He's their man': why do bikers love Trump so much?', *Guardian*, 2 July 2019, https://www.theguardian.com/us-news/2019/jul/02/bikers-for-trump-support-laconia-motorcycle-week

5 'How Garry Kasparov went from being chess champion to "terrorist" in Russia', *Firstpost*, 7 March 2024, https://www.firstpost.com/explainers/garry-kasparov-chess-champion-vladimir-putin-critic-terrorist-russia-13746334.html

6 'Stewart Brand, S P A C E W A R Fanatic Life and Symbolic Death Among the Computer Bums', *Rolling Stone*, 7 December 1972, https://www.wheels.org/spacewar/stone/rolling_stone.html

7 'Jan–June Circulation Figures', *Investegate*, 13 August 1999, https://www.investegate.co.uk/announcement/rns/future--futr/jan-june-circulation-figures-/117342

8 Keith Stuart, 'Scans for the memories: why old games magazines are a vital source of cultural history – and nostalgia', *Guardian*, 28 Janaury 2025, https://www.theguardian.com/games/2025/jan/28/video-game-history-foundation-digitised-archive-games-magazines

9 'The significance of *Starcraft*', *Prospect*, 28 July 2010, https://www.prospectmagazine.co.uk/ideas/technology/54354/the-significance-of-starcraft

10 Denis Gießler, 'The Stasi Played Along', *Die Zeit*, 21 November 2018, https://www.zeit.de/digital/games/2018-11/computer-games-gdr-stasi-surveillance-gamer-crowd

11 Aaron A. Reed, '1980: MUD', *50 Years of Text Games*, 11 March 2021, https://if50.substack.com/p/1980-mud

12 Nicole Segre, 'MUD on your Screens', *MSX User*, October 1985, https://mud.co.uk/richard/msxoct85.htm

13 Richard A. Bartle, 'Hearts, Clubs, Diamonds, Spades: Players Who Suit MUDs', April 1996 version, https://mud.co.uk/richard/hcds.htm

14 Wesley Le Blanc, '100 Billion Hours Were Spent Watching Gaming Content on YouTube in 2020', *IGN*, 31 December 2020, https://www.ign.com/articles/100-billion-hours-were-spent-watching-gaming-content-on-youtube-in-2020

15 Nathan Grayson, *Stream Big: The Triumphs and Turmoils of Twitch and the Stars behind the Screen*, Ayria Books (2025), p. 1.

16 Simon Carless, 'Who's winning video game Discords? We know!', The Game-DiscoverCo Newsletter, 24 June 2025, https://newsletter.gamediscover.co/p/whos-winning-video-game-discords

17 Cass Marshall, '*Helldivers 2* players knew how to mobilize against Sony after training in-game', *Polygon*, 6 May 2024, https://www.polygon.com/24150510/helldivers-2-psn-account-sony-response-controversy-steam-review-bombing-refunds/

18 Paul Tassi, 'EA Voted Worst Company in America, Again', *Forbes*, 9 April 2013, https://www.forbes.com/sites/insertcoin/2013/04/09/ea-voted-worst-company-in-america-again/

Part 2: The war for influence

5. Saudi Arabia's savvy gaming soft power plan

1 Tom Gerken, 'Gaming giant Electronic Arts bought in unprecedented $55bn deal', *BBC Sport*, 29 September 2025, https://www.bbc.co.uk/news/articles/cn4w3jzx807o

2 Nick Harris, 'REVEALED: the full scale of Saudi Arabia's takeover of sport, costing tens of billions', *Sporting Intelligence*, 2 December 2024, https://sporting-intelligence832.substack.com/p/revealed-the-full-scale-of-saudi

3 Stephanie Kirchgaessner, 'US finds Saudi crown prince approved Khashoggi murder but does not sanction him', *Guardian*, 26 February 2021, https://www.theguardian.com/world/2021/feb/26/jamal-khashoggi-mohammed-bin-salman-us-report

4 Will Barker, 'What Saudi Arabia wants with EA video games', *The Week*, 30 September 2025, https://theweek.com/business/what-saudi-arabia-wants-with-ea-video-games

5 Tim Marshall, *The Power of Geography*, Elliott & Thompson Limited (2021), p. 114.

6 David Rundell, *Vision or Mirage: Saudi Arabia at the Crossroads*, I. B. Taurus (2022), pp. 257–8.

7 Tabulated data can be found at https://www.stats.gov.sa/en/w/detailed-results-of-census-2010

8 'Saudi population at 32.2 million, 63% of Saudis under 30 years old, census shows', *Reuters*, 31 May 2023, https://www.reuters.com/world/middle-east/saudi-

population-322-mln-median-age-29-years-old-general-authority-statistics-2023-05-31/

9 'GASTAT: 83.83% of individuals (12 to 65 years) use internet, and 92% use cell phone', Official government website of the Government of the Kingdom of Saudi Arabia, 15 May 2018, https://www.stats.gov.sa/en/w/gastat-83.83-of-individuals-12-to-65-years-use- internet-and-92-use-cell-phone

10 Miguel Delaney, *States of Play: How Sportwashing Took Over Football*, Seven Dials (2024), p. 304.

11 Peter Snowdon, '"Game over Mubarak": the Arab Revolutions and the Gamification of Everyday Life', *Fast Capitalism*, Vol. 11, Issue 1, 1 November 2014, https://fastcapitalism.uta.edu/11_1/snowdon11_1.html

12 Jonathan Rugman, 'Power, oil and a $450m painting – insiders on the rise of Saudi's Crown Prince', *BBC News*, 19 August 2024, https://www.bbc.co.uk/news/articles/c4gz8934wrro

13 'Vision 2030', 25 April 2016, https://www.vision2030.gov.sa/media/rc0b5oyl/saudi_vision203.pdf

14 'A timeline of Saudi's Arabia's unprecedented sports investments', *ESPN*, 28 February 2024, https://www.espn.co.uk/golf/story/_/id/38162723/saudi-arabia-sports-takeover-line-30-years-making

15 Martin Chulov, 'Saudi Arabia to lift 35-year ban on cinemas', *Guardian*, 11 December 2017, https://www.theguardian.com/world/2017/dec/11/saudi-arabia-to-lift-35-year-ban-on-cinemas

16 'Economic and Social Revolution in Saudi Arabia – September 2023', New Zealand Foreign Affairs & Trade Department, https://www.mfat.govt.nz/en/trade/mfat-market-reports/economic-and-social-revolution-in-saudi-arabia-september-2023

17 Bradley Hope and Justin Scheck, *Blood and Oil: Mohammed bin Salman's Ruthless Quest for Global Power*, John Murray (2020), p. 47.

18 'Saudi Arabia bans Pokemon', *BBC News*, 26 March 2021, http://news.bbc.co.uk/1/hi/world/middle_east/1243307.stm

19 '"GOOD NEGOTIATIONS": Saudi crown prince says "every day" is a day closer to peace with Israel', *Fox News*, 22 September 2023', https://www.youtube.com/watch?v=Y_u8ghPr3HE

20 Ben Hubbard, 'MBS: The Rise of a Saudi Prince', *New York Times*, 21 March 2020, https://www.nytimes.com/2020/03/21/world/middleeast/mohammed-bin-salman-saudi-arabia.html

21 Dan De Luce, Ken Dilanian and Robert Windrem, 'How a Saudi royal crushed his rivals in a "shakedown" at the Ritz-Carlton', *NBC News*, 3 November 2018, https://www.nbcnews.com/news/mideast/how-saudi-royal-crushed-his-rivals-shakedown-ritz-carlton-n930396

22 'Lebanese PM Hariri "pressured to resign" by the Saudis', *Al-Jazeera*, 25 December 2017, https://www.aljazeera.com/news/2017/12/25/lebanese-pm-hariri-pressured-to-resign-by-the-saudis

23   Ian Black, 'Jamal Khashoggi obituary', *Guardian*, 19 October 2018, https://www.theguardian.com/world/2018/oct/19/jamal-khashoggi-obituary

24   Julian E. Barnes, 'C.I.A. Concludes That Saudi Crown Prince Ordered Khashoggi Killed', *New York Times*, 16 November 2018, https://www.nytimes.com/2018/11/16/us/politics/cia-saudi-crown-prince-khashoggi.html

25   For more on soft power in general, read Joseph S. Nye, Jr., *Soft Power: The Means to Success in World Politics*, Hachette (2005).

26   'Newcastle United reveal green and white third kit with Saudi Arabia resemblance', *BBC News*, 28 June 2022, https://www.bbc.co.uk/sport/football/61962841

27   Brian Mazique, 'Saudi Arabia Has Become The Fight Capital Of The World', *Forbes*, 21 February 2024, https://www.forbes.com/sites/brianmazique/2024/02/21/saudi-arabia-has-become-the-fight-capital-of-the-world/

28   Jonathan Jurejko, '"Hurdles" in PGA–LIV deal – but Trump "bolstering" talks', *BBC Sport*, 11 March 2025, https://www.bbc.co.uk/sport/tennis/articles/c4g0pvx9011o

29   Paul MacInnes, 'Fifa deepens Saudi Arabia ties with $1bn deal to fund global football infrastructure', *Guardian*, 24 November 2025-, https://www.theguardian.com/football/2025/nov/24/fifa-saudi-arabian-government-agency-new-partnership-fund-football-infrastructure

30   'Signing of MoU with the Public Investment Fund', Square Enix, 25 June 2021, https://www.hd.square-enix.com/eng/news/pdf/%28Web%2920210625_ENG_Signing_of_MoU_with_PIF.pdf

31   The Youth Lab, 'The rise & rise of esports', *ThinkHouse*, https://www.thinkhousehq.com/the-youth-lab/the-rise-rise-of-esports

32   Simon Hunt and Matt Hardy, 'David Beckham-backed Guild Esports put up for sale on insolvency marketplace', *CityAM*, 14 August 2025, https://www.cityam.com/david-beckham-backed-guild-esports-put-up-for-sale-on-insolvency-marketplace/

33   Prarthana Prakash, 'Saudi Arabia has gone so soccer crazy that it spent $875 million to buy top players – more than any European country except England', *Fortune*, 8 September 2023, https://fortune.com/2023/09/08/fifa-transfer-window-saudi-arabia-soccer-pro-league-fifa-875-million-buy-players/

34   Federal Ministry of Transport and Digital Infrastructure, 'Strategy for Germany as a Games Hub', June 2021, https://www.bundeswirtschaftsministerium.de/Redaktion/DE/Publikationen/Wirtschaft/games-strategy-germany.pdf?__blob=publicationFile&v=1

35   UK Games Fund, 'Games Growth Plan', 23 June 2025, https://ukgamesfund.com/ukgfnews/games-growth-plan/

36   George E. Osborn, 'How do you make a head of state care about video games policy?', *Video Games Industry Memo*, 16 January 2025, https://www.videogamesindustrymemo.com/p/what-do-heads-of-state-think-about

37   Aaron Astle, 'Monopoly Go! topped 2023 download AND revenue charts in the US', Pocket Gamer Biz, 9 January 2024, https://www.pocketgamer.biz/monopoly-go-topped-2023-download-and-revenue-charts-in-the-us/

38 Savvy Games Group, 'Scopely completes acquisition of Niantic's games business', 29 May 2025, https://www.savvygames.com/news/scopely-completes-acquisition-of-niantic-games-business

39 IT441 Game Design and Development course outline, King Saud University, https://faculty.ksu.edu.sa/en/sahali/course/230598

40 Dean Takahashi, 'Savvy Games Group invests \$265M in China's VSPO esports startup', *Gamesbeat,* 16 February 2023, https://gamesbeat.com/savvy-games-group-invests-265m-in-chinas-vspo-esports-startup/

41 Rachel Young Gu, 'From 2008 to 2017: Reflections from the stands in the Bird's Nest', ESPN, 9 November 2017, https://www.espn.com/gaming/story/_/id/21356303/league-legends-2008-2017-reflections-stands-bird-nest

42 'Al-Nassr star Cristiano Ronaldo announces collaboration with Saudi Crown Prince Mohammed bin Salman to host E-Sports World Cup in 2024', *Goal,* 23 October 2023, https://www.goal.com/en-gb/news/cristiano-ronaldo-mohamed-bin-salman-saudi-arabia-esports-world-cup-2024/bltabf7ad87dd81f681

43 Email to the Honorable Steve Besssant from Senators Elizabeth Warren and Richard Blumenthal, 14 October 2025, https://www.hsgac.senate.gov/wp-content/uploads/2025-10-14-Letter-from-Blumenthal-and-Warren-to-Secretary-Bessent-re-Electronic-Arts.pdf

44 Kenneth Shepherd, 'Team Liquid "Disappointed" CEO's Story About Growing Up Gay Was Censored From Esports Documentary In Saudi Arabia', 9 July 2025, *Kotaku,* https://kotaku.com/team-liquid-esports-world-cup-documentary-lgbtqia-queer-1851785943

6. Censoring a video game superpower

1 'Top countries and markets by video game revenues', Newzoo, https://newzoo.com/resources/rankings/top-10-countries-by-game-revenues

2 'Esports Around The World: China', *Esports Insider,* 11 August 2023, https://esportsinsider.com/2023/07/esports-around-the-world-china

3 Jonathan Fenby, *The Penguin History of Modern China: The Fall and Rise of a Great Power, 1850 to the Present,* Penguin Books (2013), p. 559.

4 Ibid., p. 561.

5 James Griffiths, *The Great Firewall of China: How to Build and Control an Alternative Version of the Internet,* Zed Books (2019), pp. 24–5.

6 Ibid., p. 32.

7 Ibid.

8 'China's Online Population Grows', Embassy of the People's Republic of China in the Republic of Bulgaria, 12 June 2004, http://bg.china-embassy.gov.cn/eng/dtxw/200406/t20040612_2181266.htm

9 Jonathan E. Hillman, *The Digital Silk Road: China's Quest to Wire the World and Win the Future,* Profile Books (2022), p. 30.

10 Geremie R. Barme and Sang Ye, 'The Great Firewall of China', *Wired*, 1 June 1997, https://www.wired.com/1997/06/china-3/

11 'Dissident who was jailed on Yahoo's information gets early release', *Reporters Sans Frontières*, 20 January 2016, https://rsf.org/en/dissident-who-was-jailed-yahoo-s-information-gets-early-release

12 Edward Wong, 'Security Law Suggests a Broadening of China's "Core Interests"', *New York Times*, 2 July 2015, https://www.nytimes.com/2015/07/03/world/asia/security-law-suggests-a-broadening-of-chinas-core-interests.html

13 Anu Bradford, *Digital Empires: The Global Battle to Regulate Technology*, OUP, New York (2023), p. 88.

14 'China bans Uyghurs from using social media apps', Radio Free Asia, 18 April 2024, https://uhrp.org/news/china-bans-uyghurs-from-using-social-media-apps/

15 Veta Chan, 'Hong Kong protesters are in "deep fear" about leaving a digital footprint', *NBC News*, 22 June 2019, https://www.nbcnews.com/news/world/hong-kong-protesters-are-deep-fear-about-leaving-digital-footprint-n1020146

16 Anu Bradford, *Digital Empires*, p. 94.

17 Josh Ye, 'Why the impact of China's 15-year console ban still lingers today', *South China Morning Post*, 23 November 2018, https://www.scmp.com/abacus/who-what/what/article/3028254/why-impact-chinas-15-year-console-ban-still-lingers-today

18 Eric Jou, 'The Chinese Gaming Console with the Jackie Chan Seal of Approval', *Kotaku*, 4 November 2013, https://kotaku.com/the-chinese-gaming-console-with-the-jackie-chan-seal-of-1457960866

19 Lulu Yilun Chen, *Influence Empire: The Story of Tencent and China's Tech Ambition*, Hodder (2023), p. 135.

20 'Chinese online gamers turn on to "Fantasy Westward Journey"', *Independent*, 14 July 2010, https://www.independent.co.uk/tech/chinese-online-gamers-turn-on-to-fantasy-westward-journey-2026389.html

21 'China's Tumultuous Relationship with Gaming', *Konvoy*, 19 January 2024, https://www.konvoy.vc/newsletters/chinas-tumultuous-relationship-with-gaming

22 Greg Pilarowski, Chao Yu and Ziwei Zhu, 'Legal Primer: Regulation of China's digital games industry', *Pillar Legal*, 1 December 2022, https://www.pillarlegalpc.com/legal-primer-regulation-of-chinas-digital-game-industry/

23 Manya Koetse, 'The Lanjisu Fire That Changed China's "Wangba" Era', *What's on Weibo*, 16 June 2018, https://www.whatsonweibo.com/the-beijing-haidian-lanjisu-internet-cafe-fire/

24 'HoI banned in China', Civilization Fanatics Forum, 29 May 2004, https://forums.civfanatics.com/threads/hoi-banned-in-china.89537/

25 'China lifts ban on foreign video games consoles', *BBC News*, 7 January 2014, https://www.bbc.co.uk/news/technology-25635719

26 'Online games sales soar in internet Internet-mad China', *China Daily*, 16 February 2005, https://www.chinadaily.com.cn/english/doc/2005-02/16/content_416887.htm

27 Mantin Lu, 'Facts and Trends You Want to Know About China Game Market 2016 to 2017 [Report]', *Game Developer*, 3 February 2017, https://www.gamedeveloper.com/business/facts-and-trends-you-want-to-know-about-china-game-market-2016-to-2017-report-

28 Matthew Handrahan, 'Kunlun offers $46m fund to Korean developers', *Games Industry Biz*, 18 August 2011, https://www.gamesindustry.biz/kunlun-offers-usd46m-fund-to-korean-developers

29 Lu, 'Facts and Trends'.

30 Tencent Holdings Ltd historic market caps can be viewed at Marketscreener: https://www.marketscreener.com/quote/stock/TENCENT-HOLDINGS-LIMITED-3045861/finances-segments/

31 Gwilym Mumford, 'China's Hollywood film quota to expand after Trump trade deal', *Guardian*, 12 April 2017, https://www.theguardian.com/film/2017/apr/12/trump-xi-trade-talks-china-hollywood-film-quota

32 Mark Strauss, 'That Time When People Thought Playing Chess Would Make You Violent', *Gizmodo*, 10 June 2014, https://gizmodo.com/chess-was-once-deemed-a-menace-to-society-1588675766

33 Wong Liang Hao, 'A Review on the Evaluation of Video Game Addiction as a Legitimate Disorder', *Open Journal of Social Sciences*, Vol. 11, No. 3, March 2023, https://www.scirp.org/journal/paperinformation?paperid=124012

34 Mark Griffiths et al., 'Working towards an international consensus on criteria for assessing internet gaming disorder: a critical commentary on Petry *et al.*' (2014), https://pmc.ncbi.nlm.nih.gov/articles/PMC5699464/

35 'Gaming disorder', World Health Organization, https://www.who.int/standards/classifications/frequently-asked-questions/gaming-disorder

36 Charlie Hall, 'World Health Organization moves closer to recognizing gaming disorder', Polygon, 28 December 2017, https://www.polygon.com/2017/12/28/16825828/who-gaming-disorder-addiction-draft-icd-11/

37 Niklas Johannes et al., 'Major new study finds little evidence for causal connection between well-being and video game playing', 27 July 2022, https://www.oii.ox.ac.uk/news-events/major-new-study-finds-little-evidence-for-causal-connection-between-well-being-and-video-game-playing/

38 Nazia Darvesh et al., 'Exploring the prevalence of gaming disorder and internet internet gaming disorder: a rapid scoping review', *Systematic Reviews*, 2 April 2020, https://link.springer.com/content/pdf/10.1186/s13643-020-01329-2. pdf

39 Niko Partners, 'Honor Of Kings Restricts Play For Minors', 11 July 2017, https://nikopartners.com/honor-kings-restricts-play-minors/

40 Yue Wang, 'As China's Regulatory Freeze Drags On, Its Gaming Industry Searches For An Answer', *Forbes*, 10 December 2018, https://www.forbes.com/sites/ywang/2018/12/10/as-chinas-regulatory-freeze-drags-on-its-gaming-industry-searches-for-an-answer/

41 Josh Ye, 'Why PUBG Mobile became Game for Peace in China', *South China Morning Post*, 7 October 2019, https://www.scmp.com/abacus/who-what/what/article/3091767/why-pubg-mobile-became-game-peace-china

42 Greg Pilarowski, Charles Yu, Zhu Ziwei, 'Legal Primer: Regulation of China's Digital Game Industry', 1 December 2022, https://www.pillarlegalpc.com/wp-content/uploads/2022/12/Pillar-Legal-Regulation-of-Chinas-Digital-Game-Industry.pdf

43 'NHS treats hundreds with gaming disorders', National Health Service, 28 March 2023, https://www.england.nhs.uk/2023/03/nhs-treats-hundreds-with-gaming-disorders/

44 Lily Kuo, 'China bans children from late-night gaming to combat addiction', *Guardian*, 7 November 2019, https://www.theguardian.com/world/2019/nov/07/china-bans-children-from-late-night-gaming-to-combat-addiction

45 Marco Rubio, 'Recognize what's happening here' X, 8 October 2019, https://x.com/marcorubio/status/1181556058659135488

46 Diksha Madhok, 'Tencent cracks down on screen time after Chinese state media says gaming is "spiritual opium"', *CNN*, 3 August 2021, https://edition.cnn.com/2021/08/03/investing/tencent-gaming-crackdown-hnk-intl

47 Iris Deng, Zhou Xin and Xinmei Shen, 'Chinese newspaper publishes, and then deletes, report that called video gaming "spiritual opium", hitting Tencent stocks', *South China Morning Post*, 3 August 2021, https://www.scmp.com/tech/policy/article/3143625/chinese-newspaper-deletes-report-called-video-gaming-spiritual-opium

48 Tom Singleton, 'China claims youth gaming addiction resolved', *BBC News*, 23 November 2022, https://www.bbc.co.uk/news/technology-63730316

49 Daniel Camilo, 'Death Stranding 2 Would Tour', X, 1 July 2025, https://x.com/DanielOlimac/status/1940147222043402297

50 Simon Carless, '4 great graphs – and 1 new feature – from Steam's GDC presentations', GameDiscoverCo, 25 March 2025, https://newsletter.gamediscover.co/p/4-great-graphs-and-1-new-feature

51 Emmanuel Rosier, 'Into the data: PC & Console Gaming Report 2025', *Newzoo*, 15 April 2025, https://newzoo.com/resources/blog/into-the-data-pc-console-gaming-report-2025

52 Josh Ye, 'Beijing takes "golden share" in a Tencent subsidiary, records show', *Reuters*, 19 October 2023, https://www.reuters.com/world/china/beijing-takes-golden-share-tencent-subsidiary-records-show-2023-10-19/

53 Josh Ye, 'China's Xi holds rare meet with business leaders amid US tech rivalry', *Reuters*, 17 February 2025, https://www.reuters.com/world/china/chinas-xi-attends-symposium-private-enterprises-delivers-speech-2025-02-17/

54 Brent Koepp, 'Wuchang Fallen Feathers Patch 1.5 Removes Major Feature – and Players Are Furious', *Vice*, 14 August 2025, https://www.vice.com/en/article/wuchang-fallen-feathers-patch-1-5-removes-major-feature-and-players-are-furious/

55 Mark Sellman, 'Marvel game "bans" the words "free Taiwan" and "Winnie-the-Pooh"', *The Times*, 6 January 2025, https://www.thetimes.com/uk/technology-uk/article/marvel-rivals-video-game-blocks-words-taiwan-winnie-the-pooh-0hj3ltkgg

7. Nothing is true and everything is playable

1 Thomas Rid, *Active Measures: The Secret History of Disinformation and Political Warfare*, Profile Books (2021), p. 9.

2 Claire Wardle, 'Understanding information disorder', *First Draft News*, 22 September 2020, https://firstdraftnews.org/long-form-article/understanding-information-disorder/

3 Rid, *Active Measures*, p. 6.

4 Ibid., pp. 234–5.

5 Ibid., pp. 157–64.

6 Catherine Belton, *Putin's People: How the KGB Took Back Russia and Then Took on the West*, William Collins (2021), pp. 34–5.

7 Ibid., p. 42.

8 Rid, *Active Measures*, pp. 329–31.

9 Michael McFaul, 'Russia's 2000 Presidential Elections: Implications for Russian Democracy and U.S.–Russian Relations', Carnegie Endowment for International Peace, 1 April 2000, https://carnegieendowment.org/posts/2000/04/russias-2000-presidential-elections-implications-for-russian-democracy-and-us-russian-relations

10 Peter Pomerantsev, *Nothing is True and Everything is Possible: Adventures in Modern Russia*, Faber & Faber (2017), p. 56.

11 Ibid., p. 220.

12 Ibid., pp. 92–123.

13 'Alexey Navalny's wife says lab tests show he was poisoned before death', *Al-Jazeera*, 17 September 2025, https://www.aljazeera.com/news/2025/9/17/alexey-navalny-wife-says-lab-tests-show-he-was-poisoned-before-death

14 Rid, *Active Measures*, p. 341.

15 Phil McCausland, 'Right-wing US influencers say they were victims of alleged Russian plot', *BBC News*, 5 September 2024, https://www.bbc.co.uk/news/articles/crrlv7jdnq8o

16 Peter Pomerantsev, *This is Not Propaganda: Adventures in the War against Reality*, Faber & Faber (2019), pp. 35–6.

17 Scott Shane, 'These Are the Ads Russia Bought on Facebook in 2016', *New York Times*, 1 November 2017, https://www.nytimes.com/2017/11/01/us/politics/russia-2016-election-facebook.html

18 Robert S. Mueller, III, 'Report On The Investigation Into Russian Interference In The 2016 Presidential Election', Volume I of II, March 2019, Department of Justice, https://www.justice.gov/archives/sco/file/1373816/dl?inline=

19 Donatienne Ruy, 'Did Russia Influence Brexit?', Center for Strategic and International Studies, 21 July 2020, https://www.csis.org/blogs/brexit-bits-bobs-and-blogs/did-russia-influence-brexit

20 Sergey Sukhankin, 'Russian Disinformation Targets the European Union', The Jamestown Foundation, 2 October 2024, https://jamestown.org/program/russian-disinformation-targets-the-european-union/

21　'77 pct of Russian internet users have played video games: survey', *Xinhua*, 7 June 2025, https://english.news.cn/20250607/9917f3e180de47798c469911b14f9dc4/c.html

22　Óscar Ontañón Docal, 'Steam's most popular languages of 2024', *Game Reactor*, 9 January 2025, https://www.gamereactor.eu/steams-most-popular-languages-of-2024-1479483/

23　Joshua Wolens, 'Steam has taken down "over 260 materials containing illegal content" from its Russian store, brags the country's media censorship agency', *PC Gamer*, 17 October 2024, https://www.pcgamer.com/gaming-industry/steam-has-taken-down-over-260-materials-containing-illegal-content-from-its-russian-store-brags-the-countrys-media-censorship-agency/

24　Cat Goodfellow, 'Beyond Tetris: a brief history of patriotic video gaming in Russia', *Guardian*, 18 December 2014, https://www.theguardian.com/world/2014/dec/18/-sp-tetris-russia-video-gaming

25　A game listing for *Confrontation: Peace Enforcement* can be found at: https://www.gamepressure.com/games/confrontation-peace-enforcement/zd2308

26　Simon Shuster, 'Russia attempts to turn the patriotic tide by funding new video games', *Telegraph*, 7 June 2010, http://www.telegraph.co.uk/news/worldnews/europe/russia/7809066/Russia-attempts-to-turn-the-patriotic-tide-by-funding-new-video-games.html

27　Michael Houston, 'Russian President Putin gives green light for esports in schools', *Inside the Games*, 24 September 2020, https://www.insidethegames.biz/articles/1098777/russia-vladimir-putin-esports-in-schools

28　Victoria Phillips Kennedy, 'Russia looking into creating its own national game engine', *Eurogamer*, 18 July 2022, https://www.eurogamer.net/russia-looking-into-creating-its-own-national-game-engine

29　'Шум и гейм' ('Noise and Game'), *Kommersant*, 19 December 2022, https://www.kommersant.ru/doc/5733186

30　'Video games must educate people, foster true patriotism, Putin believes', *TASS*, 19 July 2023, https://tass.com/society/1649169

31　'Путин одобрил идею перенести в Россию серверы популярных в стране игр' ('Putin approved the idea of moving servers of popular games to Russia'), *App2Top*, 19 October 2023, https://app2top.ru/news/putin-odobril-ideyu-perenesti-v-rossiyu-servery-populyarny-h-v-strane-igr-212178.html

32　George E. Osborn, 'Vladimir Putin's Video Games Console', *Video Games Industry Memo*, 4 April 2024, https://www.videogamesindustrymemo.com/p/vladimir-putins-video-games-console/

33　Irina Borogan and Andrei Soldatov, 'Putin and the Secret Policeman's Ball', Centre for European Policy Action, 13 May 2024, https://cepa.org/article/putin-and-the-secret-policemans-ball/

34　Although the level can be completed without directly shooting civilians, its inclusion sparked much controversy.

35 Steven Lee Myers and Kellen Browning, 'Russia Takes Its Ukraine Information War Into Video Games', *New York Times*, 30 July 2023, https://www.nytimes.com/2023/07/30/technology/russia-propaganda-video-games.html

36 CT Influence Games, LinkedIn, https://www.linkedin.com/company/ct-influence-games

37 *Squad 22*: Team page, https://squad22.online/gameteam/

38 *Squad 22: ZOV*, 'Presentation of the *Squad 22: ZOV* game to Yunarmiya and Cadet organizations', YouTube, 27 May 2025, https://www.youtube.com/watch?v=mbbLg_U5poU

39 Dr Jack Watling and Nick Reynolds, 'Meatgrinder: Russian Tactics in the Second Year of Its Invasion of Ukraine', Royal United Services Institute, 19 May 2023, https://www.rusi.org/explore-our-research/publications/special-resources/meatgrinder-russian-tactics-second-year-its-invasion-ukraine

40 Zita Whalley, 'Russian army's "official" video game promises more levels if Ukraine doesn't surrender', *Daily Star*, 29 May 2025, https://www.dailystar.co.uk/news/world-news/russian-armys-official-video-game-35309089

41 Official page of the Ministry of Digital Transformation of Ukraine, 'Мінцифра на зв'язку' ('The Ministry of Digital Affairs is in touch') X, 4 June 2025, https://x.com/mintsyfra/status/1930208779603189856

42 See the VKontakte page for *Squad 22: ZOV* for further details, https://vk.com/squad22_game

43 The *Squad 22: ZOV* Steam Community page hosted the content, https://steamcommunity.com/app/3573040

44 Vaspaan Dastoor, 'Russian Streamer Partners With Mercenary Group For Weird Propaganda Stream', *TheGamer*, 11 February 2023, https://www.thegamer.com/russian-streamer-partners-mercenary-group-propaganda-stream/

45 History Legends, 'The Russian Teenage Streamer That Infiltrated PMC Wagner', YouTube, 8 April 2024, https://www.youtube.com/watch?v=0nPfPC2uQy4

46 George Spencer Terry, 'Downstream Influence in the Russo-Ukrainian War: Grand Strategy War Gaming as a Novel Approach to Influence Operations', *Journal on Baltic Security*, Vol. 9, Issue 1 (2023), pp. 98–120, https://journalonbalticsecurity.com/journal/JOBS/article/115/info

47 r/Bokoen1, 'This has got to be the saddest shit I've ever seen lmao', Reddit, 24 August 2023, https://www.reddit.com/r/Bokoen1/comments/15zn3vx/this_has_got_to_be_the_saddest_shit_ive_ever_seen/

48 Ali Chenrose, 'Russia uses video games in Africa to spread anti-Western propaganda', *DFR Lab*, 12 August 2024, https://dfrlab.org/2024/08/12/russia-uses-video-games-in-africa-to-spread-anti-western-propaganda/

49 Joe Inwood and Jake Tacchi, 'Wagner in Africa: How the Russian mercenary group has rebranded', *BBC News*, 20 February 2024, https://www.bbc.co.uk/news/world-africa-68322230

50 Morgane Le Cam and Thomas Eydoux, 'African Initiative, the new bridgehead for Russian propaganda in Africa', *Le Monde*, 9 March 2024, https://www.lemonde.fr/en/le-monde-africa/article/2024/03/09/african-initiative-the-new-bridgehead-for-russian-propaganda-in-africa_6599556_124.html

51 'St. Petersburg State University student Grigorii Korolev on helping the front and using video games in patriotic education of youth', Saint Petersburg State University, 11 May 2025, https://english.spbu.ru/news-events/student-reviews/st-petersburg-state-university-student-grigorii-korolev-helping-front

52 Bokeon1 account, X, 2 October 2024, https://x.com/bokoen1?lang=en

53 Leo Chiu, 'Fake Waifu Artillery? Chinese Citizens Pay Russian Troops to Draw Messages on Artillery Shells', *Kyiv Post*, 17 April 2024, https://www.kyivpost.com/post/31269

54 Koch Media, 'Koch Media and GSC Game World partner up for the physical release of S.T.A.L.K.E.R. 2: Heart of Chernobyl', 11 August 2021, https://www.gamespress.com/STALKER-2-Heart-of-Chernobyl-Koch-Media-und-GSC-Game-

55 Brendan Lowry, 'STALKER 2: Heart of Chernobyl gets April 28, 2022 release date, gameplay trailer', Windows Central, 14 June 2021, https://www.windowscentral.com/stalker-2-heart-chernobyl-gets-april-28-2022-release-date-gameplay-trailer

56 Tom Regan, ' "At this point it's not just a game": the making of Ukrainian RPG Stalker 2 – during wartime', *Guardian*, 31 January 2024, https://www.theguardian.com/games/2024/jan/31/stalker-2-heart-of-chernobyl-interview-ukraine-war-gsc-game-world

57 'One of S.T.A.L.K.E.R. video game developers killed in action near Bakhmut', *Pravda*, 25 December 2022, https://www.pravda.com.ua/eng/news/2022/12/25/7382287/

58 Jack Grimshaw, 'GSC Game World raises over £600,000 for Ukraine aid', *NME*, 17 April 2022, https://www.nme.com/news/gsc-game-world-raises-over-600000-for-ukraine-aid-3206443

59 Taras Mishchenko, 'In S.T.A.L.K.E.R. 2 there will be no Russian voice acting, but only English and Ukrainian. The game was postponed to 2023', *Mezha*, 14 June 2022, https://mezha.media/en/2022/06/14/in-s-t-a-l-k-e-r-2-there-will-be-no-russian-voice-acting/

60 Defense of Ukraine, 'Volodymyr Yezhov, one of the developers of @stalkerthegame' X, 26 December 2022, https://x.com/DefenceU/status/1607400845246664704

61 Ted Litchfield, 'STALKER 2 developer suffers Russia-linked security breach: "We have been enduring constant cyberattacks for more than a year now" ', *PC Gamer*, 12 March 2023, https://www.pcgamer.com/stalker-2-developer-suffers-russia-linked-security-breach-we-have-been-enduring-constant-cyberattacks-for-more-than-a-year-now/

62 Ivan Khomenko, 'Russian Gamers Warned of Potential Criminal Liability for Purchasing S.T.A.L.K.E.R. 2', *United 24*, 11 November 2024, https://united24media.com/latest-news/russian-gamers-warned-of-potential-criminal-liability-for-purchasing-stalker-2-3666

63 Emanuel Maiberg, 'Russian Disinformation Campaign Spreads Lies About Ukraine's "Stalker 2"', *404 Media*, 27 November 2024, https://www.404media.co/stalker2-disinformation/

64 Andrea Januta, '"For some it's a game, for me it's a manifesto" – Ukrainian soldiers join S.T.A.L.K.E.R. 2 frenzy', *Kyiv Independent*, 29 November 2024, https://kyivindependent.com/for-some-its-a-game-for-me-its-a-manifesto-ukrainian-soldiers-join-s-t-a-l-k-e-r-2-frenzy/

65 'Victor Pinchuk Foundation hosts discussion with S.T.A.L.K.E.R 2 video game creators, during WEF in Davos', Victor Pinchuk Foundation, 22 January 2025, https://pinchukfund.org/en/news/29514/

66 TommyKayClips 'What's Grisha Doing Here', YouTube, 7 May 2023, https://www.youtube.com/watch?v=QQgMMUiVdt0

67 Jonathan Chadwick, 'Russia is mocked over plans to launch its own "Putindo 64" games console in a desperate attempt to shun Western technology', *Daily Mail*, 3 January 2025, https://www.dailymail.co.uk/sciencetech/article-14247003/Russia-mocked-Putindo-64-games-console.html

68 'Russian government seizes former Wargaming studio Lesta for supporting Ukraine', *Games Industry Biz*, 28 April 2025, https://www.gamesindustry.biz/russian-government-seizes-former-wargaming-studio-lesta-for-supporting-ukraine

69 Tatsiana Ashurkevich, Christo Grozev and Roman Dobrokhotov, '"We must not say it's for the war": Hundreds of thousands of Russian schoolkids are building drones that kill Ukrainians', *The Insider*, 22 July 2025, https://theins.ru/en/inv/283351

70 'Arma 3 footage being used as fake news', Bohemia Interactive, 10 October 2023, https://www.bohemia.net/blog/arma-3-footage-being-used-as-fake-news

71 Estelle Nilsson-Julien, 'Fake war in Ukraine clips from video games mislead millions on social media', *Euro News*, 10 June 2025, https://www.euronews.com/my-europe/2025/06/10/fake-war-in-ukraine-clips-from-video-games-mislead-millions-on-social-media

72 'Former Gazprom executive's investment co to acquire Volga Gas for $25 mln', Interfax, 16 November 2020, https://interfax.com/newsroom/top-stories/70361/

73 Matthew Loh, 'Russia's military is being accused of stealing video game characters from "Atomic Heart" to promote itself', *Business Insider*, 31 March 2023, https://www.businessinsider.com/russias-military-accused-stealing-atomic-heart-game-characters-posters-brand-2023-3

74 Olha Karpenko, 'The "apolitical" Russian game Atomic Heart makes fun of the killings of Ukrainians', *AIN*, 22 February 2023, https://en.ain.ua/2023/02/22/the-apolitical-russian-game-atomic-heart-makes-fun-of-the-killings-of-ukrainians/

75 Evgeny Obedkov, '"Feast in time of plague": Soviet-style presentation of Atomic Heart in Russia draws mixed reaction', *Game World Observer*, https://gameworldobserver.com/2022/11/25/atomic-heart-promo-event-russia-mundfish-reaction

76 David Gilbert, 'DOJ: Russia Aimed Propaganda at Gamers, Minorities to Swing 2024 Election', *Wired*, 5 September 2024, https://www.wired.com/story/project-good-old-usa-russia-2024-election/

8. The gamer-fication of terror

1 'Investigative Report on the role of online platforms in the tragic mass shooting in Buffalo on May 14, 2022', Office of the New York State Attorney General Letitia James, 18 October 2022, https://ag.ny.gov/sites/default/files/buffaloshooting-onlineplatformsreport.pdf

2 'Footage of Buffalo Attack Spread Quickly Across Platforms, Has Been Online for Days', *ADL*, 20 May 2022, https://www.adl.org/resources/article/footage-buffalo-attack-spread-quickly-across-platforms-has-been-online-days

3 'The 9/11 Commission Report: Final Report of the National Commission on Terrorist Attacks Upon the United States (9/11 Report)', Executive Agency Publications, 22 July 2004, https://9-11commission.gov/report/911Report.pdf

4 Clara Pellerin, 'Communicating Terrror: an Analysis of Isis Communication Strategy', paper for 'Islam and Politics in a Changing Middle East' at Sciences Po, spring 2016, https://www.sciencespo.fr/kuwait-program/wp-content/uploads/2018/05/KSP_Paper_Award_Spring_2016_PELLERIN_Clara.pdf

5 Cori E. Dauber et al., 'Call of Duty: Jihad – How the Video Game Motif Has Migrated Downstream from Islamic State Propaganda Videos', *Perspectives on Terrorism*, Vol. 12, Issue 3, June 2019, https://pt.icct.nl/sites/default/files/2023-06/02--dauber-et-al.pdf

6 Laurel Wamsley, 'ISIS Claims Responsibility For London Attack That Killed 7, Injured 48', *NPR*, 4 June 2017, https://www.npr.org/sections/thetwo-way/2017/06/04/531459784/raids-in-london-after-attack-that-killed-7-injured-48

7 Eric Levenson, 'The "serious red flag" for a potential school shooter? An obsession with other mass shooters', *CNN*, 7 September 2025, https://edition.cnn.com/2025/09/07/us/mass-shooters-obsession-school-shootings

8 'Online Sect's Influence on Teen Knife Attacks Faces Court Scrutiny', *Sweden Herald*, 3 April 2025, https://swedenherald.com/article/online-sects-influence-on-teen-knife-attacks-faces-court-scrutiny

9 James Hardy and Christopher Stewart, 'Gore and violent extremism: How extremist groups exploit "gore" sites to view and share terrorist material', Institute for Strategic Dialogue, 29 June 2023, https://www.isdglobal.org/digital_dispatches/gore-and-violent-extremism-how-extremist-groups-exploit-gore-sites-to-view-and-share-terrorist-material/

10 Jonny Humphries, 'Prevent closed Southport killer case "prematurely"', *BBC News*, 5 February 2025, https://www.bbc.co.uk/news/articles/c0rqxpg2ryvo

11 Josh Halliday, 'Axel Rudakubana: from "unassuming" schoolboy to Southport killer', *Guardian*, 25 January 2025, https://www.theguardian.com/uk-news/2025/jan/25/axel-rudakubana-from-unassuming-schoolboy-to-notorious-southport-killer

12 'Written evidence submitted by the Institute for Strategic Dialogue (COM0017)', https://committees.parliament.uk/writtenevidence/142702/pdf/

13 'Violent video games found not to be associated with adolescent aggression', University of Oxford, 13 February 2019, https://www.ox.ac.uk/news/2019-02-13-violent-video-games-found-not-be-associated-adolescent-aggression

14 Sarah Whitten, 'No evidence that violent video games are causing mass shootings, despite politicians' claims', *CNBC*, 9 August 2019, https://www.cnbc.com/2019/08/09/no-evidence-that-violent-video-games-are-causing-mass-shootings.html

15 Joe Whittaker, 'Online radicalisation: What we know', Radicalisation Awareness Network Policy Support, 2022 https://home-affairs.ec.europa.eu/system/files/2023-11/RAN-online-radicalisation_en.pdf

16 Galen Lamphere-Englund, and Menso Hartgers, 'CTRL+ALT+COLLAB-ORATE: Public–private partnerships to prevent extremism in gaming', RAN Network, February 2024, https://home-affairs.ec.europa.eu/document/download/e446f013-34e1-4f74-bce6-90f661937ce9_en

17 As yet unpublished More in Common report: Using video games to reach disengaged audiences with media literacy interventions. Findings were reported at the Cambridge Disinformation Summit in April 2025.

18 'Hate is No Game: Hate and Harrassment in Online Games 2023' Center for Technology and Society, Anti-Defamation League, 6 February 2024, https://www.adl.org/resources/report/hate-no-game-hate-and-harassment-online-games-2023

19 Debbie Elliott, 'The Charlottesville rally 5 years later: "It's what you're still trying to forget"', *NPR*, 12 August 2022, https://www.npr.org/2022/08/12/1116942725/the-charlottesville-rally-5-years-later-its-what-youre-still-trying-to-forget

20 Ebner, Julia, *Going Dark: The Secret Social Lives of Extremists*, Bloomsbury (2020), pg 173-175

21 'How Trust & Safety Addresses Violent Extremism on Discord', Discord, 25 May 2021,https://discord.com/blog/how-trust-safety-addresses-violent-extremism-on-Discord

22 Harry Cockburn, 'Mosque killer sent email to New Zealand prime minister Jacinda Ardern minutes before beginning attack', *Independent*, 16 March 2019, https://www.independent.co.uk/news/world/australasia/new-zealand-shooting-mosque-jacinda-ardern-email-prime-minister-a8826021.html

23 Robert Evans, 'Shitposting, Inspirational Terrorism, and the Christchurch Mosque Massacre', *Bellingcat*, 15 March 2019, https://www.bellingcat.com/news/rest-of-world/2019/03/15/shitposting-inspirational-terrorism-and-the-christchurch-mosque-massacre/

24 Sanya Burgess, 'New Zealand mosque shootings: Suspected killer is fascist who "had contact with Breivik"', *Sky News*, 16 March 2019, https://news.sky.com/story/new-zealand-mosque-shootings-suspected-killer-is-fascist-who-had-contact-with-breivik-11666136

25 'Royal Commission of Inquiry into the terrorist attack on Christchurch masjidain on 15 March 2019', 8 December 2020, https://christchurchattack.royalcommission.nz/the-report/firearms-licensing/preparation-for-the-terrorist-attack

26 Niraj Chokshi, 'PewDiePie Put in Spotlight After New Zealand Shooting', *New York Times*, 15 March 2019, https://www.nytimes.com/2019/03/15/technology/pewdiepie-new-zealand-shooting.html

27 Graham Macklin, 'The Christchurch Attacks: Livestream Terror in the Viral Video Age', *CTC Sentinel*, Vol. 12, Issue 6 (July 2019), https://ctc.westpoint.edu/christchurch-attacks-livestream-terror-viral-video-age/

28 Ryan Broll, 'Dark Fandoms: An Introduction and Case Study', *Deviant Behavior*, Vol. 41, Issue 6, 26 March 2019, https://www.tandfonline.com/doi/abs/10.1080/01639625.2019.1596453

29 Galen Lamphere-Englund, 'Theories of Digital Games and Radicalization', in Linda Schlegel and Rachel Kowert (eds.), *Gaming and Extremism: The Radicalisation of Digital Playgrounds*, Routledge (2024), p. 47.

30 Hannah Rose, The Bratislava Attacks: Insights from the Shooter's Manifesto, Global Network on Extremism and Technology, 14 October 2022, https://gnet-research.org/2022/10/14/the-bratislava-shooting-and-manifesto-initial-insights-and-learnings/

31 Suraj Lakhani, 'A is for Apple, B is for Bullet: The Gamification of (Violent) Extremism', in Schlegel and Kowert (eds.), *Gaming and Extremism*, pp. 47, 154–5.

32 Benjamin Goggin, X, 18 May 2022, https://x.com/BenjaminGoggin/status/1526966284294012929?lang=en

33 Gabrielle Fonrouge, 'Twisted diary of alleged Buffalo shooter Payton Gendron reveals his online radicalization', *New York Post*, 17 May 2022, https://nypost.com/2022/05/17/twisted-diary-of-alleged-buffalo-shooter-payton-gendron-reveals-his-online-radicalization/

34 'Buffalo Shooter's Weapons Covered in White Supremacist Messaging', Anti-Defamation League, 15 May 2022, https://www.adl.org/resources/article/buffalo-shooters-weapons-covered-white-supremacist-messaging

35 'Turkey Attacker Inspired by Accelerationism and Mass Killers, Manifesto Shows', Center on Extremism, Anti-Defamation League, 16 August 2024, https://www.adl.org/resources/article/turkey-attacker-inspired-accelerationism-and-mass-killers-manifesto-shows

36 George Hancorn, 'Mosque shootings and far-right skins: Teens playing Roblox exposed to extremist content', *ITV News*, 17 November 2025, https://www.itv.com/news/2025-11-14/mosque-attacks-and-far-right-skins-roblox-teens-exposed-to-extremist-content

37 Matt Kaufman, 'How Roblox Partners With Law Enforcement: Investigating Potential Threats to Safety', *Roblox* corporate blog, 7 August 2025, https://corp.roblox.com/newsroom/2025/08/how-roblox-partners-law-enforcement

38 *Hatred* Steam page, https://store.steampowered.com/app/341940/Hatred/

39 'The Dark Side of Roblox: "Active Shooter Studios" Create Maps Based on Real-Life Mass Shootings', Center on Extremism, Anti-Defamation League,

21 April 2025, https://www.adl.org/resources/article/dark-side-roblox-active-shooter-studios-create-maps-based-real-life-mass

40 Moustafa Ayad and Isabelle Frances-Wright, 'Minors exposed to mass shooter glorification across mainstream social media platforms', Institute for Strategic Dialogue, 24 January 2024, https://www.isdglobal.org/digital_dispatches/minors-exposed-to-mass-shooter-glorification-across-mainstream-social-media-platforms/

41 Michael McWhertor, 'Helldivers 2 is getting pulled into the Charlie Kirk assassination investigation', *Polygon*, 12 September 2025, https://www.polygon.com/charlie-kirk-shooter-helldivers-2-meme-tyler-robinson/

42 Herb Scribner, 'Roblox removes "over 100 experiences" tied to Charlie Kirk shooting', *Axios*, 11 September 2025, https://www.axios.com/2025/09/11/charlie-kirk-shooting-roblox-game-removed

9. The Gamergate to populism

1 Samit Sarkar, 'Blizzard reaches 100M lifetime World of Warcraft accounts', *Polygon*, 28 January 2014, https://www.polygon.com/2014/1/28/5354856/world-of-warcraft-100m-accounts-lifetime/

2 r/WOW, '9 million years of world of warcraft, has been played, since 2004!', Reddit, 22 April 2022, https://www.reddit.com/r/wow/comments/u9kci6/9_million_years_of_world_of_warcraft_has_been/

3 Jonathan Lee, 'House member cites Leeroy Jenkins meme during speaker vote', *Washington Post*, 4 January 2023, https://www.washingtonpost.com/video-games/2023/01/04/leeroy-jenkins-warcraft-congress/

4 'Charity', Wowpedia, https://wowpedia.fandom.com/wiki/Charity

5 Vicky Schaubert, 'My disabled son's amazing gaming life in the World of Warcraft', *BBC News*, 7 February 2019, https://www.bbc.co.uk/news/disability-47064773

6 Eliza Thompson, '3 Couples Talk About How World of Warcraft Brought Them Together', *Cosmopolitan*, 9 June 2016, https://www.cosmopolitan.com/entertainment/movies/a59553/world-of-warcraft-wedding-stories/

7 James Ball, *The Other Pandemic: How QAnon Contaminated the World*, Bloomsbury (2023), pp. 1–2.

8 C. C. P. Dolan, 'The Bloodbath of B-R5RB, Gaming's Most Destructive Battle Ever', EVE: Online company blog, 1 February 2014, https://www.eveonline.com/news/view/the-bloodbath-of-b-r5rb

9 Yongcheng Liu and Qinfang Ying, 'How to Reduce In-Game Inflation by Monitoring Your Economic Systems', Game Developer Conference, YouTube, 6 November 2020, https://www.youtube.com/watch?v=T55AXQEUybA

10 Barbara Scheben, 'Online gaming: a virtual paradise for money launderers', KPMG, March 2025, https://kpmg.com/de/en/home/insights/2025/03/online-gaming-a-virtual-paradise-for-money-launderers.html

11 Ellie Gibson, 'Chinese WOW players speak out', *Eurogamer*, 17 January 2006, https://www.eurogamer.net/news170106wowracism

12 Ashley Rodriguez, 'How Steve Bannon made his fortune from "Seinfeld" reruns', *Quartz*, 21 July 2022, https://qz.com/841601/steve-bannon-made-his-money-from-seinfeld-reruns

13 Julian Dibbell's superb story 'The Decline and Fall of an Ultra Rich Online Gaming Empire' for *Wired* was referenced throughout this section, 24 November 2008. It also deserves to be made into a movie, https://www.wired.com/2008/11/ff-ige/

14 Conor Friedersdorf, 'How *Breitbart* Destroyed Andrew Breitbart's Legacy', *The Atlantic*, 14 November 2017, https://www.theatlantic.com/politics/archive/2017/11/how-breitbart-destroyed-andrew-breitbarts-legacy/545807/

15 Joshua Green, *Devil's Bargain: Steve Bannon, Donald Trump, and the Storming of the Presidency*, Penguin Press (2017).

16 'Comscore Reports April 2014 U.S. Smartphone Subscriber Market Share', Comscore, 4 June 2014, https://www.comscore.com/Insights/Press-Releases/2014/6/comScore-Reports-April-2014-US-Smartphone-Subscriber-Market-Share

17 Emil Protalinski, 'Facebook passes 1.35B monthly active users and 864M daily active users, with a third now mobile-only, *VentureBeat*, 28 October 2014, https://venturebeat.com/business/facebook-passes-1-35b-monthly-active-users-and-864m-daily-active-users-with-a-third-now-mobile-only/

18 '5 things we learned about Twitter in 2014', *Digiday*, 15 December 2014, https://digiday.com/media/5-things-learned-twitter-2014/

19 Sunil Gill, 'Reddit Statistics | Revenue, User Count & Growth 2026', Priori Data, 5 January 2026, https://prioridata.com/data/reddit-statistics/

20 Snapchat Revenue and Usage Statistics (2026), David Curry, *The Business of Apps*, 6 January 2026, https://www.businessofapps.com/data/snapchat-statistics/

21 Joshua Cohen, 'Top 250 Most Viewed YouTube Channels Worldwide In 2014', Tubefilter, 30 January 2015, https://www.tubefilter.com/2015/01/30/top-250-most-viewed-youtube-channels-worldwide-2014/

22 Shannon Liao, 'On Elon Musk's Twitter, gaming offers a glimpse of a chaotic future', *Washington Post*, 11 November 2022, https://www.washingtonpost.com/video-games/2022/11/11/twitter-gaming-elon-musk/

23 Bryant Francis, 'Watch *Mass Effect 3*'s developers look back on the controversial, crunch-generating ending', *Game Developer*, 21 October 2021, https://www.gamedeveloper.com/design/watch-mass-effect-3-s-developers-look-back-on-the-controversial-crunch-generating-ending

24 Dylan Matthews, 'The alt-right is more than warmed-over white supremacy. It's that, but way way weirder', *Vox*, 25 August 2016, https://www.vox.com/2016/4/18/11434098/alt-right-explained

25 Cassidee Moser, 'How Twitter Changed the Gaming Industry', *IGN*, 14 January 2014, https://www.ign.com/articles/2014/01/14/how-twitter-changed-the-gaming-industry

26 James Delingpole and Milo Yiannopoulos, 'James's and Milo's Year in Liberal Stupid, Part One', *Breitbart*, 29 December 2014, https://www.breitbart.com/pol itics/2014/12/29/jamess-and-milos-year-in-liberal-stupid-part-one/

27 Nick Wingfield, 'Feminist Critics of Video Games Facing Threats in "GamerGate" Campaign', *New York Times*, 16 October 2014, https://www.nytimescom/ 2014/10/16/technology/gamergate-women-video-game-threats-anita-sarkeesian.html

28 Eric Johnson, 'Under Pressure From Gamers, Intel Pulls Advertising From Gamasutra', *Vox*, 1 October 2014, https://www.vox.com/2014/10/1/11631508/ under-pressure-from-gamers-intel-pulls-advertising-from-gamasutra

29 Abby Ohlheiser, 'Why "social justice warrior", a Gamergate insult, is now a dictionary entry', *Washington Post*, 7 October 2015, https://www.washingtonpost. com/news/the-intersect/wp/2015/10/07/why-social-justice-warrior-a-gamer gate-insult-is-now-a-dictionary-entry/

30 Mike Wendling, 'Trump's shock troops: Who are the "alt-right"?', *BBC News*, 26 August 2016, https://www.bbc.co.uk/news/magazine-37021991

31 Allum Bokhari and Milo Yiannopoulos, 'An Establishment Conservative's Guide to the Alt-Right', *Breitbart*, 29 March 2016, https://www.breitbart.com/tech/ 2016/03/29/an-establishment-conservatives-guide-to-the-alt-right/

32 Sarah Posner, 'How Steve Bannon Created an Online Haven for White Nationalists', *Mother Jones*, 22 August 2016, https://www.motherjones.com/politics/2016/ 08/stephen-bannon-donald-trump-alt-right-breitbart-news/

33 Matt Lees, 'What Gamergate should have taught us about the "alt-right"', *Guardian*, 1 December 2016, https://www.theguardian.com/technology/2016/dec/01/ gamergate-alt-right-hate-trump

34 'Steve Bannon's out at the White House, aftermath of white nationalist protests in Charlottesville', PBS, 18 August 2017, https://www.pbs.org/weta/washington-week/video/2017/08/steve-bannons-out-at-the-white-house-aftermath-of-white-nationalist-protests-in-charlottesville

35 Dorian Lynskey, 'The rise and fall of Milo Yiannopoulos – how a shallow actor played the bad guy for money', *Guardian*, 21 February 2017, https://www.the guardian.com/world/2017/feb/21/milo-yiannopoulos-rise-and-fall-shallow-actor-bad-guy-hate-speech

36 'Who is Ian Miles-Cheong? Meet Twitter's favourite right-wing commentator', *Times of India*, 9 July 2024, https://timesofindia.indiatimes.com/world/us/who-is-ian-miles-cheong-meet-twitters-favourite-right-wing-commentator/article show/111606114.cms

37 Grummz, X, 24 February 2025, https://x.com/Grummz/status/1894052241713 275202

38 Kyle Rowley, X, 4 March 2024, https://x.com/TimePirateNinja/status/17646971 35344202183

39 Oliver Holmes, 'Elon Musk admits cheating at video games, chat transcript appears to show', *Guardian*, 22 January 2025, https://www.theguardian.com/

technology/2025/jan/22/elon-musk-admits-cheating-at-video-games-chat-transcript-appears-to-show

40 Andrew Williams, 'What is Sweet Baby Inc? Elon Musk says video games are "woke" as debate intensifies', *Standard*, 21 March 2024, https://www.standard.co.uk/culture/gaming/what-sweet-baby-inc-gamergate-elon-musk-woke-video-games-b1146769.html

41 Kat Tenbarge, 'Andrew Tate's arrest prompted by livestreamer who said Tate was leaving Romania, law firm says', *NBC News*, 12 March 2024, https://www.nbcnews.com/tech/internet/andrew-tate-arrest-prompted-adin-ross-stream-says-law-firm-rcna143009

42 Zoe G. Phillips, 'Adin Ross' Livestream With Donald Trump Peaks at 500,000 Viewers', *Hollywood Reporter*, 5 August 2024, https://www.hollywoodreporter.com/news/politics-news/adin-ross-livestrea-donald-500000-viewers-1235966797/

43 James Johnson, 'I was the only pollster to predict the Trump landslide', *Independent*, 8 November 2024, https://www.independent.co.uk/voices/trump-harris-election-polling-b2643873.html

Part 3: Fighting back

10. A serious game for democracies to play

1 Phil Wilkinson, 'A Brief History of Serious Games', 5 October 2016, https://eprints.bournemouth.ac.uk/30697/1/A%20Brief%20History%20of%20Serious%20Games.pdf

2 Joachim Froholt, 'The Sumerian Game: The ancestor of modern city builders', Spillhistorie, 10 July 2025, https://spillhistorie.no/2025/07/10/the-sumerian-game-the-ancestor-of-modern-city-builders/

3 Clark C. Abt, *Serious Games*, University Press of America (1987).

4 Amy Bruckman, 'Can Educational Be Fun?', Game Developers Conference, 17 March 1999, https://faculty.cc.gatech.edu/~asb/papers/bruckman-gdc99.pdf

5 'Plague Inc. gives a quarter of a million dollars to fight COVID-19', NDemic Creations, 22 March 2020, https://www.ndemiccreations.com/en/news/175-plague-inc-gives-a-quarter-of-a-million-dollars-to-fight-covid-19

6 Charles Gulick, *Runway USA: A guide to destination cities in Flight Simulator* (1987), https://www.flightsimbooks.com/runwayusa/

7 Kelly Clancy, *Playing With Reality: How Games Shape Our World*, Allen Lane (2024), p. 253.

8 'Origins of the "Serious Game" name', Serious Games Society, https://seriousgamessociety.org/2016/09/21/origins-of-the-serious-game-name/

9 'Obama Buys First Video Game Campaign Ads', *Reuters*, 17 October 2008, https://www.reuters.com/article/technology/obama-buys-first-video-game-campaign-ads-idUSTRE49EAGL/

10 Lawrence Bonk, 'Indie favorite "Papers, Please" has sold 5 million copies', *Engadget*, 9 August 2023, https://www.engadget.com/indie-favorite-papers-please-has-sold-5-million-copies-171537016.html

11 'Plague Inc. gives a quarter of a million dollars to fight COVID-19', NDemic Creations, 22 March 2020, https://www.ndemiccreations.com/en/news/175-plague-inc-gives-a-quarter-of-a-million-dollars-to-fight-covid-19

12 Andrew Griffin, 'Coronavirus: World Health Organisation tells people to stay at home and play games', *Independent*, 30 March 2020, https://www.independent.co.uk/tech/coronavirus-world-health-organisation-play-games-covid-19-advice-a9438916.html

13 Robert Purchese, 'Fighting wildfires in Riders Republic – the Green Game Jam '22 had some great ideas', *Eurogamer*, 5 July 2022, https://www.eurogamer.net/fighting-wildfires-in-riders-republic-the-green-game-jam-22-had-some-great-ideas

14 Boom Beach, 'Boom Beach: Turtle Division', YouTube, 23 May 2023, https://www.youtube.com/watch?v=BoHE5fax79A

15 George E. Osborn, 'Playing for the Planet: Five Years On, Five Years Onward – Reaching players through the Green Game Jam', Playing for the Planet, 15 January 2025, https://www.playing4theplanet.org/post/playing-for-the-planet-five-years-on-part-onej

16 Green Game Jam, 'Gaming for Wildlife', Playing for the Planet, https://www.playing4theplanet.org/green-game-jam-2023

17 'Record year for the Green Game Jam as 42 games enter with a reach of 275 million', Playing for the Planet, 11 January 2022, https://www.playing4theplanet.org/post/record-year-for-the-green-game-jam-as-42-games-enter-with-a-reach-of-275-million

18 George E. Osborn, 'Playing for the Planet: Five Years On, Five Years Onward – Practical Steps to Reduce Industry Emissions', Playing for the Planet, 24 January 2025, https://www.playing4theplanet.org/post/playing-for-the-planet-five-years-on-five-years-onward---part-two

19 'Video Gaming in Lockdown: The impact of Covid-19 on video game play behaviours and attitudes', IPSOS Mori, September 2020, https://videogameseurope.eu/wp-content/uploads/2020/09/IpsosMori-Gaming-during-Lockdown-Q1-Q2-2020-report.pdf

20 Ukraine Global Game Jam Group, US Embassy Warsaw, 2022, https://artsandculture.google.com/asset/ukraine-global-game-jam-group-u-s-embassy-warsaw/gwH-0lRUq-6CDg?hl=en

21 'CTRL+ALT+DISINFO Top 20', Global Game Jam, https://unitedwithukraine.games/top_20/

22 George E. Osborn, 'NATO's video game frontline', *Video Games Industry Memo*, 9 October 2025, https://www.videogamesindustrymemo.com/p/natos-video-game-frontline-09102025

Index

GEORGE E. OSBORN is a leading expert on the video game industry who has worked in the sector for nearly fifteen years, including as Head of Communications at the UK video games trade association, Ukie. He is the creator of Video Games Industry Memo, a newsletter about the intersection of video games, business and politics. He is the founder of Half-Space Consulting, a business which advises NGOs, regulators and governments about the impact of video games on society. George has appeared on *Sky News* and *BBC World Service*, and has contributed to the *Guardian*, *New York Times*, *Politico* and *Bloomberg* on issues relating to video games.

RAISING READERS
Books Build Bright Futures

Dear Reader,

We'd love your attention for one more page to tell you about the crisis in children's reading, and what we can all do.

Studies have shown that reading for fun is the **single biggest predictor of a child's future life chances** – more than family circumstance, parents' educational background or income. It improves academic results, mental health, wealth, communication skills, ambition and happiness.[1]

The number of children reading for fun is in rapid decline. Young people have a lot of competition for their time. In 2024, 1 in 10 children and young people in the UK aged 5 to 18 did not own a single book at home.[2]

Hachette works extensively with schools, libraries and literacy charities, but here are some ways we can all raise more readers:

- Reading to children for just 10 minutes a day makes a difference
- Don't give up if children aren't regular readers – there will be books for them!
- Visit bookshops and libraries to get recommendations
- Encourage them to listen to audiobooks
- Support school libraries
- Give books as gifts

There's a lot more information about how to encourage children to read on our website: **www.RaisingReaders.co.uk**

Thank you for reading.

---

[1] OECD, '21st-Century Readers: Developing Literacy Skills in a Digital World', 2021, https://www.oecd.org/en/publications/21st-century-readers_a83d84cb-en.html

[2] National Literacy Trust, 'Book Ownership in 2024', November 2024, https://literacytrust.org.uk/research-services/research-reports/book-ownership-in-2024